Thackray's 2022 Investor's Guide

THACKRAY'S
2022
INVESTOR'S
GUIDE

Brooke Thackray MBA, CIM

Published in 2021 by: MountAlpha Media:

alphamountain.com

ISBN13: 978-1-989125-06-9

Printed and Bound in Canada by Marquis.

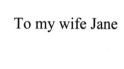
To my wife Jane

Acknowledgments

This book is the product of many years of research and could not have been written without the help of many people. I would like to thank my wife, Jane Steer-Thackray, and my children Justin, Megan, Carly and Madeleine, for the help they have given me and their patience during the many hours that I have devoted to writing this book.

INTRODUCTION

2022 THACKRAY'S INVESTOR'S GUIDE
Technical Commentary

The seasonal strategies that I have included in my previous books have proven to be very successful. The buy and sell dates are based upon iterative comparisons of different time periods measured by gain and frequency of success. Although the buy and sell dates are the optimal dates on which seasonal investors should focus on making their investment decisions, the markets have different dynamics from year to year, shifting the optimal buy and sell dates. Combining technical analysis with seasonal trends helps to adjust the decision process, allowing seasonal investors to enter and exit trades early or late, depending on market conditions.

The universe of technical indicators and techniques is huge. It is impossible to use all of the indicators. Only a small number of indicators and techniques that suit an investment style should be used. In the case of seasonal investing, a lot of long-term indicators provide little benefit. For example, the standard Moving Average Convergence Divergence (MACD), is too slow to be of use in shorter term seasonal strategies. In this book I have chosen to illustrate three technical indicators that can provide value in fine-tuning the dates for seasonal investing: Full Stochastic Oscillator (FSO), Relative Strength Index (RSI) and Relative Strength. The indicators are used in conjunction with the price pattern and moving averages of the security being considered. Investors must remember that technical analysis is not absolute and there will be exceptions when utilizing indicators and price patterns.

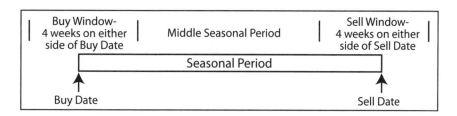

To combine technical indicators with seasonal trends, it is best that the indicators be used within the windows of the buy and sell dates. The indicators should be ignored outside the seasonal buy/sell windows. An exception to this occurs when an indicator gives a signal during its middle seasonal period, which is in the seasonal period, but after the buy window and before the sell window. In this case a technical signal can support selling a full position based upon a fundamental breakdown in the price action of a security. By itself, a FSO or RSI indicator showing weakness in a security during its middle seasonal period, does not necessarily warrant action, it can be used to support a decision being made in conjunction with underperformance relative to the broad market, or a major price action break.

Below are short descriptions of three technical indicators that can be used with seasonal analysis. Full evaluation of the indicators and their uses with seasonal analysis is beyond the scope of this book.

Full Stochastic Oscillator (FSO)

A stochastic oscillator is a range bound momentum indicator that tracks the location of the close price relative to the high-low range, over a set number of periods. It tracks the momentum of price change and helps to indicate the strength and direction of price movement.

I have found that generally the best method to combine the FSO with seasonal trends is to buy an early partial position when the FSO turns up above 20 within four weeks of the seasonal buy date. Additionally, the best time to sell an early partial position occurs when the FSO turns below 80, within four weeks of the seasonal exit date.

Relative Strength Index (RSI)

The RSI is a momentum oscillator that measures the speed and change of price movements. I have found that the best method to combine the RSI with seasonal trends is to buy an early partial position when the RSI turns up above 30 within four weeks of the seasonal buy date. The best time to sell an early partial position occurs when the RSI turns below 70, within four weeks of the seasonal exit date. Compared with the FSO, the RSI is less useful as it is slower and gives too few signals in the buy/sell windows.

Relative Strength

Relative strength calculates the performance of one security versus another security. When the relative strength is increasing, it indicates the seasonal security is outperforming. When the relative strength is declining, the seasonal security is underperforming. When a downward trend line is broken to the upside by the performance of the seasonal security, relative to the benchmark, this is a positive signal. This action carries a lot of weight and can justify a full early entry into a position if other technical evidence is positive. Likewise, if an upward trend line is broken to the downside, a negative technical signal is given and can justify a full early exit from a position if other technical evidence is negative.

THACKRAY'S 2022 INVESTOR'S GUIDE

You can choose great companies to invest in and still underperform the market. Unless you are in the market at the right time and in the best sectors, your investment expertise can be all for naught.

Successful investors know when they should be in the market. Very successful investors know when they should be in the market, and the best sectors in which to invest. *Thackray's 2022 Investor's Guide* is designed to provide investors with the knowledge of when and what to buy, and when to sell.

The goal of this book is to help investors capture extra profits by taking advantage of the seasonal trends in the markets. This book is straightforward. There are no complicated rules and there are no complex algorithms. The strategies put forward are intuitive and easy to understand.

It does not matter if you are a short-term or long-term investor, this book can be used to help establish entry and exit points. For the short-term investor, specific periods are identified that can provide profitable opportunities. For the long-term investor best buy dates are identified to launch new investments on a sound footing.

The stock market has its seasonal rhythms. Historically, the broad markets, such as the S&P 500, have a seasonal trend of outperforming during certain times of the year. Likewise, different sectors of the market have their own seasonal trends of outperformance. When oil stocks tend to do well in the springtime before "driving season," health care stocks tend to underperform the market. When utilities do well in the summertime, industrials do not. With different markets and different sectors having a tendency to outperform at different times of the year, there is always a place to invest.

Until recently, investors did not have access to the information necessary to analyse and create sector strategies. In recent years there have been a great number of sector Exchange Traded Funds (ETFs) and sector indexes introduced into the market. For the first time, investors are now able to easily implement a sector rotation strategy. This book provides a seasonal road map of what sectors tend to do well at different times of the year. It is a first of its kind, revealing new sector-based strategies that have never before been published.

In terms of market timing there are ample strategies in this book to help determine the times when equities should be over or underweight. During a favorable time for the market, investments can be purchased to overweight equities relative to their target weight in a portfolio (staying within risk tolerances). During an unfavorable time, investments can be sold to underweight equities relative to their target.

A large part of the book is devoted to sector seasonality – the underpinnings for a sector rotation strategy. The most practical rotation strategy is to create a core part of a portfolio that represents the broad market and then set aside an allocation to be rotated between favored sectors from one time period to the next.

It does not makes sense to apply any investment strategy only once with a large investment. Seasonal strategies are no exception. The best way to apply an investment strategy is to use a disciplined methodology that allows for diversification and a large enough number of investments to help remove the anomalies of the market. This reduces risk and increases the probability of a long term gain.

Following the specific buy and sell dates put forth in this book would have netted an investor large, above market returns. To "turbo-charge" gains, an investor can combine seasonality with technical analysis. As the seasonal periods are never exactly the same, technical analysis can help investors capture the extra gains when a sector turns up early, or momentum extends the trend.

IMPORTANT: Strategy Buy and Sell Dates
The beginning date of every strategy period in this book represents a full day in the market; therefore, investors should buy at the end of the preceding market day. For example the *Biotech Summer Solstice* seasonal period of strength is from June 23rd to September 13th. To be in the sector for the full seasonal period, an investor would enter the market before the closing bell on June 22nd. If the buy date landed on a weekend or holiday, then the buy would occur at the end of the preceding trading day.

The last day of a trading strategy is the sell date. For example, the Biotech sector investment would be sold at the end of the day on September 13th. If the sell date is a holiday or weekend, then the investment would be sold at the close on the preceding trading day.

What is Seasonal Investing?

In order to properly understand seasonal investing in the stock market, it is important to look briefly at its evolution. It may surprise investors to know that seasonal investing at the broad market level, i.e. Dow Jones or S&P 500, has been around for a long time. The initial seasonal strategies were written by Fields (1931, 1934) and Watchel (1942), who focused on the *January Effect*. Coincidentally, this strategy is still bantered about in the press every year.

Yale Yirsch Senior has been largely responsible for the next stage in the evolution, producing the *Stock Trader's Almanac* for more than forty years. This publication focuses on broad market trends such as the best six months of the year and tendencies of the market to do well depending on the political party in power and holiday trades.

In 2000, Brooke Thackray and Bruce Lindsay wrote, *Time In Time Out: Outsmart the Market Using Calendar Investment Strategies*. This work focused on a comprehensive analysis of the six month seasonal cycle and other shorter seasonal cycles in the broad markets such as the S&P 500.

Seasonal investing has changed over time. The focus has shifted from broad market strategies to taking advantage of sector rotation opportunities – investing in different sectors at different times of the year, depending on their seasonal strength. This has created a whole new set of investment opportunities. Rather than just being "in or out" of the market, investors can now always be invested by shifting between different sectors and asset classes, taking advantage of both up and down markets.

Definition – Seasonal investing is a method of investing in the market at the time of the year when it typically does well, or investing in a sector of the market when it typically outperforms the broad market such as the S&P 500.

The term seasonal investing is somewhat of a misnomer, and it is easy to see why some investors might believe that the discipline relates to investing based upon the seasons of the year – winter, spring, summer and autumn. Other than some agricultural commodities where the price is often correlated to growing seasons, generally seasonal investment strategies use the calendar as a reference for buy and sell dates. It is usually a specific event, i.e. Christmas sales, that occurs on a recurring annual basis that creates the seasonal opportunity.

The discipline of seasonal investing is not restricted to the stock market. It has been used successfully for a number of years in the commodities market. The opportunities in this market tend to be based upon changes in supply and/or demand that occur on a yearly basis. Most commodities, especially the agricultural commodities, tend to have cyclical supply cycles, i.e., crops are harvested only at certain times of the year. The supply bulge that occurs at the same time every year provides seasonal investors with profit opportunities. Recurring increased seasonal demand for commodities also plays a major part in providing opportunities for seasonal investors. This applies to most metals and many other commodities, whether the end-product is industrial or consumer based.

Seasonal investment strategies can be used with a lot of different types of investments. The premise is the same, outperformance during a certain period of the year based upon a repeating event in the markets or economy. In my past writings I have developed seasonal strategies that have been used successfully in the stock, commodity, bond and foreign exchange markets. Seasonal investing is still relatively new for most markets with a lot of new opportunities waiting to be discovered.

How Does Seasonal Investing Work?

Most stock market sector seasonal trends are the result of a recurring annual catalyst: an event that affects the sector positively. These events can range from a seasonal spike in demand, seasonal inventory lows, weather effects, conferences and other events. Mainstream investors very often anticipate a move in a sector and incorrectly try to take a position just before an event takes place that is supposed to drive a sector higher. A good example of this would be investors buying oil just before the cold weather sets in. Unfortunately, their efforts are usually unsuccessful as they are too late to the party and the opportunity has already passed.

By the time the anticipated event occurs, a substantial amount of investors have bought into the sector – fully pricing in the expected benefit. At this time there is little potential left in the short-term. Unless there is a strong positive surprise, the sector's outperformance tends to slowly roll over. If the event produces less than its desired result, the sector can be severely punished.

So how does the seasonal investor take advantage of this opportunity? "Be there" before the mainstream investors, and get out before they do. Seasonal investors usually enter a sector two or three months before an event is anticipated to have a positive effect on a sector and get out before the actual event takes place. In essence, seasonal investors are benefiting from the mainstream investor's tendency to "buy in" too late.

Seasonality in the markets occurs because of three major reasons: money flow, changing market analyst expectations and the *Anticipation-Realization Cycle*. First, money flows vary throughout the year and at different times of the month. Generally, money flows increase at the end of the year and into the start of the next year. This is a result of year end bonuses and tax related investments. In addition, money flows increase at month end from money managers "window dressing" their portfolios. As a result of these money flows, the months around the end of the year and the days around the end of the month, tend to have a stronger performance than the other times of the year.

Second, the analyst expectations cycle tends to push markets up at the end of the year and the beginning of the next year. Stock market analysts tend to be a positive bunch – the large investment houses pay them to be positive. They start the year with aggressive earnings for all of their favorite companies. As the year progresses, they generally back off their earnings forecast, which decreases their support for the market. After a lull in the summer and early autumn months, they start to focus on the next year with another rosy forecast. As a result, the stock market tends to rise once again at the end of the year.

Third, at the sector level, sectors of the market tend to be greatly influenced by the *Anticipation-Realization Cycle*. Although some investors may not be familiar with the term "anticipation-realization," they probably are familiar with the concept of "buy the rumor – sell the fact," or in the famous words of Lord Rothschild "Buy on the sound of the war-cannons; sell on the sound of the victory trumpets."

The *Anticipation-Realization Cycle* as it applies to human behavior has been much studied in psychology journals. In the investment world, the premise of this cycle rests on investors anticipating a positive event in the market to drive prices higher and buying in ahead of the event. When the event takes place, or is realized, upward pressure on prices decreases as there is very little impetus for further outperformance.

A good example of the *Anticipation-Realization Cycle* takes place with the "conference effect." Very often large industries have major conferences that occur at approximately the same time every year. Major companies in the industry often hold back positive announce-

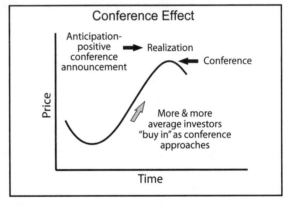

ments and product introductions to be released during the conference.

Two to three months prior to the conference, seasonal investors tend to buy into the sector. Shortly afterwards, the mainstream investors anticipate "good news" from the conference and start to buy in. As a result, prices are pushed up. Just before the conference starts, seasonal investors capture their profits by exiting their positions. As the conference unfolds, company announcements are made (realized), but as the potential good news has already been priced into the sector, there is little to push prices higher and the sector typically starts to rolls over.

The same *Anticipation-Realization Cycle* takes place with increased demand for oil to meet the "summer driving season", increased sales of goods at Christmas time, increased demand for gold jewellery to meet the autumn and winter demand, and many other events that tend to drive the outperformance of different sectors.

Does Seasonal Investing ALWAYS Work?

The simple answer to the above question is "No." There is not any investment system in the world that works all of the time. When following any investment system, it is probability of success that counts. It has often been said that "being correct in the markets 60% of the time will make you rich." Investors tend to forget this and become too emotionally attached to their losses. Just about every investment trading book states that investors typically fail to let their profits run and cut their losses quickly. I concur. In my many years in the investment industry, the biggest mistake that I have found with investors is not being able to cut their losses. Everyone wants to be right, that is how we have been raised. Investors feel that if they sell at a loss they have failed, and as a result, often suffer bigger losses by waiting for their position to trade at profit. With any investment system, investors should let probability work for them. This means that investors should be able to enter and exit positions capturing both gains and losses without becoming emotionally attached to any posi-

XOI vs S&P 500 1984 to 2019			
Feb 25 to May 9	S&P 500	positive XOI	Diff
1984	1.7 %	5.6 %	3.9 %
1985	1.4	4.9	3.5
1986	6.0	7.7	1.7
1987	3.7	25.5	21.8
1988	-3.0	5.6	8.6
1989	6.3	8.1	1.8
1990	5.8	-0.6	-6.3
1991	4.8	6.8	2.0
1992	0.9	5.8	4.9
1993	0.3	6.3	6.0
1994	-4.7	3.2	7.9
1995	7.3	10.3	3.1
1996	-2.1	2.2	4.3
1997	1.8	4.7	2.9
1998	7.5	9.8	2.3
1999	7.3	35.4	28.1
2000	4.3	22.2	17.9
2001	0.8	10.2	9.4
2002	-1.5	5.3	6.9
2003	12.1	5.7	-6.4
2004	-3.5	4.0	7.5
2005	-1.8	-1.0	0.8
2006	2.8	9.4	6.6
2007	4.2	10.1	5.8
2008	2.6	7.6	5.0
2009	20.2	15.8	-4.4
2010	0.5	-2.3	-2.8
2011	3.1	-0.6	-3.7
2012	-0.8	-13.4	-12.5
2013	7.3	3.8	-3.5
2014	1.7	9.1	7.4
2015	0.3	1.2	1.1
2016	6.7	11.1	4.4
2017	1.3	-4.0	-5.2
2018	-1.8	15.4	17.2
2019	2.8	-2.6	-5.4
Avg	2.9 %	6.9 %	4.0 %
Fq > 0	78 %	81 %	75 %

tions. Emotional attachment clouds judgement, which leads to errors. When all of the trades are put together, the goal is for profits to be larger than losses in a way that minimizes risks and beats the market.

If we examine the winter oil stock trade, we can see how probability has worked in an investor's favor. This trade is based upon the premise that at the tail end of winter, the refineries drive up demand for oil in order to produce enough gas for the approaching "driving season" that starts in the spring. As a result, oil stocks tend to increase and outperform the market (from February 25 to May 9). The oil stock sector, represented by the NYSE Arca Oil Index (XOI), has been very successful at this time of year, producing an average return of 6.9% and beating the S&P 500 by 4.0%, from 1984 to 2019. In addition it has been positive 29 out of 36 times. Investors should always evaluate the strength of seasonal trades before applying them to their own portfolios.

If an investor started using the seasonal investment discipline in 1984 and chose to invest in the winter-oil trade, they would have been very happy with the results. If an investor started using the strategy in 2010 a loss would have occurred following the strategy. The fact that the strategy did not produce gains in 2010, 2011 and 2012, does not mean that the seasonal trade no longer works. All seasonal trades go through periods, sometimes multiple years where they do not work. An investor can start any methodology of trading at the "wrong time," and be unsuccessful in a particular trade. In fact, if an investor started the oil-winter trade in 1990 and had given up in the same year, they would have missed the following successful twelve years. Investors have to remember that it is the final score that counts, after all of the gains have been weighed against the losses.

In practical terms, investors should not put all of their investment strategies in one basket. If one or two large investments were made based upon seasonal strategies, it is possible that the seasonal methodology might be inappropriately evaluated and its use discontinued. A much more prudent strategy is to use a larger number of strategic seasonal investments with smaller investments. The end result will be to put the seasonal probability to work with a much greater chance of success.

Measuring Seasonal Performance

How do you determine if a seasonal strategy has been successful? Many people feel that ten years of data is a good sample size, others feel that fifteen years is better, and yet others feel that the more data the better. I tend to fall into the camp that, if possible, it is best to use fifteen or twenty years of data for sectors and more data for the broad markets, such as the S&P 500. Although the most recent data in almost any analytical framework is the most relevant, it is important to get enough data to reflect a sector's performance across different economic conditions. Given that historically the economy has performed on an eight year cycle, four years of expansion and then four years of contraction, using a short data set does not provide for enough exposure to different economic conditions.

A data set that is too long can run into the problem of older data having too much of an influence on the numbers when fundamental factors affecting a sector have changed. It is important to look at trends over time and assess if there has been a change that should be considered in determining the dates for a seasonal cycle. Each sector should be judged on its own merit. The analysis tables in this book illustrate the performance level for each year in order to provide the opportunity for readers to determine any relevant changes.

In order to determine if a seasonal strategy is effective there are two possible benchmarks, absolute and relative performance. Absolute performance measures if a profit is made and relative performance measures the performance of a sector in relationship to a major market. Both measurements have their merits and depending on your investment style, one measurement may be more valuable than another. This book provides both sets of measurement in tables and graphs.

It is not just the average percent gain of a sector over a certain time period that determines success. It is possible that one or two spectacular years of performance skew the results substantially (particularly with a small data set). The frequency of success is also very important: the higher the percentage of success the better. Also, the fewer large drawdowns the better. There is no magic number (percent success rate) per se of what constitutes a successful strategy. The success rate should be above fifty percent, otherwise it would be better to just invest in the broad market. Ideally speaking a strategy should have a high percentage success rate on both an absolute and relative basis. Some strategies are stronger than others, but that does not mean that the weaker strategies should not be used. Prudence should be used in determining the ideal portfolio allocation.

Illustrating the strength of a sector's seasonal performance can be accomplished through either an absolute yearly average performance graph, or a relative yearly average performance graph. The absolute graph shows the average yearly cumulative gain for a set number of years. It lets a reader visually identify the strong periods during the year. The relative graph shows the average yearly cumulative gain for the sector relative to the benchmark index.

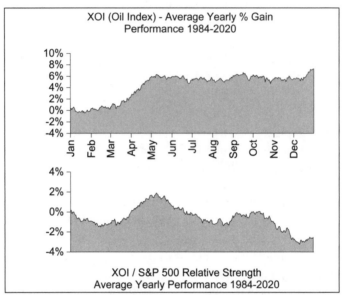

Both graphs are useful in determining the strength of a particular seasonal strategy. In the above diagram, the top graph illustrates the average year for the NYSE Arca Oil Index (XOI) from 1984 to 2020. Essentially it illustrates the cumulative average gain if an investment were made in the index. The steep rising line starting in January/February shows the overall price rise that typically occurs in this sector at this time of year. In May the line flattens out and then rises very modestly starting in July.

The bottom graph is a ratio graph, illustrating the strength of the XOI Index relative to the S&P 500. It is derived by dividing the average year of the XOI by the average year of the S&P 500. When the line in the graph is rising, the XOI is outperforming the S&P 500, and vise versa when it is declining. This is an important graph and should be used in considering seasonal investments because the S&P 500 is a viable alternative to the energy sector. If both markets are increasing, but the S&P 500 is increasing at a faster rate, the S&P 500 represents a more attractive opportunity. This is particularly true when measuring the risk of a volatile sector relative to the broad market. If both investments were expected to produce the same rate of return, generally the broad market is a better investment because of its diversification.

Who Can Use Seasonal Investing?

Any investor from novice to expert, from short-term trader to long-term investor can benefit from using seasonal analysis. Seasonal investing is unique because it is an easy to understand system that can be used by itself or as a complement to another investment discipline. For the novice it provides an easy to follow strategy that makes intuitive sense. For the expert it can be used as a stand-alone system or as a complement to an existing system.

Seasonal investing is easily understood by all levels of investors, which allows investors to make rational decisions. This may seem obvious, but it is very common for investors to listen to a "guru of the market", be impressed and blindly follow his advice. When the advice works there is no problem. When the advice does not work investors wonder why they made the investment in the first place. When investors do not understand their investments it causes stress, bad decisions and a lack of "stick-to-it ness" with any investment discipline. Even expert investors realize the importance of understanding your investments. Peter Lynch of Fidelity Investments used to say "Never invest in any idea that you can't illustrate with a crayon." Investors do not need to go that far, but they should understand their investments.

Novice investors find seasonal strategies very easy to understand because they are intuitive. They do not have to be investing for years to understand why seasonal strategies work. They understand that an increase in demand for gold every year at the same time causes a ripple effect in the stock market pushing up gold stocks at the same time every year.

Most expert investors use information from a variety of sources in making their decisions. Even experts that primarily use fundamental analysis can benefit from using seasonal trends to get an edge in the market. Fundamental analysis is a very crude tool and provides very little in the way of timing an investment. Using seasonal trends can help with the timing of the buy and sell decisions and produce extra profit.

Seasonal investing can be used by both short-term and long-term investors, but in different ways. For short-term investors it provides a complete trade – buy and sell dates. For long-term investors it can provide a buy date for a sector of interest.

Combining Seasonal Analysis with other Investment Disciplines

Seasonal investing used by itself has historically produced above average market returns. Depending on an investor's particular style, it can be combined with one of the other three investment disciplines: fundamental, quantitative and technical analysis. There are two basic ways to combine seasonal analysis with other investment methodologies – as the primary or secondary method. If it is used as a primary method, seasonally strong time periods are established for a number of sectors and then appropriate sectors are chosen based upon fundamental, quantitative or technical screens. If it is used as a secondary method, sector selections are first made based upon one of three methods and then final sectors are chosen based upon which ones are in their seasonally strong period.

Technical analysis is an ideal mate for seasonal analysis. Unlike fundamental and quantitative analysis, which are very blunt timing tools at best, seasonal and technical analysis can provide specific trigger points to buy and sell. The combination can turbo-charge investment strategies, adding extra profits by fine-tuning entry and exit dates.

Seasonal analysis provides both buy and sell dates. Although a sector in the market can sometimes bottom on the exact seasonal buy date, it more often bottoms a bit early or a bit late. After all, the seasonal buy date is based upon an average of historical performance. Depending on the sector, buying opportunities start to develop approximately one month before and after the seasonal buy date. Using technical analysis gives an investor the advantage of buying into a sector when it turns up early or waiting when it turns up late. Likewise, technical analysis can be used to trigger a sell signal when the market turns down before or after the sell date.

The sell decision can be extended with the help of a trailing stop-loss order. If a sector has strong momentum and the technical tools do not provide a sell signal, it is possible to let the sector "run." When a trailing stop-loss is used, a profitable sell point is established. If the price continues to run, then the selling point is raised. If, on the other hand, the price falls through the stop-loss point, the position is sold.

Sectors of the Market

Standard & Poor's has done an excellent job in categorizing the U.S. stock market into its different parts. Although the demand for this service initially came from institutional investors, many individual investors now seek the same information. Knowing the sector breakdown in the market allows investors to see how different their portfolio is relative to the market. As a result, they are able to make conscious decisions on what parts of the stock market to overweight based upon their beliefs of which sectors will outperform. It also helps control the amount of desired risk.

Standard & Poor's uses four levels of detail in its Global Industry Classification Standard (GICS[©]) to categorize stock markets around the world. From the most specific, it classifies companies into sub-industries, industries, industry groups and finally economic sectors. All companies in the Standard & Poor's global family of indices are classified according to the GICS structure.

This book focuses on the U.S. market, analysing the trends of the venerable S&P 500 index and its economic sectors and industry groups. The following diagram illustrates the index classified according to its economic sectors.

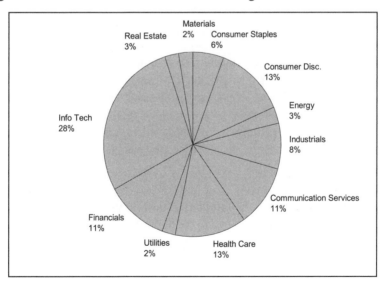

Standard and Poor's, Understanding Sectors, June 30, 2021

For more information on Standard and Poor's Global Industry Classification Standard (GICS[©]), refer to www.standardandpoors.com

Investment Products – Which One Is The Right One?

There are many ways to take advantage of the seasonal trends at the broad stock market and sector levels. Regardless of the investment products that you currently use, whether exchange traded funds, mutual funds, stocks or options, all can be used with the strategies in this book. Different investments offer different risk-reward relationships and return potential.

Exchange Traded Funds (ETFs)

Exchange Traded Funds (ETFs) offer the purest method of seasonal investment. The broad market ETFs are designed to track the major indices and the sector ETFs are designed to track specific sectors without using active management. Relatively new, ETFs are a great way to capture both market and sector trends. They were originally introduced into the Canadian market in 1993 to represent the Toronto stock market index. Shortly afterward they were introduced to the U.S. market and there are now hundreds of ETFs to represent almost every market, sector, style of investing and company capitalization. Originally ETFs were mainly of interest to institutional investors, but individual investors have fast realized the merits of ETF investing and have made some of the broad market ETFs the most heavily traded securities in the world.

An ETF is a single security that represents a market, such as the S&P 500; a sector of the market, such as the financial sector; or a commodity, such as gold. In the case of the S&P 500, an investor buying one security is buying all 500 stocks in the index. By investing into a financial ETF, an investor is buying the companies that make up the financial sector of the market. By investing into a gold commodity ETF, an investor is buying a security that represents the price of gold.

ETFs trade on the open market just like stocks. They have a bid and an ask, can be shorted and many are option eligible. They are a very low cost, tax efficient method of targeting specific parts of the market.

Mutual Funds

Mutual funds are a good way to combine market or sector investing with active management. In recent years, many mutual fund companies have added sector funds to accommodate an increasing appetite in this area.

As the seasonal strategies put forward in this book have a short-term nature, it is important to make sure that there are no fees (or a nominal charge) for getting into and out of a position in the market.

Stocks

Stocks provide an opportunity to make better returns than the market or sector. If the market increases during its seasonal period, some stocks will increase dramatically more than the index. Choosing one of the outperforming stocks will greatly enhance returns; choosing one of the underperforming stocks can create substantial loses. Using stocks requires increased attention to diversification and security selection.

Options

Disclaimer: Options involve risk and are not suitable for every investor. Because they are cash-settled, investors should be aware of the special risks associated with index options and should consult a tax advisor. Prior to buying or selling options, a person must receive a copy of Characteristics and Risks of Standardized Options and should thoroughly understand the risks involved in any use of options. Copies may be obtained from The Options Clearing Corporation, 440 S. LaSalle Street, Chicago, IL 60605.

Options, for more sophisticated investors, are a good tool to take advantage of both market and sector opportunities. An option position can be established with either stocks or ETFs. There are many different ways to use options for seasonal trends: establish a long position on the market during its seasonally strong period, establish a short position during its seasonally weak period, or create a spread trade to capture the superior gains of a sector over the market.

THACKRAY'S 2022 INVESTOR'S GUIDE

CONTENTS

JANUARY

	MONDAY	TUESDAY	WEDNESDAY
WEEK 01	**3** 28 CAN Market Closed - New Year's Day	**4** 27	**5** 26
WEEK 02	**10** 21	**11** 20	**12** 19
WEEK 03	**17** 14 USA Market Closed - Martin Luther King Jr. Day	**18** 13	**19** 12
WEEK 04	**24** 7	**25** 6	**26** 5
WEEK 05	**31**	1	2

THURSDAY	FRIDAY
6 25	**7** 24
13 18	**14** 17
20 11	**21** 10
27 4	**28** 3
3	4

FEBRUARY

M	T	W	T	F	S	S
	1	2	3	4	5	6
7	8	9	10	11	12	13
14	15	16	17	18	19	20
21	22	23	24	25	26	27
28						

MARCH

M	T	W	T	F	S	S
	1	2	3	4	5	6
7	8	9	10	11	12	13
14	15	16	17	18	19	20
21	22	23	24	25	26	27
28	29	30	31			

APRIL

M	T	W	T	F	S	S
				1	2	3
4	5	6	7	8	9	10
11	13	13	14	15	16	17
18	19	20	21	22	23	24
25	26	27	28	29	30	

MAY

M	T	W	T	F	S	S
						1
2	3	4	5	6	7	8
9	10	11	12	13	14	15
16	17	18	19	20	21	22
23	24	25	26	27	28	29
30	31					

JANUARY SUMMARY

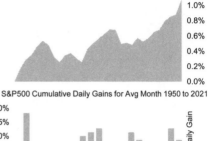

S&P500 Cumulative Daily Gains for Avg Month 1950 to 2021

	Dow Jones	S&P 500	Nasdaq	TSX Comp
Month Rank	5	5	1	3
# Up	45	43	32	23
# Down	26	28	17	13
% Pos	63	61	65	64
% Avg. Gain	1.0	1.1	2.6	1.2

Dow & S&P 1950-2020, Nasdaq 1972-2020, TSX 1985-2020

Prob. of Daily Gain

♦ Over the last ten years, the stock market in January has had large moves up or down on a number of occasions, and has increased three times by more than 5%. ♦ It has also decreased once by more than 5%. ♦ In January there is typically a lot of sector rotation. ♦ Small caps tend to perform well. ♦ The technology sector finishes its seasonal period. ♦ The industrials, materials, metals and mining sectors start the second part of their seasonal periods. ♦ The retail sector starts its strongest seasonal period.

BEST / WORST JANUARY BROAD MKTS. 2012-2021

BEST JANUARY MARKETS
- ♦ Russell 2000 (2019) 11.2%
- ♦ Nasdaq (2019) 9.7%
- ♦ TSX Comp. (2019) 8.5%

WORST JANUARY MARKETS
- ♦ Russell 2000 (2016) - 8.8%
- ♦ Nikkei 225 (2016) -8.5%
- ♦ Nikkei 225 (2016) -8.0%

Index Values End of Month

	2012	2013	2014	2015	2016	2017	2018	2019	2020	2021
Dow	12,633	13,861	15,699	17,165	16,466	19,864	26,149	25,000	28,256	29,983
S&P 500	1,312	1,498	1,783	1,995	1,940	2,279	2,824	2,704	3,226	3,714
Nasdaq	2,814	3,142	4,104	4,635	4,614	5,615	7,411	7,282	9,151	13,071
TSX Comp.	12,452	12,685	13,695	14,674	12,822	15,386	15,952	15,541	17,318	17,337
Russell 1000	726	832	996	1,112	1,070	1,265	1,562	1,498	1,784	2,101
Russell 2000	793	902	1,131	1,165	1,035	1,362	1,575	1,499	1,614	2,074
FTSE 100	5,682	6,277	6,510	6,749	6,084	7,099	7,534	6,969	7,286	6,407
Nikkei 225	8,803	11,139	14,915	17,674	17,518	19,041	23,098	20,773	23,205	27,663

Percent Gain for January

	2012	2013	2014	2015	2016	2017	2018	2019	2020	2021
Dow	3.4	5.8	-5.3	-3.7	-5.5	0.5	5.8	7.2	-1.0	-2.0
S&P 500	4.4	5.0	-3.6	-3.1	-5.1	1.8	5.6	7.9	-0.2	-1.1
Nasdaq	8.0	4.1	-1.7	-2.1	-7.9	4.3	7.4	9.7	2.0	1.4
TSX Comp.	4.2	2.0	0.5	0.3	-1.4	0.6	-1.6	8.5	1.5	-0.6
Russell 1000	4.8	5.3	-3.3	-2.8	-5.5	1.9	5.4	8.2	0.0	-0.9
Russell 2000	7.0	6.2	-2.8	-3.3	-8.8	0.3	2.6	11.2	-3.3	5.0
FTSE 100	2.0	6.4	-3.5	2.8	-2.5	-0.6	-2.0	3.6	-3.4	-0.8
Nikkei 225	4.1	7.2	-8.5	1.3	-8.0	-0.4	1.5	3.8	-1.9	0.8

January Market Avg. Performance 2012 to 2021[1]

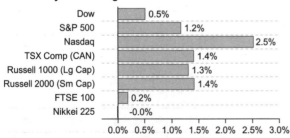

- Dow: 0.5%
- S&P 500: 1.2%
- Nasdaq: 2.5%
- TSX Comp (CAN): 1.4%
- Russell 1000 (Lg Cap): 1.3%
- Russell 2000 (Sm Cap): 1.4%
- FTSE 100: 0.2%
- Nikkei 225: -0.0%

0.0% 0.5% 1.0% 1.5% 2.0% 2.5% 3.0%

Interest Corner Jan[2]

	Fed Funds % [3]	3 Mo. T-Bill % [4]	10 Yr % [5]	20 Yr % [6]
2021	0.25	0.06	1.11	1.68
2020	1.75	1.55	1.51	1.83
2019	2.50	2.41	2.63	2.83
2018	1.50	1.46	2.72	2.83
2017	0.75	0.52	2.45	2.78

(1) Russell Data provided by Russell (2) Federal Reserve Bank of St. Louis- end of month values (3) Target rate set by FOMC (4)(5)(6) Constant yield maturities.

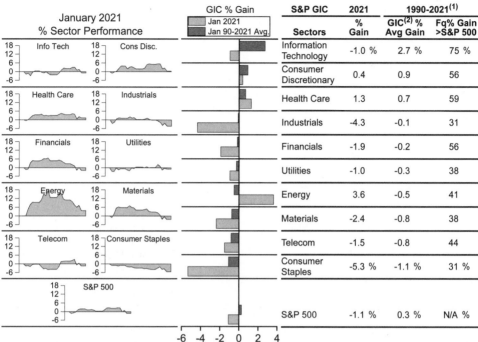

S&P GIC Sectors	2021 % Gain	1990-2021[1] GIC[2] % Avg Gain	1990-2021[1] Fq% Gain >S&P 500
Information Technology	-1.0 %	2.7 %	75 %
Consumer Discretionary	0.4	0.9	56
Health Care	1.3	0.7	59
Industrials	-4.3	-0.1	31
Financials	-1.9	-0.2	56
Utilities	-1.0	-0.3	38
Energy	3.6	-0.5	41
Materials	-2.4	-0.8	38
Telecom	-1.5	-0.8	44
Consumer Staples	-5.3 %	-1.1 %	31 %
S&P 500	-1.1 %	0.3 %	N/A %

Sector Commentary

♦ In January 2021, the S&P 500 had a loss of 1.1%.
♦ The energy sector was the most volatile sector, making a large gain in the first half of the month and then giving most of it back, but still managing to produce a gain of 3.5%. ♦ The consumer staples sector produced a big loss of 5.3%. ♦ Typically, the cyclical sectors of the market start their strong seasonal periods in late January. In 2021, the cyclical sectors lagged the stock market at the end of January.

Sub-Sector Commentary

♦ In January 2021, homebuilders performed well as the economy was expanding and interest rates remained low. ♦ On a seasonal basis, January tends to be a strong month for the homebuilders sector. ♦ The automobile sub-sector performed well as strong auto sales continued to bolster the sector. Typically, the automobile sub-sector tends to start its strong seasonal period in late February. ♦ The transportation sub-sector is typically weak for most of January and January 2021 was no exception as the sub-sector lost 5.3%.

SELECTED SUB-SECTORS[3]			
SOX (1995-2021)	3.3 %	3.6 %	59 %
Home-builders	8.5	3.4	63
Silver	3.5	3.0	66
Gold	-1.3	1.8	56
Biotech (1993-2021)	2.3	1.8	55
Railroads	-4.0	1.3	56
Automotive & Components	13.0	1.2	50
Retail	-1.2	0.7	56
Steel	-8.4	0.2	47
Transportation	-5.3	0.0	47
Pharma	1.8	0.0	53
Banks	-0.8	-0.1	50
Agriculture (1994-2021)	-0.8	-0.3	43
Metals & Mining	-0.3	-0.7	44
Chemicals	-2.6	-0.8	38

AUTOMATIC DATA PROCESSING
① SELL SHORT (Jan1-Jan31)
② LONG (Sep13-Nov17)

Hiring employees has a seasonal cycle. The trend forms a trough in January, rising in the spring and once again forming another trough in the summer and then rising in autumn and then once again declining into January.

ADP has a similar seasonal cycle. As a result, ADP tends to perform poorly in January. Since 1990 to 2020, the worst month of the year for ADP has been January on an average, median and frequency basis.

From 1990 to 2020, in the month of January, ADP has produced an average loss of 1.5% and has only been positive 35% of the time.

10% growth & 77% of the time positive

On a positive note, in the same yearly time period, October is the strongest month of the year on an average, median and frequency basis. October, is the sweet spot for ADP's strong seasonal period that lasts from September 13 to November 17. In this period, from 1990 to 2020, ADP has produced an average gain of 8.6% and has been positive 84% of the time.

Covid-19 Pandemic Update. In 2021, ADP performed poorly in January, its weak seasonal period. In late January, ADP managed to perform better and start a rally on an absolute and relative basis compared to the S&P 500. The rally continued in the first half of 2021.

ⓘ *ADP is the stock symbol for Automatic Data Processing which trades on the NYSE and is adjusted for stock splits.*

ADP vs. S&P 500 1990 to 2020

Positive Long ▢   Negative Short ▢

Year	Jan 1 to Jan 31 S&P 500	ADP	Sep 13 to Nov 17 S&P 500	ADP	Compound Growth S&P 500	ADP
1990	-6.9 %	-4.1 %	-1.7 %	9.4 %	-8.4 %	13.9 %
1991	4.2	11.4	-1.2	12.9	2.9	0.0
1992	-2.0	-6.0	-0.1	7.2	-2.1	13.7
1993	0.7	-3.3	0.7	13.3	1.4	17.0
1994	3.3	-5.2	-0.6	6.8	2.7	12.3
1995	2.4	1.3	4.1	14.6	6.6	13.1
1996	3.3	7.4	9.9	0.0	13.5	-7.4
1997	6.1	-3.5	2.4	23.5	8.7	27.8
1998	1.0	-2.5	12.9	10.8	14.1	13.6
1999	4.1	6.2	4.4	21.0	8.6	13.6
2000	-5.1	-11.9	-7.7	8.2	-12.4	21.1
2001	3.5	-5.5	4.2	8.2	7.8	14.1
2002	-1.6	-8.3	2.6	19.0	1.0	28.9
2003	-2.7	-11.7	2.5	-1.9	-0.4	9.6
2004	1.7	7.9	5.2	9.3	7.0	0.7
2005	-2.5	-2.0	0.2	13.7	-2.4	15.9
2006	2.5	-4.3	6.7	4.5	9.4	8.9
2007	1.4	-3.1	-0.9	5.6	0.5	8.9
2008	-6.1	-8.9	-32.0	-23.1	-36.2	-16.2
2009	-8.6	-7.7	6.5	14.6	-2.6	23.4
2010	-3.7	-4.7	6.2	10.9	2.3	16.2
2011	2.3	3.5	4.6	3.6	7.0	-0.1
2012	4.4	1.4	-5.3	-4.6	-1.2	-6.0
2013	5.0	4.1	6.8	4.2	12.2	-0.1
2014	-3.6	-5.2	2.8	16.4	-0.8	22.4
2015	-3.1	-1.0	4.6	9.7	1.3	10.8
2016	-5.1	-1.9	1.3	7.1	-3.8	9.1
2017	1.8	-1.7	3.3	2.9	5.1	4.7
2018	5.6	5.5	-5.3	-0.4	0.0	-5.9
2019	7.9	6.7	3.7	6.7	11.8	-0.4
2020	-0.2	0.5	8.0	32.0	7.9	31.3
Avg.	0.3 %	-1.5 %	1.6 %	8.6 %	2.0 %	10.2 %
Fq>0	58 %	35 %	71 %	84 %	68 %	77 %

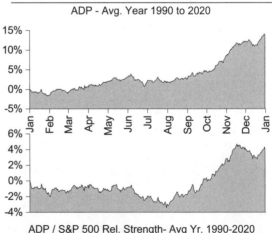

ADP - Avg. Year 1990 to 2020

ADP / S&P 500 Rel. Strength- Avg Yr. 1990-2020

ADP Performance

ADP Monthly % Gain (1990-2020)

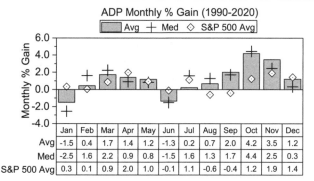

	Jan	Feb	Mar	Apr	May	Jun	Jul	Aug	Sep	Oct	Nov	Dec
Avg	-1.5	0.4	1.7	1.4	1.2	-1.3	0.2	0.7	2.0	4.2	3.5	1.2
Med	-2.5	1.6	2.2	0.9	0.8	-1.5	1.6	1.3	1.7	4.4	2.5	0.3
S&P 500 Avg	0.3	0.1	0.9	2.0	1.0	-0.1	1.1	-0.6	-0.4	1.2	1.9	1.4

Fq ADP Gain > 0% (1990-2020)

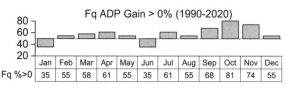

	Jan	Feb	Mar	Apr	May	Jun	Jul	Aug	Sep	Oct	Nov	Dec
Fq %>0	35	55	58	61	55	35	61	55	68	81	74	55

Fq % ADP Gain > S&P 500 % (1990-2020)

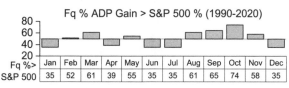

	Jan	Feb	Mar	Apr	May	Jun	Jul	Aug	Sep	Oct	Nov	Dec
Fq %> S&P 500	35	52	61	39	55	35	35	61	65	74	58	35

ADP % Gain 5 Year (2016-2020)

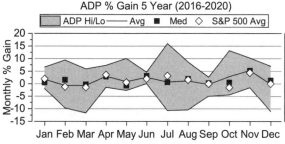

ADP Performance 2020-2021

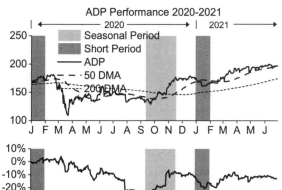

Relative Strength, % Gain vs. S&P 500

Market Indices & Rates
Weekly Values**

Stock Markets	2020	2021
Dow	28,635	31,098
S&P500	3,235	3,825
Nasdaq	9,021	13,202
TSX	17,066	18,042
FTSE	7,622	6,873
DAX	13,219	14,050
Nikkei	23,657	28,139
Hang Seng	28,452	27,878

Commodities	2020	2021
Oil	63.05	52.24
Gold	1548.8	1862.9

Bond Yields	2020	2021
USA 5 Yr Treasury	1.59	0.49
USA 10 Yr T	1.80	1.13
USA 20 Yr T	2.11	1.67
Moody's Aaa	2.94	2.48
Moody's Baa	3.79	3.32
CAN 5 Yr T	1.55	0.45
CAN 10 Yr T	1.54	0.81

Money Market	2020	2021
USA Fed Funds	1.75	0.25
USA 3 Mo T-B	1.49	0.08
CAN tgt overnight rate	1.75	0.25
CAN 3 Mo T-B	1.65	0.06

Foreign Exchange	2020	2021
EUR/USD	1.12	1.22
GBP/USD	1.31	1.36
USD/CAD	1.30	1.27
USD/JPY	108.09	103.94

JANUARY

M	T	W	T	F	S	S
					1	2
3	4	5	6	7	8	9
10	11	12	13	14	15	16
17	18	19	20	21	22	23
24	25	26	27	28	29	30
31						

FEBRUARY

M	T	W	T	F	S	S
1	1	2	3	4	5	6
7	8	9	10	11	12	13
14	15	16	17	18	19	20
21	22	23	24	25	26	27
28						

MARCH

M	T	W	T	F	S	S
	1	2	3	4	5	6
7	8	9	10	11	12	13
14	15	16	17	18	19	20
21	22	23	24	25	26	27
28	29	30	31			

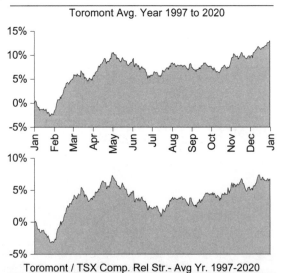

TOROMONT
① Jan31 to Mar7 ② Oct14 to Dec14

Toromont's revenue generation on average ramps up from Q1 to Q4 of the calendar year. The first quarter of the year tends to be the weakest. Revenue tends to take a large jump from Q1 to Q2 and then from Q3 to Q4. Investors try and front run these trends.

The result of the investor behavior has created two seasonal periods for Toromont. The first seasonal period is from January 31 to March 7. In this time period, from 1997 to 2020, Toromont has produced an average gain of 8.8% and has been positive 88% of the time.

14% gain

Investors should note the juxtaposition of Toromont's January 31 to March 7 strong seasonal period with the weakest month of the year– December. January, the start of the strong seasonal period is the strongest month of the year. The strong seasonal period starts at the end of January, but in any one year, could start earlier or later.

The second seasonal period is from October 14 to December 14. In this time period, from 1997 to 2020, Toromont has produced an average gain of 5.1% and has been positive 75% of the time.

It should also be noted that the end of this seasonal period, occurs just before the weakest month of the year for Toromont – January.

Covid-19 Performance Update. In 2021, Toromont outperformed the Canadian stock market up until June as it mirrored the performance of the cyclical sectors of the stock market.

*Source: TIH- stock symbol for Toromont which trades on the Toronto Stock Exchange, adjusted for stock splits.

Toromont vs TSX Comp. 1997 to 2020   Positive ☐

Year	Jan 31 to Mar 7 S&P 500	Jan 31 to Mar 7 TIH	Oct 14 to Dec 14 S&P 500	Oct 14 to Dec 14 TIH	Compound Growth S&P 500	Compound Growth TIH
1997	3.0 %	0.4 %	-6.6 %	6.2 %	-3.8 %	6.5 %
1998	7.2	23.8	12.1	4.8	20.3	29.7
1999	-4.7	6.5	12.7	-1.2	7.4	5.2
2000	12.3	8.5	-12.1	14.5	-1.3	24.2
2001	-11.2	15.8	5.6	4.7	-6.2	21.2
2002	5.4	21.1	11.5	-2.0	17.5	18.7
2003	-2.8	1.1	4.5	9.0	1.6	10.2
2004	3.8	15.8	4.1	2.3	8.0	18.5
2005	8.1	0.7	6.4	6.9	15.0	7.7
2006	-1.1	3.2	9.3	4.6	8.1	8.0
2007	-0.2	18.2	-4.3	11.5	-4.5	31.8
2008	2.2	19.8	-6.1	-2.1	-4.0	17.3
2009	-12.7	-0.9	1.2	12.5	-11.7	11.5
2010	7.9	7.9	4.8	8.0	13.1	16.6
2011	4.9	-0.9	-3.1	11.5	1.6	10.5
2012	-0.7	7.4	0.8	8.8	0.1	16.8
2013	0.3	8.1	1.8	17.4	2.1	26.9
2014	4.1	1.9	-3.5	5.9	0.5	8.0
2015	1.9	13.5	-8.3	-7.8	-6.6	4.6
2016	4.4	16.0	3.8	9.6	8.3	27.2
2017	1.3	9.2	1.3	-5.2	2.7	3.5
2018	-3.0	1.9	-5.3	-15.6	-8.2	-14.0
2019	3.7	16.5	3.6	5.6	7.4	23.0
2020	-7.5	-4.2	5.3	13.0	-2.6	8.2
Avg.	1.1 %	8.8 %	1.6 %	5.1 %	2.7 %	14.2 %
Fq>0	63 %	88 %	67 %	75 %	63 %	96 %

Toromont Avg. Year 1997 to 2020

Toromont / TSX Comp. Rel Str.- Avg Yr. 1997-2020

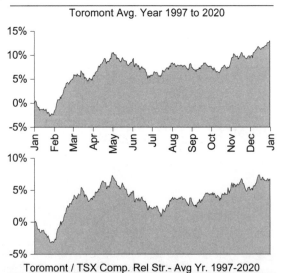

Toromont Performance

Market Indices & Rates
Weekly Values**

Toromont Monthly % Gain (1997-2020)

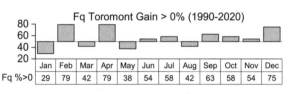

	Jan	Feb	Mar	Apr	May	Jun	Jul	Aug	Sep	Oct	Nov	Dec
Avg	-2.1	7.3	0.4	5.2	-1.6	-2.5	2.4	-0.5	0.2	0.6	1.3	3.5
Med	-2.8	7.9	-0.7	4.7	-2.2	0.2	3.5	-0.9	0.4	0.7	1.3	4.2
TSX Comp. Avg	0.9	0.4	-0.1	1.8	0.9	-0.2	0.7	-0.4	-1.1	0.0	1.1	1.4

Fq Toromont Gain > 0% (1990-2020)

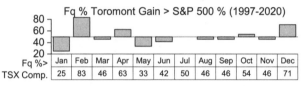

	Jan	Feb	Mar	Apr	May	Jun	Jul	Aug	Sep	Oct	Nov	Dec
Fq %>0	29	79	42	79	38	54	58	42	63	58	54	75

Fq % Toromont Gain > S&P 500 % (1997-2020)

	Jan	Feb	Mar	Apr	May	Jun	Jul	Aug	Sep	Oct	Nov	Dec
Fq %> TSX Comp.	25	83	46	63	33	42	50	46	46	54	46	71

Stock Markets	2020	2021
Dow	28,824	30,814
S&P500	3,265	3,768
Nasdaq	9,179	12,999
TSX	17,234	17,909
FTSE	7,588	6,736
DAX	13,483	13,788
Nikkei	23,851	28,519
Hang Seng	28,638	28,574

Commodities	2020	2021
Oil	59.04	52.36
Gold	1553.6	1839.0

Bond Yields	2020	2021
USA 5 Yr Treasury	1.63	0.46
USA 10 Yr T	1.83	1.11
USA 20 Yr T	2.14	1.66
Moody's Aaa	2.99	2.46
Moody's Baa	3.82	3.24
CAN 5 Yr T	1.60	0.43
CAN 10 Yr T	1.59	0.81

Money Market	2020	2021
USA Fed Funds	1.75	0.25
USA 3 Mo T-B	1.51	0.09
CAN tgt overnight rate	1.75	0.25
CAN 3 Mo T-B	1.64	0.05

Foreign Exchange	2020	2021
EUR/USD	1.11	1.21
GBP/USD	1.31	1.36
USD/CAD	1.31	1.27
USD/JPY	109.45	103.85

Toromont % Gain 5 Year (2016-2020)

Toromont Performance 2020-2021

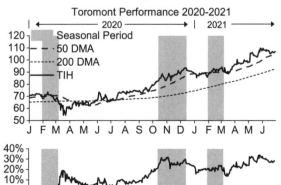

Relative Strength, % Gain vs. TSX Comp.

JANUARY

M	T	W	T	F	S	S
					1	2
3	4	5	6	7	8	9
10	11	12	13	14	15	16
17	18	19	20	21	22	23
24	25	26	27	28	29	30
31						

FEBRUARY

M	T	W	T	F	S	S
1	1	2	3	4	5	6
7	8	9	10	11	12	13
14	15	16	17	18	19	20
21	22	23	24	25	26	27
28						

MARCH

M	T	W	T	F	S	S
	1	2	3	4	5	6
7	8	9	10	11	12	13
14	15	16	17	18	19	20
21	22	23	24	25	26	27
28	29	30	31			

SILVER – SHINES
① LONG (Dec27 to Feb22)
② SELL SHORT (April12-Jun29)

Gold and silver have a high degree of price correlation, with silver typically mirroring the direction of gold's price changes. When gold increases in price, silver typically increases in price and vice versa. Despite this relationship, the seasonal profiles for gold and silver are different because of silver's use in industrial products

9% growth

Although the period of seasonal strength for silver finishes in late February, under favorable conditions of rising base metal prices, silver can perform well into late March.

Historically, when silver has corrected sharply in December, it has often rallied strongly at the beginning of its seasonal period. This phenomenon has taken place a few times over the last few years. Over the last twenty years, silver has been positive nineteen times in its strong seasonal period from late December to late February.

Covid-19 Performance Update. In 2020/21, silver was positive in its seasonal period from December 27 to February 22. Silver started to perform poorly at the end of May as the cyclical sectors of the stock market generally underperformed the S&P 500.

In 2021, silver has been in the news as investors have looked for it to play an important part in the green infrastructure build out that has been expected. It has also been a hot topic on the Reddit board, as some investors tried to force a short squeeze on silver. Nevertheless, silver performed poorly in the 1st half of 2021.

*Source: Bank of England- London PM represents the close value of silver in afternoon trading in London.

Silver* vs. S&P 500 1983/84 to 2020/21

Positive Long   Negative Short

Year	Dec 27 to Feb 22 S&P 500	Dec 27 to Feb 22 Silver	April 12 to Jun 29 S&P 500	April 12 to Jun 29 Silver	Compound Growth S&P 500	Compound Growth Silver
1983/84	-5.5	6.6 %	-1.2 %	-9.7 %	-6.6 %	17.0 %
1984/85	7.7	-6.4	6.5	-8.5	14.7	1.6
1985/86	8.4	1.7	5.8	-6.8	14.7	8.7
1986/87	15.6	2.6	5.3	0.8	21.7	1.8
1987/88	5.4	-5.1	0.3	4.7	5.7	-9.6
1988/89	4.7	-2.9	7.1	-9.4	12.1	6.2
1989/90	-6.1	-5.5	4.7	-4.8	-1.7	-1.0
1990/91	10.5	-10.4	-1.7	11.7	8.6	-20.9
1991/92	1.6	5.2	1.2	-3.4	2.8	8.7
1992/93	-1.0	-2.8	2.0	14.9	1.0	-17.3
1993/94	0.9	2.7	-0.5	-3.4	0.4	6.2
1994/95	5.5	0.1	7.6	1.0	13.5	-0.9
1995/96	7.3	9.2	6.3	-9.1	14.0	19.2
1996/97	6.1	8.2	20.3	-0.9	27.6	9.1
1997/98	10.4	7.9	2.5	-17.2	13.2	26.5
1998/99	3.7	13.7	0.2	4.8	4.0	8.2
1999/00	-7.3	1.0	-3.9	-2.7	-10.9	3.7
2000/01	-4.7	-3.8	5.0	0.1	0.0	-3.9
2001/02	-5.2	-2.1	-10.3	5.5	-15.0	-7.5
2002/03	-4.7	0.5	12.4	1.3	7.2	-0.9
2003/04	4.4	15.5	-0.3	-27.1	4.1	46.9
2004/05	-2.1	9.7	1.6	-1.6	-0.6	11.4
2005/06	1.9	12.1	-1.1	-18.1	0.8	32.4
2006/07	2.8	14.0	4.5	-9.9	7.4	25.3
2007/08	-9.7	25.0	-4.1	-3.1	-13.3	28.8
2008/09	-11.8	38.8	8.3	14.4	-4.5	18.8
2009/10	-1.6	-5.1	-12.8	1.3	-14.3	-6.3
2010/11	4.7	13.1	-1.3	-16.9	3.3	32.2
2011/12	7.3	16.6	-0.5	-14.6	6.8	33.6
2012/13	6.7	-4.6	0.8	-31.6	7.6	25.5
2013/14	-0.3	12.1	8.0	4.7	7.7	6.8
2014/15	1.0	3.6	-2.1	-4.4	-1.1	8.1
2015/16	-5.6	5.6	1.4	17.0	-4.3	-12.4
2016/17	4.4	14.4	2.8	-6.2	7.3	21.4
2017/18	0.9	1.8	2.9	-3.2	3.8	5.1
2018/19	13.2	8.1	1.9	0.4	15.3	7.7
2019/20	3.0	5.5	9.4	18.0	12.7	-13.4
2020/21	4.7	6.5	3.9	2.9	8.8	3.4
Avg.	2.0 %	5.6 %	2.4 %	-2.9 %	4.6 %	8.7 %
Fq>0	66 %	74 %	68 %	42 %	74 %	71 %

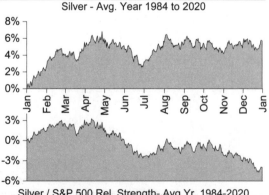

Silver - Avg. Year 1984 to 2020

Silver / S&P 500 Rel. Strength- Avg Yr. 1984-2020

Silver Performance

Silver Monthly % Gain (1984-2020)

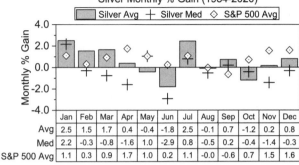

	Jan	Feb	Mar	Apr	May	Jun	Jul	Aug	Sep	Oct	Nov	Dec
Avg	2.5	1.5	1.7	0.4	-0.4	-1.8	2.5	-0.1	0.7	-1.2	0.2	0.8
Med	2.2	-0.3	-0.8	-1.6	1.0	-2.9	0.8	-0.5	0.2	-0.4	-1.4	-0.3
S&P 500 Avg	1.1	0.3	0.9	1.7	1.0	0.2	1.1	-0.0	-0.6	0.7	1.5	1.6

Fq Silver Gain > 0% (1984-2020)

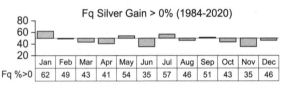

	Jan	Feb	Mar	Apr	May	Jun	Jul	Aug	Sep	Oct	Nov	Dec
Fq %>0	62	49	43	41	54	35	57	46	51	43	35	46

Fq % Silver Gain > S&P 500 % (1984-2020)

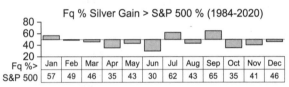

	Jan	Feb	Mar	Apr	May	Jun	Jul	Aug	Sep	Oct	Nov	Dec
Fq %> S&P 500	57	49	46	35	43	30	62	43	65	35	41	46

Silver % Gain 5 Year (2016-2020)

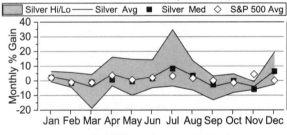

Silver Performance 2020-2021

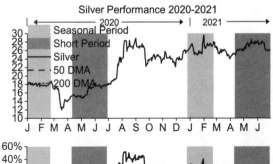

Relative Strength, % Gain vs. S&P 500

Market Indices & Rates
Weekly Values**

Stock Markets	2020	2021
Dow	29,348	30,997
S&P500	3,330	3,841
Nasdaq	9,389	13,543
TSX	17,559	17,846
FTSE	7,675	6,695
DAX	13,526	13,874
Nikkei	24,041	28,631
Hang Seng	29,056	29,448

Commodities	2020	2021
Oil	58.54	52.25
Gold	1557.6	1852.7

Bond Yields	2020	2021
USA 5 Yr Treasury	1.63	0.44
USA 10 Yr T	1.84	1.10
USA 20 Yr T	2.16	1.66
Moody's Aaa	3.01	2.51
Moody's Baa	3.82	3.24
CAN 5 Yr T	1.58	0.44
CAN 10 Yr T	1.56	0.85

Money Market	2020	2021
USA Fed Funds	1.75	0.25
USA 3 Mo T-B	1.53	0.08
CAN tgt overnight rate	1.75	0.25
CAN 3 Mo T-B	1.64	0.06

Foreign Exchange	2020	2021
EUR/USD	1.11	1.22
GBP/USD	1.30	1.37
USD/CAD	1.31	1.27
USD/JPY	110.14	103.78

JANUARY

M	T	W	T	F	S	S
					1	2
3	4	5	6	7	8	9
10	11	12	13	14	15	16
17	18	19	20	21	22	23
24	25	26	27	28	29	30
31						

FEBRUARY

M	T	W	T	F	S	S
1	1	2	3	4	5	6
7	8	9	10	11	12	13
14	15	16	17	18	19	20
21	22	23	24	25	26	27
28						

MARCH

M	T	W	T	F	S	S
	1	2	3	4	5	6
7	8	9	10	11	12	13
14	15	16	17	18	19	20
21	22	23	24	25	26	27
28	29	30	31			

TJX COMPANIES INC.
January 22 to March 30

TJX is an off-price apparel and home fashion retailer that typically reports its fourth quarter earnings in approximately the third week of February. The company, like the retail sector, benefits from investors expecting positive results from the Christmas season.

Over the long-term, TJX has typically outperformed the retail sector when the sector has been positive, making it an excellent complement to a retail sector investment during retail's strong seasonal period that also starts in January.

TJX's period of seasonal strength is similar to the seasonal period for the retail sector. The best time to invest in TJX has been from January 22 to March 30. In this time period, positive economic forecasts by investment analysts tend to increase expected consumption forecasts in the economy helping to drive the retail sector and TJX higher.

10% gain & positive 72% of the time

Since 1990, TJX has produced large gains in its seasonal period, and very few large losses. In the last thirty-one years, TJX has only had two losses of 10% or greater. In the same time period, TJX has had thirteen gains of 10% or greater.

TJX* vs. Retail vs. S&P 500
1990 to 2021

Jan 22 to Mar 30	S&P 500	Retail	TJX
1990	0.2%	6.3%	6.7%
1991	13.3	21.7	61.9
1992	-2.3	1.7	16.2
1993	3.8	3.0	21.7
1994	-6.1	-0.1	-2.8
1995	8.1	9.7	-6.9
1996	5.5	19.7	43.6
1997	-1.1	10.4	-0.3
1998	12.6	19.7	25.4
1999	5.3	16.5	18.9
2000	3.2	5.1	35.4
2001	-13.6	1.7	16.4
2002	1.8	4.7	2.9
2003	-2.7	6.6	-6.7
2004	-1.8	5.4	3.5
2005	1.2	-0.6	-1.6
2006	3.1	4.5	3.8
2007	-0.7	-2.7	-10.2
2008	-0.8	1.4	13.1
2009	-6.3	8.1	29.0
2010	5.1	12.5	17.2
2011	3.5	3.5	6.1
2012	7.1	12.9	19.3
2013	5.6	6.2	4.5
2014	0.8	-2.7	-0.2
2015	2.7	12.5	6.8
2016	10.4	10.2	16.0
2017	4.3	5.4	5.7
2018	-6.0	1.6	3.4
2019	6.1	6.7	8.2
2020	-20.9	-10.8	-23.7
2021	2.7	-0.1	-2.3
Avg	1.3%	6.2%	10.3%
Fq > 0	66%	81%	72%

Covid-19 Performance Update.
TJX performed well in the fourth quarter of 2020. In 2021, TJX underperformed in its strong seasonal period. Part of the reason is that TJX had potentially overshot its value in late 2020 and the underperformance in 2021 was a corrective move.

In addition, in 2021, TJX's e-commerce initiative failed to perform as well as other competing retailers. As the economy continues to open up and shoppers return to in-store shopping, this could potentially benefit off-label retailers such as TJX.

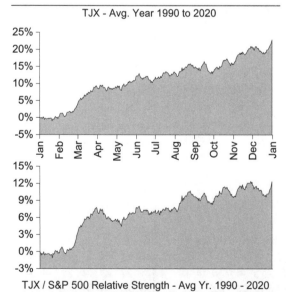

TJX - Avg. Year 1990 to 2020

TJX / S&P 500 Relative Strength - Avg Yr. 1990 - 2020

(i) * TJX - stock symbol for The TJX Companies Inc. which trades on the NYSE, adjusted for stock splits.

JANUARY

TJX Performance

TJX Monthly % Gain (1990-2020)

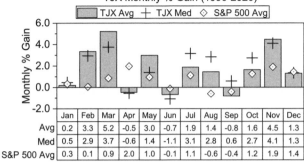

	Jan	Feb	Mar	Apr	May	Jun	Jul	Aug	Sep	Oct	Nov	Dec
Avg	0.2	3.3	5.2	-0.5	3.0	-0.7	1.9	1.4	-0.8	1.6	4.5	1.3
Med	0.5	2.9	3.7	-0.6	1.4	-1.1	3.1	2.8	0.6	2.7	4.1	1.3
S&P 500 Avg	0.3	0.1	0.9	2.0	1.0	-0.1	1.1	-0.6	-0.4	1.2	1.9	1.4

Fq TJX Gain > 0% (1990-2020)

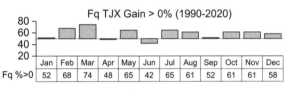

	Jan	Feb	Mar	Apr	May	Jun	Jul	Aug	Sep	Oct	Nov	Dec
Fq %>0	52	68	74	48	65	42	65	61	52	61	61	58

Fq % TJX Gain > S&P 500 % (1990-2020)

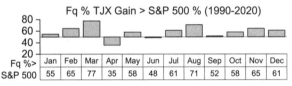

	Jan	Feb	Mar	Apr	May	Jun	Jul	Aug	Sep	Oct	Nov	Dec
Fq %> S&P 500	55	65	77	35	58	48	61	71	52	58	65	61

TJX % Gain 5 Year (2016-2020)

TJX Performance 2020-2021

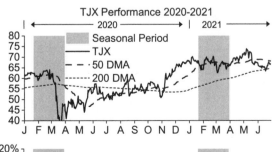

Relative Strength, % Gain vs. S&P 500

WEEK 04

Market Indices & Rates
Weekly Values**

Stock Markets	2020	2021
Dow	28,990	29,983
S&P500	3,295	3,714
Nasdaq	9,315	13,071
TSX	17,565	17,337
FTSE	7,586	6,407
DAX	13,577	13,433
Nikkei	23,827	27,663
Hang Seng	27,950	28,284

Commodities	2020	2021
Oil	54.12	52.20
Gold	1564.3	1863.8

Bond Yields	2020	2021
USA 5 Yr Treasury	1.51	0.45
USA 10 Yr T	1.70	1.11
USA 20 Yr T	2.00	1.68
Moody's Aaa	2.82	2.51
Moody's Baa	3.68	3.28
CAN 5 Yr T	1.38	0.42
CAN 10 Yr T	1.36	0.89

Money Market	2020	2021
USA Fed Funds	1.75	0.25
USA 3 Mo T-B	1.51	0.06
CAN tgt overnight rate	1.75	0.25
CAN 3 Mo T-B	1.64	0.07

Foreign Exchange	2020	2021
EUR/USD	1.10	1.21
GBP/USD	1.31	1.37
USD/CAD	1.31	1.28
USD/JPY	109.28	104.68

JANUARY

M	T	W	T	F	S	S
					1	2
3	4	5	6	7	8	9
10	11	12	13	14	15	16
17	18	19	20	21	22	23
24	25	26	27	28	29	30
31						

FEBRUARY

M	T	W	T	F	S	S
1	1	2	3	4	5	6
7	8	9	10	11	12	13
14	15	16	17	18	19	20
21	22	23	24	25	26	27
28						

MARCH

M	T	W	T	F	S	S
	1	2	3	4	5	6
7	8	9	10	11	12	13
14	15	16	17	18	19	20
21	22	23	24	25	26	27
28	29	30	31			

SNAP-ON

 ①LONG (Jan24-May5) ②SHORT SELL (Aug1-Oct8)
③LONG (Oct9-Dec31)

Snap-On has a seasonal trend that generally follows the seasonal six month trend of the stock market, performing well from October into early May. There are some differences, with Snap-On performing much worse than the S&P 500 from August into early October. This is generally a slower time for automobile maintenance and the purchase of automobile maintenance tools.

21% gain & positive 65% of the time

After its weak summer seasonal period, Snap-On tends to perform well from October 9 to the end of the year as automobile maintenance tends to increase at this time. This strong seasonal period occurs right after its weak seasonal period and as such it has typically been best to use technical indicators to help navigate the seasonal transition.

Covid-19 Performance Update. In 2021, Snap-On performed well in its strong seasonal period from late January to early May, outperforming the S&P 500. In late May, Snap-On started to dramatically underperform the S&P 500. After being out-of-sync with its seasonal pattern in 2020, Snap-On seems to have gotten back on track in 2021.

ⓘ *SNA - stock symbol for Snap-On, which trades on the NYSE, adjusted for stock splits.*

Snap-On vs. S&P 500 1990 to 2020
Negative Short ☐   Positive Long ☐

Year	Jan 24 to May 5 S&P 500	SNA	Aug 1 to Oct 8 S&P 500	SNA	Oct 9 to Dec 31 S&P 500	SNA	Compound Growth S&P 500	SNA
1990	2.0 %	8.1 %	-12.0 %	-20.3 %	5.3 %	13.4 %	-5.4 %	47.5 %
1991	15.3	7.4	-1.8	-1.9	9.6	0.8	24.0	10.3
1992	0.5	-2.2	-3.9	-4.0	6.9	3.7	3.2	5.5
1993	1.9	12.2	2.7	-11.8	1.3	-1.3	6.1	23.8
1994	-4.9	-8.8	-0.7	-5.5	0.9	-4.0	-4.7	-7.6
1995	11.7	16.3	3.6	-7.8	5.7	17.5	22.4	47.3
1996	4.7	3.3	9.5	10.7	5.7	8.8	21.2	0.3
1997	6.8	7.4	2.0	6.4	-0.4	-0.6	8.6	0.0
1998	16.5	9.4	-14.4	-17.3	28.1	18.5	27.8	52.0
1999	10.0	0.2	0.5	-7.1	10.0	-18.3	21.6	-12.3
2000	-0.6	-5.6	-1.5	-27.1	-6.3	26.7	-8.3	52.0
2001	-6.9	3.9	-12.3	-9.5	8.1	37.8	-11.7	56.8
2002	-4.9	4.1	-12.4	-17.9	10.2	26.1	-8.2	54.7
2003	4.4	14.7	4.4	2.5	7.6	11.0	17.2	24.1
2004	-1.8	7.4	1.9	-11.0	8.0	20.2	8.1	43.3
2005	0.4	-0.1	-3.1	-2.3	4.4	4.8	1.6	7.0
2006	4.9	7.4	5.7	7.0	5.1	6.0	16.5	5.8
2007	5.4	14.7	6.7	-5.4	-5.4	-2.5	6.4	17.8
2008	5.1	44.7	-22.3	-22.9	-8.3	-9.3	-25.1	61.2
2009	8.6	2.7	7.9	0.8	4.7	17.7	22.7	19.9
2010	6.8	7.2	5.8	6.0	7.9	19.5	21.9	20.4
2011	4.0	7.6	-10.6	-19.9	8.8	11.2	1.2	43.4
2012	4.0	14.5	5.6	7.4	-2.0	8.5	7.6	15.0
2013	8.0	7.4	-1.8	0.8	11.7	14.5	18.4	22.0
2014	3.1	11.8	2.0	-0.1	4.6	13.8	9.9	27.3
2015	1.8	12.7	-4.3	-1.9	1.5	6.0	-1.1	21.7
2016	7.5	3.5	-0.9	-4.4	4.0	14.0	10.8	23.1
2017	5.9	-1.8	3.2	-3.2	4.9	16.8	14.6	18.3
2018	-6.2	-20.5	2.4	5.7	-13.1	-19.0	-16.5	-39.2
2019	11.6	5.1	-2.9	-0.5	11.7	11.5	21.0	17.7
2020	-13.7	-27.8	5.4	8.6	9.0	8.1	-0.9	-28.6
Avg.	3.6 %	5.4 %	-1.2 %	-4.7 %	4.8 %	9.1 %	7.5 %	21.0 %
Fq>0	77 %	77 %	52	32 %	81 %	77 %	71 %	65 %

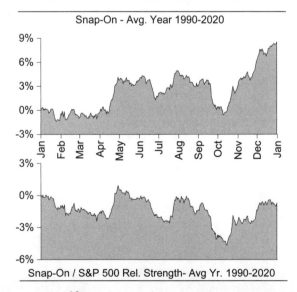

Snap-On - Avg. Year 1990-2020

Snap-On / S&P 500 Rel. Strength- Avg Yr. 1990-2020

Snap-On Performance

SNA Monthly % Gain (1990-2020)

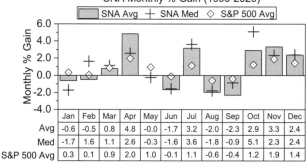

	Jan	Feb	Mar	Apr	May	Jun	Jul	Aug	Sep	Oct	Nov	Dec
Avg	-0.6	-0.5	0.8	4.8	-0.0	-1.7	3.2	-2.0	-2.3	2.9	3.3	2.4
Med	-1.7	1.6	1.1	2.6	-0.3	-1.6	3.6	-1.8	-0.9	5.1	2.3	2.4
S&P 500 Avg	0.3	0.1	0.9	2.0	1.0	-0.1	1.1	-0.6	-0.4	1.2	1.9	1.4

Fq SNA Gain > 0% (1990-2020)

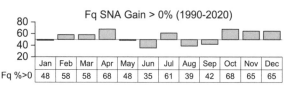

	Jan	Feb	Mar	Apr	May	Jun	Jul	Aug	Sep	Oct	Nov	Dec
Fq %>0	48	58	58	68	48	35	61	39	42	68	65	65

Fq % SNA Gain > S&P 500 % (1990-2020)

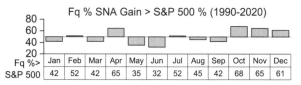

	Jan	Feb	Mar	Apr	May	Jun	Jul	Aug	Sep	Oct	Nov	Dec
Fq %> S&P 500	42	52	42	65	35	32	52	45	42	68	65	61

SNA % Gain 5 Year (2016-2020)

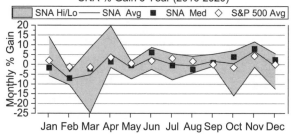

SNA Performance 2020-2021

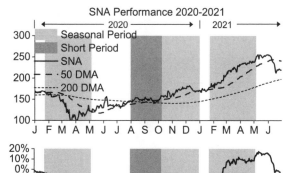

Relative Strength, % Gain vs. S&P 500

Market Indices & Rates
Weekly Values**

Stock Markets	2020	2021
Dow	28,256	31,148
S&P500	3,226	3,887
Nasdaq	9,151	13,856
TSX	17,318	18,136
FTSE	7,286	6,489
DAX	12,982	14,057
Nikkei	23,205	28,779
Hang Seng	26,313	29,289

Commodities	2020	2021
Oil	51.56	56.85
Gold	1584.2	1803.0

Bond Yields	2020	2021
USA 5 Yr Treasury	1.32	0.47
USA 10 Yr T	1.51	1.19
USA 20 Yr T	1.83	1.79
Moody's Aaa	2.82	2.63
Moody's Baa	3.64	3.37
CAN 5 Yr T	1.28	0.48
CAN 10 Yr T	1.27	1.00

Money Market	2020	2021
USA Fed Funds	1.75	0.25
USA 3 Mo T-B	1.52	0.03
CAN tgt overnight rate	1.75	0.25
CAN 3 Mo T-B	1.64	0.06

Foreign Exchange	2020	2021
EUR/USD	1.11	1.20
GBP/USD	1.32	1.37
USD/CAD	1.32	1.28
USD/JPY	108.35	105.39

JANUARY

M	T	W	T	F	S	S
					1	2
3	4	5	6	7	8	9
10	11	12	13	14	15	16
17	18	19	20	21	22	23
24	25	26	27	28	29	30
31						

FEBRUARY

M	T	W	T	F	S	S
1	1	2	3	4	5	6
7	8	9	10	11	12	13
14	15	16	17	18	19	20
21	22	23	24	25	26	27
28						

MARCH

M	T	W	T	F	S	S
	1	2	3	4	5	6
7	8	9	10	11	12	13
14	15	16	17	18	19	20
21	22	23	24	25	26	27
28	29	30	31			

FEBRUARY

	MONDAY	TUESDAY	WEDNESDAY
WEEK 05	31	**1** 27	**2** 26
WEEK 06	**7** 21	**8** 20	**9** 19
WEEK 07	**14** 14	**15** 13	**16** 12
WEEK 08	**21** 7 CAN Market Closed - Family Day USA Market Closed - Presidents' Day	**22** 6	**23** 5
WEEK 09	**28**	1	2

THURSDAY		FRIDAY	
3	25	**4**	24
10	18	**11**	17
17	11	**18**	10
24	4	**25**	3
3		4	

MARCH

M	T	W	T	F	S	S
	1	2	3	4	5	6
7	8	9	10	11	12	13
14	15	16	17	18	19	20
21	22	23	24	25	26	27
28	29	30	31			

APRIL

M	T	W	T	F	S	S
				1	2	3
4	5	6	7	8	9	10
11	13	13	14	15	16	17
18	19	20	21	22	23	24
25	26	27	28	29	30	

MAY

M	T	W	T	F	S	S
						1
2	3	4	5	6	7	8
9	10	11	12	13	14	15
16	17	18	19	20	21	22
23	24	25	26	27	28	29
30	31					

JUNE

M	T	W	T	F	S	S
		1	2	3	4	5
6	7	8	9	10	11	12
13	14	15	16	17	18	19
20	21	22	23	24	25	26
27	28	29	30			

FEBRUARY
S U M M A R Y

S&P500 Cumulative Daily Gains for Avg Month 1950 to 2021

	Dow Jones	S&P 500	Nasdaq	TSX Comp
Month Rank	8	11	10	7
# Up	41	39	26	22
# Down	30	32	23	14
% Pos	58	55	53	61
% Avg. Gain	0.2	0.0	0.6	0.8

Dow & S&P 1950-2020, Nasdaq 1972-2020, TSX 1985-2020

♦ Historically, over the long-term, February has been one of the weaker months of the year for the S&P 500. Over the last ten years, the S&P 500 has bucked this trend and has been positive eight out of ten times. ♦ The energy sector typically starts to outperform in late February, helping to boost the S&P/TSX Composite. ♦ The consumer discretionary sector tends to be one of the better performing sectors. ♦ In February 2021, the S&P 500 rallied in the first half of the month, corrected in the second half, but still ended up being positive for the month.

BEST / WORST FEBRUARY BROAD MKTS. 2012-2021

BEST FEBRUARY MARKETS
♦ Nikkei 225 (2012) 10.5%
♦ Nasdaq (2015) 7.1%
♦ Nikkei (2015) 6.4%

WORST FEBRUARY MARKETS
♦ Dow (2020) -10.1%
♦ FTSE 100 (2020) -9.7%
♦ Nikkei 225 (2020) -8.9%

Index Values End of Month

	2012	2013	2014	2015	2016	2017	2018	2019	2020	2021
Dow	12,952	14,054	16,322	18,133	16,517	20,812	25,029	25,916	25,409	30,932
S&P 500	1,366	1,515	1,859	2,105	1,932	2,364	2,714	2,784	2,954	3,811
Nasdaq	2,967	3,160	4,308	4,964	4,558	5,825	7,273	7,533	8,567	13,192
TSX Comp.	12,644	12,822	14,210	15,234	12,860	15,399	15,443	15,999	16,263	18,060
Russell 1000	756	841	1,041	1,173	1,067	1,311	1,501	1,546	1,635	2,159
Russell 2000	811	911	1,183	1,233	1,034	1,387	1,512	1,576	1,476	2,201
FTSE 100	5,872	6,361	6,810	6,947	6,097	7,263	7,232	7,075	6,581	6,483
Nikkei 225	9,723	11,559	14,841	18,798	16,027	19,119	22,068	21,385	21,143	28,966

Percent Gain for February

	2012	2013	2014	2015	2016	2017	2018	2019	2020	2021
Dow	2.5	1.4	4.0	5.6	0.3	4.8	-4.3	3.7	-10.1	3.2
S&P 500	4.1	1.1	4.3	5.5	-0.4	3.7	-3.9	3.0	-8.4	2.6
Nasdaq	5.4	0.6	5.0	7.1	-1.2	3.8	-1.9	3.4	-6.4	0.9
TSX Comp.	1.5	1.1	3.8	3.8	0.3	0.1	-3.2	2.9	-6.1	4.2
Russell 1000	4.1	1.1	4.5	5.5	-0.3	3.6	-3.9	3.2	-8.3	2.8
Russell 2000	2.3	1.0	4.6	5.8	-0.1	1.8	-4.0	5.1	-8.5	6.1
FTSE 100	3.3	1.3	4.6	2.9	0.2	2.3	-4.0	1.5	-9.7	1.2
Nikkei 225	10.5	3.8	-0.5	6.4	-8.5	0.4	-4.5	2.9	-8.9	4.7

February Market Avg. Performance 2012 to 2021[1]

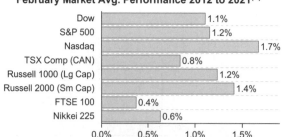

- Dow 1.1%
- S&P 500 1.2%
- Nasdaq 1.7%
- TSX Comp (CAN) 0.8%
- Russell 1000 (Lg Cap) 1.2%
- Russell 2000 (Sm Cap) 1.4%
- FTSE 100 0.4%
- Nikkei 225 0.6%

Interest Corner Feb[2]

	Fed Funds %[3]	3 Mo. T-Bill %[4]	10 Yr %[5]	20 Yr %[6]
2021	0.25	0.04	1.44	2.08
2020	1.75	1.27	1.13	1.46
2019	2.50	2.45	2.73	2.94
2018	1.50	1.65	2.87	3.02
2017	0.75	0.53	2.36	2.70

(1) Russell Data provided by Russell (2) Federal Reserve Bank of St. Louis- end of month values (3) Target rate set by FOMC (4)(5)(6) Constant yield maturities.

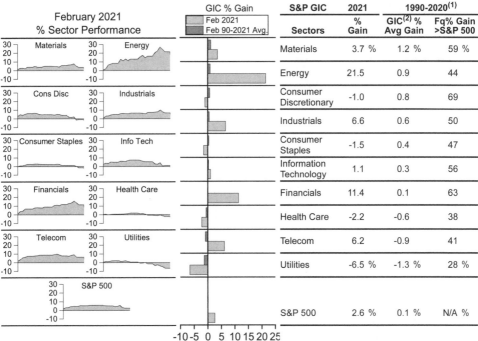

S&P GIC Sectors	2021 % Gain	1990-2020[1] GIC[2] % Avg Gain	1990-2020[1] Fq% Gain >S&P 500
Materials	3.7 %	1.2 %	59 %
Energy	21.5	0.9	44
Consumer Discretionary	-1.0	0.8	69
Industrials	6.6	0.6	50
Consumer Staples	-1.5	0.4	47
Information Technology	1.1	0.3	56
Financials	11.4	0.1	63
Health Care	-2.2	-0.6	38
Telecom	6.2	-0.9	41
Utilities	-6.5 %	-1.3 %	28 %
S&P 500	2.6 %	0.1 %	N/A %

Sector Commentary

♦ In February 2021, most of the sectors were positive. ♦ Generally, most sectors followed their seasonal trends with their relative performance compared to the S&P 500. ♦ The energy sector performed particularly well with a gain of 21.5%. ♦ The defensive sectors were the worst performing sectors. ♦ The utilities sector was the biggest loser, with a loss of 2.2%.

Sub-Sector Commentary

♦ In February 2021, the stock market was in a risk-on mode and the cyclical sub-sectors performed particularly well. ♦ The steel sub-sector produced a gain of 22.8%. ♦ The banking sub-sector produced a gain of 16.4%. ♦ The worst performing sub-sector from the list was the auto sector which starts its strong seasonal period late in the month. Typically, the auto sub-sector is one of the weaker sub-sectors in February. The biotech sector typically performs poorly in February and in 2021 the biotech sector followed its seasonal trend of negative performance.

SELECTED SUB-SECTORS[3]			
SOX (1995-2021)	6.3 %	2.8 %	67 %
Silver	-2.7	2.0	50
Metals & Mining	9.2	1.7	56
Retail	-1.2	1.5	69
Chemicals	2.4	1.4	66
Steel	22.8	1.0	53
Gold	-6.5	0.9	47
Transportation	8.4	0.5	53
Railroads	5.4	0.4	47
Banks	16.4	0.4	56
Agriculture (1994-2021)	13.1	0.4	50
Automotive & Components	-10.5	-0.2	41
Homebuilders	0.8	-0.3	53
Pharma	-3.4	-0.7	38
Biotech (1993-2021)	-3.1	-0.8	48

COPPER

Cu ① Jan29 to Mar5 ② Jun24 to Jul31

Copper has a strong seasonal period early in the year as economic activity tends to increase at this time. In addition, copper demand tends to increase in China before the Chinese New Year' holidays. Investor's front run the increase in Chinese copper demand. As a result, once the Chinese economy starts to increase after the holidays, copper tends to lose momentum. From 1990 to 2020, in the period from January 29 to March 5, copper has produced an average gain of 3.9% and has been positive 65% of the time.

> ### *8% gain &*
> ### *74% of the time positive*

Copper also tends to perform well from late June until the end of July. The positive trend in copper somewhat aligns with strong stock market performance that tends to occur from late June into mid-July as investors move to a risk-on mode, in the period leading up to the Q2 earnings season.

From 1990 to 2020, in the period from June 24 to Jul 31, copper has produced an average gain of 3.9% and has been positive 71% of the time. It should be noted that after the strong seasonal period finishes, copper on average has declined in price in August, which tends to be one of the weaker months of the year for copper.

Covid-19 Performance Update. In 2021, copper performed well in its late January to early March seasonal period as the cyclical sectors of the stock market performed well in the Covid-19 pandemic recovery. Copper corrected from early May to late June before performing well in its late June to late July seasonal period.

ⓘ *Source: Copper. Source data: Bloomberg*

Copper vs S&P 500 - 1990 to 2020   Positive ☐

Year	Jan 29-Mar 5 S&P 500	Jan 29-Mar 5 Cop-per	Jun 24-Jul 31 S&P 500	Jun 24-Jul 31 Cop-per	Compound Growth S&P 500	Compound Growth Cop-per
1990	2.4 %	18.8 %	0.2 %	12.1 %	2.6 %	33.1 %
1991	12.1	4.0	2.7	0.4	15.1	4.4
1992	-2.0	2.8	5.0	6.7	2.9	9.6
1993	1.7	-4.8	1.1	4.7	2.8	-0.4
1994	-2.9	4.5	1.9	-1.9	-1.1	2.6
1995	3.2	-3.9	2.2	-2.5	5.5	-6.4
1996	5.5	3.1	-4.0	2.2	1.2	5.4
1997	4.8	4.0	8.6	-7.9	13.9	-4.2
1998	5.9	-0.2	0.1	2.5	6.0	2.3
1999	0.8	-1.5	-0.3	15.5	0.5	13.8
2000	3.6	-3.8	-0.7	7.9	2.8	3.8
2001	-8.4	-0.2	-1.2	-4.5	-9.4	-4.7
2002	1.2	5.7	-7.8	-8.3	-6.8	-3.1
2003	-3.3	1.0	0.9	7.0	-2.5	8.0
2004	2.5	18.6	-3.7	9.3	-1.3	29.6
2005	4.3	3.9	2.8	7.7	7.2	11.8
2006	0.3	1.4	2.6	13.3	2.9	14.9
2007	-3.4	1.3	-3.1	7.8	-6.4	9.2
2008	-1.5	24.8	-3.8	-3.8	-5.3	20.0
2009	-21.9	10.5	10.3	19.3	-13.9	31.9
2010	5.0	10.3	0.9	12.8	5.9	24.4
2011	3.5	2.6	0.7	11.0	4.2	13.9
2012	3.6	-0.6	3.3	3.5	7.1	2.9
2013	2.6	-3.9	5.9	0.6	8.7	-3.3
2014	4.5	-1.5	-1.6	2.4	2.8	0.8
2015	4.9	7.9	-1.0	-9.9	3.9	-2.8
2016	5.6	10.0	2.9	2.5	8.6	12.8
2017	3.9	0.3	1.3	10.2	5.2	10.5
2018	-5.3	-2.2	2.2	-6.5	-3.2	-8.5
2019	5.5	9.5	1.0	-1.4	6.6	7.9
2020	-7.7	-0.3	4.5	7.9	-3.6	7.6
Avg.	1.0 %	3.9 %	1.1 %	3.9 %	2.0 %	8.0 %
Fq>0	71 %	65 %	68 %	71 %	68 %	74 %

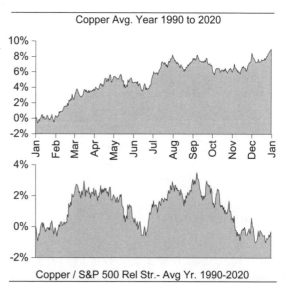

Copper Avg. Year 1990 to 2020

Copper / S&P 500 Rel Str.- Avg Yr. 1990-2020

- 19 -

Copper Performance

Copper Monthly % Gain (1990-2020)

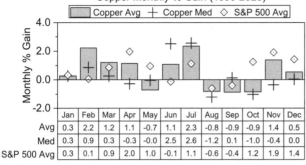

	Jan	Feb	Mar	Apr	May	Jun	Jul	Aug	Sep	Oct	Nov	Dec
Avg	0.3	2.2	1.2	1.1	-0.7	1.1	2.3	-0.8	-0.9	-0.9	1.4	0.5
Med	0.3	0.9	0.3	-0.3	-0.0	2.5	2.6	-1.2	0.1	-1.0	-0.4	0.0
S&P 500 Avg	0.3	0.1	0.9	2.0	1.0	-0.1	1.1	-0.6	-0.4	1.2	1.9	1.4

Fq Copper Gain > 0% (1990-2020)

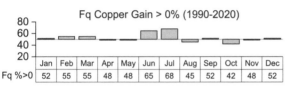

	Jan	Feb	Mar	Apr	May	Jun	Jul	Aug	Sep	Oct	Nov	Dec
Fq %>0	52	55	55	48	48	65	68	45	52	42	48	52

Fq % Copper Gain > S&P 500 % (1990-2020)

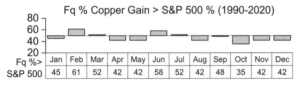

	Jan	Feb	Mar	Apr	May	Jun	Jul	Aug	Sep	Oct	Nov	Dec
Fq %> S&P 500	45	61	52	42	42	58	52	42	48	35	42	42

Copper % Gain 5 Year (2016-2020)

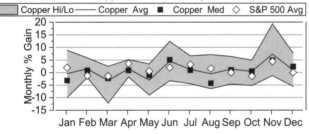

Copper Performance 2020-2021

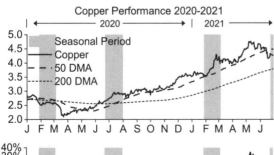

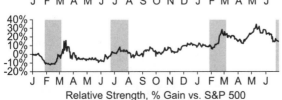

Relative Strength, % Gain vs. S&P 500

Market Indices & Rates
Weekly Values**

Stock Markets	2020	2021
Dow	29,103	31,458
S&P500	3,328	3,935
Nasdaq	9,521	14,095
TSX	17,655	18,460
FTSE	7,467	6,590
DAX	13,514	14,050
Nikkei	23,828	29,520
Hang Seng	27,404	30,174

Commodities	2020	2021
Oil	50.32	59.47
Gold	1572.7	1816.4

Bond Yields	2020	2021
USA 5 Yr Treasury	1.41	0.50
USA 10 Yr T	1.59	1.20
USA 20 Yr T	1.89	1.83
Moody's Aaa	2.77	2.65
Moody's Baa	3.64	3.39
CAN 5 Yr T	1.34	0.50
CAN 10 Yr T	1.33	1.03

Money Market	2020	2021
USA Fed Funds	1.75	0.25
USA 3 Mo T-B	1.53	0.04
CAN tgt overnight rate	1.75	0.25
CAN 3 Mo T-B	1.64	0.07

Foreign Exchange	2020	2021
EUR/USD	1.09	1.21
GBP/USD	1.29	1.38
USD/CAD	1.33	1.27
USD/JPY	109.75	104.94

FEBRUARY

M	T	W	T	F	S	S
1	1	2	3	4	5	6
7	8	9	10	11	12	13
14	15	16	17	18	19	20
21	22	23	24	25	26	27
28						

MARCH

M	T	W	T	F	S	S
	1	2	3	4	5	6
7	8	9	10	11	12	13
14	15	16	17	18	19	20
21	22	23	24	25	26	27
28	29	30	31			

APRIL

M	T	W	T	F	S	S
				1	2	3
4	5	6	7	8	9	10
11	13	13	14	15	16	17
18	20	20	21	22	23	24
25	27	27	28	29	30	

EASTMAN CHEMICAL COMPANY
① LONG (Jan28 to May5)
② SELL SHORT (May30-Oct27)

In its positive seasonal period from January 28 to May 5, Eastman Chemical during the period from 1994 to 2020, has produced an average 11.2% gain and has been positive 81% of the time.

In its short sell seasonal period from May 30 to October 27, in the same yearly period, Eastman Chemical has produced an average loss of 4.5% and has been positive 41% of the time.

17% growth

Eastman Chemical, in its 10-K report filed with regulators in 2013, outlines the seasonal trends in its business. *"The Company's earnings are typically greater in second and third quarters."* This is a bit different than many other cyclical companies, that tend to have weaker earnings over the summer months.

The net result is for Eastman Chemical to outperform into May and then underperform at the tail end of Q2, and Q3, as investors anticipate a weaker Q4 earnings report. In Q4, Eastman tends to perform at market.

Covid-19 Performance Update. In 2021, Eastman Chemical outperformed the S&P 500 in its strong seasonal period from late January to early May. It then underperformed the S&P 500 in its weak seasonal period that started in late May. As investors started to realize that economic growth was subsiding, many of the cyclical stocks such as Eastman Chemical started to underperform in May.

(i) *Eastman Chemical Company manufactures and sells chemicals, fibers, and plastics, globally. It trades on the NYSE, adjusted for splits.*

Eastman Chemical* vs. S&P 500 1994 to 2020

Positive Long ▢   Negative Short ▢

Year	Jan 28 to May 5 S&P 500	Jan 28 to May 5 EMN	May 30 to Oct 27 S&P 500	May 30 to Oct 27 EMN	Compound Growth S&P 500	Compound Growth EMN
1994	-5.4	7.8 %	1.9 %	8.7 %	-3.6 %	-1.6 %
1995	10.6	11.0	10.7	2.6	22.4	8.2
1996	3.2	7.1	4.9	-21.8	8.3	30.5
1997	8.5	-1.1	3.9	2.7	12.8	-3.8
1998	15.1	18.7	-2.3	-15.3	12.4	36.8
1999	8.4	32.1	-0.4	-24.5	8.0	64.4
2000	2.4	21.9	0.1	-19.3	2.6	45.3
2001	-6.5	22.7	-12.9	-33.1	-18.6	63.2
2002	-5.3	13.1	-15.9	-21.2	-20.4	37.0
2003	9.3	-11.4	8.6	-0.6	18.7	-10.9
2004	-2.0	16.4	0.4	-1.9	-1.6	18.6
2005	-0.2	10.5	-1.7	-15.7	-1.8	27.9
2006	3.3	17.3	7.6	5.5	11.1	10.9
2007	5.9	11.8	1.1	-0.1	7.1	11.9
2008	5.8	14.9	-39.3	-55.6	-35.8	78.8
2009	6.9	52.4	15.7	34.3	23.6	0.2
2010	6.2	12.4	8.5	33.0	15.3	-24.7
2011	2.7	9.2	-3.5	-23.1	-0.8	34.5
2012	4.0	0.6	6.0	21.6	10.2	-21.1
2013	7.4	-5.6	6.8	8.4	14.7	-13.5
2014	5.8	15.5	2.2	-15.6	8.1	33.4
2015	3.0	13.1	-2.0	-6.0	0.9	19.9
2016	8.9	21.5	1.6	-8.8	10.7	32.1
2017	4.6	2.5	6.8	16.4	11.7	-14.3
2018	-7.3	2.4	-1.2	-25.0	-8.4	28.0
2019	10.5	-1.6	8.6	12.7	20.1	-14.2
2020	-11.6	-13.9	11.4	21.1	-1.5	-32.1
Avg.	3.4 %	11.2 %	1.0 %	-4.5 %	4.7 %	16.5 %
Fq>0	74 %	81 %	67 %	41 %	67 %	67 %

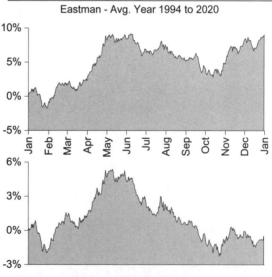

Eastman - Avg. Year 1994 to 2020

Eastman / S&P 500 Rel. Strength- Avg Yr. 1994-2020

- 21 -

Eastman Chemical Performance

EMN Monthly % Gain (1994-2020)

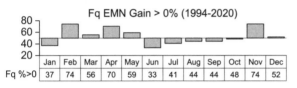

	Jan	Feb	Mar	Apr	May	Jun	Jul	Aug	Sep	Oct	Nov	Dec
Avg	-1.2	2.5	1.2	6.9	0.7	-1.2	0.8	-2.4	-1.2	0.9	3.0	0.5
Med	-1.5	3.5	0.7	5.1	1.3	-2.4	-1.8	-1.4	-0.3	-0.1	1.7	0.1
S&P 500 Avg	0.5	-0.3	0.8	2.3	0.5	0.1	1.0	-0.5	-0.2	1.3	2.1	1.1

Fq EMN Gain > 0% (1994-2020)

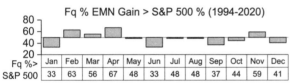

	Jan	Feb	Mar	Apr	May	Jun	Jul	Aug	Sep	Oct	Nov	Dec
Fq %>0	37	74	56	70	59	33	41	44	44	48	74	52

Fq % EMN Gain > S&P 500 % (1994-2020)

	Jan	Feb	Mar	Apr	May	Jun	Jul	Aug	Sep	Oct	Nov	Dec
Fq %> S&P 500	33	63	56	67	48	33	48	48	37	44	59	41

EMN % Gain 5 Year (2016-2020)

EMN Performance 2020-2021

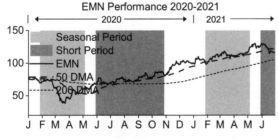

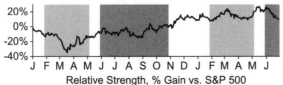

Relative Strength, % Gain vs. S&P 500

Market Indices & Rates
Weekly Values**

Stock Markets	2020	2021
Dow	29,398	31,494
S&P500	3,380	3,907
Nasdaq	9,731	13,874
TSX	17,848	18,384
FTSE	7,409	6,624
DAX	13,744	13,993
Nikkei	23,688	30,018
Hang Seng	27,816	30,645

Commodities	2020	2021
Oil	52.05	59.24
Gold	1581.4	1786.2

Bond Yields	2020	2021
USA 5 Yr Treasury	1.42	0.59
USA 10 Yr T	1.59	1.34
USA 20 Yr T	1.89	1.98
Moody's Aaa	2.79	2.76
Moody's Baa	3.63	3.48
CAN 5 Yr T	1.37	0.64
CAN 10 Yr T	1.37	1.21

Money Market	2020	2021
USA Fed Funds	1.75	0.25
USA 3 Mo T-B	1.55	0.04
CAN tgt overnight rate	1.75	0.25
CAN 3 Mo T-B	1.64	0.09

Foreign Exchange	2020	2021
EUR/USD	1.08	1.21
GBP/USD	1.30	1.40
USD/CAD	1.33	1.26
USD/JPY	109.78	105.45

FEBRUARY

M	T	W	T	F	S	S
1	2	3	4	5	6	
7	8	9	10	11	12	13
14	15	16	17	18	19	20
21	22	23	24	25	26	27
28						

MARCH

M	T	W	T	F	S	S
	1	2	3	4	5	6
7	8	9	10	11	12	13
14	15	16	17	18	19	20
21	22	23	24	25	26	27
28	29	30	31			

APRIL

M	T	W	T	F	S	S
			1	2	3
4	5	6	7	8	9	10
11	13	13	14	15	16	17
18	20	20	21	22	23	24
25	27	27	28	29	30	

ADOBE
① Feb1 to May23 ② Oct10 to Nov17

Adobe's strongest fiscal quarter is its first quarter which ends in February. Adobe tends to report on the quarter in late March. Investors tend to front run the quarter reporting, helping to push Adobe stock price higher in February and March.

The trend continues on into May. It is a bit unusual for a seasonal trend to continue to perform strongly past the event that is being front run.

Adobe's strength tends to fade fast in late May as it gets ready to report its second fiscal quarter, which tends to be its weakest revenue quarter. From February 1 to May 23, in the period from 1990 to 2020, Adobe has produced an average gain of 23% and has been positive 87% of the time.

38% gain & 87% of the time positive

Adobe also tends to perform well leading up to its fourth fiscal quarter which ends in November and is typically reported in mid-December.

On average, Adobe's fourth fiscal quarter is its second best revenue generating quarter. From October 10 to November 17, in the period from 1990 to 2020, Adobe has produced an average gain of 11% and has been positive 74% of the time.

Covid-19 Performance Update. In 2021, Adobe continued its underperformance compared to the S&P 500 from 2020 into the first part of the year. It underperformed in its late winter seasonal period. In May 2021, it resumed its outperformance.

*Adobe is a software company. It trades on the Nasdaq, adjusted for splits.

Adobe vs S&P 500 - 1990 to 2020

Year	Feb 1- May 23 S&P 500	Feb 1- May 23 Adobe	Oct 10- Nov 17 S&P 500	Oct 10- Nov 17 Adobe	Compound Growth S&P 500	Compound Growth Adobe
1990	9.2 %	108.5 %	3.9 %	38.7 %	13.5 %	189.1 %
1991	9.0	26.3	1.5	3.4	10.7	30.6
1992	1.3	-27.1	4.1	22.9	5.5	-10.4
1993	1.6	57.8	1.0	7.8	2.6	70.1
1994	-5.9	-2.9	1.9	-2.5	-4.1	-5.3
1995	12.4	96.1	3.8	26.3	16.6	147.8
1996	6.3	23.2	5.9	17.2	12.5	44.4
1997	7.7	22.4	-2.5	-5.3	5.0	15.9
1998	13.3	12.7	15.7	34.7	31.1	51.8
1999	4.0	66.0	5.6	30.9	9.8	117.2
2000	-1.5	97.8	-2.4	10.6	-3.9	118.7
2001	-5.6	1.8	7.8	10.6	1.7	12.6
2002	-2.9	10.1	17.1	59.3	13.7	75.5
2003	9.1	31.1	0.5	-3.6	9.6	26.3
2004	-3.3	16.0	5.3	17.8	1.8	36.7
2005	1.1	10.2	3.9	16.0	5.0	27.8
2006	-1.8	-27.0	3.7	10.9	1.8	-19.0
2007	5.8	11.2	-6.8	-6.2	-1.4	4.3
2008	-0.2	18.1	-6.5	-18.5	-6.7	-3.8
2009	7.4	37.1	3.6	6.5	11.3	46.1
2010	1.3	-0.4	1.2	7.1	2.5	6.7
2011	2.4	4.2	5.3	9.5	7.8	14.1
2012	0.5	4.0	-5.7	3.0	-5.2	7.1
2013	10.2	13.1	8.6	16.0	19.6	31.1
2014	6.6	8.6	5.9	6.6	12.9	15.8
2015	6.6	14.1	1.8	7.7	8.5	22.9
2016	5.6	8.4	1.6	-2.6	7.2	5.6
2017	5.2	23.1	1.3	20.3	6.7	48.0
2018	-3.2	22.1	-5.0	-6.0	-8.0	14.8
2019	4.4	10.7	6.9	8.5	11.6	20.0
2020	-8.4	9.7	3.8	-6.8	-4.9	2.2
Avg.	3.2 %	22.8 %	3.0 %	11.0 %	6.3 %	37.6 %
Fq>0	71 %	87 %	81 %	74 %	77 %	87 %

Positive

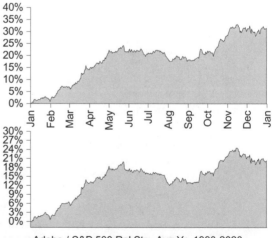

Adobe Avg. Year 1990 to 2020

Adobe / S&P 500 Rel Str.- Avg Yr. 1990-2020

Adobe Performance

Adobe Monthly % Gain (1990-2020)

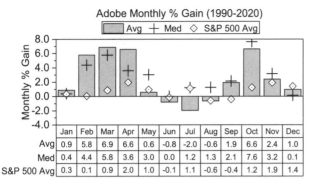

	Jan	Feb	Mar	Apr	May	Jun	Jul	Aug	Sep	Oct	Nov	Dec
Avg	0.9	5.8	6.9	6.6	0.6	-0.8	-2.0	-0.6	1.9	6.6	2.4	1.0
Med	0.4	4.4	5.8	3.6	3.0	0.0	1.2	1.3	2.1	7.6	3.2	0.1
S&P 500 Avg	0.3	0.1	0.9	2.0	1.0	-0.1	1.1	-0.6	-0.4	1.2	1.9	1.4

Fq Adobe Gain > 0% (1990-2020)

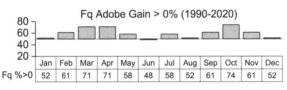

	Jan	Feb	Mar	Apr	May	Jun	Jul	Aug	Sep	Oct	Nov	Dec
Fq %>0	52	61	71	71	58	48	58	52	61	74	61	52

Fq % Adobe Gain > S&P 500 % (1990-2020)

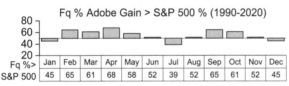

	Jan	Feb	Mar	Apr	May	Jun	Jul	Aug	Sep	Oct	Nov	Dec
Fq %> S&P 500	45	65	61	68	58	52	39	52	65	61	52	45

Adobe % Gain 5 Year (2016-2020)

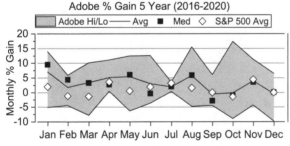

Adobe Performance 2020-2021

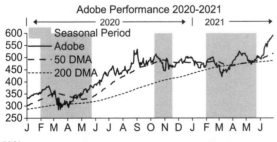

Relative Strength, % Gain vs. S&P 500

Market Indices & Rates
Weekly Values**

Stock Markets	2020	2021
Dow	28,992	30,932
S&P500	3,338	3,811
Nasdaq	9,577	13,192
TSX	17,844	18,060
FTSE	7,404	6,483
DAX	13,579	13,786
Nikkei	23,387	28,966
Hang Seng	27,309	28,980

Commodities	2020	2021
Oil	53.30	61.50
Gold	1643.3	1742.9

Bond Yields	2020	2021
USA 5 Yr Treasury	1.30	0.75
USA 10 Yr T	1.46	1.44
USA 20 Yr T	1.75	2.08
Moody's Aaa	2.74	2.86
Moody's Baa	3.55	3.56
CAN 5 Yr T	1.30	0.88
CAN 10 Yr T	1.28	1.36

Money Market	2020	2021
USA Fed Funds	1.75	0.25
USA 3 Mo T-B	1.53	0.04
CAN tgt overnight rate	1.75	0.25
CAN 3 Mo T-B	1.63	0.13

Foreign Exchange	2020	2021
EUR/USD	1.08	1.21
GBP/USD	1.30	1.39
USD/CAD	1.32	1.27
USD/JPY	111.61	106.57

FEBRUARY

M	T	W	T	F	S	S
1	2	3	4	5	6	
7	8	9	10	11	12	13
14	15	16	17	18	19	20
21	22	23	24	25	26	27
28						

MARCH

M	T	W	T	F	S	S
	1	2	3	4	5	6
7	8	9	10	11	12	13
14	15	16	17	18	19	20
21	22	23	24	25	26	27
28	29	30	31			

APRIL

M	T	W	T	F	S	S
				1	2	3
4	5	6	7	8	9	10
11	13	13	14	15	16	17
18	20	20	21	22	23	24
25	27	27	28	29	30	

OIL STOCKS

①LONG (Feb25-May9) ②SELL SHORT (May10-Jun26)
③LONG (Jul24-Oct3)

Oil stocks have two seasonal periods largely based upon the supply and demand cycles oil. The highest demand for oil on a seasonal basis occurs in May as the US driving season kicks off. This tends to drive the value of oil stocks higher in the months leading up to the US driving season.

As the driving season gets underway, investors become less interested in oil stocks and as a result, oil stocks tend to perform poorly from mid-May until late June.

9% gain & positive 78% of the time positive

In addition, oil stocks have another strong seasonal period from late July to early October. This is a minor seasonal period and is not as strong as the February to May seasonal period. This seasonal period is based upon the increased demand for oil in the winter heating season.

Covid-19 Performance Update. In 2021, oil stocks started to outperform the S&P 500 in January. On an absolute basis, oil stocks started to roll over in late May and underperformed the S&P 500 in its weak seasonal late spring, summer period.

ℹ️ **NYSE Arca Oil Index (XOI):**
An index designed to represent a cross section of widely held oil corporations involved in various phases of the oil industry.
For more information on the XOI index, see www.cboe.com

XOI* vs. S&P 500 1984 to 2020

Negative Short ☐   Positive Long ▨

Year	Feb 25 to May 9 S&P 500	Feb 25 to May 9 XOI	May 10 to Jun 26 S&P 500	May 10 to Jun 26 XOI	Jul 24 to Oct 3 S&P 500	Jul 24 to Oct 3 XOI	Compound Growth S&P 500	Compound Growth XOI
1984	1.7 %	5.6 %	-4.6 %	-8.0 %	9.1 %	9.0 %	5.7 %	24.3 %
1985	1.4	4.9	4.5	-2.8	-4.3	6.7	1.5	15.1
1986	6.0	7.7	4.6	-3.2	-2.1	15.7	8.6	28.5
1987	3.7	25.5	4.7	1.3	6.6	-1.2	15.7	22.4
1988	-3.0	5.6	6.7	-1.8	3.0	-3.6	6.6	3.7
1989	6.3	8.1	7.0	1.9	5.6	5.7	20.1	12.0
1990	5.8	-0.6	2.7	-1.3	-12.4	-0.5	-4.8	0.2
1991	4.8	6.8	-3.0	-8.1	1.3	0.7	3.0	16.3
1992	0.9	5.8	-3.0	-1.5	-0.4	2.9	-2.5	10.6
1993	0.3	6.3	1.2	-2.5	3.2	7.8	4.7	17.5
1994	-4.7	3.2	0.1	-1.8	1.9	-3.6	-2.8	1.2
1995	7.3	10.3	3.9	-3.4	5.2	-2.2	17.3	11.6
1996	-2.1	2.2	2.9	1.8	10.5	7.7	11.4	8.1
1997	1.8	4.7	7.1	4.4	3.0	8.9	12.4	8.9
1998	7.5	9.8	2.3	-3.6	-12.0	1.4	-3.3	15.5
1999	7.3	35.4	-2.2	-4.4	-5.5	-2.1	-0.8	38.3
2000	4.3	22.2	3.1	3.3	-3.6	12.2	3.6	32.6
2001	0.8	10.2	-3.1	-2.5	-10.0	-5.1	-12.1	7.1
2002	-1.5	5.3	-9.3	-2.6	2.7	7.3	-8.3	15.9
2003	12.1	5.7	5.6	5.8	4.2	5.5	23.3	5.1
2004	-3.5	4.0	3.3	4.9	4.2	10.9	3.7	9.7
2005	-1.8	-1.0	1.1	7.0	-0.6	14.3	-1.3	5.4
2006	2.8	9.4	-5.6	-4.9	7.6	-8.5	4.3	4.9
2007	4.2	10.1	-1.3	6.5	-0.1	-4.2	2.7	-1.4
2008	2.6	7.6	-7.6	-1.7	-14.3	-18.1	-18.7	-10.4
2009	20.2	15.8	-1.1	-7.6	5.0	3.0	24.8	28.3
2010	0.5	-2.3	-3.1	-7.9	4.0	8.5	1.3	14.3
2011	3.1	-0.6	-5.8	-7.6	-18.3	-26.0	-20.6	-20.8
2012	-0.8	-13.4	-2.6	-4.9	7.4	6.1	3.8	-3.6
2013	7.3	3.8	-1.4	-4.0	-0.8	-0.8	4.9	7.2
2014	1.7	9.1	4.2	4.5	-1.0	-10.7	4.9	-7.1
2015	0.0	1.2	-0.7	-5.9	-7.2	-9.5	-7.8	-3.1
2016	6.7	11.1	-1.0	1.9	-0.6	2.1	4.9	11.4
2017	1.3	-4.0	1.8	-4.2	2.5	8.9	5.6	9.0
2018	-1.8	15.4	0.9	-2.3	4.2	7.4	3.3	26.8
2019	2.8	-2.6	1.5	0.6	-3.2	-7.9	1.0	-10.9
2020	-9.2	-25.2	2.7	-4.6	3.5	-24.0	-3.5	-40.5
Avg.	2.6 %	6.0 %	0.4 %	-1.6 %	0.0 %	0.7 %	3.1 %	8.5 %
Fq>0	76 %	78 %	57	32 %	54 %	57 %	68 %	78 %

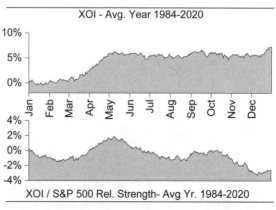

XOI - Avg. Year 1984-2020

XOI / S&P 500 Rel. Strength- Avg Yr. 1984-2020

NYSE Arca Oil Index (XOI) Performance

Market Indices & Rates
Weekly Values**

XOI Monthly % Gain (1984-2020)

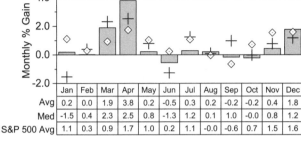

	Jan	Feb	Mar	Apr	May	Jun	Jul	Aug	Sep	Oct	Nov	Dec
Avg	0.2	0.0	1.9	3.8	0.2	-0.5	0.3	0.2	-0.2	-0.2	0.4	1.8
Med	-1.5	0.4	2.3	2.5	0.8	-1.3	1.2	0.1	1.0	-0.0	0.8	1.2
S&P 500 Avg	1.1	0.3	0.9	1.7	1.0	0.2	1.1	-0.0	-0.6	0.7	1.5	1.6

Fq XOI Gain > 0% (1984-2020)

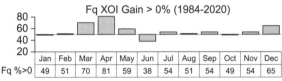

	Jan	Feb	Mar	Apr	May	Jun	Jul	Aug	Sep	Oct	Nov	Dec
Fq %>0	49	51	70	81	59	38	54	51	54	49	54	65

Fq % XOI Gain > S&P 500 % (1984-2020)

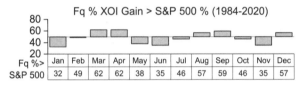

	Jan	Feb	Mar	Apr	May	Jun	Jul	Aug	Sep	Oct	Nov	Dec
Fq %> S&P 500	32	49	62	62	38	35	46	57	59	46	35	57

XOI % Gain 5 Year (2016-2020)

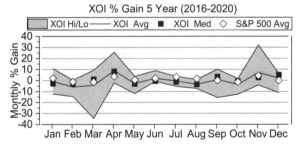

XOI Performance 2020-2021

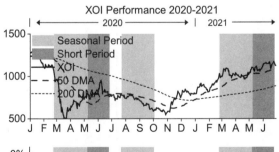

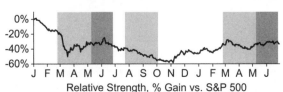

Relative Strength, % Gain vs. S&P 500

Stock Markets	2020	2021
Dow	25,409	31,496
S&P500	2,954	3,842
Nasdaq	8,567	12,920
TSX	16,263	18,381
FTSE	6,581	6,631
DAX	11,890	13,921
Nikkei	21,143	28,864
Hang Seng	26,130	29,098

Commodities	2020	2021
Oil	44.76	66.09
Gold	1609.9	1696.3

Bond Yields	2020	2021
USA 5 Yr Treasury	0.89	0.79
USA 10 Yr T	1.13	1.56
USA 20 Yr T	1.46	2.18
Moody's Aaa	2.70	2.97
Moody's Baa	3.51	3.69
CAN 5 Yr T	1.08	0.91
CAN 10 Yr T	1.13	1.50

Money Market	2020	2021
USA Fed Funds	1.75	0.25
USA 3 Mo T-B	1.25	0.04
CAN tgt overnight rate	1.75	0.25
CAN 3 Mo T-B	1.46	0.11

Foreign Exchange	2020	2021
EUR/USD	1.10	1.19
GBP/USD	1.28	1.38
USD/CAD	1.34	1.27
USD/JPY	107.89	108.31

FEBRUARY

M	T	W	T	F	S	S
1	1	2	3	4	5	6
7	8	9	10	11	12	13
14	15	16	17	18	19	20
21	22	23	24	25	26	27
28						

MARCH

M	T	W	T	F	S	S
	1	2	3	4	5	6
7	8	9	10	11	12	13
14	15	16	17	18	19	20
21	22	23	24	25	26	27
28	29	30	31			

APRIL

M	T	W	T	F	S	S
				1	2	3
4	5	6	7	8	9	10
11	13	13	14	15	16	17
18	20	20	21	22	23	24
25	27	27	28	29	30	

MARCH

	MONDAY	TUESDAY	WEDNESDAY
WEEK 09	28	**1** 30	**2** 29
WEEK 10	**7** 24	**8** 23	**9** 22
WEEK 11	**14** 17	**15** 16	**16** 15
WEEK 12	**21** 10	**22** 9	**23** 8
WEEK 13	**28** 3	**29** 2	**30** 1

THURSDAY	FRIDAY
3 28	**4** 27
10 20	**11** 20
17 14	**18** 13
24 7	**25** 6
31	1

APRIL

M	T	W	T	F	S	S
				1	2	3
4	5	6	7	8	9	10
11	13	13	14	15	16	17
18	19	20	21	22	23	24
25	26	27	28	29	30	

MAY

M	T	W	T	F	S	S
						1
2	3	4	5	6	7	8
9	10	11	12	13	14	15
16	17	18	19	20	21	22
23	24	25	26	27	28	29
30	31					

JUNE

M	T	W	T	F	S	S
		1	2	3	4	5
6	7	8	9	10	11	12
13	14	15	16	17	18	19
20	21	22	23	24	25	26
27	28	29	30			

JULY

M	T	W	T	F	S	S
				1	2	3
4	5	6	7	8	9	10
11	12	13	14	15	16	17
18	19	20	21	22	23	24
25	26	27	28	29	30	31

MARCH SUMMARY

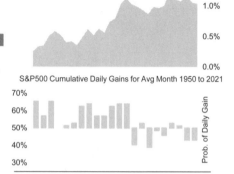

S&P500 Cumulative Daily Gains for Avg Month 1950 to 2021

	Dow Jones	S&P 500	Nasdaq	TSX Comp
Month Rank	6	6	9	8
# Up	45	45	30	21
# Down	26	26	19	15
% Pos	63	63	61	58
% Avg. Gain	0.9	1.0	0.6	0.5

Dow & S&P 1950-2020, Nasdaq 1972-2020, TSX 1985-2020

♦ March tends to be a strong month for stocks. ♦ Typically, in March, it is the cyclical sectors that perform well and the defensive sectors that underperform. ♦ The energy, consumer discretionary and the financial sectors are typically strong performing sectors in March. ♦ Retail, also tends to perform well in March. ♦ The information technology sector tends to be a laggard in March.

BEST / WORST MARCH BROAD MKTS. 2012-2021

BEST MARCH MARKETS
- ♦ Russell 2000 (2016) 7.7%
- ♦ Nikkei 225 (2013) 7.3%
- ♦ Dow (2016) 7.1%

WORST MARCH MARKETS
- ♦ Russell 2000 (2020) -21.9%
- ♦ TSX Comp. (2020) -17.7%
- ♦ FTSE 100 (2020) -13.8%

Index Values End of Month

	2012	2013	2014	2015	2016	2017	2018	2019	2020	2021
Dow	13,212	14,579	16,458	17,776	17,685	20,663	24,103	25,929	21,917	32,982
S&P 500	1,408	1,569	1,872	2,068	2,060	2,363	2,641	2,834	2,585	3,973
Nasdaq	3,092	3,268	4,199	4,901	4,870	5,912	7,063	7,729	7,700	13,247
TSX	12,392	12,750	14,335	14,902	13,494	15,548	15,367	16,102	13,379	18,701
Russell 1000	779	872	1,046	1,157	1,139	1,310	1,465	1,570	1,416	2,238
Russell 2000	830	952	1,173	1,253	1,114	1,386	1,529	1,540	1,153	2,221
FTSE 100	5,768	6,412	6,598	6,773	6,175	7,323	7,057	7,279	5,672	6,714
Nikkei 225	10,084	12,398	14,828	19,207	16,759	18,909	21,454	21,206	18,917	29,179

Percent Gain for March

	2012	2013	2014	2015	2016	2017	2018	2019	2020	2021
Dow	2.0	3.7	0.8	-2.0	7.1	-0.7	-3.7	0.0	-13.7	6.6
S&P 500	3.1	3.6	0.7	-1.7	6.6	0.0	-2.7	1.8	-12.5	4.2
Nasdaq	4.2	3.4	-2.5	-1.3	6.8	1.5	-2.9	2.6	-10.1	0.4
TSX	-2.0	-0.6	0.9	-2.2	4.9	1.0	-0.5	0.6	-17.7	3.5
Russell 1000	3.0	3.7	0.5	-1.4	6.8	-0.1	-2.4	1.6	-13.4	3.7
Russell 2000	2.4	4.4	-0.8	1.6	7.8	-0.1	1.1	-2.3	-21.9	0.9
FTSE 100	-1.8	0.8	-3.1	-2.5	1.3	0.8	-2.4	2.9	-13.8	3.6
Nikkei 225	3.7	7.3	-0.1	2.2	4.6	-1.1	-2.8	-0.8	-10.5	0.7

March Market Avg. Performance 2012 to 2021[1]

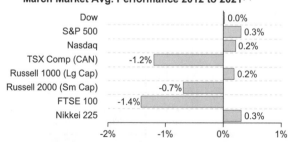

- Dow 0.0%
- S&P 500 0.3%
- Nasdaq 0.2%
- TSX Comp (CAN) -1.2%
- Russell 1000 (Lg Cap) 0.2%
- Russell 2000 (Sm Cap) -0.7%
- FTSE 100 -1.4%
- Nikkei 225 0.3%

Interest Corner Mar[2]

	Fed Funds % [3]	3 Mo. T-Bill % [4]	10 Yr % [5]	20 Yr % [6]
2021	0.25	0.03	1.74	2.31
2020	0.25	0.11	0.70	1.15
2019	2.50	2.40	2.41	2.63
2018	1.75	1.73	2.74	2.85
2017	1.00	0.76	2.40	2.76

(1) Russell Data provided by Russell (2) Federal Reserve Bank of St. Louis- end of month values (3) Target rate set by FOMC (4)(5)(6) Constant yield maturities.

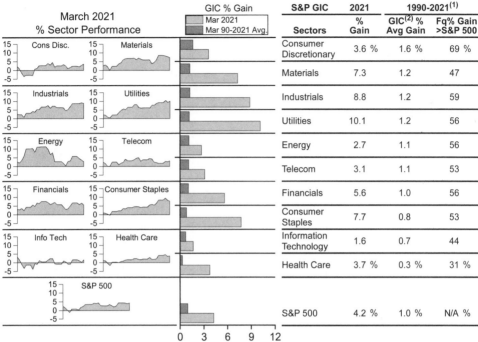

S&P GIC Sectors	2021 % Gain	1990-2021[1] GIC[2] % Avg Gain	Fq% Gain >S&P 500
Consumer Discretionary	3.6 %	1.6 %	69 %
Materials	7.3	1.2	47
Industrials	8.8	1.2	59
Utilities	10.1	1.2	56
Energy	2.7	1.1	56
Telecom	3.1	1.1	53
Financials	5.6	1.0	56
Consumer Staples	7.7	0.8	53
Information Technology	1.6	0.7	44
Health Care	3.7 %	0.3 %	31 %
S&P 500	4.2 %	1.0 %	N/A %

Sector Commentary

♦ In March 2021, all of the major sectors of the stock market were positive. ♦ The top performing sector was utilities, gaining over 10%. Although the utilities sector on average performs well in March, the strength of the sector was surprising given that the yield on the US Treasury 10-Year Note rose during the month.♦ Similarly, the consumer staples sector also performed well, gaining over 7% during the month. ♦ The weakest performing sector was the information technology sector, which only managed to gain 1.6%.

Sub-Sector Commentary

♦ In March 2021, the cyclical sub-sectors of the stock market performed well. ♦ From the selected sub-sectors, steel was at the top of the list, gaining over 34%. ♦ Homebuilders also managed to gain over 15%. ♦ The biggest loser was silver, losing over 10%. ♦ Gold also lost ground with a 3% loss. Both gold and silver typically do not perform well in March.

SELECTED SUB-SECTORS[3]

Retail	4.9 %	3.0 %	78 %
Steel	34.2	2.8	56
Transportation	8.1	1.6	59
Chemicals	7.8	1.5	50
Railroads	7.7	1.5	53
SOX (1995-2021)	1.9	1.2	52
Metals & Mining	8.5	0.8	44
Homebuilders	15.5	0.7	53
Agriculture (1994-2021)	0.7	0.6	36
Pharma	2.5	0.5	34
Silver	-10.1	0.4	44
Banks	6.2	0.4	47
Automotive & Components	0.2	0.1	47
Biotech (1993-2021)	4.0	-0.3	34
Gold	-3.0	-1.0	34

NIKE – RUNS INTO EARNINGS
①Mar1-Mar20 ②Sep1-Sep25 ③Dec12-Dec24

Nike has had a strong run in the stock market since it went public in 1980. A lot of the gains in it's stock price can be accounted for in the two to three week periods leading up to its first, second and third quarters earnings reports.

Nike's year-end is May 31, and although from year to year the actual report dates for Nike's earnings changes, generally speaking, Nike reports its earnings in the third or fourth week in the months of March, June, September and December.

There are large differences in Nike's pattern of seasonal strength compared with the seasonal pattern of the consumer discretionary sector. First, Nike has a period of seasonal strength that includes September, a month that is not favorable to consumer discretionary stocks. Second, Nike's outperformance is focused on very short periods in the weeks leading up to three of its earnings reports. In contrast, the consumer discretionary sector has a much longer seasonal period and has a more gradual transition from its favorable seasonal period to its unfavorable seasonal period and vice versa.

From 1990 to 2020, Nike produced an average annual gain of 21%. In comparison, its three short seasonal periods within the year have produced an average compound gain of 13%. The seasonal periods for Nike, in total are approximately eight weeks and yet, they have produced most of the average annual gains of Nike. Investors have been well served investing in Nike in its seasonal periods and then running to another investment during its "off-season."

Nike Inc* Seasonal Gains 1990 to 2020

	Year %	Mar 1 to Mar 20	Sep 1 to Sep 25	Dec 12 to Dec 24	Positive Compound Growth
1990	51.2 %	14.5 %	1.3 %	11.5 %	29.5 %
1991	79.8	-5.7	9.3	12.7	12.4
1992	14.7	-8.4	6.0	-2.9	-6.8
1993	-44.3	5.7	-13.5	0.6	-9.0
1994	61.4	10.4	-7.0	14.5	17.3
1995	86.6	5.3	18.8	10.7	34.4
1996	72.4	22.1	13.7	13.0	56.9
1997	-34.9	-6.1	0.9	-14.1	-18.6
1998	3.8	1.0	18.0	14.8	36.8
1999	22.2	15.6	15.1	18.2	57.3
2000	12.6	16.0	1.5	16.3	37.1
2001	0.8	-2.6	-8.7	3.7	-7.8
2002	-20.9	8.7	2.8	2.1	14.0
2003	53.9	14.0	6.0	4.4	26.1
2004	32.5	4.9	5.8	5.3	17.0
2005	-4.3	-1.8	3.0	1.3	2.5
2006	14.1	-1.5	7.1	2.6	8.3
2007	29.7	4.6	3.8	4.2	13.0
2008	-20.6	11.7	7.3	0.8	20.8
2009	29.5	8.4	5.9	2.2	17.3
2010	29.3	8.8	13.7	-2.0	21.2
2011	12.8	-12.9	2.3	-0.8	-11.6
2012	7.1	3.5	-2.3	6.2	7.4
2013	52.4	0.7	9.7	1.1	11.6
2014	22.3	1.2	1.5	-0.7	2.1
2015	30.0	5.0	11.9	0.1	17.5
2016	-18.7	2.3	-4.3	0.4	-1.8
2017	23.1	2.7	0.8	2.2	5.8
2018	18.5	-0.3	3.2	-7.4	-4.8
2019	36.6	1.1	7.5	3.0	12.0
2020	39.6	-24.5	11.0	3.0	-13.7
Avg.	21.4 %	3.4 %	4.9 %	4.1 %	13.4 %

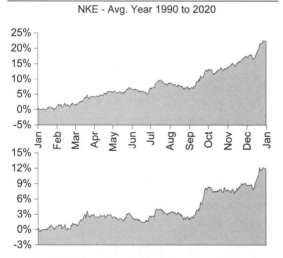

NKE - Avg. Year 1990 to 2020

25%
20%
15%
10%
5%
0%
-5%

Jan Feb Mar Apr May Jun Jul Aug Sep Oct Nov Dec Jan

15%
12%
9%
6%
3%
0%
-3%

NKE / S&P 500 Relative Strength - Avg Yr. 1990 - 2020

Covid-19 Performance Update. In 2021, Nike has had a roller coaster ride relative to the S&P 500. For most of the first half of the year, Nike underperformed. A strong earnings report in June helped to rally the value of Nike relative to the S&P 500.

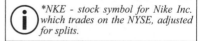

*NKE - stock symbol for Nike Inc. which trades on the NYSE, adjusted for splits.

Nike Performance

NKE Monthly % Gain (1990-2020)

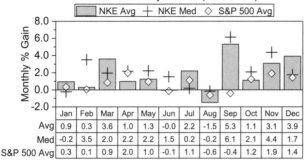

	Jan	Feb	Mar	Apr	May	Jun	Jul	Aug	Sep	Oct	Nov	Dec
Avg	0.9	0.3	3.6	1.0	1.3	-0.0	2.2	-1.5	5.3	1.1	3.1	3.9
Med	-0.2	3.5	2.0	2.2	2.2	1.5	0.2	-0.2	6.1	2.1	4.4	1.7
S&P 500 Avg	0.3	0.1	0.9	2.0	1.0	-0.1	1.1	-0.6	-0.4	1.2	1.9	1.4

Fq NKE Gain > 0% (1990-2020)

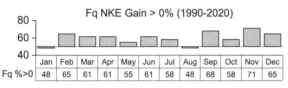

	Jan	Feb	Mar	Apr	May	Jun	Jul	Aug	Sep	Oct	Nov	Dec
Fq %>0	48	65	61	61	55	61	58	48	68	58	71	65

Fq % NKE Gain > S&P 500 % (1990-2020)

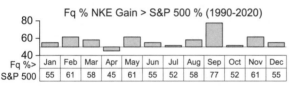

	Jan	Feb	Mar	Apr	May	Jun	Jul	Aug	Sep	Oct	Nov	Dec
Fq %> S&P 500	55	61	58	45	61	55	52	58	77	52	61	55

NKE % Gain 5 Year (2016-2020)

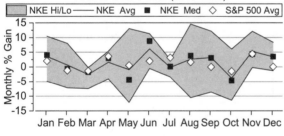

NKE Performance 2020-2021

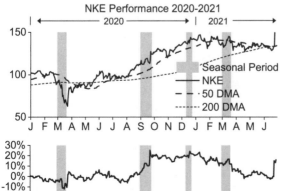

Relative Strength, % Gain vs. S&P 500

Market Indices & Rates
Weekly Values**

Stock Markets	2020	2021
Dow	25,865	32,779
S&P500	2,972	3,943
Nasdaq	8,576	13,320
TSX	16,175	18,851
FTSE	6,463	6,761
DAX	11,542	14,502
Nikkei	20,750	29,718
Hang Seng	26,147	28,740

Commodities	2020	2021
Oil	41.28	65.61
Gold	1683.7	1704.8

Bond Yields	2020	2021
USA 5 Yr Treasury	0.58	0.85
USA 10 Yr T	0.74	1.64
USA 20 Yr T	1.09	2.31
Moody's Aaa	2.36	3.13
Moody's Baa	3.29	3.83
CAN 5 Yr T	0.68	1.04
CAN 10 Yr T	0.73	1.59

Money Market	2020	2021
USA Fed Funds	1.25	0.25
USA 3 Mo T-B	0.45	0.04
CAN tgt overnight rate	1.25	0.25
CAN 3 Mo T-B	0.76	0.11

Foreign Exchange	2020	2021
EUR/USD	1.13	1.20
GBP/USD	1.30	1.39
USD/CAD	1.34	1.25
USD/JPY	105.39	109.03

MARCH

M	T	W	T	F	S	S
	1	2	3	4	5	6
7	8	9	10	11	12	13
14	15	16	17	18	19	20
21	22	23	24	25	26	27
28	29	30	31			

APRIL

M	T	W	T	F	S	S
				1	2	3
4	5	6	7	8	9	10
11	13	13	14	15	16	17
18	20	20	21	22	23	24
25	27	27	28	29	30	

MAY

M	T	W	T	F	S	S
						1
2	3	4	5	6	7	8
9	11	11	12	13	14	15
16	18	18	19	20	21	22
21	25	25	26	27	28	29
30	31					

LOBLAW
April 25 to May 18

Loblaw is considered to be a defensive stock due to its major source of revenue coming from its grocery store business. Although Loblaw pays a healthy dividend and many Canadian investors see this as a company to hold over the long-term, on a seasonal basis Loblaw tends to perform well from late April to mid-May. This is a relatively short period, but the gains and frequency of outperformance in this period have been strong compared to the S&P/TSX Composite Index.

3% extra & 77% of the time better than the TSX Composite

Loblaw typically announces its Q1 earnings in late April or early May. The month of May is a transition month for the stock market from its favorable season to its unfavorable season. During this time, investors tend to favor defensive stocks. In addition, seasonally, bond yields on average have tended to decrease at this time of the year, which helps boost high dividend paying stocks such as Loblaw.

Loblaw vs.
S&P/TSX Comp. 1996 to 2021

Apr 25 to May 18	TSX	Positive Loblaw	Diff
1996	2.0 %	5.3 %	3.3 %
1997	6.5	8.6	2.0
1998	-0.3	7.7	8.0
1999	-1.5	5.6	7.0
2000	8.2	5.8	-2.4
2001	4.8	-4.5	-9.3
2002	0.2	5.7	5.5
2003	2.8	10.1	7.3
2004	-5.8	0.2	6.1
2005	0.4	-2.8	-3.2
2006	-6.5	-1.9	4.6
2007	3.8	1.3	-2.5
2008	7.3	13.6	6.3
2009	2.2	7.9	5.6
2010	-3.9	1.1	5.0
2011	-2.6	4.0	6.6
2012	-5.8	-1.3	4.6
2013	2.8	17.9	15.1
2014	-0.3	2.2	2.5
2015	-1.9	1.6	3.6
2016	-0.3	-0.2	0.1
2017	-2.8	3.3	6.1
2018	4.4	1.9	-2.5
2019	-1.1	7.8	9.0
2020	1.5	-9.6	-11.1
2021	2.1	4.8	2.7
Avg.	0.6 %	3.7 %	3.1 %
Fq > 0	54 %	77 %	77 %

Loblaw - Avg. Year 1996 to 2020

Loblaw / S&P/TSX Comp Rel. Strength- Avg Yr. 1996 - 2020

tends to perform poorly shortly after its strong seasonal period, extra consideration should be given to using technical analysis in exiting a position in Loblaw at the end of its seasonal period.

Covid-19 Performance Update. In 2021, Loblaw started to outperform the S&P/TSX Composite Index in late February and continued to outperform right through its strong seasonal period from late April to mid-May.

It should be noted that June, which falls right after Loblaw's strong seasonal period, is one of the weaker months of the year for Loblaw. In June, from 1996 to 2021, Loblaw produced an average loss of 1.0% and was only positive 35% of the time. Given that Loblaw

(i) *Loblaw Companies Limited, a food and pharmacy company, engages in the grocery, pharmacy, health and beauty, apparel, general merchandise, financial services, and wireless mobile products and services businesses in Canada.*

Loblaw Performance

Loblaw Monthly % Gain (1996-2020)

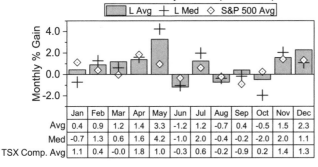

L Avg + L Med ◇ S&P 500 Avg

	Jan	Feb	Mar	Apr	May	Jun	Jul	Aug	Sep	Oct	Nov	Dec
Avg	0.4	0.9	1.2	1.4	3.3	-1.2	1.2	-0.7	0.4	-0.5	1.5	2.3
Med	-0.7	1.3	0.6	1.6	4.2	-1.0	2.0	-0.4	-0.2	-2.0	2.0	1.1
TSX Comp. Avg	1.1	0.4	-0.0	1.8	1.0	-0.3	0.6	-0.2	-0.9	0.2	1.4	1.3

Fq Loblaw Gain > 0% (1996-2020)

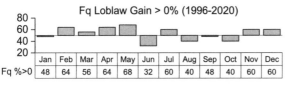

	Jan	Feb	Mar	Apr	May	Jun	Jul	Aug	Sep	Oct	Nov	Dec
Fq %>0	48	64	56	64	68	32	60	40	48	40	60	60

Fq % Loblaw Gain > S&P 500 % (1996-2020)

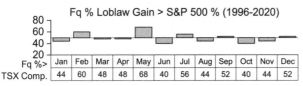

	Jan	Feb	Mar	Apr	May	Jun	Jul	Aug	Sep	Oct	Nov	Dec
Fq %> TSX Comp.	44	60	48	48	68	40	56	44	52	40	44	52

Loblaw % Gain 5 Year (2016-2020)

L Hi/Lo —— L Avg ■ L Med ◇ S&P 500 Avg

Loblaw Performance 2020-2021

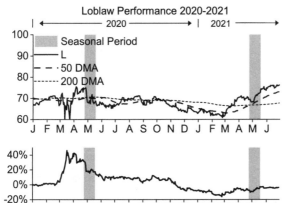

Relative Strength, % Gain vs. TSX Composite Index

Market Indices & Rates
Weekly Values**

Stock Markets	2020	2021
Dow	23,186	32,628
S&P500	2,711	3,913
Nasdaq	7,875	13,215
TSX	13,716	18,854
FTSE	5,366	6,709
DAX	9,232	14,621
Nikkei	17,431	29,792
Hang Seng	24,033	28,991

Commodities	2020	2021
Oil	31.73	61.42
Gold	1562.8	1735.2

Bond Yields	2020	2021
USA 5 Yr Treasury	0.70	0.90
USA 10 Yr T	0.94	1.74
USA 20 Yr T	1.31	2.36
Moody's Aaa	3.03	3.13
Moody's Baa	4.24	3.84
CAN 5 Yr T	0.67	1.01
CAN 10 Yr T	0.85	1.59

Money Market	2020	2021
USA Fed Funds	1.25	0.25
USA 3 Mo T-B	0.27	0.01
CAN tgt overnight rate	0.75	0.25
CAN 3 Mo T-B	0.61	0.09

Foreign Exchange	2020	2021
EUR/USD	1.11	1.19
GBP/USD	1.23	1.39
USD/CAD	1.38	1.25
USD/JPY	107.62	108.88

MARCH

M	T	W	T	F	S	S
	1	2	3	4	5	6
7	8	9	10	11	12	13
14	15	16	17	18	19	20
21	22	23	24	25	26	27
28	29	30	31			

APRIL

M	T	W	T	F	S	S
				1	2	3
4	5	6	7	8	9	10
11	13	13	14	15	16	17
18	20	20	21	22	23	24
25	27	27	28	29	30	

MAY

M	T	W	T	F	S	S
						1
2	3	4	5	6	7	8
9	11	11	12	13	14	15
16	18	18	19	20	21	22
21	25	25	26	27	28	29
30	31					

NATURAL GAS – FIRES UP AND DOWN
①LONG (Mar22-Jun19) & ②LONG (Sep5-Dec21)
③SELL SHORT (Dec22-Dec31)

There are two high consumption times for natural gas: winter and summer. The colder it gets in winter, the more natural gas is consumed to keep the furnaces going. The warmer it gets in summer, the more natural gas is used to produce power for air conditioners.

On the supply side, weather plays a large factor in determining price. During the hurricane season in the Gulf of Mexico, the price of natural gas is affected by the number and severity of hurricanes.

March 22 to June 19, the spot price of natural gas has on average increased 10% and has been positive 65% of the time. The price of natural gas also tends to rise between September 5 and December 21, due to the demands of the heating season. In this period, from 1995 to 2020, natural gas has produced an average gain of 34.0% and has been positive 73% of the time.

56% Gain & Positive 81% of the time

Natural gas tends to fall in price from December 22 to December 31. Although this is a short time period, for the years from 1995 to 2020, natural gas has produced an average loss of 3.8% and has only been positive 38% of the time. Also, in this period, when gains did occur, they were relatively small. The poor performance of natural gas at this time is largely driven by southern U.S. refiners dumping inventory on the market to help mitigate year-end taxes on their inventory.

Covid-19 Performance Update. In 2021, natural gas started to rally strongly in April, just after its strong seasonal period started. Natural gas continued to rally into the summer. Demand for natural gas increased as a hotter than normal summer increased electricity demand and the need for natural gas. Logistics problems also helped to crimp supply, and drive the price higher.

Natural Gas (Cash) Henry Hub LA*
Seasonal Gains 1995 to 2020

Year %	Pos. Mar 22 to Jun 19	Pos. Sep 5 to Dec 21	Neg. (Short) Dec 22 to Dec 31	Pos. Compound Growth
1995	99.4 %	13.0 %	103.0 %	1.2 %	126.7 %
1996	-27.4	-6.6	170.4	-46.2	269.2
1997	-9.4	16.8	-13.1	-6.3	7.9
1998	-13.0	-2.6	20.9	-6.7	25.7
1999	18.6	28.9	5.3	-11.2	50.9
2000	356.5	57.1	121.9	0.7	246.3
2001	-74.3	-24.1	21.5	1.5	-9.2
2002	70.0	0.6	61.3	-9.1	77.1
2003	26.4	9.5	47.1	-16.3	87.4
2004	3.6	18.2	54.6	-11.6	103.9
2005	58.4	6.3	14.5	-29.6	57.7
2006	-42.2	-1.8	17.4	-9.5	26.3
2007	30.2	9.2	32.7	2.0	42.1
2008	-21.4	52.2	-21.4	-0.9	20.6
2009	3.6	1.5	208.0	0.7	210.4
2010	-27.4	28.6	10.4	2.4	38.6
2011	-29.6	10.0	-26.1	-1.7	-17.3
2012	15.4	18.7	21.7	0.6	43.7
2013	26.3	-1.4	18.2	-0.2	16.8
2014	-31.1	7.7	-11.8	-12.9	7.2
2015	-22.8	-0.5	-36.1	35.6	-59.0
2016	59.2	46.6	21.9	5.8	68.3
2017	-3.9	-6.6	-10.4	36.0	-46.4
2018	-9.9	9.1	16.7	-7.7	37.1
2019	-34.4	-13.2	-8.5	-7.9	-14.3
2020	14.4	-17.0	47.2	-9.8	34.1
Avg.	16.8 %	10.0 %	34.0 %	-3.8 %	55.6 %

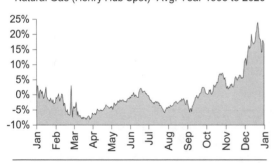

Natural Gas (Henry Hub Spot)- Avg. Year 1995 to 2020

Natural gas prices tend to rise from mid-March to mid-June ahead of the cooling season demands in the summer. From 1995 to 2020, during the period of

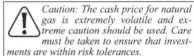

⚠ Caution: The cash price for natural gas is extremely volatile and extreme caution should be used. Care must be taken to ensure that investments are within risk tolerances.

ⓘ *Source: New York Mercantile Exchange. NYMX is an exchange provider of futures and options.*

Natural Gas Performance

Natural Gas Monthly % Gain (1995-2020)

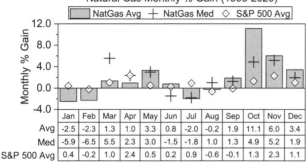

	Jan	Feb	Mar	Apr	May	Jun	Jul	Aug	Sep	Oct	Nov	Dec
Avg	-2.5	-2.3	1.3	1.0	3.3	0.8	-2.0	-0.2	1.9	11.1	6.0	3.4
Med	-5.9	-6.5	5.5	2.3	3.0	-1.5	-1.8	1.0	1.3	4.9	5.2	1.9
S&P 500 Avg	0.4	-0.2	1.0	2.4	0.5	0.2	0.9	-0.6	-0.1	1.3	2.3	1.1

Fq Natural Gas Gain > 0% (1995-2020)

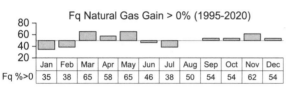

	Jan	Feb	Mar	Apr	May	Jun	Jul	Aug	Sep	Oct	Nov	Dec
Fq %>0	35	38	65	58	65	46	38	50	54	54	62	54

Fq % Natural Gas Gain > S&P 500 % (1995-2020)

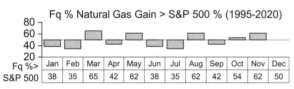

	Jan	Feb	Mar	Apr	May	Jun	Jul	Aug	Sep	Oct	Nov	Dec
Fq %> S&P 500	38	35	65	42	62	38	35	62	42	54	62	50

Natural Gas % Gain 5 Year (2016-2020)

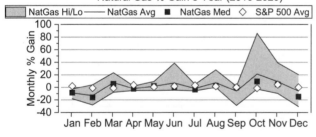

Natural Gas Performance 2020-2021

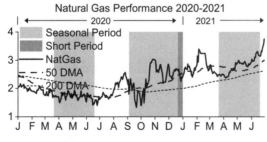

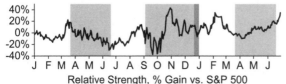

Relative Strength, % Gain vs. S&P 500

Stock Markets	2020	2021
Dow	19,174	33,073
S&P500	2,305	3,975
Nasdaq	6,880	13,139
TSX	11,852	18,753
FTSE	5,191	6,741
DAX	8,929	14,749
Nikkei	16,553	29,177
Hang Seng	22,805	28,336

Commodities	2020	2021
Oil	22.43	60.97
Gold	1494.4	1731.8

Bond Yields	2020	2021
USA 5 Yr Treasury	0.52	0.85
USA 10 Yr T	0.92	1.67
USA 20 Yr T	1.35	2.27
Moody's Aaa	4.12	3.06
Moody's Baa	5.15	3.76
CAN 5 Yr T	0.75	0.94
CAN 10 Yr T	0.87	1.50

Money Market	2020	2021
USA Fed Funds	0.25	0.25
USA 3 Mo T-B	0.05	0.02
CAN tgt overnight rate	0.75	0.25
CAN 3 Mo T-B	0.42	0.09

Foreign Exchange	2020	2021
EUR/USD	1.07	1.18
GBP/USD	1.16	1.38
USD/CAD	1.44	1.26
USD/JPY	110.93	109.64

MARCH

M	T	W	T	F	S	S
	1	2	3	4	5	6
7	8	9	10	11	12	13
14	15	16	17	18	19	20
21	22	23	24	25	26	27
28	29	30	31			

APRIL

M	T	W	T	F	S	S
				1	2	3
4	5	6	7	8	9	10
11	13	13	14	15	16	17
18	20	20	21	22	23	24
25	27	27	28	29	30	

MAY

M	T	W	T	F	S	S
						1
2	3	4	5	6	7	8
9	11	11	12	13	14	15
16	18	18	19	20	21	22
21	25	25	26	27	28	29
30	31					

CANADIANS GIVE 3 CHEERS FOR AMERICAN HOLIDAYS

When I used to work on the retail side of the investment business, I was always amazed at how often the Canadian stock market increased on U.S. holidays, when the US market was closed.

The Canadian stock market on U.S. holidays had light volume, tended to have small increases or decreases, but usually ended the day with a gain.

1% average gain

How the trade works

For the three big holidays in the United States that do not exist in Canada (Memorial, Independence and U.S. Thanksgiving Days), buy at the end of the market day before the holiday (TSX Composite) and sell at the end of the U.S. holiday when the U.S markets are closed.

For U.S. investors to take advantage of this trade, they must have access to the TSX Composite. Unfortunately, SEC regulations do not allow most Americans to purchase foreign ETFs.

Generally, markets perform well around most major U.S. holidays, hence the trading strategies for U.S holidays included in this book. The typical U.S. holiday trade is to get into the stock market the day before the holiday and then exit the day after the holiday. The main reason for the strong performance around these holidays is a lack of institutional involvement in the markets, allowing bullish retail investors to push up the markets.

On the actual American holidays, economic reports are not released in the U.S. and are very seldom released in Canada. During market hours on U.S. holidays, without any strong influences, the TSX Composite tends to float, as investors wait until the next day before making any significant moves. Despite this lackadaisical action during the day, the TSX Composite tends to end the day on a gain. This is true for the three major U.S. holidays: Memorial Day, Independence Day and U.S. Thanksgiving.

From a theoretical perspective, a lot of the gain that is captured on the U.S. holidays in the Canadian stock market is realized the next day when the U.S stock market is open. This does not invalidate the *Canadians Give 3 Cheers* trade – it

presents more alternatives for the astute investor.

For example, an investor can allocate a portion of money to a standard U.S. holiday trade and another portion to the *Canadian Give 3 Cheers* version. By spreading out the exit days, the overall risk in the trade is reduced.

S&P/TSX Comp
Gain 1977-2020   Positive

	Memorial	Independence	Thanksgiving	Compound Growth
1977	0.10 %	-0.08 %	0.61 %	0.63 %
1978	-0.05	-0.16	0.57	0.36
1979	1.11	0.23	0.58	1.93
1980	1.64	0.76	0.89	3.32
1981	0.51	-0.15	1.03	1.40
1982	-0.18	-0.01	0.35	0.17
1983	0.29	0.53	0.15	0.97
1984	0.86	-0.11	0.73	1.48
1985	0.61	0.31	0.31	1.24
1986	0.23	-0.02	0.22	0.44
1987	-0.11	1.08	1.57	2.55
1988	0.44	0.08	0.58	1.11
1989	0.10	-0.12	-0.11	-0.13
1990	0.11	0.43	0.02	0.57
1991	0.02	0.18	-0.09	0.11
1992	-0.06	0.35	0.36	0.65
1993	0.42	-0.18	0.14	0.38
1994	-0.19	0.70	0.91	1.43
1995	0.14	0.25	0.29	0.68
1996	0.11	0.25	0.54	0.90
1997	1.08	-0.04	-0.85	0.18
1998	0.56	0.18	0.51	1.25
1999	0.57	1.63	1.14	3.39
2000	0.43	1.04	0.91	2.40
2001	-0.02	-0.23	0.70	0.45
2002	-0.01	0.08	0.38	0.45
2003	0.03	0.03	0.26	0.31
2004	0.84	-0.02	0.55	1.39
2005	0.56	0.39	1.48	2.45
2006	0.70	1.04	0.70	2.46
2007	0.35	-0.03	0.76	1.08
2008	0.24	-0.94	1.28	0.56
2009	0.76	0.36	-1.29	-0.18
2010	0.78	-0.92	0.34	0.19
2011	0.23	0.64	-0.75	0.12
2012	-0.09	0.55	0.44	0.90
2013	0.23	0.17	0.07	0.47
2014	0.05	0.05	-0.77	-0.67
2015	-0.09	0.30	0.16	0.38
2016	-0.13	1.48	-0.04	1.21
2017	0.03	-0.34	0.00	-0.30
2018	-0.37	0.26	-0.02	-0.14
2019	0.72	0.08	0.08	0.88
2020	1.08	-0.16	0.22	1.14
Avg	0.33 %	0.22 %	0.36 %	0.92 %
Fq > 0	75 %	64 %	82 %	89 %

Canadians Give 3 Cheers Performance

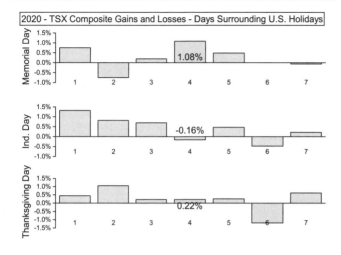

2020 - TSX Composite Gains and Losses - Days Surrounding U.S. Holidays

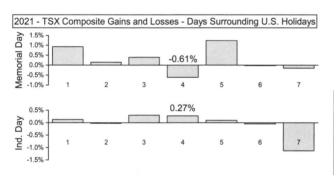

2021 - TSX Composite Gains and Losses - Days Surrounding U.S. Holidays

Market Indices & Rates
Weekly Values**

Stock Markets	2020	2021
Dow	21,637	33,153
S&P500	2,541	4,020
Nasdaq	7,502	13,480
TSX	12,688	18,990
FTSE	5,510	6,737
DAX	9,633	15,107
Nikkei	19,389	29,854
Hang Seng	23,484	28,939

Commodities	2020	2021
Oil	21.51	61.45
Gold	1617.3	1726.1

Bond Yields	2020	2021
USA 5 Yr Treasury	0.41	0.97
USA 10 Yr T	0.72	1.72
USA 20 Yr T	1.09	2.27
Moody's Aaa	2.95	2.91
Moody's Baa	4.70	3.67
CAN 5 Yr T	0.64	0.97
CAN 10 Yr T	0.74	1.51

Money Market	2020	2021
USA Fed Funds	0.25	0.25
USA 3 Mo T-B	0.03	0.02
CAN tgt overnight rate	0.25	0.25
CAN 3 Mo T-B	0.21	0.09

Foreign Exchange	2020	2021
EUR/USD	1.11	1.18
GBP/USD	1.25	1.38
USD/CAD	1.40	1.26
USD/JPY	107.94	110.69

Canadians Give 3 Cheers Performance

In 2020, the TSX Composite produced a large gain on Memorial Day. On Independence Day, the TSX Composite was slightly negative. On Thanksgiving Day, the TSX was slightly positive. Overall, the combination of the three holidays produced a gain of more than 1%.

In 2021, the TSX Composite produced a loss of 0.6% on Memorial Day. The day following Memorial Day produced a large gain. On Independence Day, the TSX Composite was positive, but the gain did not make up for the loss on Memorial Day.

MARCH

M	T	W	T	F	S	S
	1	2	3	4	5	6
7	8	9	10	11	12	13
14	15	16	17	18	19	20
21	22	23	24	25	26	27
28	29	30	31			

APRIL

M	T	W	T	F	S	S
			1	2	3
4	5	6	7	8	9	10
11	13	13	14	15	16	17
18	20	20	21	22	23	24
25	27	27	28	29	30	

MAY

M	T	W	T	F	S	S
						1
2	3	4	5	6	7	8
9	11	11	12	13	14	15
16	18	18	19	20	21	22
21	25	25	26	27	28	29
30	31					

APRIL

	MONDAY	TUESDAY	WEDNESDAY
WEEK 13	28	29	30 29
WEEK 14	4 26	5 25	6 24
WEEK 15	11 19	12 18	13 17
WEEK 16	18 12	19 11	20 10
WEEK 17	25 5	26 4	27 3

THURSDAY	FRIDAY
31	**1** 29
7 23	**8** 22
14 16	**15** 15
	USA Market Closed- Good Friday CAN Market Closed- Good Friday
21 9	**22** 8
28 2	**29** 1

MAY

M	T	W	T	F	S	S
						1
2	3	4	5	6	7	8
9	10	11	12	13	14	15
16	17	18	19	20	21	22
23	24	25	26	27	28	29
30	31					

JUNE

M	T	W	T	F	S	S
		1	2	3	4	5
6	7	8	9	10	11	12
13	14	15	16	17	18	19
20	21	22	23	24	25	26
27	28	29	30			

JULY

M	T	W	T	F	S	S
				1	2	3
4	5	6	7	8	9	10
11	12	13	14	15	16	17
18	19	20	21	22	23	24
25	26	27	28	29	30	31

AUGUST

M	T	W	T	F	S	S
1	2	3	4	5	6	7
8	9	10	11	12	13	14
15	16	17	18	19	20	21
22	23	24	25	26	27	28
29	30	31				

APRIL
S U M M A R Y

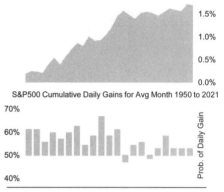

S&P500 Cumulative Daily Gains for Avg Month 1950 to 2021

	Dow Jones	S&P 500	Nasdaq	TSX Comp
Month Rank	1	2	3	4
# Up	49	50	32	23
# Down	22	21	17	13
% Pos	69	70	65	64
% Avg. Gain	2.0	1.6	1.6	1.2

Dow & S&P 1950-2020, Nasdaq 1972-2020, TSX 1985-2020

♦ The first part of April tends to be the strongest (see *18 Day Earnings Month Effect strategy*). ♦ The last part of April tends to be "flat." ♦ Overall, April tends to be a volatile month with the cyclical sectors outperforming. ♦ In 2021, all of the major sectors of the stock market were positive. Investors pushed the stock market higher based upon the narrative that the economy was recovering. Generally, the cyclical sectors performed well.

BEST / WORST APRIL BROAD MKTS. 2012-2021

BEST APRIL MARKETS
- Nasdaq (2020) 15.4%
- Russell 2000 (2020) 13.7%
- Russell 1000 (2020) 13.1%

WORST APRIL MARKETS
- Nikkei 225 (2012) -5.6%
- Russell 2000 (2014) -3.9%
- Nikkei 225 (2014) -3.5%

Index Values End of Month

	2012	2013	2014	2015	2016	2017	2018	2019	2020	2021
Dow	13,214	14,840	16,581	17,841	17,774	20,941	24,163	26,593	24,346	33,875
S&P 500	1,398	1,598	1,884	2,086	2,065	2,384	2,648	2,946	2,912	4,181
Nasdaq	3,046	3,329	4,115	4,941	4,775	6,048	7,066	8,095	8,890	13,963
TSX	12,293	12,457	14,652	15,225	13,951	15,586	15,608	16,581	14,781	19,108
Russell 1000	774	887	1,050	1,164	1,144	1,322	1,468	1,632	1,602	2,357
Russell 2000	817	947	1,127	1,220	1,131	1,400	1,542	1,591	1,311	2,266
FTSE 100	5,738	6,430	6,780	6,961	6,242	7,204	7,509	7,418	5,901	6,970
Nikkei 225	9,521	13,861	14,304	19,520	16,666	19,197	22,468	22,259	20,194	28,813

Percent Gain for April

	2012	2013	2014	2015	2016	2017	2018	2019	2020	2021
Dow	0.0	1.8	0.7	0.4	0.5	1.3	0.2	2.6	11.1	2.7
S&P 500	-0.7	1.8	0.6	0.9	0.3	0.9	0.3	3.9	12.7	5.2
Nasdaq	-1.5	1.9	-2.0	0.8	-1.9	2.3	0.0	4.7	15.4	5.4
TSX	-0.8	-2.3	2.2	2.2	3.4	0.2	1.6	3.0	10.5	2.2
Russell 1000	-0.7	1.7	0.4	0.6	0.4	0.9	0.2	3.9	13.1	5.3
Russell 2000	-1.6	-0.4	-3.9	-2.6	1.5	1.0	0.8	3.3	13.7	2.1
FTSE 100	-0.5	0.3	2.8	2.8	1.1	-1.6	6.4	1.9	4.0	3.8
Nikkei 225	-5.6	11.8	-3.5	1.6	-0.6	1.5	4.7	5.0	6.7	-1.3

April Market Avg. Performance 2012 to 2021[(1)]

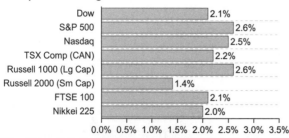

	Dow	2.1%
S&P 500	2.6%
Nasdaq	2.5%
TSX Comp (CAN)	2.2%
Russell 1000 (Lg Cap)	2.6%
Russell 2000 (Sm Cap)	1.4%
FTSE 100	2.1%
Nikkei 225	2.0%

0.0% 0.5% 1.0% 1.5% 2.0% 2.5% 3.0% 3.5%

Interest Corner Apr[(2)]

	Fed Funds % [(3)]	3 Mo. T-Bill % [(4)]	10 Yr % [(5)]	20 Yr % [(6)]
2021	0.25	0.01	1.65	2.19
2020	0.25	0.09	0.64	1.05
2019	2.50	2.43	2.51	2.75
2018	1.75	1.87	2.95	3.01
2017	1.00	0.80	2.29	2.67

(1) Russell Data provided by Russell (2) Federal Reserve Bank of St. Louis- end of month values (3) Target rate set by FOMC (4)(5)(6) Constant yield maturities.

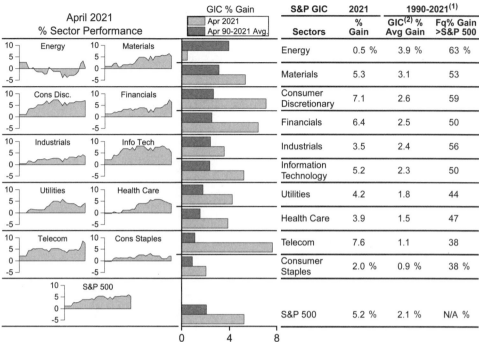

S&P GIC	2021	1990-2021[1]	
Sectors	% Gain	GIC[2] % Avg Gain	Fq% Gain >S&P 500
Energy	0.5 %	3.9 %	63 %
Materials	5.3	3.1	53
Consumer Discretionary	7.1	2.6	59
Financials	6.4	2.5	50
Industrials	3.5	2.4	56
Information Technology	5.2	2.3	50
Utilities	4.2	1.8	44
Health Care	3.9	1.5	47
Telecom	7.6	1.1	38
Consumer Staples	2.0 %	0.9 %	38 %
S&P 500	5.2 %	2.1 %	N/A %

Sector Commentary

♦ In April 2021, the stock market rallied sharply. ♦ The telecom sector was the big winner with a gain of 7.6%. ♦ The consumer discretionary sector performed well with a 7.1% gain. A rally in Amazon, a large part of the consumer discretionary sector, helped to drive the sector higher. ♦ The energy sector barely managed to remain positive for the month. After performing well in the previous months, the energy sector faded in April. It was negative for most of the month and a late month rally helped to bring it into positive territory.

Sub-Sector Commentary

♦ In April 2021, the agriculture sub-sector was the strongest from the selected sub-sectors, producing a gain of 10.8%. ♦ Silver performed well, with a gain of 7.8%. Typically, silver is not a strong performer in April, but it benefited from a strong performance in the metals and mining sector. ♦ The biotech sub-sector barely managed to produce a gain. Typically, biotech is one of the weaker performing sub-sectors.

SELECTED SUB-SECTORS[3]			
Automotive & Components	4.5 %	5.8 %	50 %
Railroads	3.1	3.9	63
Chemicals	4.3	3.5	72
SOX (1995-2021)	-0.5	3.4	48
Banks	4.4	2.9	50
Metals & Mining	7.7	2.8	44
Transportation	5.3	2.5	59
Homebuilders	7.5	2.3	47
Retail	9.0	2.1	53
Steel	2.5	1.9	50
Pharma	0.5	1.8	47
Agriculture (1994-2021)	10.8	1.2	54
Silver	7.8	0.7	41
Gold	4.5	0.6	41
Biotech (1993-2021)	0.5	0.4	34

(1) Sector data provided by Standard and Poors (2) GIC is short form for Global Industry Classification (3) Sub Sector data provided by Standard and Poors, except where marked by symbol.

18 DAY EARNINGS MONTH EFFECT
Markets Outperform 1st 18 Calendar Days of Earnings Months

Earnings season occurs the first month of every quarter. At this time, public companies report their financials for the previous quarter and give guidance on future expectations. As a result, investors tend to bid up stocks, anticipating good earnings. Earnings are a major driver of stock market prices as investors generally get in the stock market early, in anticipation of favorable results, which helps to run stock prices up in the first half of the month.

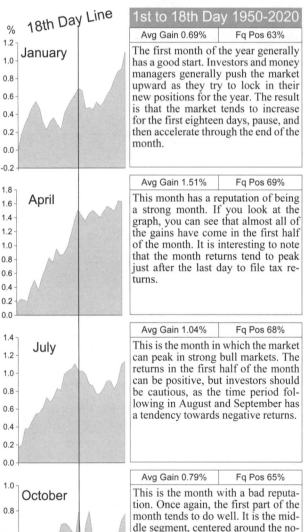

18th Day Line

January

1st to 18th Day 1950-2020

Avg Gain 0.69%	Fq Pos 63%

The first month of the year generally has a good start. Investors and money managers generally push the market upward as they try to lock in their new positions for the year. The result is that the market tends to increase for the first eighteen days, pause, and then accelerate through the end of the month.

April

Avg Gain 1.51%	Fq Pos 69%

This month has a reputation of being a strong month. If you look at the graph, you can see that almost all of the gains have come in the first half of the month. It is interesting to note that the month returns tend to peak just after the last day to file tax returns.

July

Avg Gain 1.04%	Fq Pos 68%

This is the month in which the market can peak in strong bull markets. The returns in the first half of the month can be positive, but investors should be cautious, as the time period following in August and September has a tendency towards negative returns.

October

Avg Gain 0.79%	Fq Pos 65%

This is the month with a bad reputation. Once again, the first part of the month tends to do well. It is the middle segment, centered around the notorious Black Monday, that brings down the results. Toward the end of the month, investors realize that the world has not ended and start to buy stocks again, providing a strong finish to the month.

1st to 18th Day Gain S&P500

	JAN	APR	JUL	OCT
1950	0.36 %	4.28 %	-3.56 %	2.88 %
1951	4.75	3.41	4.39	1.76
1952	2.02	-3.57	-0.44	-1.39
1953	-2.07	-2.65	0.87	3.38
1954	2.50	3.71	2.91	-1.49
1955	-3.28	4.62	3.24	-4.63
1956	-2.88	-1.53	4.96	2.18
1957	-4.35	2.95	2.45	-4.93
1958	2.78	1.45	1.17	2.80
1959	1.09	4.47	1.23	0.79
1960	-3.34	2.26	-2.14	1.55
1961	2.70	1.75	-0.36	2.22
1962	-4.42	-1.84	2.65	0.12
1963	3.30	3.49	-1.27	2.26
1964	2.05	1.99	2.84	0.77
1965	2.05	2.31	1.87	1.91
1966	1.64	2.63	2.66	2.77
1967	6.80	1.84	3.16	-1.51
1968	-0.94	7.63	1.87	2.09
1969	-1.76	-0.27	-2.82	3.37
1970	-1.24	-4.42	6.83	-0.02
1971	1.37	3.17	0.42	-1.01
1972	1.92	2.40	-1.22	-2.13
1973	0.68	0.02	2.00	1.46
1974	-2.04	0.85	-2.58	13.76
1975	3.50	3.53	-2.09	5.95
1976	7.55	-2.04	0.38	-3.58
1977	-3.85	2.15	0.47	-3.18
1978	-4.77	4.73	1.40	-2.00
1979	3.76	0.11	-1.19	-5.22
1980	2.90	-1.51	6.83	4.83
1981	-0.73	-0.96	-0.34	2.59
1982	-4.35	4.33	1.33	13.54
1983	4.10	4.43	-2.20	1.05
1984	1.59	-0.80	-1.16	1.20
1985	2.44	0.10	1.32	2.72
1986	-1.35	1.46	-5.77	3.25
1987	9.96	-1.64	3.48	-12.16
1988	1.94	0.12	-1.09	2.75
1989	3.17	3.78	4.20	-2.12
1990	-4.30	0.23	1.73	-0.10
1991	0.61	3.53	3.83	1.20
1992	0.42	3.06	1.83	-1.45
1993	0.26	-0.60	-1.06	2.07
1994	1.67	-0.74	2.46	1.07
1995	2.27	0.93	2.52	0.52
1996	-1.25	-0.29	-4.04	3.42
1997	4.78	1.22	3.41	-0.33
1998	-0.92	1.90	4.67	3.88
1999	1.14	2.54	3.36	-2.23
2000	-0.96	-3.80	2.69	-6.57
2001	2.10	6.71	-1.36	2.66
2002	-1.79	-2.00	-10.94	8.48
2003	2.50	5.35	1.93	4.35
2004	2.51	0.75	-3.46	-0.05
2005	-1.32	-2.93	2.50	-4.12
2006	2.55	1.22	0.51	3.15
2007	1.41	4.33	-3.20	1.48
2008	-9.75	5.11	-1.51	-19.36
2009	-5.88	8.99	2.29	2.89
2010	1.88	1.94	3.32	3.81
2011	2.97	-1.56	-1.15	8.30
2012	4.01	-1.66	0.78	1.16
2013	4.2	-1.76	5.17	3.74
2014	-0.52	-0.4	0.92	-4.34
2015	-1.92	0.64	3.08	5.89
2016	-8.0	1.68	3.21	-1.32
2017	1.48	-0.87	1.54	1.66
2018	4.65	2.57	3.58	-4.98
2019	6.54	2.49	1.81	0.32
2020	3.06	11.21	4.01	3.59
Avg	0.69 %	1.51 %	1.04 %	0.79 %

Earnings Month Effect Performance

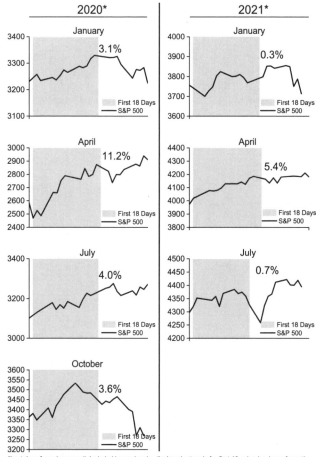

*Last day of previous month included in graph only, displayed return is for first 18 calendar days of month

Market Indices & Rates
Weekly Values**

Stock Markets	2020	2021
Dow	21,053	33,801
S&P500	2,489	4,129
Nasdaq	7,373	13,900
TSX	12,938	19,228
FTSE	5,416	6,916
DAX	9,526	15,234
Nikkei	17,820	29,768
Hang Seng	23,236	28,699

Commodities	2020	2021
Oil	28.34	59.32
Gold	1613.1	1741.2

Bond Yields	2020	2021
USA 5 Yr Treasury	0.39	0.87
USA 10 Yr T	0.62	1.67
USA 20 Yr T	1.05	2.23
Moody's Aaa	2.63	2.92
Moody's Baa	4.54	3.63
CAN 5 Yr T	0.59	0.96
CAN 10 Yr T	0.71	1.50

Money Market	2020	2021
USA Fed Funds	0.25	0.25
USA 3 Mo T-B	0.10	0.02
CAN tgt overnight rate	0.25	0.25
CAN 3 Mo T-B	0.17	0.09

Foreign Exchange	2020	2021
EUR/USD	1.08	1.19
GBP/USD	1.23	1.37
USD/CAD	1.42	1.25
USD/JPY	108.55	109.67

APRIL

M	T	W	T	F	S	S
				1	2	3
4	5	6	7	8	9	10
11	13	13	14	15	16	17
18	20	20	21	22	23	24
25	27	27	28	29	30	

MAY

M	T	W	T	F	S	S
						1
2	3	4	5	6	7	8
9	11	11	12	13	14	15
16	18	18	19	20	21	22
21	25	25	26	27	28	29
30	31					

JUNE

M	T	W	T	F	S	S
	1	2	3	4	5
6	7	8	9	10	11	12
13	14	15	16	17	18	19
20	21	22	23	24	25	26
27	28	29	30			

Earnings Month Effect Performance

In 2020, all of the first three earnings months were positive in the first eighteen calendar days. The first eighteen days in April were particularly strong as the stock market rebounded after Federal Reserve loose monetary policy and increased government support payments to the Covid-19 pandemic helped to increase economic growth expectations.

In 2021, the Earnings Month Effect was positive in the first three earnings months. The biggest performance gain was made in April with the first eighteen calendar days producing a gain of 5.4% in the S&P 500. The earnings month effect in July was also positive.

CONSUMER STAPLES
① Apr25 to May31 ② Sep25 to Oct27

The consumer staples sector is not an attractive sector for a lot of investors, as it is typically not fast moving. Nevertheless, it can play an important part in an investment portfolio.

There are two times of the year when the consumer staples sector tends to perform well relative to the S&P 500. The first period overlaps the transition period out of the favorable six-month period for the stock market, which takes place in early May. The second period leads into the favorable six-month period for the stock market in late October.

3.7% gain & 74% of the time positive

From April 25 to May 31, in the period from 1990 to 2020, the consumer staples sector has produced an average gain of 2.1% and has been positive 74% of the time. This is by no means a huge gain, but it is better than the average 1.3% that the S&P 500 has produced in the same time period. In the same yearly period, from September 25 to October 27, the consumer staples sector has produced an average gain of 1.6% compared to a gain of 0.5% for the S&P 500. The gain in the consumer staples sector is fairly moderate, but the sector can provide a more defensive profile than many of the other sectors of the S&P 500.

Covid-19 Performance Update. In 2021, the consumer staples sector underperformed the S&P 500 at the beginning of the year. It bounced in its strong seasonal period from April 25 to May 31 and outperformed the S&P 500.

ⓘ *The SP GICS Consumer Staples sector encompasses a wide range consumer staples based companies. For more information, see www.standardandpoors.com*

Cons. Staples vs S&P 500 - 1990 to 2020 Positive ▢

Year	Apr 25 to May 31 S&P 500	Apr 25 to May 31 Cons Staples	Sep 25 Oct 27 S&P 500	Sep 25 Oct 27 Cons Staples	Compound Growth S&P 500	Compound Growth Cons Staples
1990	9.3 %	10.9 %	0.0 %	7.6 %	9.4 %	19.3 %
1991	1.8	1.5	-0.9	-2.1	0.9	-0.6
1992	1.5	2.6	0.0	-0.5	1.6	2.0
1993	3.0	3.7	1.5	4.4	4.6	8.2
1994	2.0	-0.1	1.3	4.9	3.4	4.8
1995	4.0	3.9	-0.3	2.7	3.6	6.7
1996	2.9	7.5	2.2	0.6	5.2	8.2
1997	10.0	7.8	-7.1	-5.7	2.1	1.6
1998	-1.5	1.5	2.2	11.2	0.6	12.8
1999	-4.1	1.1	1.5	-0.2	-2.6	1.0
2000	-0.6	3.8	-4.8	11.7	-5.4	15.9
2001	3.8	5.0	10.1	4.1	14.3	9.3
2002	-2.4	0.5	9.6	4.2	7.0	4.7
2003	5.7	4.7	2.2	2.2	8.0	6.9
2004	-1.7	-1.9	1.4	1.0	-0.4	-0.9
2005	3.4	2.7	-3.0	-0.1	0.3	2.6
2006	-2.9	1.8	4.8	1.7	1.7	3.5
2007	3.4	0.5	1.2	2.8	4.6	3.3
2008	0.8	0.9	-28.4	-19.2	-27.8	-18.5
2009	6.1	7.3	1.2	2.3	7.4	9.7
2010	-10.5	-6.1	2.9	1.7	-7.9	-4.5
2011	0.6	4.2	13.0	6.4	13.7	10.8
2012	-4.5	-0.3	-3.1	-2.3	-7.4	-2.7
2013	3.3	-1.9	3.7	3.4	7.1	1.4
2014	2.4	3.0	-1.8	0.9	0.5	3.9
2015	-0.5	-0.9	6.9	7.4	6.4	6.5
2016	0.3	1.4	-1.5	-1.9	-1.2	-0.5
2017	1.6	2.0	3.2	-1.6	4.8	0.4
2018	2.7	-1.1	-8.9	-0.7	-6.5	-1.8
2019	-6.0	-2.6	1.9	0.7	-4.2	-1.9
2020	7.3	0.6	4.4	2.5	12.1	3.1
Avg.	1.3 %	2.1 %	0.5 %	1.6 %	1.8 %	3.7 %
Fq>0	68 %	74 %	68 %	68 %	71 %	74 %

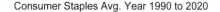

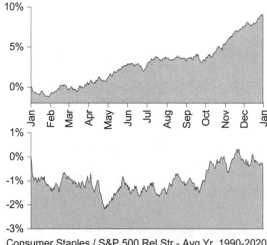

Consumer Staples Avg. Year 1990 to 2020

Consumer Staples / S&P 500 Rel Str.- Avg Yr. 1990-2020

- 45 -

Consumer Staples Performance

Consumer Staples Monthly % Gain (1990-2020)

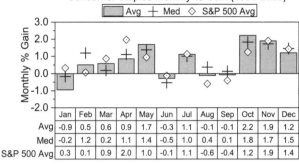

	Jan	Feb	Mar	Apr	May	Jun	Jul	Aug	Sep	Oct	Nov	Dec
Avg	-0.9	0.5	0.6	0.9	1.7	-0.3	1.1	-0.1	-0.1	2.2	1.9	1.2
Med	-0.2	1.2	0.2	1.1	1.4	-0.5	1.0	0.4	0.1	1.8	1.7	1.5
S&P 500 Avg	0.3	0.1	0.9	2.0	1.0	-0.1	1.1	-0.6	-0.4	1.2	1.9	1.4

Fq Consumer Staples Gain > 0% (1990-2020)

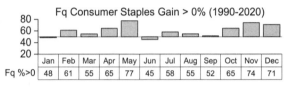

	Jan	Feb	Mar	Apr	May	Jun	Jul	Aug	Sep	Oct	Nov	Dec
Fq %>0	48	61	55	65	77	45	58	55	52	65	74	71

Fq % Consumer Staples Gain > S&P 500 % (1990-2020)

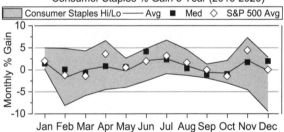

	Jan	Feb	Mar	Apr	May	Jun	Jul	Aug	Sep	Oct	Nov	Dec
Fq %> S&P 500	32	48	52	39	55	35	58	58	55	55	42	42

Consumer Staples % Gain 5 Year (2016-2020)

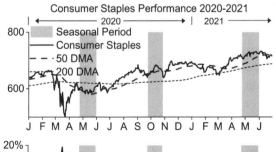

Jan Feb Mar Apr May Jun Jul Aug Sep Oct Nov Dec

Consumer Staples Performance 2020-2021

Relative Strength, % Gain vs. S&P 500

Market Indices & Rates
Weekly Values**

Stock Markets	2020	2021
Dow	23,719	34,201
S&P500	2,790	4,185
Nasdaq	8,154	14,052
TSX	14,167	19,351
FTSE	5,843	7,020
DAX	10,565	15,460
Nikkei	19,499	29,683
Hang Seng	24,300	28,970

Commodities	2020	2021
Oil	22.76	63.13
Gold	1680.7	1774.5

Bond Yields	2020	2021
USA 5 Yr Treasury	0.41	0.84
USA 10 Yr T	0.73	1.59
USA 20 Yr T	1.15	2.15
Moody's Aaa	2.46	2.85
Moody's Baa	4.34	3.56
CAN 5 Yr T	0.60	0.96
CAN 10 Yr T	0.76	1.54

Money Market	2020	2021
USA Fed Funds	0.25	0.25
USA 3 Mo T-B	0.25	0.02
CAN tgt overnight rate	0.25	0.25
CAN 3 Mo T-B	0.24	0.09

Foreign Exchange	2020	2021
EUR/USD	1.09	1.20
GBP/USD	1.25	1.38
USD/CAD	1.40	1.25
USD/JPY	108.47	108.80

APRIL

M	T	W	T	F	S	S
				1	2	3
4	5	6	7	8	9	10
11	13	13	14	15	16	17
18	20	20	21	22	23	24
25	27	27	28	29	30	

MAY

M	T	W	T	F	S	S
						1
2	3	4	5	6	7	8
9	11	11	12	13	14	15
16	18	18	19	20	21	22
21	25	25	26	27	28	29
30	31					

JUNE

M	T	W	T	F	S	S
	1	2	3	4	5	
6	7	8	9	10	11	12
13	14	15	16	17	18	19
20	21	22	23	24	25	26
27	28	29	30			

U.S. GOVERNMENT BONDS (7-10 YEARS)
May 6 to October 3

The following government bond seasonal period analysis has been broken down into two contiguous periods in order to demonstrate the relative strength of the first part of the trade compared with the second part. Although both the May 6 to August 8 and the August 9 to October 3 periods provide value, the sweet spot to the government bond trade is in the latter period from August 9 to October 3.

Bonds tend to outperform from late spring into autumn for three reasons. First, governments and companies tend to raise more money through bond issuance at the beginning of the year to meet their needs for the rest of the year. With more bonds competing in the market for money, bond prices tend to decrease. Less bonds tend to be issued in late spring and early summer during their seasonal period, helping to support bond prices.

4% gain & positive 78% of the time

Second, optimistic forecasts at the beginning of the year for stronger GDP growth tend to increase inflation expectations and as a result interest rates respond by increasing. As economic growth expectations tend to decrease in the summer, interest rates respond by retreating.

Third, the stock market often peaks in May and investors rotate their money into bonds. As the demand for bonds increases, interest rates decrease and bonds increase in value. For seasonal investors looking to put their money to work in the unfavora-

ble six months of the year, buying bonds in the summer months fits perfectly with their strategy.

In periods when the stock market rallies in the early summer months, positive bond performance can be delayed until later in the summer, typically early August, which coincides with the bond seasonal period sweet spot, from August 9 to October 3.

Covid-19 Performance Update. In 2021, government bonds started to perform well in late March, ahead of their strong seasonal period. Government bonds performed well for most of their strong seasonal period.

(i) Source: Barclays Capital Inc.
The U.S. Treasury: 7-10 Year is a total return index, which includes both interest and capital appreciation. For more information on fixed income indices, see www.barcap.com.

U.S. Gov. Bonds* vs. S&P 500 1998 to 2020   Positive [ ]

Year	May 6 to Aug 8 S&P 500	May 6 to Aug 8 Gov. Bonds	Aug 9 to Oct 3 S&P 500	Aug 9 to Oct 3 Gov. Bonds	Total Growth S&P 500	Total Growth Gov. Bonds
1998	-2.3 %	3.3 %	-8.0 %	8.3 %	-10.1 %	11.9 %
1999	-3.5	-3.0	-1.3	0.9	-4.8	-2.1
2000	3.5	5.8	-3.8	0.9	-0.4	6.7
2001	-6.6	2.6	-9.4	4.4	-15.3	7.1
2002	-15.7	6.5	-9.6	5.0	-23.7	11.9
2003	5.5	-1.3	5.4	1.3	11.2	0.0
2004	-5.1	3.6	6.4	0.8	0.9	4.4
2005	4.3	-0.9	0.3	0.7	4.6	-0.2
2006	-4.1	2.6	4.9	2.7	0.6	5.3
2007	-0.5	-0.3	2.8	3.3	2.3	3.0
2008	-7.9	0.9	-15.2	2.4	-21.9	3.4
2009	11.8	-4.0	1.5	5.4	13.4	1.1
2010	-3.8	7.1	2.2	2.6	-1.7	9.8
2011	-16.2	7.6	-1.8	4.6	-17.7	12.6
2012	2.4	2.3	3.5	0.9	6.0	3.3
2013	5.1	-5.2	-1.1	0.3	4.0	-4.9
2014	2.5	2.3	1.9	0.1	4.4	2.4
2015	-0.6	0.6	-6.1	2.1	-6.6	2.6
2016	6.4	1.6	-0.9	-0.1	5.4	1.6
2017	3.2	1.3	2.4	-0.1	5.6	1.2
2018	7.3	0.6	2.4	-1.0	9.8	-0.4
2019	-0.2	7.1	-0.9	1.5	-1.2	8.7
2020	16.8	1.1	0.0	-0.6	16.7	0.6
Avg.	0.1 %	1.8 %	-1.1 %	2.0 %	-0.1 %	3.9 %
Fq>0	48 %	74 %	48 %	83 %	57 %	78 %

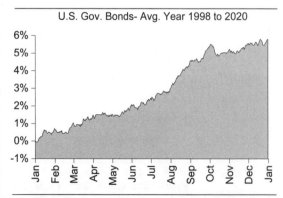

U.S. Gov. Bonds- Avg. Year 1998 to 2020

(Chart y-axis: 6%, 5%, 4%, 3%, 2%, 1%, 0%, -1%; x-axis: Jan, Feb, Mar, Apr, May, Jun, Jul, Aug, Sep, Oct, Nov, Dec, Jan)

U.S. Government Bond Performance

UST 7-10YR Monthly % Gain (1998-2020)

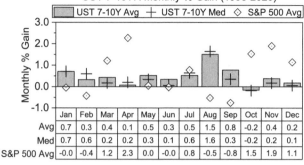

	Jan	Feb	Mar	Apr	May	Jun	Jul	Aug	Sep	Oct	Nov	Dec
Avg	0.7	0.3	0.4	0.1	0.5	0.3	0.5	1.5	0.8	-0.2	0.4	0.2
Med	0.7	0.6	0.2	0.2	0.3	0.1	0.6	1.6	0.3	-0.2	0.2	0.1
S&P 500 Avg	-0.0	-0.4	1.2	2.3	0.0	-0.0	0.8	-0.5	-0.8	1.5	1.9	1.1

Fq UST 7-10YR Gain > 0% (1998-2020)

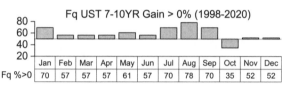

	Jan	Feb	Mar	Apr	May	Jun	Jul	Aug	Sep	Oct	Nov	Dec
Fq %>0	70	57	57	57	61	57	70	78	70	35	52	52

Fq % UST 7-10YR Gain > S&P 500 % (1998-2020)

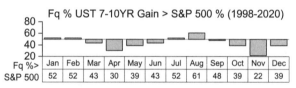

	Jan	Feb	Mar	Apr	May	Jun	Jul	Aug	Sep	Oct	Nov	Dec
Fq %> S&P 500	52	52	43	30	39	43	52	61	48	39	22	39

UST 7-10YR % Gain 5 Year (2016-2020)

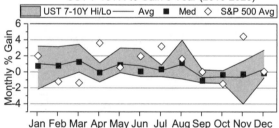

Jan Feb Mar Apr May Jun Jul Aug Sep Oct Nov Dec

UST 7-10YR Performance 2020-2021

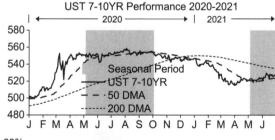

Relative Strength, % Gain vs. S&P 500

Market Indices & Rates
Weekly Values**

Stock Markets	2020	2021
Dow	24,242	34,043
S&P500	2,875	4,180
Nasdaq	8,650	14,017
TSX	14,360	19,102
FTSE	5,787	6,939
DAX	10,626	15,280
Nikkei	19,897	29,021
Hang Seng	24,380	29,079

Commodities	2020	2021
Oil	18.27	62.18
Gold	1692.6	1781.8

Bond Yields	2020	2021
USA 5 Yr Treasury	0.36	0.83
USA 10 Yr T	0.65	1.58
USA 20 Yr T	1.08	2.14
Moody's Aaa	2.41	2.88
Moody's Baa	3.92	3.57
CAN 5 Yr T	0.46	0.94
CAN 10 Yr T	0.65	1.52

Money Market	2020	2021
USA Fed Funds	0.25	0.25
USA 3 Mo T-B	0.12	0.03
CAN tgt overnight rate	0.25	0.25
CAN 3 Mo T-B	0.20	0.09

Foreign Exchange	2020	2021
EUR/USD	1.09	1.21
GBP/USD	1.25	1.39
USD/CAD	1.40	1.25
USD/JPY	107.54	107.88

APRIL

M	T	W	T	F	S	S
				1	2	3
4	5	6	7	8	9	10
11	13	13	14	15	16	17
18	20	20	21	22	23	24
25	27	27	28	29	30	

MAY

M	T	W	T	F	S	S
						1
2	3	4	5	6	7	8
9	11	11	12	13	14	15
16	18	18	19	20	21	22
21	25	25	26	27	28	29
30	31					

JUNE

M	T	W	T	F	S	S
	1	2	3	4	5	
6	7	8	9	10	11	12
13	14	15	16	17	18	19
20	21	22	23	24	25	26
27	28	29	30			

CAD VS US DOLLAR ①SELL SHORT (Jan6-Mar7)
②LONG (Mar15-Apr30) ③LONG(Aug12-Sep22)
④SELL SHORT (Oct13-Dec18) ⑤LONG(Dec19-Jan5)

The Canadian dollar versus the US dollar has many drivers of valuation, but two of the bigger drivers are the price of oil and the spread on the two year differential government bonds between the two countries.

Although the energy sector seasonal period does not line up exactly with the seasonality for the Canadian dollar, there is an overlap. The energy sector tends to perform well from late February into early May. Correspondingly, the Canadian dollar tends to perform well from mid-March to the end of April. In addition, the energy sector tends to perform well from late July to early October, and the Canadian dollar tends to perform well from early August to late September.

The Canadian dollar also performs well from mid-December to early January. The US dollar tends to perform poorly against most currencies in late December.

The US dollar's strongest period relative to the Canadian dollar is from mid-October to mid-December. Overall, this is one of the weaker seasonal periods for oil.

The US dollar also tends to perform well relative to the Canadian dollar from early January to early March. The US dollar tends to perform well against most major world currencies at this time.

Covid-19 Performance Update. In the first part of 2021, the Canadian dollar was strong as the price of oil strengthened. The Canadian dollar started to correct in June.

Canadian Dollar vs. US Dollar 1990/91 to 2020/21

Negative Short ☐ Positive Long ▭

Year	Jan6 Mar7	Mar15 Apr30	Aug12 Sep22	Oct13 Dec18	Dec19 Jan5	Compound
1990/91	-2.1 %	0.8 %	-0.5 %	-0.9 %	0.5 %	3.9 %
1991/92	-0.8	0.2	1.0	-1.5	0.0	3.4
1992/93	-3.5	0.3	-4.1	-2.8	0.1	2.4
1993/94	2.5	-2.1	-1.0	-0.8	1.4	-3.4
1994/95	-2.7	-1.5	2.8	-3.3	-0.6	6.8
1995/96	-1.0	4.3	0.8	-2.9	1.5	10.9
1996/97	-1.0	0.5	0.2	-1.1	-0.2	2.6
1997/98	0.1	-2.3	0.3	-3.4	0.2	1.5
1998/99	0.3	-1.3	-0.4	-0.2	2.1	0.3
1999/00	-0.4	4.6	1.0	-0.2	1.9	8.4
2001/01	-0.4	-1.0	-0.3	-0.6	1.7	1.4
2001/02	-3.3	1.4	-2.1	-0.7	-1.3	2.0
2002/03	0.8	1.5	0.0	2.1	-0.7	-2.0
2003/04	6.7	3.0	2.3	-0.6	3.7	2.6
2004/05	-3.0	-2.8	3.4	2.1	0.3	1.6
2005/06	-0.3	-4.1	2.5	1.0	-0.3	-2.7
2006/07	1.0	3.6	0.7	-2.0	-1.4	3.9
2007/08	-0.5	6.0	5.2	-3.4	0.3	16.2
2008/09	1.2	-1.8	3.2	-2.6	1.3	4.1
2009/10	-7.6	6.7	3.0	-3.0	2.6	25.0
2010/11	1.0	0.1	1.5	-0.4	1.8	2.9
2011/12	2.3	3.0	-4.3	-2.0	1.8	0.1
2012/13	2.2	0.5	1.5	-0.6	-0.2	0.2
2013/14	-4.1	1.5	-0.1	-3.3	0.6	9.7
2014/15	-4.1	1.3	-1.1	-3.3	-1.6	5.9
2015/16	-6.8	5.8	-1.2	-6.9	-0.3	19.1
2016/17	5.4	5.6	-0.4	-0.5	0.8	0.8
2017/18	-1.4	-1.3	2.7	-3.0	3.6	9.8
2018/19	-3.9	0.9	1.7	-3.3	0.7	10.9
2019/20	-0.6	-0.4	-0.3	0.7	0.9	0.1
2020/21	-3.1	-0.9	0.0	2.5	0.9	0.4
Avg.	-0.8 %	1.0 %	0.5 %	-1.4 %	0.7 %	4.8 %
Fq>0	11 %	20 %	54 %	16 %	68 %	90 %

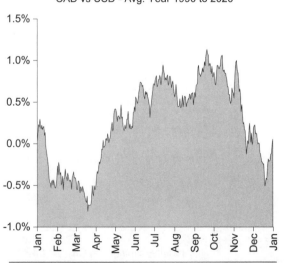

CAD vs USD - Avg. Year 1990 to 2020

CAD/USD Performance

CADUSD Monthly % Gain (1990-2020)

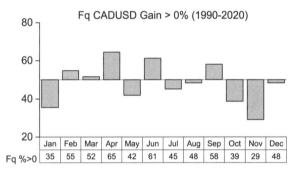

	Jan	Feb	Mar	Apr	May	Jun	Jul	Aug	Sep	Oct	Nov	Dec
CADUSD Avg	-0.4	0.0	-0.1	1.0	0.0	0.3	-0.1	-0.1	0.2	-0.2	-0.6	0.0
CADUSD Med	-0.4	0.2	0.1	0.8	-0.2	0.5	-0.2	-0.0	0.3	-0.4	-0.9	-0.0

Fq CADUSD Gain > 0% (1990-2020)

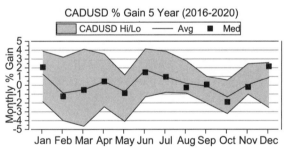

	Jan	Feb	Mar	Apr	May	Jun	Jul	Aug	Sep	Oct	Nov	Dec
Fq %>0	35	55	52	65	42	61	45	48	58	39	29	48

CADUSD % Gain 5 Year (2016-2020)

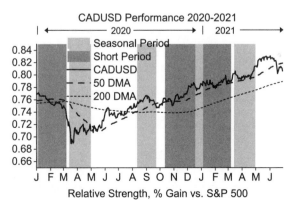

CADUSD Performance 2020-2021

Relative Strength, % Gain vs. S&P 500

Market Indices & Rates
Weekly Values**

Stock Markets	2020	2021
Dow	23,775	33,875
S&P500	2,837	4,181
Nasdaq	8,635	13,963
TSX	14,420	19,108
FTSE	5,752	6,970
DAX	10,336	15,136
Nikkei	19,262	28,813
Hang Seng	23,831	28,725

Commodities	2020	2021
Oil	16.04	63.58
Gold	1715.9	1767.7

Bond Yields	2020	2021
USA 5 Yr Treasury	0.36	0.86
USA 10 Yr T	0.60	1.65
USA 20 Yr T	0.98	2.19
Moody's Aaa	2.30	2.94
Moody's Baa	3.85	3.61
CAN 5 Yr T	0.44	0.93
CAN 10 Yr T	0.58	1.55

Money Market	2020	2021
USA Fed Funds	0.25	0.25
USA 3 Mo T-B	0.12	0.01
CAN tgt overnight rate	0.25	0.25
CAN 3 Mo T-B	0.23	0.11

Foreign Exchange	2020	2021
EUR/USD	1.08	1.20
GBP/USD	1.24	1.38
USD/CAD	1.41	1.23
USD/JPY	107.51	109.31

APRIL

M	T	W	T	F	S	S
				1	2	3
4	5	6	7	8	9	10
11	13	13	14	15	16	17
18	20	20	21	22	23	24
25	27	27	28	29	30	

MAY

M	T	W	T	F	S	S
						1
2	3	4	5	6	7	8
9	11	11	12	13	14	15
16	18	18	19	20	21	22
21	25	25	26	27	28	29
30	31					

JUNE

M	T	W	T	F	S	S
	1	2	3	4	5	
6	7	8	9	10	11	12
13	14	15	16	17	18	19
20	21	22	23	24	25	26
27	28	29	30			

MAY

	MONDAY	TUESDAY	WEDNESDAY
WEEK 18	**2** 29	**3** 28	**4** 27
WEEK 19	**9** 22	**10** 21	**11** 20
WEEK 20	**16** 15	**17** 14	**18** 13
WEEK 21	**23** 8 CAN Market Closed- Victoria Day	**24** 7	**25** 6
WEEK 22	**30** 1 USA Market Closed- Memorial Day	**31**	1

THURSDAY	FRIDAY
5 26	**6** 25
12 19	**13** 18
19 12	**20** 11
26 5	**27** 4
2	3

JUNE

M	T	W	T	F	S	S
		1	2	3	4	5
6	7	8	9	10	11	12
13	14	15	16	17	18	19
20	21	22	23	24	25	26
27	28	29	30			

JULY

M	T	W	T	F	S	S
				1	2	3
4	5	6	7	8	9	10
11	12	13	14	15	16	17
18	19	20	21	22	23	24
25	26	27	28	29	30	31

AUGUST

M	T	W	T	F	S	S
1	2	3	4	5	6	7
8	9	10	11	12	13	14
15	16	17	18	19	20	21
22	23	24	25	26	27	28
29	30	31				

SEPTEMBER

M	T	W	T	F	S	S
			1	2	3	4
5	6	7	8	9	10	11
12	13	14	15	16	17	18
19	20	21	22	23	24	25
26	27	28	29	30		

- 52 -

MAY
S U M M A R Y

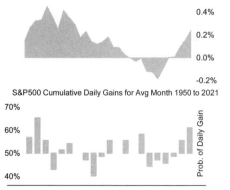

S&P500 Cumulative Daily Gains for Avg Month 1950 to 2021

	Dow Jones	S&P 500	Nasdaq	TSX Comp
Month Rank	9	8	5	2
# Up	38	42	31	22
# Down	33	29	18	14
% Pos	54	59	63	61
% Avg. Gain	0.0	0.2	1.1	1.3

Dow & S&P 1950-2020, Nasdaq 1972-2020 TSX 1985-2020

♦ The first few days and the last few days in May tend to be strong and the period in between tends to be negative. ♦ A lot of the cyclical sectors finish their seasonal periods at the beginning of May. Some of the defensive sectors start their strong seasonal period in May. ♦ Government bonds start their strong seasonal period in May. ♦ In May 2021, the S&P 500 increased in volatility, and only managed to produce a small gain. ♦ Generally, cyclicals managed to extend their rally in May.

BEST / WORST MAY BROAD MKTS. 2012-2021

BEST MAY MARKETS
- ♦ Nikkei 225 (2020) 8.3%
- ♦ Nasdaq (2020) 6.8%
- ♦ Russell 2000 (2020) 6.4%

WORST MAY MARKETS
- ♦ Nikkei 225 (2012) -10.3%
- ♦ Nasdaq (2019) -7.9%
- ♦ Russell 2000 (2019) -7.9%

Index Values End of Month

	2012	2013	2014	2015	2016	2017	2018	2019	2020	2021
Dow	12,393	15,116	16,717	18,011	17,787	21,009	24,416	24,815	25,383	34,529
S&P 500	1,310	1,631	1,924	2,107	2,097	2,412	2,663	2,752	3,044	4,204
Nasdaq	2,827	3,456	4,243	5,070	4,948	6,199	7,442	7,453	9,490	13,749
TSX Comp.	11,513	12,650	14,604	15,014	14,066	15,350	16,062	16,037	15,193	19,731
Russell 1000	724	904	1,072	1,177	1,161	1,336	1,502	1,524	1,683	2,365
Russell 2000	762	984	1,135	1,247	1,155	1,370	1,634	1,465	1,394	2,269
FTSE 100	5,321	6,583	6,845	6,984	6,231	7,520	7,678	7,162	6,077	7,023
Nikkei 225	8,543	13,775	14,632	20,563	17,235	19,651	22,202	20,601	21,878	28,860

Percent Gain for May

	2012	2013	2014	2015	2016	2017	2018	2019	2020	2021
Dow	-6.2	1.9	0.8	1.0	0.1	0.3	1.0	-6.7	4.3	1.9
S&P 500	-6.3	2.1	2.1	1.0	1.5	1.2	0.6	-6.6	4.5	0.5
Nasdaq	-7.2	3.8	3.1	2.6	3.6	2.5	5.3	-7.9	6.8	-1.5
TSX Comp.	-6.3	1.6	-0.3	-1.4	0.8	-1.5	2.9	-3.3	2.8	3.3
Russell 1000	-6.4	2.0	2.1	1.1	1.5	1.0	2.3	-6.6	5.1	0.3
Russell 2000	-6.7	3.9	0.7	2.2	2.1	-2.2	5.9	-7.9	6.4	0.1
FTSE 100	-7.3	2.4	1.0	0.3	-0.2	4.4	2.2	-3.5	3.0	0.8
Nikkei 225	-10.3	-0.6	2.3	5.3	3.4	2.4	-1.2	-7.4	8.3	0.2

May Market Avg. Performance 2012 to 2021[1]

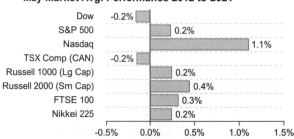

Dow	-0.2%
S&P 500	0.2%
Nasdaq	1.1%
TSX Comp (CAN)	-0.2%
Russell 1000 (Lg Cap)	0.2%
Russell 2000 (Sm Cap)	0.4%
FTSE 100	0.3%
Nikkei 225	0.2%

Interest Corner May[2]

	Fed Funds %[3]	3 Mo. T-Bill %[4]	10 Yr %[5]	20 Yr %[6]
2021	0.25	0.01	1.58	2.18
2020	0.25	0.14	0.65	1.18
2019	2.50	2.35	2.14	2.39
2018	1.75	1.93	2.83	2.91
2017	1.00	0.98	2.21	2.60

(1) Russell Data provided by Russell (2) Federal Reserve Bank of St. Louis- end of month values (3) Target rate set by FOMC (4)(5)(6) Constant yield maturities.

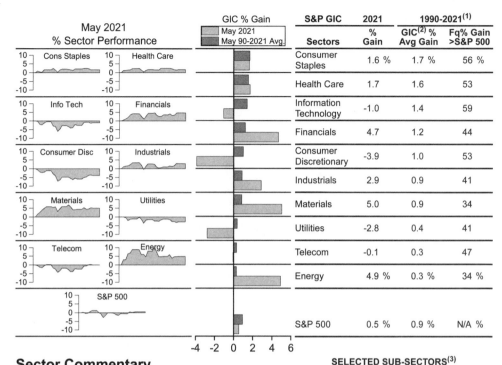

May 2021 % Sector Performance

GIC % Gain
May 2021
May 90-2021 Avg.

S&P GIC Sectors	2021 % Gain	1990-2021[1] GIC[2] % Avg Gain	Fq% Gain >S&P 500
Consumer Staples	1.6 %	1.7 %	56 %
Health Care	1.7	1.6	53
Information Technology	-1.0	1.4	59
Financials	4.7	1.2	44
Consumer Discretionary	-3.9	1.0	53
Industrials	2.9	0.9	41
Materials	5.0	0.9	34
Utilities	-2.8	0.4	41
Telecom	-0.1	0.3	47
Energy	4.9 %	0.3 %	34 %
S&P 500	0.5 %	0.9 %	N/A %

Sector Commentary

♦ In May 2021, the cyclical sectors performed well. Typically, the sectors finish their strong seasonal period early in the month, but in 2021, the sectors managed to perform into month end, despite market volatility. ♦ The top performing sector was the energy sector, with a gain of 4.9%. ♦ The next best performing sector was the financial sector with a gain of 4.7%. ♦ The growth sectors of the stock market performed poorly. ♦ The consumer discretionary sector lost 3.9%. ♦ The information technology sector lost 1.0%.

Sub-Sector Commentary

♦ In May 2021, the cyclical sub-sectors in the list performed well. The steel sub-sector gained 24.7% and the metals and mining sub-sector gained 17.2%. Gold, which is usually a mediocre performer in May, gained 7.5%. Silver, which is typically also a mediocre performer in May, produced a gain of 6.8%. The auto sector lost 6.7%. The homebuilders sub-sector, which typically produces a loss in May, followed its seasonal trend and produced a loss of 3.3%.

SELECTED SUB-SECTORS[3]

Biotech (1993-2021)	1.1 %	1.8 %	66 %
Agriculture (1994-2021)	5.4	1.6	54
Banks	5.5	1.5	47
Railroads	0.7	1.4	63
Retail	-4.5	1.4	56
SOX (1995-2021)	2.5	1.1	59
Pharma	3.7	1.1	47
Chemicals	3.6	0.9	47
Steel	24.7	0.9	47
Metals & Mining	17.2	0.6	44
Transportation	3.1	0.6	53
Gold	7.5	0.4	50
Automotive & Components	-6.7	0.2	28
Silver	6.8	0.1	47
Homebuilders	-3.3	-0.5	47

DISNEY–TIME TO STAY AWAY & TIME TO VISIT
①SELL SHORT (Jun5-Sep30) ②LONG(Oct1-Feb15)

Disney has two seasonal periods, one positive and one negative. The positive (strong) seasonal period for Disney, from October 1 to February 15, is stronger in magnitude than its weak seasonal period which takes place from June 5 to September 30.

Gain of 27%

According to Disney's Form 10-K filed with the Securities and Exchange Commission for the year ended September 29, 2012: *"Revenues in our Media Networks segment are subject to seasonal advertising patterns... these commitments are typically satisfied during the second half of the Company's fiscal year."* The media segment is the biggest driver of revenue for Disney. In addition, their other business segments are skewed towards revenue generation in the summer.

Disney's year-end occurs at the end of September and it typically reports its results in the first week of November. Investors start to increase their positions at the beginning of October in anticipation of positive year-end news.

Do not "visit" the Disney stock from June 5 to September 30. For the period from 1990 to 2020, Disney has produced an average loss of 6.8% and has only beaten the S&P 500, 32% of the time.

Covid-19 Performance Update. In 2021, Disney started to perform poorly in March and continued its poor performance in its weak seasonal period in June.

(i) *DIS - stock symbol for Walt Disney Company which trades on the NYSE. is a diversified worldwide entertainment company. Price is adjusted for stock splits.*

Disney vs. S&P 500 1990/91 to 2020/21

Negative Short ☐   Positive Long ☐

Year	Jun 5 to Sep 30 S&P 500	Jun 5 to Sep 30 Disney	Oct 1 to Feb 15 S&P 500	Oct 1 to Feb 15 Disney	Compound Growth S&P 500	Compound Growth Disney
1990/91	-16.7 %	-29.7 %	20.6 %	30.1 %	0.5 %	68.2 %
1991/92	0.0	-3.0	6.4	25.4	6.4	29.2
1992/93	1.1	-2.7	6.4	29.7	7.6	33.1
1993/94	2.0	-14.7	3.0	23.9	5.0	42.0
1994/95	0.6	-13.2	4.7	38.5	5.3	56.6
1995/96	9.8	2.7	11.5	11.3	22.3	8.3
1996/97	2.2	5.2	17.6	23.6	20.2	17.1
1997/98	12.8	0.9	7.7	38.2	21.4	36.9
1998/99	-7.1	-30.4	21.0	39.6	12.4	82.3
1999/00	-3.4	-15.1	9.3	41.9	5.6	63.2
2001/01	-2.8	-5.4	-7.7	-15.3	-10.2	-10.7
2001/02	-17.9	-41.1	6.1	28.4	-12.9	81.1
2002/03	-21.7	-31.9	2.4	10.5	-19.8	45.8
2003/04	1.0	-2.7	15.0	33.5	16.2	37.1
2004/05	-0.7	-6.3	8.6	31.2	7.8	39.4
2005/06	2.7	-11.7	4.2	11.4	7.0	24.4
2006/07	3.7	1.0	9.1	12.2	13.1	11.1
2007/08	-0.8	-3.7	-11.6	-5.5	-12.3	-2.1
2008/09	-15.3	-10.7	-29.1	-39.7	-40.0	-33.2
2009/10	12.2	9.2	1.7	9.5	14.1	0.6
2010/11	7.2	-1.8	16.4	30.2	24.7	32.5
2011/12	-13.0	-23.4	18.7	36.8	3.3	68.8
2012/13	12.7	17.7	5.5	6.4	18.9	-12.5
2013/14	3.1	0.2	9.3	22.9	12.7	22.6
2014/15	2.3	5.7	6.3	17.0	8.8	10.4
2015/16	-8.4	-7.3	-2.9	-10.8	-11.0	-4.3
2016/17	3.3	-6.0	8.4	18.7	11.9	25.7
2017/18	3.3	-8.0	8.4	6.7	12.0	15.3
2018/19	6.1	16.7	-4.8	-3.7	1.0	-19.8
2019/20	6.2	-3.3	13.6	7.1	20.6	10.6
2020/21	8.1	3.2	17.0	51.2	26.4	50.8
Avg.	-0.2 %	-6.8 %	6.5 %	18.1 %	6.4 %	26.7 %
Fq>0	65 %	68 %	84 %	84 %	81 %	77 %

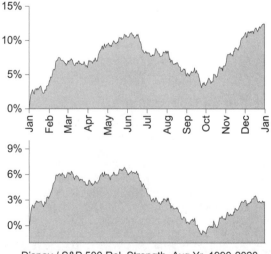

Disney - Avg. Year 1990 to 2020

Disney / S&P 500 Rel. Strength- Avg Yr. 1990-2020

Disney - Performance

DIS Monthly % Gain (1990-2020)

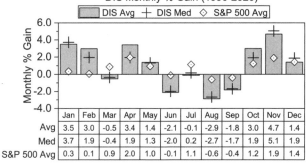

	Jan	Feb	Mar	Apr	May	Jun	Jul	Aug	Sep	Oct	Nov	Dec
Avg	3.5	3.0	-0.5	3.4	1.4	-2.1	-0.1	-2.9	-1.8	3.0	4.7	1.4
Med	3.7	1.9	-0.4	1.9	1.3	-2.0	0.2	-2.7	-1.7	1.9	5.1	1.9
S&P 500 Avg	0.3	0.1	0.9	2.0	1.0	-0.1	1.1	-0.6	-0.4	1.2	1.9	1.4

Fq DIS Gain > 0% (1990-2020)

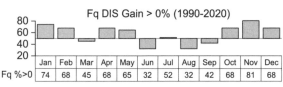

	Jan	Feb	Mar	Apr	May	Jun	Jul	Aug	Sep	Oct	Nov	Dec
Fq %>0	74	68	45	68	65	32	52	32	42	68	81	68

Fq % DIS Gain > S&P 500 % (1990-2020)

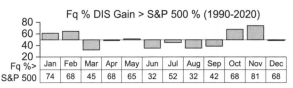

	Jan	Feb	Mar	Apr	May	Jun	Jul	Aug	Sep	Oct	Nov	Dec
Fq %> S&P 500	74	68	45	68	65	32	52	32	42	68	81	68

DIS % Gain 5 Year (2016-2020)

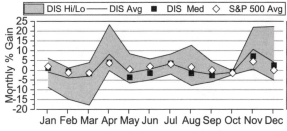

DIS Performance 2020-2021

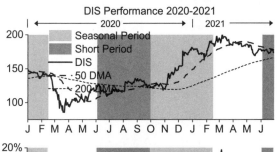

Relative Strength, % Gain vs. S&P 500

WEEK 18

Market Indices & Rates
Weekly Values**

Stock Markets	2020	2021
Dow	23,724	34,778
S&P500	2,831	4,233
Nasdaq	8,605	13,752
TSX	14,620	19,473
FTSE	5,763	7,130
DAX	10,862	15,400
Nikkei	19,619	29,358
Hang Seng	24,644	28,611

Commodities	2020	2021
Oil	19.78	64.90
Gold	1686.3	1836.6

Bond Yields	2020	2021
USA 5 Yr Treasury	0.36	0.77
USA 10 Yr T	0.64	1.60
USA 20 Yr T	1.04	2.17
Moody's Aaa	2.42	2.91
Moody's Baa	3.89	3.57
CAN 5 Yr T	0.38	0.88
CAN 10 Yr T	0.53	1.50

Money Market	2020	2021
USA Fed Funds	0.25	0.25
USA 3 Mo T-B	0.12	0.02
CAN tgt overnight rate	0.25	0.25
CAN 3 Mo T-B	0.25	0.11

Foreign Exchange	2020	2021
EUR/USD	1.10	1.22
GBP/USD	1.25	1.40
USD/CAD	1.41	1.21
USD/JPY	106.91	108.60

MAY

M	T	W	T	F	S	S
						1
2	3	4	5	6	7	8
9	11	11	12	13	14	15
16	18	18	19	20	21	22
21	25	25	26	27	28	29
30	31					

JUNE

M	T	W	T	F	S	S
	1	2	3	4	5	
6	7	8	9	10	11	12
13	14	15	16	17	18	19
20	21	22	23	24	25	26
27	28	29	30			

JULY

M	T	W	T	F	S	S
				1	2	3
4	5	6	7	8	9	10
11	12	13	14	15	16	17
18	19	20	21	22	23	24
25	26	27	28	29	30	31

SIX 'N' SIX
Take a Break for Six Months - May 6th to October 27th

The six-month cycle is the result of several factors but is mainly driven by the investor liquidity preference cycle (investors tending to decrease risk in the summer months).

Most pundits do not grasp the full value of the favorable six month period for stocks from October 28 to May 5, compared with the other six months: the unfavorable six month period.

Not only does the favorable period on average have bigger gains more frequently and smaller losses, but also on a yearly basis, outperforms the unfavorable period 72% of the time (last column in the table with YES values). There is no question which six month period seasonal investors should favor.

$2,189,154 gain on $10,000

The accompanying table uses the S&P 500 to compare the returns made from Oct 28 to May 5, to the returns made during the remainder of the year.

Starting with $10,000 and investing from October 28 to May 5 every year (October 28, 1950, to May 5, 2021) has produced a gain of $2,189,154. On the flip side, being invested from May 6 to October 27, an initial investment of $10,000 has gained $401 over the same time period.

	S&P 500 % May 6 to Oct 27	$10,000 Start	S&P 500 % Oct 28 to May 5	$10,000 Start	Oct28-May5 > May6-Oct27
1950/51	8.5 %	10,851	15.2 %	11,517	YES
1951/52	0.2	10,870	3.7	11,947	YES
1952/53	1.8	11,067	3.9	12,413	YES
1953/54	-3.1	10,727	16.6	14,475	YES
1954/55	13.2	12,141	18.1	17,097	YES
1955/56	11.4	13,528	15.1	19,681	YES
1956/57	-4.6	12,903	0.2	19,711	YES
1957/58	-12.4	11,302	7.9	21,265	YES
1958/59	15.1	13,013	14.5	24,356	
1959/60	-0.6	12,939	-4.5	23,270	
1960/61	-2.3	12,647	24.1	28,869	YES
1961/62	2.7	12,993	-3.1	27,982	
1962/63	-17.7	10,698	28.4	35,929	YES
1963/64	5.7	11,306	9.3	39,264	YES
1964/65	5.1	11,882	5.5	41,440	YES
1965/66	3.1	12,253	-5.0	39,388	
1966/67	-8.8	11,180	17.7	46,364	YES
1967/68	0.6	11,241	3.9	48,171	YES
1968/69	5.6	11,872	0.2	48,249	
1969/70	-6.2	11,141	-19.7	38,722	
1970/71	5.8	11,782	24.9	48,346	YES
1971/72	-9.6	10,647	13.7	54,965	YES
1972/73	3.7	11,046	0.3	55,154	
1973/74	0.3	11,084	-18.0	45,205	
1974/75	-23.2	8,513	28.5	58,073	YES
1975/76	-0.4	8,480	12.4	65,290	YES
1976/77	0.9	8,554	-1.6	64,231	
1977/78	-7.8	7,890	4.5	67,146	YES
1978/79	-2.0	7,732	6.4	71,476	YES
1979/80	-0.1	7,723	5.8	75,605	YES
1980/81	20.2	9,283	1.9	77,047	
1981/82	-8.5	8,498	-1.4	76,001	YES
1982/83	15.0	9,769	21.4	92,293	YES
1983/84	0.3	9,803	-3.5	89,085	
1984/85	3.9	10,183	8.9	97,057	YES
1985/86	4.1	10,604	26.8	123,044	YES
1986/87	0.4	10,651	23.7	152,196	YES
1987/88	-21.0	8,409	11.0	168,904	YES
1988/89	7.1	9,010	10.9	187,380	YES
1989/90	8.9	9,814	1.0	189,242	
1990/91	-10.0	8,837	25.0	236,498	YES
1991/92	0.9	8,916	8.5	256,590	YES
1992/93	0.4	8,952	6.2	272,550	YES
1993/94	4.5	9,356	-2.8	264,789	
1994/95	3.2	9,656	11.6	295,636	YES
1995/96	11.5	10,762	10.7	327,219	
1996/97	9.2	11,757	18.5	387,591	YES
1997/98	5.6	12,419	27.2	493,003	YES
1998/99	-4.5	11,860	26.5	623,489	YES
1999/00	-3.8	11,415	10.5	688,842	YES
2000/01	-3.7	10,992	-8.2	632,435	
2001/02	-12.8	9,586	-2.8	614,583	YES
2002/03	-16.4	8,016	3.2	634,369	YES
2003/04	11.3	8,921	8.8	689,985	
2004/05	0.3	8,952	4.2	718,942	YES
2005/06	0.5	9,000	12.5	808,503	YES
2006/07	3.9	9,350	9.3	883,804	YES
2007/08	2.0	9,534	-8.3	810,240	
2008/09	-39.7	5,750	6.5	862,619	YES
2009/10	17.7	6,766	9.6	934,470	
2010/11	1.4	6,862	12.9	1,067,851	YES
2011/12	-3.8	6,602	6.6	1,138,103	YES
2012/13	3.1	6,809	14.3	1,301,313	YES
2013/14	9.0	7,422	7.1	1,393,667	
2014/15	4.1	7,725	6.5	1,484,478	YES
2015/16	-1.1	7,638	-0.7	1,473,513	YES
2016/17	4.0	7,985	12.5	1,649,048	YES
2017/18	7.6	8,591	3.2	1,701,662	
2018/19	-0.2	8,575	10.8	1,885,321	YES
2019/20	2.6	8,799	-5.1	1,789,194	
2020/21	18.2	10,401	22.9	2,199,154	YES
Total Gain (Loss)		**$401**		**$2,189,154**	

S&P 500 Unfavorable 6 Month Avg. Gain vs Favorable 6 Month Avg. Gain (1950-2021)

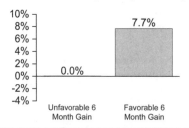

0.0%	7.7%
Unfavorable 6 Month Gain	Favorable 6 Month Gain

ⓘ *The above growth rates are geometric averages in order to represent the cumulative growth of a dollar investment over time. These figures differ from the arithmetic mean calculations used in the Six 'N' Six Take a Break Strategy, which are used to represent an average year.*

6 'n' 6 Strategy Performance

Market Indices & Rates
Weekly Values**

Stock Markets	2020	2021
Dow	24,331	34,382
S&P500	2,930	4,174
Nasdaq	9,121	13,430
TSX	14,967	19,367
FTSE	5,936	7,044
DAX	10,904	15,417
Nikkei	20,179	28,084
Hang Seng	24,230	28,028

Commodities	2020	2021
Oil	24.48	65.37
Gold	1704.1	1838.1

Bond Yields	2020	2021
USA 5 Yr Treasury	0.33	0.82
USA 10 Yr T	0.69	1.63
USA 20 Yr T	1.12	2.25
Moody's Aaa	2.54	3.00
Moody's Baa	4.06	3.66
CAN 5 Yr T	0.39	0.95
CAN 10 Yr T	0.58	1.56

Money Market	2020	2021
USA Fed Funds	0.25	0.25
USA 3 Mo T-B	0.12	0.01
CAN tgt overnight rate	0.25	0.25
CAN 3 Mo T-B	0.22	0.09

Foreign Exchange	2020	2021
EUR/USD	1.08	1.21
GBP/USD	1.24	1.41
USD/CAD	1.39	1.21
USD/JPY	106.65	109.35

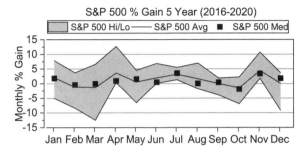

S&P 500 % Gain 5 Year (2016-2020)

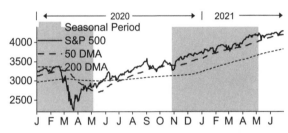

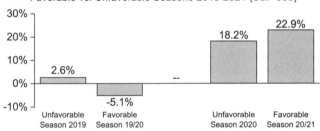

Favorable vs. Unfavorable Seasons 2019-2021 (S&P 500)

MAY

M	T	W	T	F	S	S
						1
2	3	4	5	6	7	8
9	11	11	12	13	14	15
16	18	18	19	20	21	22
21	25	25	26	27	28	29
30	31					

JUNE

M	T	W	T	F	S	S
		1	2	3	4	5
6	7	8	9	10	11	12
13	14	15	16	17	18	19
20	21	22	23	24	25	26
27	28	29	30			

JULY

M	T	W	T	F	S	S
				1	2	3
4	5	6	7	8	9	10
11	12	13	14	15	16	17
18	19	20	21	22	23	24
25	26	27	28	29	30	31

Over the last five years, the six month seasonal strategy for the stock market generally has followed its seasonal pattern. The months in the six month favorable seasonal period have generally been better than the other six months of the year. The outperformance in the favorable period has been weaker than its long-term average.

In 2019/20, the S&P 500 in its favorable six month period produced a loss of 5.1% versus a small gain of 2.6 in the unfavorable period. In 2020/21, the S&P 500 in its favorable six month period produced a large gain of 22.9%, which was larger than the gain of 18.2% that was made in the unfavorable period.

CANADIAN SIX 'N' SIX
Take a Break for Six Months - May 6th to October 27th

In analyzing long-term trends for the broad markets such as the S&P 500 or the TSX Composite, a large data set is preferable because it incorporates various economic cycles. The daily data set for the TSX Composite starts in 1977.

Over this time period, investors have been rewarded for following the six month cycle of investing from October 28 to May 5, versus the unfavorable six month period, May 6 to October 27.

Starting with an investment of $10,000 in 1977, investing in the unfavorable six months has produced a loss of $3,041, versus investing in the favorable six month period which has produced a gain of $266,355.

$266,355 gain on $10,000 since 1977

The TSX Composite Average Year 1977 to 2020 graph (below), indicates that the market tended to peak in mid-July or the end of August. In our book *Time In Time Out, Outsmart the Stock Market Using Calendar Investment Strategies*, Bruce Lindsay and I analyzed a number of market trends and peaks over different decades.

What we found was that the markets tend to peak at the beginning of May or mid-July. The mid-July peak was usually the result of a strong bull market in place that had a lot of momentum.

The main reason that the TSX Composite data shows a peak occurring in July-August is that the data is primarily from the biggest bull market in history, starting in 1982.

TSX Composite % Gain Avg. Year 1977 to 2020

intervals, the period from October to May is far superior compared with the other half of the year. The table below illustrates the superiority of the best six months over the worst six months. Going down the table year by year, the period from October 28 to May 5 outperforms the period from May 6 to October 27 on a regular basis. In a strong bull market, investors always have the choice of using a stop loss or technical indicators to help extend the exit point past the May date.

	TSX Comp May 6 to Oct 27	$10,000 Start	TSX Comp Oct 28 to May 5	$10,000 Start
1977/78	-3.9 %	9,608	13.1 %	11,313
1978/79	12.1	10,775	21.3	13,728
1979/80	2.9	11,084	23.0	16,883
1980/81	22.5	13,579	-2.4	16,479
1981/82	-17.0	11,272	-18.2	13,488
1982/83	16.6	13,138	34.6	18,150
1983/84	-0.9	13,015	-1.9	17,811
1984/85	1.6	13,226	10.7	19,718
1985/86	0.5	13,299	16.5	22,978
1986/87	-1.9	13,045	24.8	28,666
1987/88	-23.4	9,992	15.3	33,050
1988/89	2.7	10,260	5.7	34,939
1989/90	7.9	11,072	-13.3	30,294
1990/91	-8.4	10,148	13.1	34,266
1991/92	-1.6	9,982	-2.0	33,571
1992/93	-2.3	9,750	15.3	38,704
1993/94	10.8	10,801	1.7	39,365
1994/95	-0.1	10,792	0.3	39,483
1995/96	1.3	10,936	18.2	46,671
1996/97	8.3	11,843	10.8	51,725
1997/98	7.3	12,707	17.0	60,510
1998/99	-22.3	9,870	17.1	70,871
1999/00	-0.2	9,853	36.9	97,009
2000/01	-2.9	9,570	-14.4	83,062
2001/02	-12.2	8,399	9.4	90,875
2002/03	-16.4	7,020	4.0	94,476
2003/04	15.1	8,079	10.3	104,252
2004/05	3.9	8,398	7.8	112,379
2005/06	8.1	9,080	19.8	134,587
2006/07	0.0	9,079	12.2	151,053
2007/08	3.8	9,426	-0.2	150,820
2008/09	-40.2	5,638	15.7	174,551
2009/10	11.9	6,307	7.4	187,526
2010/11	5.8	6,674	7.1	200,778
2011/12	-7.4	6,183	-4.8	191,207
2012/13	3.6	6,407	1.1	193,348
2013/14	7.7	6,902	9.7	212,072
2014/15	-1.6	6,795	4.9	222,404
2015/16	-9.7	6,135	-4.9	221,307
2016/17	8.8	6,676	5.0	232,470
2017/18	2.4	6,835	-1.4	229,205
2018/19	-5.3	6,733	10.8	253,932
2019/20	-0.5	6,696	-9.7	229,275
2020/21	8.2	6,959	20.5	276,355
Total Gain (Loss)	**(3,041)**			**266,355**

8%

6%

4%

2%

0%

Jan Feb Mar Apr May Jun Jul Aug Sep Oct Nov Dec Jan

Does a later average peak in the stock market mean that the best six month cycle does not work? No. Dividing the year up into six month

6n6 Canada Strategy Performance

Market Indices & Rates
Weekly Values**

Stock Markets	2020	2021
Dow	23,685	34,208
S&P500	2,864	4,156
Nasdaq	9,015	13,471
TSX	14,639	19,527
FTSE	5,800	7,018
DAX	10,465	15,438
Nikkei	20,037	28,318
Hang Seng	23,797	28,458

Commodities	2020	2021
Oil	29.43	63.70
Gold	1735.4	1875.9

Bond Yields	2020	2021
USA 5 Yr Treasury	0.31	0.84
USA 10 Yr T	0.64	1.63
USA 20 Yr T	1.05	2.24
Moody's Aaa	2.51	2.97
Moody's Baa	4.05	3.64
CAN 5 Yr T	0.38	0.93
CAN 10 Yr T	0.54	1.54

Money Market	2020	2021
USA Fed Funds	0.25	0.25
USA 3 Mo T-B	0.12	0.01
CAN tgt overnight rate	0.25	0.25
CAN 3 Mo T-B	0.25	0.09

Foreign Exchange	2020	2021
EUR/USD	1.08	1.22
GBP/USD	1.21	1.42
USD/CAD	1.41	1.21
USD/JPY	107.06	108.96

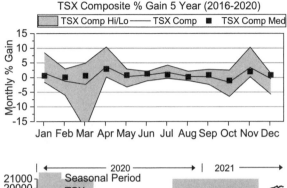

TSX Composite % Gain 5 Year (2016-2020)

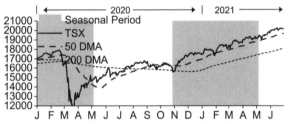

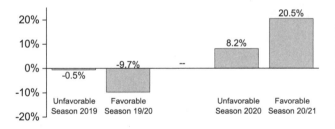

Favorable vs. Unfavorable Seasons 2019-2021 (TSX Composite)

MAY

M	T	W	T	F	S	S
						1
2	3	4	5	6	7	8
9	11	11	12	13	14	15
16	18	18	19	20	21	22
21	25	25	26	27	28	29
30	31					

Over the last five years, the TSX Composite generally followed its six month favorable/unfavorable cycle.

In 2019, the unfavorable six month period produced a loss of 0.5% for the TSX Composite. The following six month favorable period produced a loss of 9.7%. In 2020, the unfavorable period produced a gain of 8.2% for the TSX Composite, which was lower than the gain of 20.5% in the 2020/21 favorable period. Overall, between the two years, the favorable period produced a better gain profile.

JUNE

M	T	W	T	F	S	S
	1	2	3	4	5
6	7	8	9	10	11	12
13	14	15	16	17	18	19
20	21	22	23	24	25	26
27	28	29	30			

JULY

M	T	W	T	F	S	S
				1	2	3
4	5	6	7	8	9	10
11	12	13	14	15	16	17
18	19	20	21	22	23	24
25	26	27	28	29	30	31

COSTCO – BUY AT A DISCOUNT
① May26-Jun30 ② Oct4-Dec1

Shoppers are attracted to Costco because of its consistently low prices. They take comfort in the fact that although the prices may not always be the lowest, they are consistently in the lower range.

Costco performs well in late spring into early summer, and in autumn into early winter. These two periods are considered to be transition periods where the stock market is moving to and from its unfavorable and favorable seasons. Companies such as Costco that have stable earnings are desirable at these times.

There are two times when Costco is a seasonal bargain: May 26 to June 30 and October 4 to December 1.

13% gain & positive 96% of the time

Putting both seasonal periods together, from 1994 to 2020, has produced a 96% positive success rate and an average gain of 13.1%. Although the earlier strong years in the 1990's skews the data to the high-side, Costco has still maintained its strong seasonal performances in both the May to June and the October to December time periods.

Covid-19 Performance Update. In 2021, after underperforming the S&P 500 in January and February, Costco started to outperform in March. It continued its outperformance in its spring/summer strong seasonal period.

Costco* vs. S&P 500 1994 to 2020 Positive

Year	May 26 to Jun 30 S&P 500	COST	Oct 4 to Dec 1 S&P 500	COST	Compound Growth S&P 500	COST
1994	-2.6 %	10.7 %	-2.8	-6.3 %	-5.3	3.7 %
1995	3.1	19.3	4.2	-2.2	7.4	16.7
1996	-1.2	9.5	9.3	15.5	8.0	26.5
1997	4.5	3.1	1.0	16.5	5.6	20.2
1998	2.1	17.6	17.2	41.1	19.7	66.0
1999	6.9	8.1	9.0	30.7	16.5	41.3
2000	5.3	10.0	-7.8	-3.6	-2.9	6.1
2001	-4.2	9.3	6.3	12.3	1.8	22.6
2002	-8.7	-0.8	14.3	4.6	4.4	3.8
2003	4.4	5.3	3.9	13.5	8.5	19.4
2004	2.5	10.3	5.3	17.4	7.9	29.4
2005	0.1	-1.5	3.1	13.9	3.2	12.2
2006	-0.2	5.0	4.7	6.0	4.5	11.3
2007	-0.8	3.8	-3.8	8.9	-4.6	12.9
2008	-7.0	-1.7	-25.8	-23.5	-30.9	-24.7
2009	3.6	-5.2	8.2	7.5	12.1	1.9
2010	-4.0	-3.0	5.2	5.0	1.0	1.9
2011	0.0	1.2	13.2	6.7	13.2	7.9
2012	3.4	12.5	-2.4	4.3	0.9	17.3
2013	-2.6	-3.3	7.6	9.6	4.7	6.0
2014	3.1	0.2	4.4	11.7	7.6	11.9
2015	-3.0	-6.0	7.8	10.6	4.6	3.9
2016	0.4	8.7	1.4	0.5	1.8	9.2
2017	0.4	-8.5	4.3	12.1	4.6	2.7
2018	-0.1	5.4	-5.7	-0.8	-5.8	4.5
2019	4.1	6.9	7.9	3.7	12.3	10.9
2020	4.9	0.3	9.4	9.2	14.7	9.5
Avg.	0.5 %	4.3 %	3.7 %	8.3 %	4.3 %	13.1 %
Fq>0	59 %	70 %	78 %	81 %	81 %	96 %

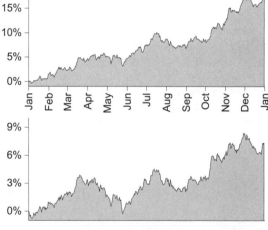

Costco - Avg. Year 1994 to 2020

Costco / S&P 500 Rel. Strength- Avg Yr. 1994-2020

Costco Performance

COST Monthly % Gain (1994-2020)

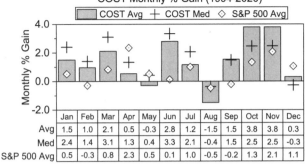

	Jan	Feb	Mar	Apr	May	Jun	Jul	Aug	Sep	Oct	Nov	Dec
Avg	1.5	1.0	2.1	0.5	-0.3	2.8	1.2	-1.5	1.5	3.8	3.8	0.3
Med	2.4	1.4	3.1	1.3	0.4	3.3	2.1	-0.4	1.5	2.5	2.5	-0.3
S&P 500 Avg	0.5	-0.3	0.8	2.3	0.5	0.1	1.0	-0.5	-0.2	1.3	2.1	1.1

Fq COST Gain > 0% (1994-2020)

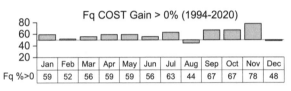

	Jan	Feb	Mar	Apr	May	Jun	Jul	Aug	Sep	Oct	Nov	Dec
Fq %>0	59	52	56	59	59	56	63	44	67	67	78	48

Fq % COST Gain > S&P 500 % (1994-2020)

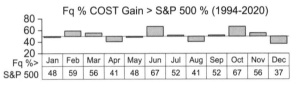

	Jan	Feb	Mar	Apr	May	Jun	Jul	Aug	Sep	Oct	Nov	Dec
Fq %> S&P 500	48	59	56	41	48	67	52	41	52	67	56	37

COST % Gain 5 Year (2016-2020)

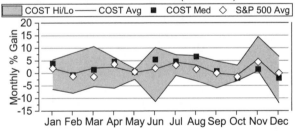

COST Performance 2020-2021

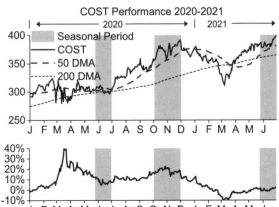

Relative Strength, % Gain vs. S&P 500

Market Indices & Rates
Weekly Values**

Stock Markets	2020	2021
Dow	24,465	34,529
S&P500	2,955	4,204
Nasdaq	9,325	13,749
TSX	14,914	19,852
FTSE	5,993	7,023
DAX	11,074	15,520
Nikkei	20,388	29,149
Hang Seng	22,930	29,124

Commodities	2020	2021
Oil	33.55	66.32
Gold	1733.6	1900.0

Bond Yields	2020	2021
USA 5 Yr Treasury	0.34	0.79
USA 10 Yr T	0.66	1.58
USA 20 Yr T	1.12	2.18
Moody's Aaa	2.41	2.90
Moody's Baa	3.84	3.57
CAN 5 Yr T	0.38	0.92
CAN 10 Yr T	0.51	1.50

Money Market	2020	2021
USA Fed Funds	0.25	0.25
USA 3 Mo T-B	0.12	0.01
CAN tgt overnight rate	0.25	0.25
CAN 3 Mo T-B	0.25	0.11

Foreign Exchange	2020	2021
EUR/USD	1.09	1.22
GBP/USD	1.22	1.42
USD/CAD	1.40	1.21
USD/JPY	107.64	109.85

MAY

M	T	W	T	F	S	S
						1
2	3	4	5	6	7	8
9	11	11	12	13	14	15
16	18	18	19	20	21	22
21	25	25	26	27	28	29
30	31					

JUNE

M	T	W	T	F	S	S
	1	2	3	4	5	
6	7	8	9	10	11	12
13	14	15	16	17	18	19
20	21	22	23	24	25	26
27	28	29	30			

JULY

M	T	W	T	F	S	S
				1	2	3
4	5	6	7	8	9	10
11	12	13	14	15	16	17
18	19	20	21	22	23	24
25	26	27	28	29	30	31

US REITS – ONE BRICK AT A TIME

US REITS
① LONG (Mar8-Sep20)
② SELL SHORT (Sep21-Oct9)

US REITS have two seasonal periods, one positive and one negative. The positive seasonal period is much longer and lasts from March 8 to September 20, compared to the negative period which lasts just over two weeks, from September 21 to October 9.

The seasonal period for REITs generally follows the seasonal trend for government bonds, which tend to perform well from early May to early October. REITs on average turn down a bit earlier than government bonds. Although REITs benefit from lower interest rates, they do have somewhat of a positive correlation with equities. As equities tend to head lower in late September, any sign of higher interest rates at this time can strongly affect REIT prices.

11% growth & positive 76% of the time

In contrast, the weak seasonal period has produced a much smaller loss than the gain in the strong seasonal period. The strong seasonal period is juxtaposed against the negative period. Although it is not suitable for most investors to short sell REITs in their negative seasonal period, the profile of this period highlights the seasonal strategy of exiting the REIT sector when it has finished its strong seasonal period.

Covid-19 Performance Update. In 2021, the REIT sector started to outperform the S&P 500 in January, as investors anticipated workers returning to work and helping to support commercial real estate prices. The sector continued to perform well as its seasonal period started in March.

*MSCI US REIT Index (RMZ). For more information, please refer to msci.com

US REITS vs. S&P 500- 1996 to 2020

Negative Short　　　　　　　　Positive Long

	Mar 8 to Sep 20		Sep 21 to Oct 9		Compound Growth	
Year	S&P 500	US REITS	S&P 500	US REITS	S&P 500	US REITS
1996	5.1 %	8.7 %	1.4	1.7 %	6.6 %	6.8 %
1997	18.1	8.9	2.1	5.2	20.6	3.2
1998	-3.4	-16.0	-3.5	-4.8	-6.8	-12.0
1999	4.7	1.4	0.0	-1.8	4.8	3.2
2000	7.1	23.8	-3.4	-2.1	3.4	26.4
2001	-22.0	2.3	7.3	3.7	-16.3	-1.5
2002	-27.0	-0.9	-8.1	-11.4	-32.9	10.4
2003	25.0	25.8	0.2	5.0	25.3	19.5
2004	-3.0	2.9	0.0	3.2	-3.0	-0.3
2005	-0.3	10.8	-2.1	-3.9	-2.4	15.1
2006	3.9	10.8	1.9	2.0	5.9	8.5
2007	9.1	-8.5	3.1	6.9	12.4	-14.8
2008	-3.0	12.5	-27.5	-35.9	-29.7	52.9
2009	56.3	107.4	0.3	-4.6	56.8	116.9
2010	0.4	17.4	2.0	-1.3	2.3	18.9
2011	-8.3	-3.0	-3.9	-10.2	-11.8	6.9
2012	8.0	7.9	-1.3	-2.0	6.6	10.1
2013	10.7	-2.9	-3.1	-3.1	7.3	0.1
2014	7.1	4.2	-4.1	0.2	2.7	3.9
2015	-5.5	-5.5	2.9	4.2	-2.7	-9.4
2016	6.9	7.7	0.7	-4.6	7.6	12.7
2017	5.9	0.4	1.5	-0.1	7.5	0.5
2018	7.5	11.5	-1.7	-2.7	5.6	14.6
2019	8.8	9.6	-2.4	0.5	6.2	9.0
2020	11.7	-14.6	4.8	4.3	17.0	-18.3
Avg.	5.0 %	8.9 %	-1.3	-2.1 %	3.7 %	11.3 %
Fq>0	68 %	72 %	52 %	44 %	68 %	76 %

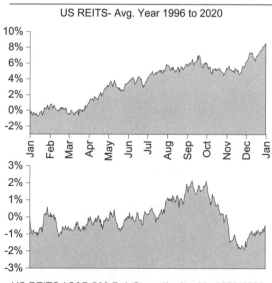

US REITS- Avg. Year 1996 to 2020

US REITS / S&P 500 Rel. Strength- Avg Yr. 1996-2020

US REITS Strategy Performance

RMZ Monthly % Gain (1996-2020)

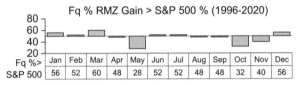

	Jan	Feb	Mar	Apr	May	Jun	Jul	Aug	Sep	Oct	Nov	Dec
Avg	0.4	-1.1	1.4	2.6	0.6	0.4	1.8	0.2	0.2	-0.7	0.4	2.3
Med	0.4	-0.4	2.4	2.3	1.0	1.9	1.4	0.2	-0.0	-1.2	1.7	2.6
S&P 500 Avg	0.1	0.1	1.4	1.7	1.0	-0.5	0.7	-0.8	-0.4	1.5	1.5	1.8

Fq RMZ Gain > 0% (1996-2020)

	Jan	Feb	Mar	Apr	May	Jun	Jul	Aug	Sep	Oct	Nov	Dec
Fq %>0	56	48	72	64	60	64	76	52	48	44	60	68

Fq % RMZ Gain > S&P 500 % (1996-2020)

	Jan	Feb	Mar	Apr	May	Jun	Jul	Aug	Sep	Oct	Nov	Dec
Fq %> S&P 500	56	52	60	48	28	52	52	48	48	32	40	56

RMZ % Gain 5 Year (2016-2020)

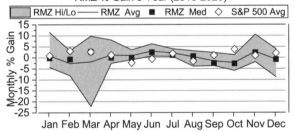

RMZ Performance 2020-2021

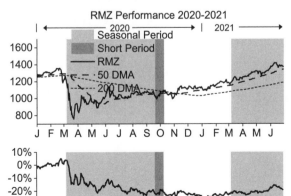

Relative Strength, % Gain vs. S&P 500

Market Indices & Rates
Weekly Values**

Stock Markets	2020	2021
Dow	25,383	34,756
S&P500	3,044	4,230
Nasdaq	9,490	13,814
TSX	15,193	20,029
FTSE	6,077	7,069
DAX	11,587	15,693
Nikkei	21,878	28,942
Hang Seng	22,961	28,918

Commodities	2020	2021
Oil	35.49	69.62
Gold	1728.7	1890.6

Bond Yields	2020	2021
USA 5 Yr Treasury	0.30	0.78
USA 10 Yr T	0.65	1.56
USA 20 Yr T	1.18	2.16
Moody's Aaa	2.41	2.88
Moody's Baa	3.76	3.54
CAN 5 Yr T	0.40	0.86
CAN 10 Yr T	0.53	1.46

Money Market	2020	2021
USA Fed Funds	0.25	0.25
USA 3 Mo T-B	0.14	0.02
CAN tgt overnight rate	0.25	0.25
CAN 3 Mo T-B	0.18	0.12

Foreign Exchange	2020	2021
EUR/USD	1.11	1.22
GBP/USD	1.23	1.42
USD/CAD	1.38	1.21
USD/JPY	107.83	109.52

MAY

M	T	W	T	F	S	S
						1
2	3	4	5	6	7	8
9	11	11	12	13	14	15
16	18	18	19	20	21	22
21	25	25	26	27	28	29
30	31					

JUNE

M	T	W	T	F	S	S
	1	2	3	4	5	
6	7	8	9	10	11	12
13	14	15	16	17	18	19
20	21	22	23	24	25	26
27	28	29	30			

JULY

M	T	W	T	F	S	S
					1	2	3
4	5	6	7	8	9	10
11	12	13	14	15	16	17
18	19	20	21	22	23	24
25	26	27	28	29	30	31

JUNE

	MONDAY	TUESDAY	WEDNESDAY
WEEK 22	30	31 29	**1** 29
WEEK 23	**6** 24	**7** 23	**8** 22
WEEK 24	**13** 17	**14** 16	**15** 15
WEEK 25	**20** 10 USA Market Closed - Juneteenth National Independence Day	**21** 9	**22** 8
WEEK 26	**27** 3	**28** 2	**29** 1

THURSDAY		FRIDAY	
2	28	**3**	27
9	21	**10**	20
16	14	**17**	13
23	7	**24**	6
30		1	

JULY

M	T	W	T	F	S	S
				1	2	3
4	5	6	7	8	9	10
11	12	13	14	15	16	17
18	19	20	21	22	23	24
25	26	27	28	29	30	31

AUGUST

M	T	W	T	F	S	S
1	2	3	4	5	6	7
8	9	10	11	12	13	14
15	16	17	18	19	20	21
22	23	24	25	26	27	28
29	30	31				

SEPTEMBER

M	T	W	T	F	S	S
			1	2	3	4
5	6	7	8	9	10	11
12	13	14	15	16	17	18
19	20	21	22	23	24	25
26	27	28	29	30		

OCTOBER

M	T	W	T	F	S	S
					1	2
3	4	5	6	7	8	9
10	11	12	13	14	15	16
17	18	19	20	21	22	23
24	25	26	27	28	29	30
31						

JUNE
S U M M A R Y

	Dow Jones	S&P 500	Nasdaq	TSX Comp
Month Rank	11	9	6	11
# Up	34	39	28	17
# Down	37	32	21	19
% Pos	48	55	57	47
% Avg. Gain	-0.1	0.1	0.9	-0.2

Dow & S&P 1950-2020, Nasdaq 1972-2020 TSX 1985-2020

S&P500 Cumulative Daily Gains for Avg Month 1950 to 2021

♦ On average, June is not a strong month for the S&P 500. From 1950 to 2020, June was the fourth worst month of the year, producing a nominal gain of 0.1%. ♦ From year to year, different sectors of the market tend to lead in June as there is not a strong consistent outperforming major sector. ♦ The last few days of June, the start of the successful *Summer Sizzler Trade,* tend to be positive. ♦ In 2021, the S&P 500 dipped in price mid-month, and managed to rally in late June into the period for the *Summer Sizzler Trade.*

BEST / WORST JUNE BROAD MKTS. 2012-2021

BEST JUNE MARKETS
- ♦ Nasdaq (2019) 7.4%
- ♦ Dow (2019) 7.2%
- ♦ Russell 2000 (2019) 6.9%

WORST JUNE MARKETS
- ♦ Nikkei 225 (2016) - 9.6%
- ♦ FTSE 100 (2015) - 6.6%
- ♦ FTSE 100 (2013) -5.6%

Index Values End of Month

	2012	2013	2014	2015	2016	2017	2018	2019	2020	2021
Dow	12,880	14,910	16,827	17,620	17,930	21,350	24,271	26,600	25,813	34,503
S&P 500	1,362	1,606	1,960	2,063	2,099	2,423	2,663	2,942	3,100	4,298
Nasdaq	2,935	3,403	4,408	4,987	4,843	6,140	7,510	8,006	10,059	14,504
TSX Comp.	11,597	12,129	15,146	14,553	14,065	15,182	16,278	16,382	15,515	20,166
Russell 1000	751	891	1,095	1,153	1,162	1,344	1,510	1,629	1,717	2,421
Russell 2000	798	977	1,193	1,254	1,152	1,415	1,643	1,567	1,441	2,311
FTSE 100	5,571	6,215	6,744	6,521	6,504	7,313	7,637	7,426	6,170	7,037
Nikkei 225	9,007	13,677	15,162	20,236	15,576	20,033	22,305	21,276	22,288	28,792

Percent Gain for June

	2012	2013	2014	2015	2016	2017	2018	2019	2020	2021
Dow	3.9	-1.4	0.7	-2.2	0.8	1.6	-0.6	7.2	1.7	-0.1
S&P 500	4.0	-1.5	1.9	-2.1	0.1	0.5	0.0	6.9	1.8	2.2
Nasdaq	3.8	-1.5	3.9	-1.6	-2.1	-0.9	0.9	7.4	6.0	5.5
TSX Comp.	0.7	-4.1	3.7	-3.1	0.0	-1.1	1.3	2.1	2.1	2.2
Russell 1000	3.7	-1.5	2.1	-2.0	0.1	0.5	0.5	6.9	2.1	2.4
Russell 2000	4.8	-0.7	5.2	0.6	-0.2	3.3	0.6	6.9	3.4	1.8
FTSE 100	4.7	-5.6	-1.5	-6.6	4.4	-2.8	-0.5	3.7	1.5	0.2
Nikkei 225	5.4	-0.7	3.6	-1.6	-9.6	1.9	0.5	3.3	1.9	-0.2

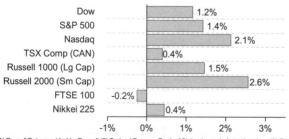

June Market Avg. Performance 2012 to 2021[1]

Dow	1.2%
S&P 500	1.4%
Nasdaq	2.1%
TSX Comp (CAN)	0.4%
Russell 1000 (Lg Cap)	1.5%
Russell 2000 (Sm Cap)	2.6%
FTSE 100	-0.2%
Nikkei 225	0.4%

Interest Corner Jun[2]

	Fed Funds % [3]	3 Mo. T-Bill % [4]	10 Yr % [5]	20 Yr % [6]
2021	0.25	0.05	1.45	2.00
2020	0.25	0.16	0.66	1.18
2019	2.50	2.12	2.00	2.31
2018	2.00	1.93	2.85	2.91
2017	1.25	1.03	2.31	2.61

(1) Russell Data provided by Russell (2) Federal Reserve Bank of St. Louis- end of month values (3) Target rate set by FOMC (4)(5)(6) Constant yield maturities.

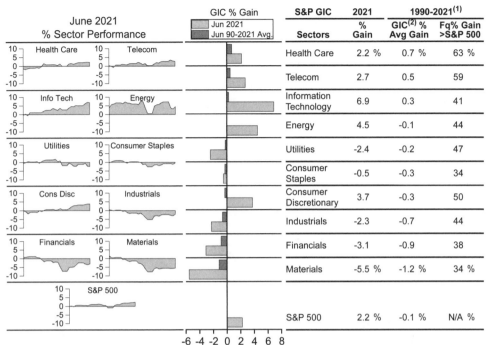

S&P GIC Sectors	2021 % Gain	1990-2021[1] GIC[2] % Avg Gain	1990-2021[1] Fq% Gain >S&P 500
Health Care	2.2 %	0.7 %	63 %
Telecom	2.7	0.5	59
Information Technology	6.9	0.3	41
Energy	4.5	-0.1	44
Utilities	-2.4	-0.2	47
Consumer Staples	-0.5	-0.3	34
Consumer Discretionary	3.7	-0.3	50
Industrials	-2.3	-0.7	44
Financials	-3.1	-0.9	38
Materials	-5.5 %	-1.2 %	34 %
S&P 500	2.2 %	-0.1 %	N/A %

Sector Commentary

♦ In June 2021, the growth sectors of the stock market rebounded from the previous month's poor performance and led the market higher. ♦ The technology sector gained 6.9% and the consumer discretionary sector gained 3.7%. ♦ The cyclical stocks were generally lower for the month. ♦ The exception to this trend was the energy sector, which gained 4.5%. ♦ The materials sector ended up producing a loss of 5.5%. ♦ The performance of the defensive sectors was mixed, with the health care sector gaining 2.2% and utilities loosing 2.4%.

Sub-Sector Commentary

♦ In June 2021, the retail sub-sector performed particularly well with a gain of 4.9%. ♦ The biotech sector started its strong seasonal period early and performed well in June. ♦ The semi-conductor sector performed well with a gain of 5.0%. ♦ The agriculture sector typically performs poorly in June and in 2021, it followed its monthly trend, with a loss of 8.9%. ♦ Gold can perform well in June when it starts its strong seasonal period early. In 2021, gold performed poorly in June.

SELECTED SUB-SECTORS[3]

Pharma	2.6 %	0.8 %	66 %
Retail	4.9	0.2	59
Gold	-7.2	-0.2	50
Biotech (1993-2021)	3.8	-0.2	48
SOX (1995-2021)	5.0	-0.2	41
Metals & Mining	-12.0	-0.3	53
Steel	-6.4	-0.9	41
Automotive & Components	6.6	-1.0	50
Homebuilders	-2.3	-1.0	41
Railroads	-3.5	-1.0	34
Transportation	-4.7	-1.1	31
Chemicals	-4.5	-1.2	34
Agriculture (1994-2021)	-8.9	-1.2	32
Banks	-5.5	-1.7	31
Silver	-6.8	-1.7	34

(1) Sector data provided by Standard and Poors (2) GIC is short form for Global Industry Classification (3) Sub Sector data provided by Standard and Poors, except where marked by symbol.

BIOTECH SUMMER SOLSTICE
June 23 to September 13

The *Biotech Summer Solstice* trade starts on June 23 and lasts until September 13. The trade is aptly named as its outperformance starts approximately when summer solstice starts– the longest day of the year.

There are two main drivers of the trade: biotech is a good substitute for technology stocks in the summer, and investors want to take a position in the biotech sector before the autumn conferences.

Positive 82% of the time

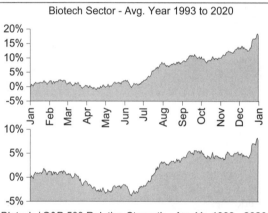

Biotech Sector - Avg. Year 1993 to 2020

Biotech / S&P 500 Relative Strength - Avg Yr. 1993 - 2020

Biotech* vs. S&P 500 1992 to 2020			
		Positive	
Jun 23 to Sep 13	S&P 500	Biotech	Diff
1992	4.0 %	17.9 %	13.8 %
1993	3.6	3.6	0.0
1994	3.2	24.2	21.0
1995	5.0	31.5	26.5
1996	2.1	7.0	4.9
1997	2.8	-18.9	-21.7
1998	-8.5	20.6	29.1
1999	0.6	64.3	63.7
2000	2.3	7.6	5.4
2001	-10.8	-3.6	7.2
2002	-10.0	8.1	18.2
2003	2.3	6.4	4.1
2004	-0.8	8.9	9.6
2005	1.4	26.0	24.5
2006	5.8	7.4	1.6
2007	-1.2	6.0	7.2
2008	-5.0	11.4	16.5
2009	16.8	7.7	-9.1
2010	2.4	2.8	0.4
2011	-8.9	-3.7	5.2
2012	9.4	15.6	6.2
2013	6.0	24.9	18.9
2014	1.2	14.8	13.6
2015	-7.6	-7.2	0.5
2016	2.0	7.3	5.3
2017	2.6	11.1	8.5
2018	5.4	7.5	2.1
2019	1.9	-4.5	-6.4
2020	7.2	-6.9	-14.1
Avg	1.2 %	10.3 %	9.0 %
Fq>0	72 %	79 %	83 %

The biotechnology sector is often considered the cousin of the technology sector, a good place for speculative investments. The sectors are similar as both include concept companies (companies without a product, but with good potential).

Despite their similarity, investors view the sectors differently. The technology sector is viewed as being much more dependent on the economy compared with the biotech sector. The end product of biotechnology companies is mainly medicine, which is not economically sensitive.

As a result, in the summer months when investors tend to be more cautious, they are more willing to commit speculative money into the biotech sector, compared with the technology sector.

The biotech sector is one of the few sectors that starts its outperformance in June. This is in part because of the biotech conferences that occur in autumn and with the possibility of positive announcements, the price of biotech companies can increase dramatically. As a re-

sult, investors try to lock in positions early.

Covid-19 Performance Update. In 2021, the biotech sector started to underperform in February into May. The sector bottomed in May, setting up well for its seasonal period, which started in late June.

(i) *Biotech SP GIC Sector # 352010: Companies primarily engaged in the research, development, manufacturing and/or marketing of products based on genetic analysis and genetic engineering.*

Biotech Performance

Biotech Monthly % Gain (1993-2020)

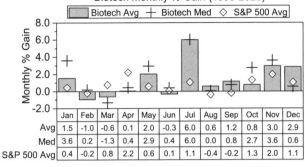

Legend: Biotech Avg ＋ Biotech Med ◇ S&P 500 Avg

	Jan	Feb	Mar	Apr	May	Jun	Jul	Aug	Sep	Oct	Nov	Dec
Avg	1.5	-1.0	-0.6	0.1	2.0	-0.3	6.0	0.6	1.2	0.8	3.0	2.9
Med	3.6	0.2	-1.3	0.4	2.9	0.4	6.0	0.0	0.8	2.7	3.6	0.6
S&P 500 Avg	0.4	-0.2	0.8	2.2	0.6	0.1	1.1	-0.4	-0.2	1.3	2.0	1.1

Fq Biotech Gain > 0% (1993-2020)

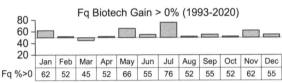

	Jan	Feb	Mar	Apr	May	Jun	Jul	Aug	Sep	Oct	Nov	Dec
Fq %>0	62	52	45	52	66	55	76	52	55	52	62	55

Fq % Biotech Gain > S&P 500 % (1993-2020)

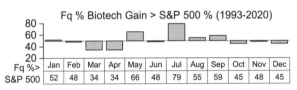

	Jan	Feb	Mar	Apr	May	Jun	Jul	Aug	Sep	Oct	Nov	Dec
Fq %> S&P 500	52	48	34	34	66	48	79	55	59	45	48	45

Biotech % Gain 5 Year (2016-2020)

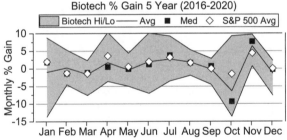

Legend: Biotech Hi/Lo — Avg ■ Med ◇ S&P 500 Avg

Biotech Performance 2020-2021

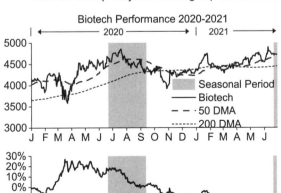

2020 → | 2021 →

Seasonal Period
Biotech
— · 50 DMA
---- 200 DMA

Relative Strength, % Gain vs. S&P 500

Market Indices & Rates
Weekly Values**

Stock Markets	2020	2021
Dow	27,111	34,480
S&P500	3,194	4,247
Nasdaq	9,814	14,069
TSX	15,854	20,138
FTSE	6,484	7,134
DAX	12,848	15,693
Nikkei	22,864	28,949
Hang Seng	24,770	28,842

Commodities	2020	2021
Oil	39.55	70.91
Gold	1683.5	1881.1

Bond Yields	2020	2021
USA 5 Yr Treasury	0.47	0.76
USA 10 Yr T	0.91	1.47
USA 20 Yr T	1.46	2.08
Moody's Aaa	2.41	2.80
Moody's Baa	3.82	3.44
CAN 5 Yr T	0.53	0.82
CAN 10 Yr T	0.73	1.37

Money Market	2020	2021
USA Fed Funds	0.25	0.25
USA 3 Mo T-B	0.15	0.03
CAN tgt overnight rate	0.25	0.25
CAN 3 Mo T-B	0.18	0.11

Foreign Exchange	2020	2021
EUR/USD	1.13	1.21
GBP/USD	1.27	1.41
USD/CAD	1.34	1.22
USD/JPY	109.59	109.66

JUNE

M	T	W	T	F	S	S
		1	2	3	4	5
6	7	8	9	10	11	12
13	14	15	16	17	18	19
20	21	22	23	24	25	26
27	28	29	30			

JULY

M	T	W	T	F	S	S
				1	2	3
4	5	6	7	8	9	10
11	12	13	14	15	16	17
18	19	20	21	22	23	24
25	26	27	28	29	30	31

AUGUST

M	T	W	T	F	S	S
1	2	3	4	5	6	7
8	9	10	11	12	13	14
15	16	17	18	19	20	21
22	23	24	25	26	27	28
29	30	31				

CAMECO – CHARGES DOWN AND UP
① SELL SHORT (Jun5-Aug7)
② LONG (Oct4-Jan24)

Cameco is the world's largest publicly traded uranium company. It trades on both the NYSE stock exchange (ticker: CCJ) and the Toronto Stock Exchange (ticker: CCO).

Cameco has a very narrow market for its product: countries that need uranium to power their nuclear reactors. Mining operations do not vary much throughout the year, so supply is fairly constant. In addition actual usage of uranium does not change much throughout the year as nuclear reactors are run most efficiently at one constant level over time. Yet, there is a seasonal tendency for Cameco to perform well from October 4 to January 24.

22% growth & positive 85% of the time

The seasonal trend for Cameco can be partly explained by the overall tendency of the stock market to perform well during Cameco's strong seasonal period, and poorly during Cameco's weak seasonal period.

The seasonal trend for Cameco can also be explained somewhat with buyer behavior. The World Nuclear Association (WNA) has an annual conference that takes place in the middle of September of each year. As a result of the conference, buyers tend to be reassured of the future demand of uranium, helping to give Cameco a boost starting in October. Likewise, investors often have a low interest level in Cameco in the summer months ahead of the WNA conference in mid-September.

Cameco Corporation is in the materials sector. Its stock symbol is CCO, which trades on the Toronto Stock Exchange, adjusted for splits.

Cameco vs. TSX Composite Index - 1995/96 to 2020/21

Negative Short ☐   Positive Long ▦

Year	Jun 5 to Aug 7 TSX	Jun 5 to Aug 7 CCO	Oct 4 to Jan 24 TSX	Oct 4 to Jan 24 CCO	Compound Growth TSX	Compound Growth CCO
1995/96	3.7 %	1.8 %	8.1 %	42.7 %	12.1 %	40.1 %
1996/97	-3.7	-6.1	12.2	-16.5	8.0	-11.5
1997/98	8.0	1.1	-8.5	-22.6	-1.1	-23.4
1998/99	-11.3	-23.2	19.5	44.4	6.0	77.9
1999/00	-0.9	-16.9	22.0	-24.8	21.0	-12.1
2000/01	8.4	-13.7	-11.0	25.0	-3.5	42.1
2001/02	-6.4	-20.3	10.9	14.6	3.9	37.9
2002/03	-14.3	-28.6	10.6	27.9	-5.2	64.5
2003/04	2.6	4.9	14.4	35.7	17.4	29.1
2004/05	-2.1	8.9	3.8	30.6	1.7	19.0
2005/06	9.1	5.7	5.5	38.3	15.1	30.4
2006/07	0.3	-9.1	12.9	18.6	13.2	29.4
2007/08	-4.1	-30.2	-7.9	-15.7	-11.8	9.8
2008/09	-8.9	-15.0	-20.1	-6.5	-27.2	7.5
2009/10	3.9	0.5	3.5	6.2	7.5	5.6
2010/11	2.0	11.2	8.0	35.6	10.1	20.4
2011/12	-10.0	-13.7	10.2	29.0	-0.9	45.0
2012/13	4.7	9.0	3.8	12.6	8.6	2.4
2013/14	-1.4	-10.3	7.7	29.6	6.2	42.9
2014/15	2.2	-3.1	-0.1	-8.9	2.1	-6.0
2015/16	-4.8	-6.2	-7.1	-0.9	-11.6	5.3
2016/17	3.0	-17.3	6.3	54.0	9.4	80.7
2017/18	-1.2	3.7	3.5	8.0	2.3	4.0
2018/19	1.5	1.7	-4.9	4.0	-3.5	2.3
2019/20	0.6	-16.1	7.3	-11.5	8.0	2.9
2020/21	6.5	-0.3	10.2	21.5	17.4	21.9
Avg.	-0.4 %	-7.0 %	4.6	14.3 %	4.0 %	21.9 %
Fq>0	54 %	38 %	73 %	69 %	69 %	85 %

Covid-19 Performance Update. In 2021, Cameco rallied from early in the year, into the beginning of June. As the weak seasonal period started for Cameco in June, the stock turned lower and underperformed the Canadian stock market.

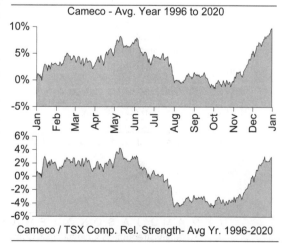

Cameco - Avg. Year 1996 to 2020

Cameco / TSX Comp. Rel. Strength- Avg Yr. 1996-2020

Cameco Performance

CCO Monthly % Gain (1996-2020)

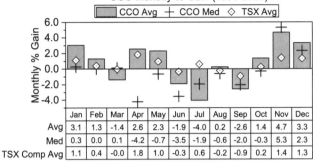

	Jan	Feb	Mar	Apr	May	Jun	Jul	Aug	Sep	Oct	Nov	Dec
Avg	3.1	1.3	-1.4	2.6	2.3	-1.9	-4.0	0.2	-2.6	1.4	4.7	3.3
Med	0.3	0.0	0.1	-4.2	-0.7	-3.5	-1.9	-0.6	-2.0	-0.3	5.3	2.3
TSX Comp Avg	1.1	0.4	-0.0	1.8	1.0	-0.3	0.6	-0.2	-0.9	0.2	1.4	1.3

Fq CCO Gain > 0% (1996-2020)

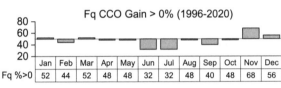

	Jan	Feb	Mar	Apr	May	Jun	Jul	Aug	Sep	Oct	Nov	Dec
Fq %>0	52	44	52	48	48	32	32	48	40	48	68	56

Fq % CCO Gain > TSX Comp. % (1996-2020)

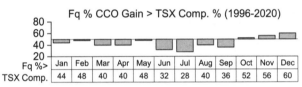

	Jan	Feb	Mar	Apr	May	Jun	Jul	Aug	Sep	Oct	Nov	Dec
Fq %> TSX Comp.	44	48	40	40	48	32	28	40	36	52	56	60

CCO % Gain 5 Year (2016-2020)

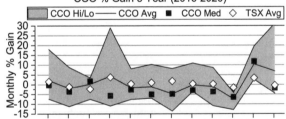

CCO Performance 2020-2021

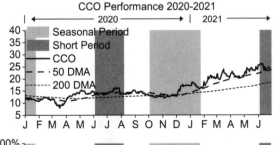

Relative Strength, % Gain vs. TSX Comp.

Market Indices & Rates
Weekly Values**

Stock Markets	2020	2021
Dow	25,606	33,290
S&P500	3,041	4,166
Nasdaq	9,589	14,030
TSX	15,257	20,000
FTSE	6,105	7,017
DAX	11,949	15,448
Nikkei	22,305	28,964
Hang Seng	24,301	28,801

Commodities	2020	2021
Oil	36.26	71.64
Gold	1733.5	1773.1

Bond Yields	2020	2021
USA 5 Yr Treasury	0.33	0.89
USA 10 Yr T	0.71	1.45
USA 20 Yr T	1.24	1.97
Moody's Aaa	2.42	2.64
Moody's Baa	3.62	3.30
CAN 5 Yr T	0.37	0.96
CAN 10 Yr T	0.54	1.37

Money Market	2020	2021
USA Fed Funds	0.25	0.25
USA 3 Mo T-B	0.16	0.05
CAN tgt overnight rate	0.25	0.25
CAN 3 Mo T-B	0.18	0.13

Foreign Exchange	2020	2021
EUR/USD	1.13	1.19
GBP/USD	1.25	1.38
USD/CAD	1.36	1.25
USD/JPY	107.38	110.21

JUNE

M	T	W	T	F	S	S
		1	2	3	4	5
6	7	8	9	10	11	12
13	14	15	16	17	18	19
20	21	22	23	24	25	26
27	28	29	30			

JULY

M	T	W	T	F	S	S
			1	2	3	
4	5	6	7	8	9	10
11	12	13	14	15	16	17
18	19	20	21	22	23	24
25	26	27	28	29	30	31

AUGUST

M	T	W	T	F	S	S
1	2	3	4	5	6	7
8	9	10	11	12	13	14
15	16	17	18	19	20	21
22	23	24	25	26	27	28
29	30	31				

SUMMER SIZZLER – THE FULL TRADE
PROFIT BEFORE & AFTER FIREWORKS
Two Market Days Before June Month End
To 5 Market Days After Independence Day

The beginning of July is a time for celebration and the markets tend to agree.

Based on previous market data, the best way to take advantage of this trend is to be invested for the two market days prior to June month end and hold until five market days after Independence Day. This time period has produced above average returns on a fairly consistent basis.

Since 1950, 1.0% avg. gain & 74% of the time positive

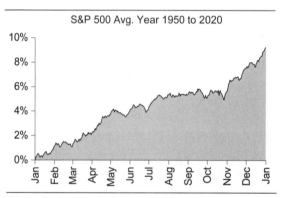

S&P 500 Avg. Year 1950 to 2020

The typical strategy to take advantage of the tendency of positive performance around Independence Day has been to invest one or two days before the holiday and take profits one or two days after the holiday.

Although this strategy has produced profits, it has left a lot of money on the table. This strategy misses out on the positive days at the end of June and on the full slate of positive days after Independence Day.

The beginning part of the *Summer Sizzler Trade's* positive trend is driven by portfolio managers who "window dress" their portfolios, buying stocks at month end that have a favorable perception in the market in order to make their portfolios look good on month and quarter end statements. This is particularly true at quarter ends. The result is typically increased buying pressure that lifts the stock market.

Depending on market conditions at the time, investors should consider extending the exit date of the *Summer Sizzler Trade* until eighteen calendar days into July. With July being an earnings month, the market can continue to rally until mid-month (see *18 Day Earnings Month Strategy*).

Covid-19 Performance Update. In 2021, the stock market performed well in its Summer Sizzler period as the stock market dipped in mid-June, which setup for a strong run into Q2 earnings season.

S&P 500, 2 Market Days Before June Month End To 5 Market Days after Independence Day % Gain 1950 to 2021 — Positive

Year		Year		Year		Year		Year		Year		Year		Year	
1950	-4.4	1960	-0.1	1970	1.5	1980	1.4	1990	1.7	2000	1.8	2010	0.4	2020	5.5
1951	1.5	1961	1.7	1971	3.2	1981	-2.4	1991	1.4	2001	-2.6	2011	1.8	2021	2.1
1952	0.9	1962	9.8	1972	0.3	1982	-0.6	1992	2.8	2002	-4.7	2012	0.7		
1953	0.8	1963	0.5	1973	2.1	1983	1.5	1993	-0.6	2003	1.2	2013	4.5		
1954	2.9	1964	2.3	1974	-8.8	1984	-0.7	1994	0.4	2004	-1.7	2014	0.5		
1955	4.9	1965	5.0	1975	-0.2	1985	1.5	1995	1.8	2005	1.5	2015	-1.2		
1956	3.4	1966	2.1	1976	2.4	1986	-2.6	1996	-2.8	2006	2.1	2016	5.0		
1957	3.8	1967	1.3	1977	-0.6	1987	0.4	1997	3.7	2007	0.8	2017	0.2		
1958	2.0	1968	2.3	1978	0.6	1988	-0.6	1998	2.7	2008	-3.4	2018	2.8		
1959	3.3	1969	-1.5	1979	1.3	1989	0.9	1999	5.1	2009	-4.3	2019	3.0		
Avg.	1.9		2.3		0.2		-0.1		1.8		-0.9		1.8		3.8

Summer Sizzler Strategy (S&P 500) Performance

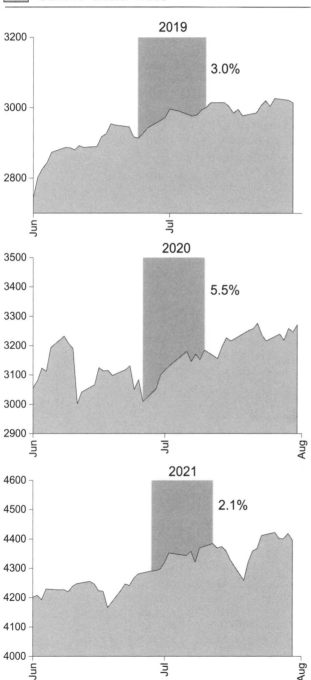

☐ Summer Sizzler Trade

2019 — 3.0%

2020 — 5.5%

2021 — 2.1%

Market Indices & Rates
Weekly Values**

Stock Markets	2020	2021
Dow	25,871	34,434
S&P500	3,098	4,281
Nasdaq	9,946	14,360
TSX	15,474	20,230
FTSE	6,293	7,136
DAX	12,331	15,608
Nikkei	22,479	29,066
Hang Seng	24,644	29,288

Commodities	2020	2021
Oil	39.75	74.25
Gold	1734.8	1786.7

Bond Yields	2020	2021
USA 5 Yr Treasury	0.33	0.92
USA 10 Yr T	0.70	1.54
USA 20 Yr T	1.23	2.09
Moody's Aaa	2.43	2.77
Moody's Baa	3.57	3.44
CAN 5 Yr T	0.38	1.01
CAN 10 Yr T	0.54	1.45

Money Market	2020	2021
USA Fed Funds	0.25	0.25
USA 3 Mo T-B	0.15	0.06
CAN tgt overnight rate	0.25	0.25
CAN 3 Mo T-B	0.20	0.14

Foreign Exchange	2020	2021
EUR/USD	1.12	1.19
GBP/USD	1.24	1.39
USD/CAD	1.36	1.23
USD/JPY	106.87	110.75

JUNE

M	T	W	T	F	S	S
		1	2	3	4	5
6	7	8	9	10	11	12
13	14	15	16	17	18	19
20	21	22	23	24	25	26
27	28	29	30			

JULY

M	T	W	T	F	S	S
				1	2	3
4	5	6	7	8	9	10
11	12	13	14	15	16	17
18	19	20	21	22	23	24
25	26	27	28	29	30	31

AUGUST

M	T	W	T	F	S	S
1	2	3	4	5	6	7
8	9	10	11	12	13	14
15	16	17	18	19	20	21
22	23	24	25	26	27	28
29	30	31				

ORACLE
June 1 to July 1

Oracle's stock price performance exhibits a positive seasonal trend in the run-up to and after reporting on its fiscal year-end. Oracle's year-end is on May 31 and it typically reports its full-year earnings in mid-to-late June.

Selling software is instantly scalable, which provides an incentive to increase sales at year-end without disrupting operations. Oracle places a lot of emphasis on providing its sales force with incentives to increase sales before its year-end closes.

Oracle's May 31, 2020 SEC Filing 10-K Annual Report states: *"Our quarterly revenues have historically been affected by a variety of seasonal factors, including the structure of our sales force incentive compensation plans, which are common in the technology industry. In each fiscal year, our total revenues and operating margins are typically highest in our fourth fiscal quarter and lowest in our first fiscal quarter."*

7% gain & positive 72% of the time

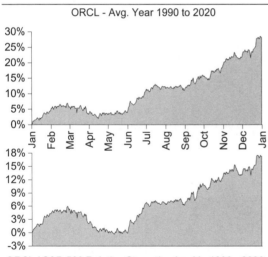

ORCL - Avg. Year 1990 to 2020

ORCL / S&P 500 Relative Strength - Avg Yr. 1990 - 2020

Investors tend to front-run Oracle's full-year earnings report pushing up Oracle's stock price. Oracle tends to be conservative in managing financial analyst expectations around year-end. The result is that its period of seasonal strength tends to last past the earnings report and finish at the beginning of July.

ORCL* vs. S&P 500 - 1990 to 2020

Jun 1 to Jul1	S&P 500	ORCL	Positive Diff
1990	-0.9%	17.1%	18.0%
1991	-3.1	13.3	16.4
1992	-0.6	16.8	17.4
1993	-0.3	19.8	20.0
1994	-2.3	10.9	13.2
1995	2.1	11.2	9.0
1996	1.0	18.1	17.1
1997	5.0	4.2	-0.9
1998	5.3	1.9	-3.4
1999	6.1	52.1	46.1
2000	2.4	17.0	14.6
2001	-2.5	24.2	26.7
2002	-9.2	13.6	22.9
2003	1.9	-5.2	-7.2
2004	0.7	3.6	2.9
2005	0.2	3.8	3.6
2006	0.0	1.9	1.9
2007	-1.8	1.7	3.5
2008	-8.2	-6.7	1.5
2009	0.5	11.0	10.5
2010	-5.7	-4.5	1.2
2011	-0.4	-3.4	-3.0
2012	4.0	12.2	8.2
2013	-1.0	-10.9	-9.9
2014	2.6	-3.0	-5.6
2015	-1.4	-7.5	-6.1
2016	0.3	1.6	1.4
2017	0.5	10.5	10.0
2018	0.5	-5.7	-6.2
2019	7.7	14.6	6.9
2020	2.4	3.2	0.8
2021	2.8	1.0	-1.8
Avg	0.2%	4.0%	7.2%
Fq > 0	59%	75%	72%

Covid-19 Performance Update.

In 2021, Oracle started to outperform the S&P 500 in February. It's performance was very volatile. June was particularly volatile, with Oracle rising sharply in price at the beginning of the month, falling sharply mid-month and then rallying sharply at the end of the month. In its seasonal period, Oracle managed to produce a gain of 1.0%, which fell short of the S&P 500, which produced a gain of 2.8%.

 * Oracle is a technology company. Oracle trades on Nasdaq Exchange. Data adjusted for stock splits.

ORCL Performance

Market Indices & Rates
Weekly Values**

ORCL Monthly % Gain (1990-2020)

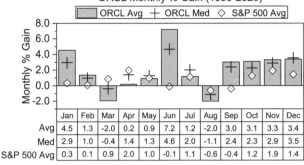

	Jan	Feb	Mar	Apr	May	Jun	Jul	Aug	Sep	Oct	Nov	Dec
Avg	4.5	1.3	-2.0	0.2	0.9	7.2	1.2	-2.0	3.0	3.1	3.3	3.4
Med	2.9	1.0	-0.4	1.4	1.3	4.6	2.0	-1.1	2.4	2.3	2.9	3.5
S&P 500 Avg	0.3	0.1	0.9	2.0	1.0	-0.1	1.1	-0.6	-0.4	1.2	1.9	1.4

Fq ORCL Gain > 0% (1990-2020)

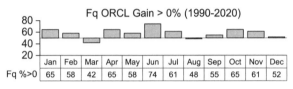

	Jan	Feb	Mar	Apr	May	Jun	Jul	Aug	Sep	Oct	Nov	Dec
Fq %>0	65	58	42	65	58	74	61	48	55	65	61	52

Fq % ORCL Gain > S&P 500 % (1990-2020)

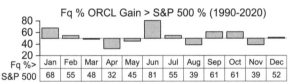

	Jan	Feb	Mar	Apr	May	Jun	Jul	Aug	Sep	Oct	Nov	Dec
Fq %> S&P 500	68	55	48	32	45	81	55	39	61	61	39	52

ORCL % Gain 5 Year (2016-2020)

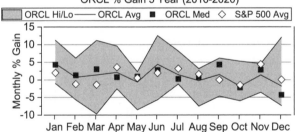

ORCL Performance 2020-2021

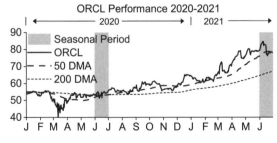

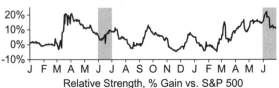

Relative Strength, % Gain vs. S&P 500

Stock Markets	2020	2021
Dow	25,016	34,786
S&P500	3,009	4,352
Nasdaq	9,757	14,639
TSX	15,189	20,226
FTSE	6,159	7,123
DAX	12,089	15,650
Nikkei	22,512	28,783
Hang Seng	24,550	28,310

Commodities	2020	2021
Oil	38.49	75.16
Gold	1747.6	1786.2

Bond Yields	2020	2021
USA 5 Yr Treasury	0.30	0.86
USA 10 Yr T	0.64	1.44
USA 20 Yr T	1.15	1.98
Moody's Aaa	2.35	2.62
Moody's Baa	3.56	3.31
CAN 5 Yr T	0.36	0.97
CAN 10 Yr T	0.51	1.37

Money Market	2020	2021
USA Fed Funds	0.25	0.25
USA 3 Mo T-B	0.14	0.05
CAN tgt overnight rate	0.25	0.25
CAN 3 Mo T-B	0.20	0.14

Foreign Exchange	2020	2021
EUR/USD	1.12	1.19
GBP/USD	1.23	1.38
USD/CAD	1.37	1.23
USD/JPY	107.22	111.05

JUNE

M	T	W	T	F	S	S
		1	2	3	4	5
6	7	8	9	10	11	12
13	14	15	16	17	18	19
20	21	22	23	24	25	26
27	28	29	30			

JULY

M	T	W	T	F	S	S
			1	2	3	
4	5	6	7	8	9	10
11	12	13	14	15	16	17
18	19	20	21	22	23	24
25	26	27	28	29	30	31

AUGUST

M	T	W	T	F	S	S
1	2	3	4	5	6	7
8	9	10	11	12	13	14
15	16	17	18	19	20	21
22	23	24	25	26	27	28
29	30	31				

JULY

MONDAY	TUESDAY	WEDNESDAY
27	28	29
4 27 USA Market Closed - Independence Day	**5** 26	**6** 25
11 20	**12** 19	**13** 18
18 13	**19** 12	**20** 11
25 6	**26** 5	**27** 4

THURSDAY	FRIDAY
30	**1** 30
	CAN Market Closed- Canada Day
7 24	**8** 23
14 17	**15** 16
21 10	**22** 9
28 3	**29** 2

AUGUST

M	T	W	T	F	S	S
1	2	3	4	5	6	7
8	9	10	11	12	13	14
15	16	17	18	19	20	21
22	23	24	25	26	27	28
29	30	31				

SEPTEMBER

M	T	W	T	F	S	S
			1	2	3	4
5	6	7	8	9	10	11
12	13	14	15	16	17	18
19	20	21	22	23	24	25
26	27	28	29	30		

OCTOBER

M	T	W	T	F	S	S
					1	2
3	4	5	6	7	8	9
10	11	12	13	14	15	16
17	18	19	20	21	22	23
24	25	26	27	28	29	30
31						

NOVEMBER

M	T	W	T	F	S	S
	1	2	3	4	5	6
7	8	9	10	11	12	13
14	15	16	17	18	19	20
21	22	23	24	25	26	27
28	29	30				

JULY
SUMMARY

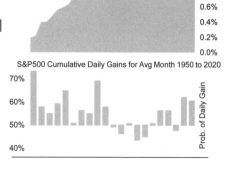

	Dow Jones	S&P 500	Nasdaq	TSX Comp
Month Rank	4	4	8	6
# Up	46	41	28	24
# Down	25	30	21	12
% Pos	65	58	57	67
% Avg. Gain	1.3	1.1	0.7	1.0

Dow & S&P 1950-2020 Nasdaq 1972-2020, TSX 1985-2020

S&P500 Cumulative Daily Gains for Avg Month 1950 to 2020

♦ When a summer rally occurs in the stock market, the gains are usually made in July. ♦ Typically, it is the first part of July that produces the gains as the market tends to rally before Independence Day and into the first eighteen calendar days of July (see the *18 Days Earnings Month Effect*). In 2020, July produced a strong gain of 5.5% in July. ♦ On average, volatility starts to increase in July and continues this trend into October.

BEST / WORST JULY BROAD MKTS. 2011-2020

BEST JULY MARKETS
♦ Russell 2000 (2013) 6.9%
♦ Nasdaq (2020) 6.8%
♦ Nasdaq (2016) 6.6%

WORST JULY MARKETS
♦ Russell 2000 (2014) -6.1%
♦ FTSE 100 (2020) -4.4%
♦ Russell 2000 (2011) -3.7%

Index Values End of Month

	2011	2012	2013	2014	2015	2016	2017	2018	2019	2020
Dow	12,143	13,009	15,500	16,563	17,690	18,432	21,891	25,415	26,864	26,428
S&P 500	1,292	1,379	1,686	1,931	2,104	2,174	2,470	2,816	2,980	3,271
Nasdaq	2,756	2,940	3,626	4,370	5,128	5,162	6,348	7,672	8,175	10,745
TSX Comp.	12,946	11,665	12,487	15,331	14,468	14,583	15,144	16,434	16,407	16,169
Russell 1000	718	759	937	1,076	1,174	1,204	1,369	1,560	1,652	1,816
Russell 2000	797	787	1,045	1,120	1,239	1,220	1,425	1,671	1,575	1,480
FTSE 100	5,815	5,635	6,621	6,730	6,696	6,724	7,372	7,749	7,587	5,898
Nikkei 225	9,833	8,695	13,668	15,621	20,585	16,569	19,925	22,554	21,522	21,710

Percent Gain for July

	2011	2012	2013	2014	2015	2016	2017	2018	2019	2020
Dow	-2.2	1.0	4.0	-1.6	0.4	2.8	2.5	4.7	1.0	2.4
S&P 500	-2.1	1.3	4.9	-1.5	2.0	3.6	1.9	3.6	1.3	5.5
Nasdaq	-0.6	0.2	6.6	-0.9	2.8	6.6	3.4	2.2	2.1	6.8
TSX Comp.	-2.7	0.6	2.9	1.2	-0.6	3.7	-0.3	1.0	0.1	4.2
Russell 1000	-2.3	1.1	5.2	-1.7	1.8	3.7	1.9	3.3	1.4	5.7
Russell 2000	-3.7	-1.4	6.9	-6.1	-1.2	5.9	0.7	1.7	0.5	2.7
FTSE 100	-2.2	1.2	6.5	-0.2	2.7	3.4	0.8	1.5	2.2	-4.4
Nikkei 225	0.2	-3.5	-0.1	3.0	1.7	6.4	-0.5	1.1	1.2	-2.6

July Market Avg. Performance 2011 to 2020[1]

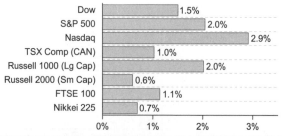

Dow	1.5%
S&P 500	2.0%
Nasdaq	2.9%
TSX Comp (CAN)	1.0%
Russell 1000 (Lg Cap)	2.0%
Russell 2000 (Sm Cap)	0.6%
FTSE 100	1.1%
Nikkei 225	0.7%

Interest Corner Jul[2]

	Fed Funds % [3]	3 Mo. T-Bill % [4]	10 Yr % [5]	20 Yr % [6]
2020	0.25	0.09	0.55	0.98
2019	2.25	2.08	2.02	2.31
2018	2.00	2.03	2.96	3.03
2017	1.25	1.07	2.30	2.66
2016	0.50	0.28	1.46	1.78

(1) Russell Data provided by Russell (2) Federal Reserve Bank of St. Louis- end of month values (3) Target rate set by FOMC (4)(5)(6) Constant yield maturities.

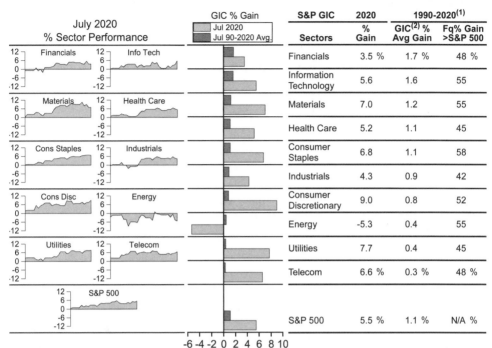

| S&P GIC | 2020 | 1990-2020[1] | |
Sectors	% Gain	GIC[2] % Avg Gain	Fq% Gain >S&P 500
Financials	3.5 %	1.7 %	48 %
Information Technology	5.6	1.6	55
Materials	7.0	1.2	55
Health Care	5.2	1.1	45
Consumer Staples	6.8	1.1	58
Industrials	4.3	0.9	42
Consumer Discretionary	9.0	0.8	52
Energy	-5.3	0.4	55
Utilities	7.7	0.4	45
Telecom	6.6 %	0.3 %	48 %
S&P 500	5.5 %	1.1 %	N/A %

Sector Commentary

♦ July is an earnings month and the S&P 500 was positive into the start of the earnings season in July 2020 and continued to perform well into the end of the month. ♦ Performance across the sectors of the market was broad based. ♦ The only sector that was an anomaly, was the energy sector, producing a loss of 5.3%.

Sub-Sector Commentary

♦ In July 2020, silver, which often performs well in the month, did exceptionally well, with a gain of 34.9%. ♦ Homebuilders also performed well with a gain of 20.4%. ♦ Falling interest rates helped to support both of these sectors. ♦ The metals and mining sector performed well, as generally the cyclical sectors performed well. ♦ The biotech sector typically is a strong performer in July. After performing well earlier in the year, the biotech sector performed poorly in July.

SELECTED SUB-SECTORS[3]			
Biotech (1993-2020)	-2.5 %	6.0 %	79 %
Silver	34.9	2.7	61
Railroads	4.6	2.4	58
Banks	1.2	1.7	65
Transportation	8.9	1.7	52
Homebuilders	20.4	1.5	48
Retail	10.9	1.5	58
Chemicals	7.9	1.5	55
Automotive & Components	2.1	1.3	45
SOX (1995-2020)	7.0	1.2	50
Metals & Mining	10.3	0.7	48
Gold	11.1	0.6	52
Pharma	4.3	0.6	48
Steel	1.3	0.1	45
Agriculture (1994-2020)	7.3	-0.2	48

(1) Sector data provided by Standard and Poors (2) GIC is short form for Global Industry Classification (3) Sub Sector data provided by Standard and Poors, except where marked by symbol.

GOLD SHINES
(Metal) ① Jul12-Oct9 ② Dec27-Jan26

Most of the gold produced each year is consumed in jewelery fabrication. The time of the year with the highest demand for gold is in the fourth quarter, particularly around Indian Diwali, the festival of lights. The demand for gold bullion takes place in previous months as gold fabricators purchase gold bullion to fashion into jewelery for Diwali.

6% gain & 68% of the time positive

The result is that gold bullion tends to rise from July 12 to October 9. In this period, from 1984 to 2020, gold bullion has increased on average 3.3% and has been positive 65% of the time.

In more recent years, the Chinese have become large consumers of gold and have vied with India for the top gold consuming country. The Chinese consume most of their gold around the Chinese New Year, which takes place early in the calendar year. In the yearly period from 1984 to 2021, from December 27 to January 26, gold bullion has produced an average gain of 2.3% and has been positive 59% of the time. Gains in this period have been more frequent in recent years as the Chinese population has increased its consumption of gold.

Covid-19 Performance Update. In 2021, gold started to perform well in March, and then started to correct in early June. The level of real interest rates were a big factor in the gold trend. As the yield on the 10-year US Treasury Note declined, starting in March, it helped to support a move higher in the price of gold.

ⓘ *Source: Bank of England- London PM represents the close value of gold in afternoon trading in London.*

Gold* vs. S&P 500 - 1984/85 to 2020/21   Positive ☐

Year	Jul 12 to Oct 9 S&P 500	Gold	Dec 27 to Jan 26 S&P 500	Gold	Compound Growth S&P 500	Gold
1984/85	7.4 %	0.5 %	6.5 %	-3.9 %	14.4 %	-3.4 %
1985/86	-5.4	4.2	-0.4	9.0	-5.7	13.5
1986/87	-2.6	25.2	9.2	4.3	6.3	30.6
1987/88	0.9	3.9	-1.0	-2.4	-0.1	1.4
1988/89	2.8	-7.5	5.0	-2.6	7.9	-10.0
1989/90	9.4	-4.2	-6.1	1.3	2.8	-3.0
1990/91	-15.5	12.1	1.6	-2.5	-14.2	9.3
1991/92	-0.1	-2.9	2.6	-1.8	2.6	-4.6
1992/93	-2.9	0.4	0.0	-0.6	-2.8	-0.2
1993/94	2.7	-8.8	1.3	-0.5	4.0	-9.3
1994/95	1.6	1.6	1.9	-0.1	3.4	1.6
1995/96	4.3	-0.1	1.2	4.8	5.5	4.7
1996/97	7.9	-0.4	1.9	-4.4	10.0	-4.7
1997/98	5.9	4.4	2.2	3.5	8.2	8.0
1998/99	-15.5	2.8	2.1	0.5	-13.7	3.3
1999/00	-4.8	25.6	-3.7	-0.5	-8.3	25.0
2000/01	-5.3	-4.5	3.0	-3.5	-2.5	-7.9
2001/02	-10.5	8.4	-1.4	0.5	-11.7	9.0
2002/03	-16.2	1.7	-3.2	6.4	-18.9	8.2
2003/04	4.1	7.8	5.4	-0.3	9.7	7.5
2004/05	0.8	3.8	-3.0	-3.5	-2.2	0.1
2005/06	-1.9	11.4	0.4	11.3	-1.5	24.0
2006/07	6.1	-8.8	0.4	4.0	6.5	-5.1
2007/08	3.1	11.0	-11.2	13.3	-8.4	25.8
2008/09	-26.6	-8.2	-4.2	7.9	-29.6	-1.0
2009/10	21.9	15.2	-3.1	0.7	18.2	16.0
2010/11	8.1	11.0	3.2	-3.3	11.5	7.3
2011/12	-12.4	6.2	4.2	7.5	-8.8	14.2
2012/13	7.5	12.5	5.9	0.5	13.7	13.1
2013/14	-1.1	1.5	-2.8	5.7	-3.9	7.2
2014/15	-2.0	-8.1	-1.5	9.0	-3.5	0.1
2015/16	-3.0	-0.7	-7.6	4.3	-10.4	3.6
2016/17	0.8	-7.3	1.5	5.2	2.2	-2.5
2017/18	4.9	5.6	7.2	7.0	12.4	13.0
2018/19	3.8	-5.3	8.0	2.8	12.1	-2.6
2019/20	-2.6	6.6	1.7	5.5	-1.1	12.5
2020/21	9.2	6.7	4.0	-1.0	13.5	5.6
Avg.	-0.4 %	3.3 %	0.8 %	2.3 %	0.5 %	5.7 %
Fq>0	54 %	65 %	64 %	59 %	51 %	68 %

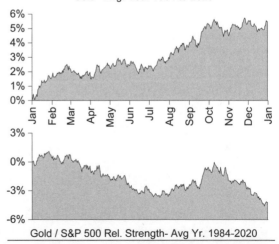

Gold - Avg. Year 1984 to 2020

Gold / S&P 500 Rel. Strength- Avg Yr. 1984-2020

Gold Performance

Gold Monthly % Gain (1984-2020)

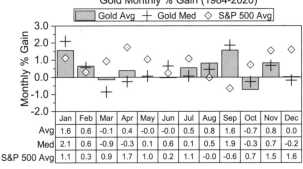

	Jan	Feb	Mar	Apr	May	Jun	Jul	Aug	Sep	Oct	Nov	Dec
Avg	1.6	0.6	-0.1	0.4	-0.0	-0.0	0.5	0.8	1.6	-0.7	0.8	0.0
Med	2.1	0.6	-0.9	-0.3	0.1	0.6	0.1	0.5	1.9	-0.3	0.7	-0.2
S&P 500 Avg	1.1	0.3	0.9	1.7	1.0	0.2	1.1	-0.0	-0.6	0.7	1.5	1.6

Fq Gold Gain > 0% (1984-2020)

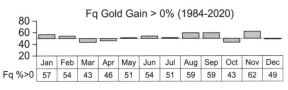

	Jan	Feb	Mar	Apr	May	Jun	Jul	Aug	Sep	Oct	Nov	Dec
Fq %>0	57	54	43	46	51	54	51	59	59	43	62	49

Fq % Gold Gain > S&P 500 % (1984-2020)

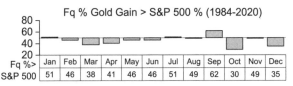

	Jan	Feb	Mar	Apr	May	Jun	Jul	Aug	Sep	Oct	Nov	Dec
Fq %> S&P 500	51	46	38	41	46	46	51	49	62	30	49	35

Gold % Gain 5 Year (2016-2020)

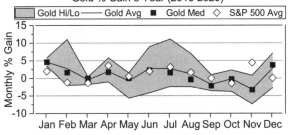

Gold Performance 2020-2021

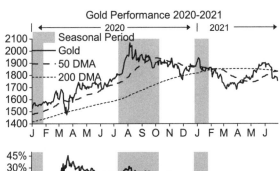

Relative Strength, % Gain vs. S&P 500

Market Indices & Rates
Weekly Values**

Stock Markets	2019	2020
Dow	26,922	25,827
S&P500	2,990	3,130
Nasdaq	8,162	10,208
TSX	16,542	15,597
FTSE	7,553	6,157
DAX	12,569	12,528
Nikkei	21,746	22,306
Hang Seng	28,775	25,373

Commodities	2019	2020
Oil	57.34	40.65
Gold	1388.7	1772.9

Bond Yields	2019	2020
USA 5 Yr Treasury	1.84	0.29
USA 10 Yr T	2.04	0.68
USA 20 Yr T	2.34	1.20
Moody's Aaa	3.26	2.37
Moody's Baa	4.30	3.55
CAN 5 Yr T	1.53	0.38
CAN 10 Yr T	1.57	0.56

Money Market	2019	2020
USA Fed Funds	2.50	0.25
USA 3 Mo T-B	2.18	0.14
CAN tgt overnight rate	1.75	0.25
CAN 3 Mo T-B	1.66	0.20

Foreign Exchange	2019	2020
EUR/USD	1.12	1.12
GBP/USD	1.25	1.25
USD/CAD	1.31	1.35
USD/JPY	108.47	107.51

JULY

M	T	W	T	F	S	S
				1	2	3
4	5	6	7	8	9	10
11	12	13	14	15	16	17
18	19	20	21	22	23	24
25	26	27	28	29	30	31

AUGUST

M	T	W	T	F	S	S
1	2	3	4	5	6	7
8	9	10	11	12	13	14
15	16	17	18	19	20	21
22	23	24	25	26	27	28
29	30	31				

SEPTEMBER

M	T	W	T	F	S	S
		1	2	3	4	5
6	7	8	9	10	11	12
13	14	15	16	17	18	19
20	21	22	23	24	25	26
27	28	29	30			

GOLD MINERS – DIG GAINS

(Stocks) ① Jul27-Sep25 ② Dec23-Feb14

The gold miners sector tends to perform well at approximately the same time of the year that gold bullion performs well. As gold bullion moves higher in price, gold miners benefit from their gold in the ground increasing in value.

Gold miners have their main seasonal period of strength from July 27 to September 25. Gold miners tend to perform well as gold bullion tends to increase at this time due to increased demand to make gold jewelery for fourth quarter consumption.

10% gain & 68% of the time positive

Gold miners also tend to perform well at the beginning of the year as Chinese New Year approaches. The Chinese buy a large amount of their gold in the period leading up to Chinese New Year. Over the years, this trend has become more predominant as the wealth of Chinese citizens has increased.

Combining the two gold seasonal trades together has proven to be beneficial as the frequency of gains for the combined trade of 68% is higher than the 54% and 62% success rates of the summer and winter trades respectively.

Covid-19 Pandemic Update. In 2021, gold miners started the year with fairly flat performance. In April, as the stock market moved higher and the price of gold moved higher, gold miners performed well. Gold miners peaked in late May and moved lower in June.

XAU* vs. S&P 500 - 1984/85 to 2020/21   Positive ▢

	Jul 27 to Sep 25		Dec 23 to Feb 14		Compound Growth	
Year	S&P 500	XAU	S&P 500	XAU	S&P 500	XAU
1984/85	10.4 %	20.8 %	10.2 %	10.6 %	21.6 %	33.6 %
1985/86	-6.1	-5.5	4.2	-2.0	-2.2	-7.2
1986/87	-3.5	36.9	12.4	14.4	8.5	56.6
1987/88	3.5	23.0	3.1	-15.9	6.7	3.4
1988/89	1.7	-11.9	5.4	12.1	7.2	-1.3
1989/90	1.8	10.5	-4.4	6.8	-2.7	18.1
1990/91	-13.4	3.8	9.8	-0.8	-4.9	3.1
1991/92	1.6	-11.9	6.6	9.8	8.2	-3.3
1992/93	0.7	-3.8	1.0	8.9	1.6	4.8
1993/94	1.9	-7.3	0.6	-1.4	2.5	-8.6
1994/95	1.4	18.2	5.0	-4.4	6.4	13.0
1995/96	3.6	-1.0	7.1	20.8	11.0	19.6
1996/97	7.9	-1.0	8.0	-2.2	16.4	-3.2
1997/98	-0.1	8.7	7.0	6.9	6.9	16.2
1998/99	-8.4	12.0	2.2	8.8	-6.4	21.9
1999/00	-5.2	16.9	-3.2	-1.3	-8.3	15.3
2000/01	-0.9	-2.8	0.8	-12.5	-0.2	-15.0
2001/02	-15.9	3.2	-2.5	23.7	-17.9	27.6
2002/03	-1.6	29.8	-6.8	-3.7	-8.2	25.1
2003/04	0.5	11.0	4.8	-0.8	5.3	10.1
2004/05	2.4	16.5	-0.3	-3.8	2.1	12.1
2005/06	-1.3	20.6	0.6	10.0	-0.7	32.6
2006/07	4.6	-11.8	3.2	3.7	7.9	-8.5
2007/08	2.3	14.0	-9.1	5.3	-7.0	20.1
2008/09	-3.9	-18.5	-5.1	19.2	-8.8	-2.8
2009/10	6.7	6.0	-3.8	-3.8	2.6	2.0
2010/11	3.0	14.7	5.8	-5.0	9.0	8.9
2011/12	-14.7	-13.7	7.7	3.8	-8.1	-10.4
2012/13	6.0	24.0	6.4	-7.2	12.8	15.1
2013/14	0.1	-5.6	1.1	26.8	1.2	19.8
2014/15	-0.6	-16.4	0.9	18.0	0.3	-1.3
2015/16	-7.1	-2.6	-8.5	33.7	-15.1	30.2
2016/17	-0.2	-7.0	3.4	29.1	3.2	20.0
2017/18	0.8	1.5	0.6	1.8	1.3	3.3
2018/19	2.8	-13.5	13.6	8.5	16.7	-6.0
2019/20	-1.4	4.3	4.9	4.6	3.5	9.0
2020/21	2.6	-7.1	6.7	0.8	9.5	-6.3
Avg.	-0.5 %	4.2 %	2.7 %	6.0 %	2.2 %	9.9 %
Fq>0	57 %	54 %	76 %	62 %	65 %	68 %

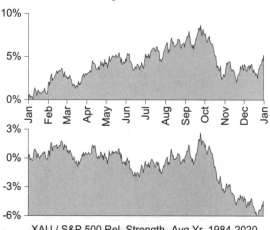

XAU - Avg. Year 1984 to 2020

XAU / S&P 500 Rel. Strength- Avg Yr. 1984-2020

ⓘ *XAU- PHLX Gold Silver Index consists of 12 precious metal mining companies.*

- 83 -

Gold Miners Performance

XAU Monthly % Gain (1984-2020)

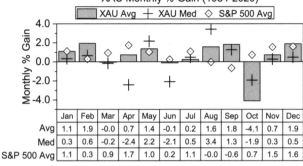

	Jan	Feb	Mar	Apr	May	Jun	Jul	Aug	Sep	Oct	Nov	Dec
Avg	1.1	1.9	-0.0	0.7	1.4	-0.1	0.2	1.6	1.8	-4.1	0.7	1.9
Med	0.3	0.6	-0.2	-2.4	2.2	-2.1	0.5	3.4	1.3	-1.9	0.3	0.5
S&P 500 Avg	1.1	0.3	0.9	1.7	1.0	0.2	1.1	-0.0	-0.6	0.7	1.5	1.6

Fq XAU Gain > 0% (1984-2020)

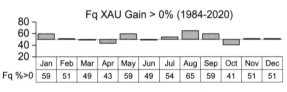

	Jan	Feb	Mar	Apr	May	Jun	Jul	Aug	Sep	Oct	Nov	Dec
Fq %>0	59	51	49	43	59	49	54	65	59	41	51	51

Fq % XAU Gain > S&P 500 % (1984-2020)

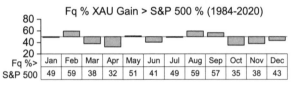

	Jan	Feb	Mar	Apr	May	Jun	Jul	Aug	Sep	Oct	Nov	Dec
Fq %> S&P 500	49	59	38	32	51	41	49	59	57	35	38	43

XAU % Gain 5 Year (2016-2020)

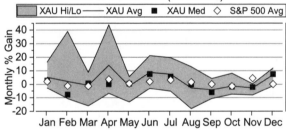

XAU Performance 2020-2021

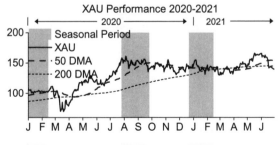

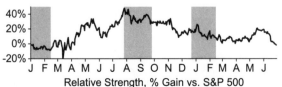

Relative Strength, % Gain vs. S&P 500

Market Indices & Rates
Weekly Values**

Stock Markets	2019	2020
Dow	27,332	26,075
S&P500	3,014	3,185
Nasdaq	8,244	10,617
TSX	16,488	15,714
FTSE	7,506	6,095
DAX	12,323	12,634
Nikkei	21,686	22,291
Hang Seng	28,472	25,727

Commodities	2019	2020
Oil	60.21	40.55
Gold	1407.6	1803.1

Bond Yields	2019	2020
USA 5 Yr Treasury	1.86	0.30
USA 10 Yr T	2.12	0.65
USA 20 Yr T	2.42	1.12
Moody's Aaa	3.34	2.19
Moody's Baa	4.37	3.39
CAN 5 Yr T	1.55	0.36
CAN 10 Yr T	1.61	0.55

Money Market	2019	2020
USA Fed Funds	2.50	0.25
USA 3 Mo T-B	2.10	0.13
CAN tgt overnight rate	1.75	0.25
CAN 3 Mo T-B	1.66	0.18

Foreign Exchange	2019	2020
EUR/USD	1.13	1.13
GBP/USD	1.26	1.26
USD/CAD	1.30	1.36
USD/JPY	107.91	106.93

JULY

M	T	W	T	F	S	S
				1	2	3
4	5	6	7	8	9	10
11	12	13	14	15	16	17
18	19	20	21	22	23	24
25	26	27	28	29	30	31

AUGUST

M	T	W	T	F	S	S
1	2	3	4	5	6	7
8	9	10	11	12	13	14
15	16	17	18	19	20	21
22	23	24	25	26	27	28
29	30	31				

SEPTEMBER

M	T	W	T	F	S	S
		1	2	3	4	5
6	7	8	9	10	11	12
13	14	15	16	17	18	19
20	21	22	23	24	25	26
27	28	29	30			

VOLATILITY INDEX
July 3rd to October 9th

The Chicago Board Options Exchange Market Volatility Index (VIX) is often referred to as a fear index as it measures investors' expectations of market volatility over the next thirty day period. The higher the VIX value, the greater the expectation of volatility and vice versa.

From 1990 to June 2021, the long-term average of the VIX is 19.5. In this time period, the VIX has bottomed at approximately 10 in the mid-90's, and the mid-2000's. In both cases, the VIX dropped below 10 for a few days.

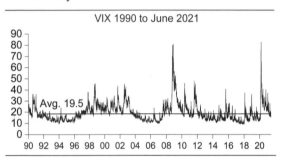

VIX 1990 to June 2021

Avg. 19.5

VIX - Avg. Year 1990 to 2020

S&P 500 Avg Yr. 1990 - 2020

VIX* vs. S&P 500 1990 to 2020		
		Positive
July 3 to Oct 9	S&P 500	VIX %Gain
1990	-15.1%	88.9%
1991	-0.2	5.2
1992	-2.2	47.8
1993	3.3	6.3
1994	2.0	3.9
1995	6.2	30.5
1996	3.4	13.4
1997	7.4	13.3
1998	-14.1	138.8
1999	-4.0	9.8
2000	-3.6	22.9
2001	-14.6	85.7
2002	-18.1	45.5
2003	4.5	-1.1
2004	-0.3	-0.2
2005	0.1	28.0
2006	6.3	-10.7
2007	3.0	4.7
2008	-27.9	146.6
2009	19.5	-17.3
2010	13.9	-31.2
2011	-13.8	128.1
2012	5.6	-2.6
2013	2.6	19.2
2014	-2.4	73.4
2015	-2.9	1.7
2016	2.4	-8.7
2017	5.0	-7.6
2018	5.6	2.2
2019	-1.8	44.2
2020	11.1	-9.7
Avg	-0.6%	28%
Fq > 0	55%	71%

Levels below 15 are often associated with investor complacency, as investors are expecting very little volatility. Very often when a stock market correction occurs in this state, it can be sharp and severe. Knowing the trends of the VIX can be useful in adjusting the amount of risk in a portfolio.

From 1990 to 2020, during the period of July 3 to October 9, the VIX has increased 71% of the time. On average, the VIX tends to start increasing in July, particularly after the earnings season gets underway. After mid-July, without the expectation of strong earnings ahead, investors tend to focus on economic forecasts that often become more dire in the second half of the year.

In addition, stock market analysts tend to reduce their earnings forecasts at this time. Both of these effects tend to add volatility in the markets, increasing the VIX. The VIX tends to peak in October as the stock market often starts to establish a rising trend at this time.

(i) * VIX - ticker symbol for the Chicago Board Options Exchange Market Volatility Index, measure implied volatility of S&P 500 index options

VIX Performance

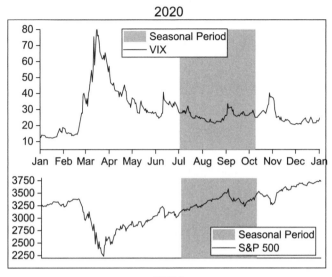

2020

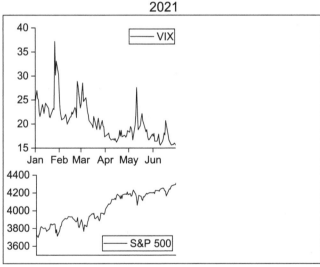

2021

Market Indices & Rates
Weekly Values**

Stock Markets	2019	2020
Dow	27,154	26,672
S&P500	2,977	3,225
Nasdaq	8,146	10,503
TSX	16,486	16,123
FTSE	7,509	6,290
DAX	12,260	12,920
Nikkei	21,467	22,696
Hang Seng	28,765	25,089

Commodities	2019	2020
Oil	55.63	40.59
Gold	1439.7	1807.4

Bond Yields	2019	2020
USA 5 Yr Treasury	1.80	0.29
USA 10 Yr T	2.05	0.64
USA 20 Yr T	2.35	1.11
Moody's Aaa	3.31	2.13
Moody's Baa	4.31	3.32
CAN 5 Yr T	1.42	0.35
CAN 10 Yr T	1.51	0.53

Money Market	2019	2020
USA Fed Funds	2.50	0.25
USA 3 Mo T-B	2.02	0.11
CAN tgt overnight rate	1.75	0.25
CAN 3 Mo T-B	1.65	0.17

Foreign Exchange	2019	2020
EUR/USD	1.12	1.14
GBP/USD	1.25	1.26
USD/CAD	1.31	1.36
USD/JPY	107.71	107.02

JULY

M	T	W	T	F	S	S
				1	2	3
4	5	6	7	8	9	10
11	12	13	14	15	16	17
18	19	20	21	22	23	24
25	26	27	28	29	30	31

AUGUST

M	T	W	T	F	S	S
1	2	3	4	5	6	7
8	9	10	11	12	13	14
15	16	17	18	19	20	21
22	23	24	25	26	27	28
29	30	31				

SEPTEMBER

M	T	W	T	F	S	S
		1	2	3	4	5
6	7	8	9	10	11	12
13	14	15	16	17	18	19
20	21	22	23	24	25	26
27	28	29	30			

In 2020, the VIX rose sharply in February and March as the stock market plummeted due to the Covid-19 pandemic. After the stock market bottomed on March 23 VIX declined into the summer months and marginally declined in its positive seasonal period.

In 2021, the VIX peaked in February and moved lower into the summer months.

VERIZON

①SELL SHORT (Dec30-Mar12)
②SELL SHORT (May2-May25) ③LONG (Aug24-Oct3)

Verizon pays a much higher dividend than the average company in the stock market. When the stock market heads lower, higher dividend paying companies tend to be more attractive.

One of the weakest months of the year for the stock market is September. It is also a time period when interest rates tend to decline on a seasonal basis, benefiting high dividend paying companies.

9% gain

Both of these factors help to drive Verizon higher from August 24 to October 3. In addition, Verizon's busiest quarter for revenue generation is the fourth quarter of the year. Investor's try to front run this trend, which helps to push Verizon up in its strong seasonal period.

Verizon has weak seasonal periods from December 30 to March 12 and from May 2 to May 25.

Covid-19 Performance Update. In 2021, in the first half of the year, Verizon was a poor performer relative to the S&P 500. It underperformed in both of its weak seasonal periods.

*VZ - stock symbol for Verizon, which trades on the NYSE, adjusted for stock splits.

Verizon vs. S&P 500 1990 to 2020

Negative Short ☐   Positive Long ▦

Year	Dec 30 to Mar 12 S&P 500	VZ	May 2 to May 25 S&P 500	VZ	Aug 24 to Oct 3 S&P 500	VZ	Compound Growth S&P 500	VZ
1990	-4.2 %	-16.4 %	6.7 %	7.9 %	1.4 %	16.0 %	3.7 %	24.3 %
1991	12.6	-12.5	-0.7	-8.7	-2.5	-8.9	9.0	11.5
1992	-0.6	-10.6	0.4	-2.0	-1.1	-2.5	-1.3	9.9
1993	2.7	0.2	2.0	4.9	1.3	11.7	6.1	6.0
1994	-0.9	-13.6	1.2	1.0	-0.6	-3.2	-0.3	8.9
1995	6.2	5.2	2.8	-1.4	4.5	6.7	14.1	2.5
1996	3.4	-6.4	3.7	-1.4	3.9	5.3	11.4	13.6
1997	6.3	-3.9	6.1	2.2	4.5	12.1	17.8	13.9
1998	12.2	5.4	-0.9	-4.4	-7.3	18.8	3.1	17.3
1999	4.3	-7.6	-3.8	-4.2	-5.7	6.8	-5.4	19.9
2000	-4.7	-7.2	-5.9	-12.7	-5.3	17.6	-15.0	42.1
2001	-10.6	-5.3	0.9	-4.8	-7.7	5.5	-16.8	16.4
2002	0.4	-1.7	-0.2	4.7	-13.0	4.0	-12.8	0.7
2003	-8.1	-14.0	1.8	-1.8	3.7	-4.2	-3.0	11.2
2004	1.0	10.5	0.5	-6.1	3.3	1.5	4.8	-3.6
2005	-1.1	-11.7	2.9	-1.1	0.7	-2.5	2.5	10.1
2006	2.2	13.0	-2.5	-5.0	3.2	9.0	2.8	-0.4
2007	-0.8	-1.8	2.0	10.4	5.3	7.3	6.5	-2.1
2008	-11.5	-22.5	-2.4	-5.7	-14.9	-11.5	-26.5	14.6
2009	-13.7	-15.1	1.1	-5.7	-0.1	-4.7	-12.8	15.9
2010	2.1	-11.1	-9.5	-5.2	7.4	11.8	-0.8	30.7
2011	3.5	0.8	-3.2	-3.7	-5.4	1.1	-5.2	4.0
2012	8.6	-1.8	-6.3	2.2	3.5	9.5	5.3	9.1
2013	10.7	12.7	4.2	-1.9	0.9	-1.3	16.4	-12.2
2014	1.5	-5.7	0.9	5.3	-1.0	2.2	1.3	2.3
2015	-1.2	2.5	0.8	-1.6	-1.0	-7.1	-1.3	-7.9
2016	-2.7	11.3	1.2	-2.1	-1.2	-1.4	-2.7	-10.7
2017	5.5	-8.2	1.1	-1.2	3.7	3.3	10.6	13.1
2018	4.1	-7.8	2.5	-0.6	2.4	0.0	9.3	8.5
2019	12.3	3.9	-3.3	5.0	2.2	5.5	11.0	-3.6
2020	-23.4	-16.8	4.4	-4.8	-1.4	0.4	-21.2	22.9
Avg.	0.5 %	-4.4 %	0.3 %	-1.4 %	-0.5 %	3.5 %	0.3 %	9.3 %
Fq>0	58 %	32 %	65 %	29 %	52 %	68 %	55 %	77 %

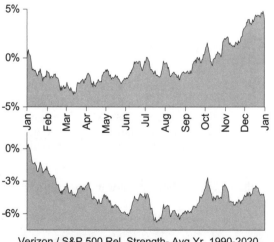

Verizon - Avg. Year 1990-2020

Verizon / S&P 500 Rel. Strength- Avg Yr. 1990-2020

Verizon Performance

Verizon Monthly % Gain (1990-2020)

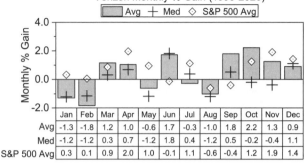

	Jan	Feb	Mar	Apr	May	Jun	Jul	Aug	Sep	Oct	Nov	Dec
Avg	-1.3	-1.8	1.2	1.0	-0.6	1.7	-0.3	-1.0	1.8	2.2	1.3	0.9
Med	-1.2	-1.2	0.3	0.7	-1.2	1.8	0.4	-1.2	0.5	-0.2	-0.4	1.1
S&P 500 Avg	0.3	0.1	0.9	2.0	1.0	-0.1	1.1	-0.6	-0.4	1.2	1.9	1.4

Fq Verizon Gain > 0% (1990-2020)

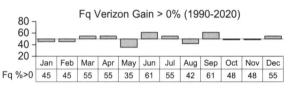

	Jan	Feb	Mar	Apr	May	Jun	Jul	Aug	Sep	Oct	Nov	Dec
Fq %>0	45	45	55	55	35	61	55	42	61	48	48	55

Fq % Verizon Gain > S&P 500 % (1990-2020)

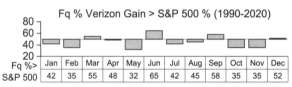

	Jan	Feb	Mar	Apr	May	Jun	Jul	Aug	Sep	Oct	Nov	Dec
Fq %> S&P 500	42	35	55	48	32	65	42	45	58	35	35	52

Verizon % Gain 5 Year (2016-2020)

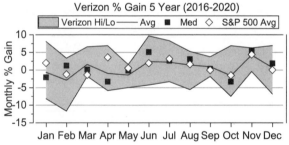

Verizon Performance 2020-2021

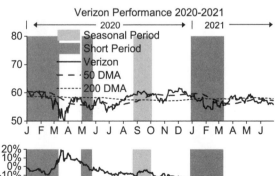

Relative Strength, % Gain vs. S&P 500

Market Indices & Rates
Weekly Values**

Stock Markets	2019	2020
Dow	27,192	26,470
S&P500	3,026	3,216
Nasdaq	8,330	10,363
TSX	16,531	15,997
FTSE	7,549	6,124
DAX	12,420	12,838
Nikkei	21,658	22,752
Hang Seng	28,398	24,705

Commodities	2019	2020
Oil	56.20	41.14
Gold	1420.4	1902.1

Bond Yields	2019	2020
USA 5 Yr Treasury	1.85	0.27
USA 10 Yr T	2.08	0.59
USA 20 Yr T	2.38	1.03
Moody's Aaa	3.31	2.01
Moody's Baa	4.21	3.17
CAN 5 Yr T	1.40	0.35
CAN 10 Yr T	1.47	0.50

Money Market	2019	2020
USA Fed Funds	2.50	0.25
USA 3 Mo T-B	2.08	0.11
CAN tgt overnight rate	1.75	0.25
CAN 3 Mo T-B	1.65	0.17

Foreign Exchange	2019	2020
EUR/USD	1.11	1.17
GBP/USD	1.24	1.28
USD/CAD	1.32	1.34
USD/JPY	108.68	106.14

JULY

M	T	W	T	F	S	S
				1	2	3
4	5	6	7	8	9	10
11	12	13	14	15	16	17
18	19	20	21	22	23	24
25	26	27	28	29	30	31

AUGUST

M	T	W	T	F	S	S
1	2	3	4	5	6	7
8	9	10	11	12	13	14
15	16	17	18	19	20	21
22	23	24	25	26	27	28
29	30	31				

SEPTEMBER

M	T	W	T	F	S	S
		1	2	3	4	
5	6	7	8	9	10	11
12	13	14	15	16	17	18
19	20	21	22	23	24	25
26	27	28	29	30		

Seasonal Investment Timeline[1]

Investment	Season		2021 2022
Core Positions			O N D J F M A M J J A S O N D
S&P 500	Oct 28 - May 5		
TSX Composite	Oct 28 - May 5		
Cash	May 6 - Oct 27		
Primary Sectors			
[4]Consumer Staples			
Financials	Dec 15 - Apr 13		
Energy	Feb 25 - May 9	Jul 24 - Oct 3	
[2]Utilities	Jul 17 - Oct 3	Jan 1 - Mar 13 (S)	
Health Care	Aug 15 - Oct 18		
Information Tech	Oct 9 - Jan 17	Apr 16 - Apr 30	
Consumer Disc.	Oct 28 - Apr 22		
Industrials	Oct 28 - Dec 31	Jan 23- May 5	
Materials	Oct 28 - Jan 6	Jan 23 - May 5	
Small Cap	Dec 19 - Mar 7		
Secondary Sectors			
Silver Bullion	Dec 27- Feb 22		
[2]Platinum	Jan 1 - May 31		
Software Jan1 - Jan19	Jun 1 - Jun 30	Oct 10 - Dec 5	
[3]Semiconductors	Jan 1 - Mar 7	Oct 28 - Nov 6	
Canadian Dollar	Apr 1 - Apr 30	Aug 20 - Sep 25	
Biotech	Jun 23 - Sep 13		
Gold Bullion	Jul 12 - Oct 9	Dec 27 - Jan 26	
Gold Miners	Jul 27 - Sep 25	Dec 23 - Feb 14	
Agriculture	Sep 26 - Nov 11		
Transportation Jan23-Apr16	Aug 3 - Oct 9 (S)	Oct 10 - Nov 13	
Natural Gas Mar22 - Jun19	Sep 6 - Dec 21	Dec 22 - Dec 31(S)	
Airlines	Oct 3 - Nov 6	Aug 1- Aug 31 (S)	
Canadian Banks	Oct 10 - Dec 31	Jan 23 - Apr 13	
Retail	Oct 28 - Nov 29	Jan 21 - Apr 12	
Homebuilders	Oct 28 - Feb 3	Apr 27- Jun 13(S)	
Metals & Mining	Nov 19 - Jan 5	Jan 23 - May 5	
Emerging Markets	Nov 24 - April 18		
[9]Aerospace & Defense	Dec 12 - May 5		
[9]Automotive Dec14 - Jan7	Feb 24 - Apr 24	Aug 3 - Oct 3 (S)	
US REITS	Mar 8 - Sep 20	Sep 21- Oct 9 (S)	
Other Market / Sector Trades			
Nikkei 225	May 6 - Nov 19 (S)		
VIX (CBOE)	Jul 3 - Oct 9		
[7]Canadian Snowbird Trade	Oct 28 - Dec 18		
[9]Mid Caps Jan 9 - Mar 7	Jun 3 - Jun 26 (S)	Nov 23 - Dec 31	
Value vs Growth	Feb 26 - Apr 19	Nov 29 - Jan 6	
Commodities			
Copper	Jan 29 - Mar 5	Jun 24 - Jul 31	
Currency			
CAD / USD	Apr 1 - Apr 30	Aug 20 - Sep 25	
EUR / USD	Nov 17 - Dec 31		
USD / EUR	Jan 1 - Feb 7		
Fixed Income			
[3]U.S. Gov. Bonds	May 9 - Oct 3		
[3]U.S. High Yield	Nov 24 - Jan 8		
10YR Inflation Break-Even	Dec 20 - Mar 7		

Long Investment ▓▓▓▓▓   Short Investment (S) ▭

[2]Thackray's 2012 Investor's Guide [3]Thackray's 2013 Investor's Guide [4]Thackray's 2014 Investor's Guide [5]Thackray's 2015 Investor's Guide [6]Thackray's 2016 Investor's Guide [7]Thackray's 2017 Investor's Guide [8]Thackray's 2018 Investor's Guide [9]Thackray's 2019 Investor's Guide

Seasonal Investment Timeline[1]

Investment Stocks	Season			2021	2022
				O N D J F M A M	J J A S O N D

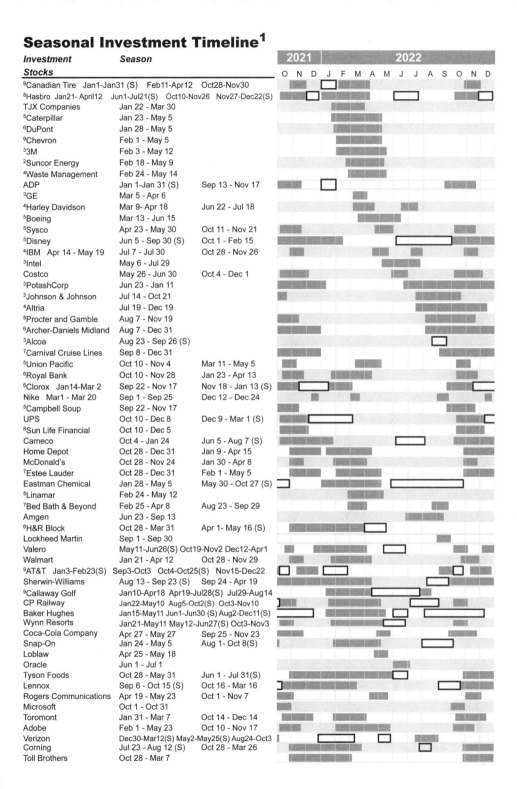

Investment Stocks	Season		
[9]Canadian Tire	Jan1-Jan31 (S)	Feb11-Apr12	Oct28-Nov30
[8]Hasbro	Jan21- April12	Jun1-Jul21(S)	Oct10-Nov26 Nov27-Dec22(S)
TJX Companies	Jan 22 - Mar 30		
[5]Caterpillar	Jan 23 - May 5		
[6]DuPont	Jan 28 - May 5		
[9]Chevron	Feb 1 - May 5		
[3]3M	Feb 3 - May 12		
[2]Suncor Energy	Feb 18 - May 9		
[4]Waste Management	Feb 24 - May 14		
ADP	Jan 1-Jan 31 (S)	Sep 13 - Nov 17	
[3]GE	Mar 5 - Apr 6		
[4]Harley Davidson	Mar 9- Apr 18	Jun 22 - Jul 18	
[5]Boeing	Mar 13 - Jun 15		
[5]Sysco	Apr 23 - May 30	Oct 11 - Nov 21	
[5]Disney	Jun 5 - Sep 30 (S)	Oct 1 - Feb 15	
[4]IBM Apr 14 - May 19	Jul 7 - Jul 30	Oct 28 - Nov 26	
[3]Intel	May 6 - Jul 29		
Costco	May 26 - Jun 30	Oct 4 - Dec 1	
[3]PotashCorp	Jun 23 - Jan 11		
[3]Johnson & Johnson	Jul 14 - Oct 21		
[4]Altria	Jul 19 - Dec 19		
[8]Procter and Gamble	Aug 7 - Nov 19		
[6]Archer-Daniels Midland	Aug 7 - Dec 31		
[3]Alcoa	Aug 23 - Sep 26 (S)		
[7]Carnival Cruise Lines	Sep 8 - Dec 31		
[5]Union Pacific	Oct 10 - Nov 4	Mar 11 - May 5	
[6]Royal Bank	Oct 10 - Nov 28	Jan 23 - Apr 13	
[6]Clorox Jan14-Mar 2	Sep 22 - Nov 17	Nov 18 - Jan 13 (S)	
Nike Mar1 - Mar 20	Sep 1 - Sep 25	Dec 12 - Dec 24	
[5]Campbell Soup	Sep 22 - Nov 17		
UPS	Oct 10 - Dec 8	Dec 9 - Mar 1 (S)	
[8]Sun Life Financial	Oct 10 - Dec 5		
Cameco	Oct 4 - Jan 24	Jun 5 - Aug 7 (S)	
Home Depot	Oct 28 - Dec 31	Jan 9 - Apr 15	
McDonald's	Oct 28 - Nov 24	Jan 30 - Apr 8	
[7]Estee Lauder	Oct 28 - Dec 31	Feb 1 - May 5	
Eastman Chemical	Jan 28 - May 5	May 30 - Oct 27 (S)	
[5]Linamar	Feb 24 - May 12		
[7]Bed Bath & Beyond	Feb 25 - Apr 8	Aug 23 - Sep 29	
Amgen	Jun 23 - Sep 13		
[6]H&R Block	Oct 28 - Mar 31	Apr 1- May 16 (S)	
Lockheed Martin	Sep 1 - Sep 30		
Valero	May11-Jun26(S)	Oct19-Nov2	Dec12-Apr1
Walmart	Jan 21 - Apr 12	Oct 28 - Nov 29	
[9]AT&T Jan3-Feb23(S)	Sep3-Oct3	Oct4-Oct25(S)	Nov15-Dec22
Sherwin-Williams	Aug 13 - Sep 23 (S)	Sep 24 - Apr 19	
[9]Callaway Golf	Jan10-Apr18	Apr19-Jul28(S)	Jul29-Aug14
CP Railway	Jan22-May10	Aug5-Oct2(S)	Oct3-Nov10
Baker Hughes	Jan15-May11	Jun1-Jun30 (S)	Aug2-Dec11(S)
Wynn Resorts	Jan21-May11	May12-Jun27(S)	Oct3-Nov3
Coca-Cola Company	Apr 27 - May 27	Sep 25 - Nov 23	
Snap-On	Jan 24 - May 5	Aug 1- Oct 8(S)	
Loblaw	Apr 25 - May 18		
Oracle	Jun 1 - Jul 1		
Tyson Foods	Oct 28 - May 31	Jun 1 - Jul 31(S)	
Lennox	Sep 6 - Oct 15 (S)	Oct 16 - Mar 16	
Rogers Communications	Apr 19 - May 23	Oct 1 - Nov 7	
Microsoft	Oct 1 - Oct 31		
Toromont	Jan 31 - Mar 7	Oct 14 - Dec 14	
Adobe	Feb 1 - May 23	Oct 10 - Nov 17	
Verizon	Dec30-Mar12(S)	May2-May25(S)	Aug24-Oct3
Corning	Jul 23 - Aug 12 (S)	Oct 28 - Mar 26	
Toll Brothers	Oct 28 - Mar 7		

Long Investment ▨▨▨▨   Short Investment (S) ▭

[2]Thackray's 2012 Investor's Guide [3]Thackray's 2013 Investor's Guide [4]Thackray's 2014 Investor's Guide [5]Thackray's 2015 Investor's Guide
[6]Thackray's 2016 Investor's Guide [7]Thackray's 2017 Investor's Guide [8]Thackray's 2018 Investor's Guide [9]Thackray's 2019 Investor's Guide

AUGUST

	MONDAY	TUESDAY	WEDNESDAY
WEEK 31	**1** 30 CAN Market Closed- Civic Day	**2** 29	**3** 28
WEEK 32	**8** 23	**9** 22	**10** 21
WEEK 33	**15** 16	**16** 15	**17** 14
WEEK 34	**22** 9	**23** 8	**24** 7
WEEK 35	**29** 2	**30** 1	**31**

THURSDAY	FRIDAY
4 27	**5** 26
11 20	**12** 19
18 13	**19** 12
25 6	**26** 5
1	2

SEPTEMBER

M	T	W	T	F	S	S
			1	2	3	4
5	6	7	8	9	10	11
12	13	14	15	16	17	18
19	20	21	22	23	24	25
26	27	28	29	30		

OCTOBER

M	T	W	T	F	S	S
					1	2
3	4	5	6	7	8	9
10	11	12	13	14	15	16
17	18	19	20	21	22	23
24	25	26	27	28	29	30
31						

NOVEMBER

M	T	W	T	F	S	S
	1	2	3	4	5	6
7	8	9	10	11	12	13
14	15	16	17	18	19	20
21	22	23	24	25	26	27
28	29	30				

DECEMBER

M	T	W	T	F	S	S
			1	2	3	4
5	6	7	8	9	10	11
12	13	14	15	16	17	18
19	20	21	22	23	24	25
26	27	28	29	30	31	

AUGUST
S U M M A R Y

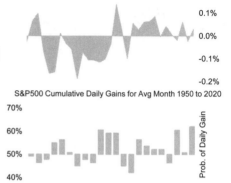

S&P500 Cumulative Daily Gains for Avg Month 1950 to 2020

Prob. of Daily Gain

	Dow Jones	S&P 500	Nasdaq	TSX Comp
Month Rank	10	10	11	10
# Up	40	39	27	21
# Down	31	32	22	15
% Pos	56	55	55	58
% Avg. Gain	0.0	0.0	0.3	-0.1

Dow & S&P 1950-2020, Nasdaq 1972-2020, TSX 1985-2020

♦ August is typically a marginal month and it has been the third worst month on average for the S&P 500 from 1950 to 2020. ♦ If there is a summer rally in July, it is often in jeopardy in August. ♦ In 2020, the S&P 500 rallied sharply in August. ♦ The TSX Composite is usually one of the better performing markets in August, but its strength is largely dependent on oil and gold stocks. In 2020, the TSX Composite lagged the S&P 500 in August.

BEST / WORST AUGUST BROAD MKTS. 2011-2020

BEST AUGUST MARKETS
- ♦ Nasdaq (2020) 9.6%
- ♦ Dow (2020) 7.6%
- ♦ Russell 1000 (2020) 7.2%

WORST AUGUST MARKETS
- ♦ Nikkei 225 (2011) -8.9%
- ♦ Russell 2000 (2011) -8.8%
- ♦ Nikkei 225 (2015) - 8.2%

Index Values End of Month

	2011	2012	2013	2014	2015	2016	2017	2018	2019	2021
Dow	11,614	13,091	14,810	17,098	16,528	18,401	21,948	25,965	26,403	28,430
S&P 500	1,219	1,407	1,633	2,003	1,972	2,171	2,472	2,902	2,926	3,500
Nasdaq	2,579	3,067	3,590	4,580	4,777	5,213	6,429	8,110	7,963	11,775
TSX Comp.	12,769	11,949	12,654	15,626	13,859	14,598	15,212	16,263	16,442	16,514
Russell 1000	675	775	909	1,118	1,101	1,203	1,370	1,611	1,619	1,946
Russell 2000	727	812	1,011	1,174	1,159	1,240	1,405	1,741	1,495	1,562
FTSE 100	5,395	5,711	6,413	6,820	6,248	6,782	7,431	7,432	7,207	5,964
Nikkei 225	8,955	8,840	13,389	15,425	18,890	16,887	19,646	22,865	20,704	23,140

Percent Gain for August

	2011	2012	2013	2014	2015	2016	2017	2018	2019	2021
Dow	-4.4	0.6	-4.4	3.2	-6.6	-0.2	0.3	2.2	-1.7	7.6
S&P 500	-5.7	2.0	-3.1	3.8	-6.3	-0.1	0.1	3.0	-1.8	7.0
Nasdaq	-6.4	4.3	-1.0	4.8	-6.9	1.0	1.3	5.7	-2.6	9.6
TSX Comp.	-1.4	2.4	1.3	1.9	-4.2	0.1	0.4	-1.0	0.2	2.1
Russell 1000	-6.0	2.2	-3.0	3.9	-6.2	-0.1	0.1	3.2	-2.0	7.2
Russell 2000	-8.8	3.2	-3.3	4.8	-6.4	1.6	-1.4	4.2	-5.1	5.5
FTSE 100	-7.2	1.4	-3.1	1.3	-6.7	0.8	0.8	-4.1	-5.0	1.1
Nikkei 225	-8.9	1.7	-2.0	-1.3	-8.2	1.9	-1.4	1.4	-3.8	6.6

August Market Avg. Performance 2011 to 2020[1]

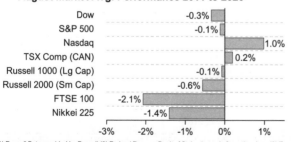

Dow	-0.3%
S&P 500	-0.1%
Nasdaq	1.0%
TSX Comp (CAN)	0.2%
Russell 1000 (Lg Cap)	-0.1%
Russell 2000 (Sm Cap)	-0.6%
FTSE 100	-2.1%
Nikkei 225	-1.4%

Interest Corner Aug[2]

	Fed Funds % [3]	3 Mo. T-Bill % [4]	10 Yr % [5]	20 Yr % [6]
2020	0.25	0.05	0.72	1.26
2019	2.25	1.99	1.50	1.78
2018	2.00	2.11	2.86	2.95
2017	1.25	1.01	2.12	2.47
2016	0.50	0.33	1.58	1.90

(1) Russell Data provided by Russell (2) Federal Reserve Bank of St. Louis- end of month values (3) Target rate set by FOMC (4)(5)(6) Constant yield maturities.

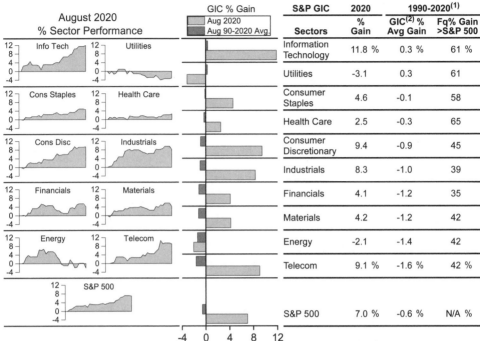

August 2020
% Sector Performance

GIC % Gain
Aug 2020
Aug 90-2020 Avg.

S&P GIC Sectors	2020 % Gain	1990-2020[1] GIC[2] % Avg Gain	1990-2020[1] Fq% Gain >S&P 500
Information Technology	11.8 %	0.3 %	61 %
Utilities	-3.1	0.3	61
Consumer Staples	4.6	-0.1	58
Health Care	2.5	-0.3	65
Consumer Discretionary	9.4	-0.9	45
Industrials	8.3	-1.0	39
Financials	4.1	-1.2	35
Materials	4.2	-1.2	42
Energy	-2.1	-1.4	42
Telecom	9.1 %	-1.6 %	42 %
S&P 500	7.0 %	-0.6 %	N/A %

Sector Commentary

♦ In August 2020, the growth sectors were largely the top performing sectors. ♦ The technology sector produced a gain of 11.8%. ♦ The consumer discretionary sector produced a gain of 9.4%. ♦ The cyclical sectors of the stock market also performed well. ♦ The worst performing sector of the stock market was the utilities sector with a loss of 3.1%. Most sectors of the stock market produced gains in August 2020.

Sub-Sector Commentary

♦ In August 2020, silver produced a large gain of 13.6%, which was largely driven by strong expectations of economic growth and strong performances from some of the cyclical sectors of the stock market. ♦ The transportation sector produced a gain of 13.2%. ♦ The auto sector produced a gain of 11.5%. ♦ On the negative side, gold produced a loss of 0.4%. Gold's negative performance and silver's strong positive performance indicates that the industrial properties of silver were the important characteristics driving the price of silver higher.

SELECTED SUB-SECTORS[3]

Gold	-0.4 %	0.8 %	48 %
Biotech (1993-2020)	1.3	0.7	57
Home-builders	5.2	0.5	55
Silver	13.6	0.2	52
Agriculture (1994-2020)	4.5	0.1	48
SOX (1995-2020)	5.8	0.1	50
Retail	8.7	0.0	61
Pharma	3.4	-0.5	55
Banks	2.8	-1.2	32
Chemicals	3.9	-1.3	42
Metals & Mining	3.9	-1.8	42
Railroads	9.7	-1.9	45
Transportation	13.2	-2.0	35
Automotive & Components	11.5	-2.9	35
Steel	8.4	-3.5	45

(1) Sector data provided by Standard and Poors (2) GIC is short form for Global Industry Classification (3) Sub Sector data provided by Standard and Poors, except where marked by symbol.

CORNING
① SELL SHORT (Jul23-Aug12)
② LONG (Oct28-Mar26)

Corning is an industrial company and as such has a similar seasonal cycle as the industrial sector.

The two strongest months of the year for Corning since 1990 have been November and March. Both of these months are the bookends of the strong seasonal period for Corning, which lasts from October 28 to March 26. In this period, from 1990 to 2020, Corning has produced an average gain of 23% and has been positive 74% of the time.

It should be noted that Corning's performance slips in April and May, underperforming the S&P 500 in both of these months. In general, Corning tends not to perform well in the summer months.

32% growth & 74% of the time positive

The weakest seasonal period for Corning from 1990 to 2020 has been from July 23 to August 12. In this period, Corning has produced an average loss of 4.6% and has only been positive 32% of the time.

Covid-19 Pandemic Update. In 2021, Corning had a slow start in January, but then rallied strongly in February and March and as a result outperformed the S&P 500 in its strong seasonal period that started in October 2020. In April 2021, Corning started to turn lower and underperform the S&P 500. Corning continued to perform poorly in May and June.

Corning vs. S&P 500 1990 to 2020

Positive Long   Negative Short

Year	Jul 23 to Aug 12 S&P 500	Jul 23 to Aug 12 GLW	Oct 28 to Mar 26 S&P 500	Oct 28 to Mar 26 GLW	Compound Growth S&P 500	Compound Growth GLW
1990	-7.2 %	-10.7 %	23.5 %	48.8 %	14.6 %	64.7 %
1991	1.3	1.3	6.2	-16.0	7.6	-17.1
1992	1.7	-2.7	7.0	-12.1	8.8	-9.7
1993	1.0	-2.3	-0.9	24.1	0.1	26.9
1994	1.9	-3.9	7.5	8.6	9.6	12.8
1995	0.3	-2.4	12.6	34.6	12.9	37.7
1996	5.0	6.0	12.8	20.7	18.5	13.4
1997	-0.8	3.7	25.5	3.3	24.5	-0.5
1998	-6.9	-8.7	20.4	63.8	12.2	78.0
1999	-4.6	-16.0	17.8	206.0	12.4	254.9
2000	-0.6	-2.9	-16.4	-68.3	-16.9	-67.4
2001	-1.7	18.8	3.1	-16.0	1.3	-31.8
2002	10.2	-51.5	-3.1	204.6	6.8	361.5
2003	0.2	-7.3	7.5	2.7	7.7	10.2
2004	-3.1	-20.2	4.1	-4.6	0.9	14.7
2005	-0.3	9.4	10.5	45.3	10.2	31.7
2006	2.1	-13.5	4.4	11.2	6.6	26.2
2007	-5.2	-11.6	-12.6	2.6	-17.2	14.5
2008	1.0	6.7	-1.9	40.2	-0.9	30.9
2009	5.4	-1.3	9.7	31.1	15.7	32.8
2010	-0.9	-3.3	11.1	16.4	10.1	20.3
2011	-12.4	-16.0	10.3	-6.6	-3.4	8.4
2012	3.2	-5.7	10.8	10.9	14.3	17.2
2013	-0.4	0.8	5.3	17.8	4.9	16.8
2014	-2.5	-8.9	4.8	19.2	2.2	29.9
2015	-1.3	-4.5	-1.5	10.9	-2.8	15.9
2016	0.4	5.6	9.9	19.6	10.3	12.9
2017	-1.3	-9.0	3.0	-10.2	1.7	-2.1
2018	1.1	12.4	6.0	9.5	7.2	-4.1
2019	-3.4	-16.8	-13.0	-28.5	-16.0	-16.5
2020	3.2	10.6	17.2	32.1	21.0	18.2
Avg.	-0.5 %	-4.6 %	6.5 %	23.3 %	6.0 %	32.3 %
Fq>0	48 %	32 %	77 %	74 %	81 %	74 %

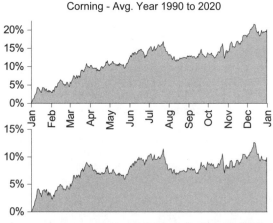

Corning - Avg. Year 1990 to 2020

Corning / S&P 500 Rel. Strength- Avg Yr. 1990-2020

ⓘ *GLW - stock symbol for Corning, which trades on the NYSE, adjusted for stock splits.*

Corning Performance

GLW Monthly % Gain (1990-2020)

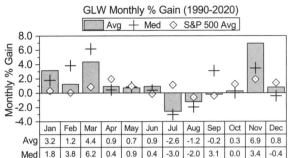

	Jan	Feb	Mar	Apr	May	Jun	Jul	Aug	Sep	Oct	Nov	Dec
Avg	3.2	1.2	4.4	0.9	0.7	0.9	-2.6	-1.2	-0.2	0.3	6.9	0.8
Med	1.8	3.8	6.2	0.4	0.9	0.4	-3.0	-2.0	3.1	0.0	3.4	-0.4
S&P 500 Avg	0.3	0.1	0.9	2.0	1.0	-0.1	1.1	-0.6	-0.4	1.2	1.9	1.4

Fq GLW Gain > 0% (1990-2020)

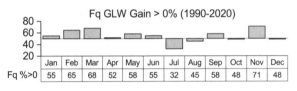

	Jan	Feb	Mar	Apr	May	Jun	Jul	Aug	Sep	Oct	Nov	Dec
Fq %>0	55	65	68	52	58	55	32	45	58	48	71	48

Fq % GLW Gain > S&P 500 % (1990-2020)

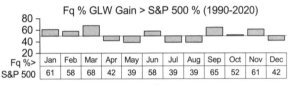

	Jan	Feb	Mar	Apr	May	Jun	Jul	Aug	Sep	Oct	Nov	Dec
Fq %> S&P 500	61	58	68	42	39	58	39	39	65	52	61	42

GLW % Gain 5 Year (2016-2020)

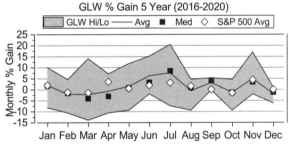

GLW Performance 2020-2021

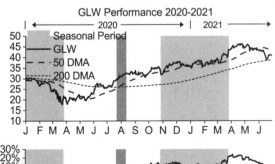

Relative Strength, % Gain vs. S&P 500

WEEK 31

Market Indices & Rates
Weekly Values**

Stock Markets	2019	2020
Dow	26,485	26,428
S&P500	2,932	3,271
Nasdaq	8,004	10,745
TSX	16,272	16,169
FTSE	7,407	5,898
DAX	11,872	12,313
Nikkei	21,087	21,710
Hang Seng	26,919	24,595

Commodities	2019	2020
Oil	55.66	40.27
Gold	1441.8	1964.9

Bond Yields	2019	2020
USA 5 Yr Treasury	1.66	0.21
USA 10 Yr T	1.86	0.55
USA 20 Yr T	2.16	0.98
Moody's Aaa	3.17	2.03
Moody's Baa	4.04	3.15
CAN 5 Yr T	1.36	0.32
CAN 10 Yr T	1.37	0.47

Money Market	2019	2020
USA Fed Funds	2.25	0.25
USA 3 Mo T-B	2.02	0.09
CAN tgt overnight rate	1.75	0.25
CAN 3 Mo T-B	1.64	0.17

Foreign Exchange	2019	2020
EUR/USD	1.11	1.18
GBP/USD	1.22	1.31
USD/CAD	1.32	1.34
USD/JPY	106.59	105.83

AUGUST

M	T	W	T	F	S	S
1	2	3	4	5	6	7
8	9	10	11	12	13	14
15	16	17	18	19	20	21
22	23	24	25	26	27	28
29	30	31				

SEPTEMBER

M	T	W	T	F	S	S
			1	2	3	4
5	6	7	8	9	10	11
12	13	14	15	16	17	18
19	20	21	22	23	24	25
26	27	28	29	30		

OCTOBER

M	T	W	T	F	S	S
					1	2
3	4	5	6	7	8	9
10	11	12	13	14	15	16
17	18	19	20	21	22	23
24	25	26	27	28	29	30
31						

TRANSPORTATION – ON A ROLL
①LONG (Jan23-Apr16) ②SELL SHORT (Aug1-Oct9)
③LONG (Oct10-Nov13)

The transportation sector can provide a "hilly" ride as the seasonal trends rise and fall throughout the year.

Activity in the transportation sub-sectors; railroads, airlines and freight, tends to bottom in January.

13% gain

Increased transportation activity in the spring, coupled with a typically positive economic outlook in the first part of the year, creates a positive seasonal trend, starting January 23 and lasting until April 16.

The next seasonal period is a weak period, giving investors an opportunity to sell short the sector and profit from its decline lasts from August 1 to October 9.

The third seasonal period is positive and occurs from October 10 to November 13. This trend is the result of a generally improved economic outlook at this time of the year.

Covid-19 Performance Update. In 2021, the transportation sector performed well as investors were anticipating a fast growing economy. The sector turned lower in May relative to the S&P 500 as economic growth expectations receded.

(i) *The SP GICS Transportation Sector encompasses a wide range transportation based companies. For more information, see www.standardandpoors.com*

Transportation Sector* vs. S&P 500 1990 to 2020

Negative Short ☐   Positive Long ☐

Year	Jan 23 to Apr 16		Aug 1 to Oct 9		Oct 10 to Nov 13		Compound Growth	
	S&P 500	Trans port	S&P 500	Trans port	S&P 500	Trans port	S&P 500	Trans port
1990	4.4 %	4.1 %	-14.3 %	-19.2 %	4.1 %	3.3 %	-6.9 %	28.1 %
1991	18.1	11.4	-2.8	0.5	5.5	9.6	21.0	21.5
1992	-0.5	3.7	-5.1	-9.1	4.9	14.1	-0.9	29.1
1993	2.9	9.1	2.7	-0.3	1.1	6.4	6.9	16.5
1994	-6.0	-10.7	-0.7	-9.3	1.6	0.8	-5.2	-1.6
1995	9.6	10.5	2.9	-1.3	2.4	5.0	15.5	17.6
1996	5.2	9.4	8.9	4.9	4.9	6.1	20.1	10.4
1997	-2.9	-2.0	1.7	0.9	-5.6	-5.4	-6.7	-8.2
1998	15.1	12.2	-12.2	-16.5	14.4	12.5	15.6	47.0
1999	7.7	17.7	0.6	-11.0	4.5	4.0	13.1	35.8
2000	-5.9	-2.7	-2.0	-6.0	-3.6	13.0	-11.1	16.6
2001	12.2	0.1	-12.8	-20.0	7.8	14.1	-17.4	37.0
2002	0.8	6.9	-14.8	-11.2	13.6	8.2	-2.4	28.6
2003	0.2	0.6	4.9	4.9	1.9	8.0	7.1	3.3
2004	-0.8	-2.9	1.9	6.6	5.5	11.1	6.6	0.7
2005	-2.2	-5.1	-3.1	-0.5	3.3	9.0	-2.1	3.9
2006	2.2	13.2	5.8	6.4	2.5	3.8	10.8	9.9
2007	3.2	4.8	7.6	-0.2	-5.4	-2.9	5.0	1.9
2008	4.1	19.1	-28.2	-23.5	0.2	4.0	-25.1	52.9
2009	4.6	7.2	8.5	6.7	2.1	5.9	15.8	5.9
2010	9.2	17.4	5.8	7.9	2.9	2.5	18.9	10.9
2011	2.8	2.2	-10.6	-11.8	9.4	11.4	0.6	26.9
2012	4.1	-2.0	4.5	-3.5	-4.6	-1.1	3.8	0.3
2013	5.5	3.5	-1.7	1.8	7.6	10.9	11.5	12.7
2014	1.0	1.7	-0.1	2.6	5.8	14.9	6.6	13.8
2015	2.0	-10.0	-4.2	-0.7	0.4	-2.0	-1.9	-11.2
2016	9.1	16.4	-0.9	4.3	0.5	6.4	8.7	18.6
2017	2.5	-4.0	3.0	6.5	1.6	-2.8	7.3	-12.7
2018	-5.5	-9.0	2.3	1.2	-5.5	-4.6	-8.6	-14.2
2019	10.4	10.7	-2.0	-9.0	6.0	10.0	14.6	32.7
2020	-15.7	-25.0	6.2	20.7	3.1	1.4	-7.6	-39.7
Avg.	2.3 %	3.5 %	-1.6 %	-2.5 %	3.0 %	5.7 %	3.7 %	12.7 %
Fq>0	71 %	68 %	48 %	45 %	84 %	81 %	61 %	81 %

Transportation Sector - Avg. Year 1990 to 2020

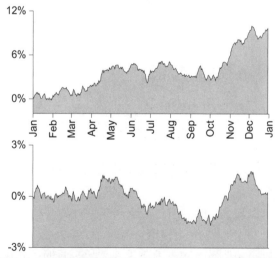

Transportation / S&P 500 Rel. Strength- Avg Yr. 1990-2020

Transportation Performance

Transportation Monthly % Gain (1990-2020)

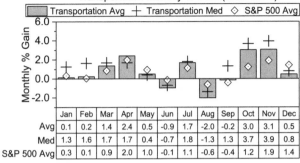

	Jan	Feb	Mar	Apr	May	Jun	Jul	Aug	Sep	Oct	Nov	Dec
Avg	0.1	0.2	1.4	2.4	0.5	-0.9	1.7	-2.0	-0.2	3.0	3.1	0.5
Med	1.3	1.6	1.7	1.7	0.4	-0.7	1.8	-1.3	1.3	3.7	3.9	0.8
S&P 500 Avg	0.3	0.1	0.9	2.0	1.0	-0.1	1.1	-0.6	-0.4	1.2	1.9	1.4

Fq Transportation Gain > 0% (1990-2020)

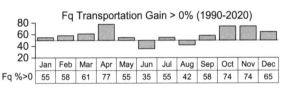

	Jan	Feb	Mar	Apr	May	Jun	Jul	Aug	Sep	Oct	Nov	Dec
Fq %>0	55	58	61	77	55	35	55	42	58	74	74	65

Fq % Transportation Gain > S&P 500 % (1990-2020)

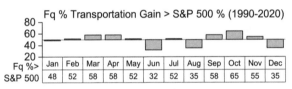

	Jan	Feb	Mar	Apr	May	Jun	Jul	Aug	Sep	Oct	Nov	Dec
Fq %> S&P 500	48	52	58	58	52	32	52	35	58	65	55	35

Transportation % Gain 5 Year (2016-2020)

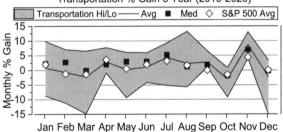

Transportation Performance 2020-2021

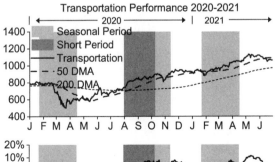

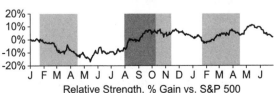

Relative Strength, % Gain vs. S&P 500

Market Indices & Rates
Weekly Values**

Stock Markets	2019	2020
Dow	26,287	27,433
S&P500	2,919	3,351
Nasdaq	7,959	11,011
TSX	16,341	16,544
FTSE	7,254	6,032
DAX	11,694	12,675
Nikkei	20,685	22,330
Hang Seng	25,939	24,532

Commodities	2019	2020
Oil	54.50	41.22
Gold	1497.7	2031.2

Bond Yields	2019	2020
USA 5 Yr Treasury	1.57	0.23
USA 10 Yr T	1.74	0.57
USA 20 Yr T	2.03	1.01
Moody's Aaa	3.09	2.03
Moody's Baa	3.97	3.14
CAN 5 Yr T	1.26	0.32
CAN 10 Yr T	1.27	0.48

Money Market	2019	2020
USA Fed Funds	2.25	0.25
USA 3 Mo T-B	1.96	0.10
CAN tgt overnight rate	1.75	0.25
CAN 3 Mo T-B	1.63	0.16

Foreign Exchange	2019	2020
EUR/USD	1.12	1.18
GBP/USD	1.20	1.31
USD/CAD	1.32	1.34
USD/JPY	105.69	105.92

AUGUST

M	T	W	T	F	S	S
1	2	3	4	5	6	7
8	9	10	11	12	13	14
15	16	17	18	19	20	21
22	23	24	25	26	27	28
29	30	31				

SEPTEMBER

M	T	W	T	F	S	S
		1	2	3	4	5
6	7	8	9	10	11	12
13	14	15	16	17	18	19
20	21	22	23	24	25	26
27	28	29	30			

OCTOBER

M	T	W	T	F	S	S
			1	2	3
4	5	6	7	8	9	10
11	12	13	14	15	16	17
18	19	20	21	22	23	24
25	26	27	28	29	30	31

AGRICULTURE MOOOVES
September 26 to November 11

The agriculture seasonal trade is the result of the major summer growing season in the northern hemisphere producing cash for growers and subsequently, increasing sales for farming suppliers typically in the third and fourth quarters of the year.

Late in the third quarter, farmers have a good idea on the viability of their crops and their cash position. This is the time period when farmers spend the most on their equipment and supplies for the upcoming year. Investors tend to front run this seasonal effect and push up the price of agriculture stocks.

63% of the time
better than the S&P 500

From September 26 to November 11, in the yearly period from 1994 to 2020, the agriculture sector has produced an average gain of 6.9% and has been positive 67% of the time. It has also outperformed the S&P 500, 63% of the time in this period.

Agriculture* vs. S&P 500 1994 to 2020

Sep 26 to Nov 11	S&P 500	Positive Agri	Diff
1994	0.6 %	5.7 %	5.1 %
1995	1.9	12.0	10.2
1996	6.7	24.7	18.0
1997	-1.5	-6.9	-5.4
1998	7.3	-1.7	-9.0
1999	8.2	1.4	-6.8
2000	-5.1	35.3	40.4
2001	10.7	18.1	7.5
2002	4.4	13.7	9.3
2003	4.3	9.8	5.5
2004	5.7	25.0	19.2
2005	1.6	7.2	5.6
2006	4.1	-5.7	-9.9
2007	-4.2	12.6	16.8
2008	-25.7	2.3	28.0
2009	5.2	17.8	12.6
2010	5.7	-4.9	-10.6
2011	11.2	17.9	6.7
2012	-4.3	-8.2	-3.9
2013	4.7	12.2	7.5
2014	3.8	1.3	-2.5
2015	7.4	-4.7	-12.1
2016	0.0	-1.7	-1.7
2017	3.4	-8.4	-11.8
2018	-4.6	-2.8	1.8
2019	3.4	7.5	4.1
2020	8.3	8.7	3.9
Avg.	2.3 %	6.9 %	4.6 %
Fq > 0	74 %	67 %	63 %

The world population is still increasing and imbalances in food supply and demand will continue to exist in the future, helping to support the agriculture seasonal trade.

Covid-19 Performance Update. In 2021, the agriculture sector performed well into May, but then started to underperform the S&P 500. On an absolute basis, the sector started to consolidate sideways.

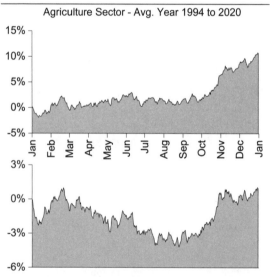

Agriculture Sector - Avg. Year 1994 to 2020

Agriculture / S&P 500 Relative Strength - Avg Yr. 1994-2020

In its strong seasonal period from September 26 to November 11, the agriculture sector has produced some large gains. Out of the twenty-seven cycles from 1994 to 2020, during its seasonal period, the agriculture sector has had ten years of returns greater than +10%. In other words, this sector is very volatile.

*The SP GICS Agriculture Sector # 30202010
For more information on the agriculture sector, see www.standardandpoors.com

Agriculture Performance

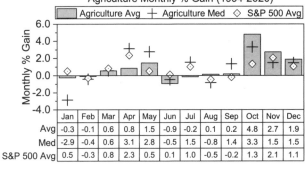

Agriculture Monthly % Gain (1994-2020)

Legend: Agriculture Avg | + Agriculture Med | ◇ S&P 500 Avg

	Jan	Feb	Mar	Apr	May	Jun	Jul	Aug	Sep	Oct	Nov	Dec
Avg	-0.3	-0.1	0.6	0.8	1.5	-0.9	-0.2	0.1	0.2	4.8	2.7	1.9
Med	-2.9	-0.4	0.6	3.1	2.8	-0.5	1.5	-0.8	1.4	3.3	1.5	1.5
S&P 500 Avg	0.5	-0.3	0.8	2.3	0.5	0.1	1.0	-0.5	-0.2	1.3	2.1	1.1

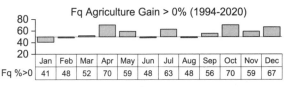

Fq Agriculture Gain > 0% (1994-2020)

	Jan	Feb	Mar	Apr	May	Jun	Jul	Aug	Sep	Oct	Nov	Dec
Fq %>0	41	48	52	70	59	48	63	48	56	70	59	67

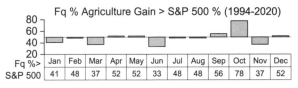

Fq % Agriculture Gain > S&P 500 % (1994-2020)

	Jan	Feb	Mar	Apr	May	Jun	Jul	Aug	Sep	Oct	Nov	Dec
Fq %> S&P 500	41	48	37	52	52	33	48	48	56	78	37	52

Agriculture % Gain 5 Year (2016-2020)

Legend: Agriculture Hi/Lo — Avg | ■ Med | ◇ S&P 500 Avg

Agriculture Performance 2020-2021

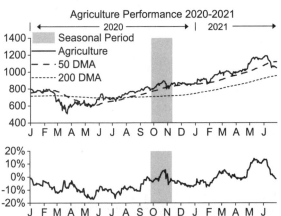

Legend: Seasonal Period | Agriculture | 50 DMA | 200 DMA

Relative Strength, % Gain vs. S&P 500

Stock Markets	2019	2020
Dow	25,886	27,931
S&P500	2,889	3,373
Nasdaq	7,896	11,019
TSX	16,150	16,515
FTSE	7,117	6,090
DAX	11,563	12,901
Nikkei	20,419	23,289
Hang Seng	25,734	25,183

Commodities	2019	2020
Oil	54.87	42.01
Gold	1515.3	1944.8

Bond Yields	2019	2020
USA 5 Yr Treasury	1.42	0.29
USA 10 Yr T	1.55	0.71
USA 20 Yr T	1.82	1.21
Moody's Aaa	2.91	2.30
Moody's Baa	3.81	3.32
CAN 5 Yr T	1.20	0.42
CAN 10 Yr T	1.16	0.61

Money Market	2019	2020
USA Fed Funds	2.25	0.25
USA 3 Mo T-B	1.83	0.10
CAN tgt overnight rate	1.75	0.25
CAN 3 Mo T-B	1.64	0.16

Foreign Exchange	2019	2020
EUR/USD	1.11	1.18
GBP/USD	1.21	1.31
USD/CAD	1.33	1.33
USD/JPY	106.38	106.60

AUGUST

M	T	W	T	F	S	S
1	2	3	4	5	6	7
8	9	10	11	12	13	14
15	16	17	18	19	20	21
22	23	24	25	26	27	28
29	30	31				

SEPTEMBER

M	T	W	T	F	S	S
			1	2	3	4
5	6	7	8	9	10	11
12	13	14	15	16	17	18
19	20	21	22	23	24	25
26	27	28	29	30		

OCTOBER

M	T	W	T	F	S	S
					1	2
3	4	5	6	7	8	9
10	11	12	13	14	15	16
17	18	19	20	21	22	23
24	25	26	27	28	29	30
31						

MICROSOFT
October 1 to October 31

If there were only one month of the year for an investor to invest in Microsoft, October would be the best choice. Microsoft can perform well in other months of the year, but historically October has been its best month on an average gain basis and frequency of positivity.

According to Microsoft's 10-K filing for the period ended June 30, 2021, the company has seasonal revenue trends.

"Our revenue fluctuates quarterly and is generally higher in the second and fourth quarters of our fiscal year. Second quarter revenue is driven by corporate year-end spending trends in our major markets and holiday season spending by consumers, and fourth quarter revenue is driven by the volume of multi-year on-premises contracts executed during the period."

5% gain

The fourth quarter of the calendar (Microsoft's second fiscal quarter) tends to be the strongest of the year. Investors are attracted to Microsoft during the month of October, ahead of its first quarter earnings report and the completion of its strongest fiscal quarter. The result is often a strong performance by Microsoft in October.

Oct 1 to Oct 31	S&P 500	Positive MSFT	Diff
1990	-0.7 %	1.2 %	1.9 %
1991	1.2	5.5	4.3
1992	0.2	10.2	10.0
1993	1.9	-2.9	-4.8
1994	2.1	12.2	10.2
1995	-0.5	10.5	11.0
1996	2.6	4.1	1.5
1997	-3.4	-1.7	1.7
1998	8.0	-3.8	-11.8
1999	6.3	2.2	-4.0
2000	-0.5	14.2	14.7
2001	1.8	13.6	11.8
2002	8.6	22.2	13.6
2003	5.5	-6.0	-11.5
2004	1.4	1.2	-0.2
2005	-1.8	-0.1	1.7
2006	3.2	5.0	1.8
2007	1.5	24.9	23.5
2008	-16.9	-16.3	0.6
2009	-2.0	7.8	9.8
2010	3.7	8.9	5.2
2011	10.8	7.0	-3.8
2012	-2.0	-4.1	-2.1
2013	4.5	6.4	1.9
2014	2.3	1.3	-1.0
2015	8.3	18.9	10.6
2016	-1.9	4.0	6.0
2017	2.2	11.7	9.4
2018	-6.9	-6.6	0.3
2019	2.0	3.1	1.1
2020	-2.8	-3.7	-1.0
Avg.	1.2 %	4.9 %	3.6 %
Fq > 0	65 %	71 %	71 %

Microsoft vs. S&P 500 1990 to 2020

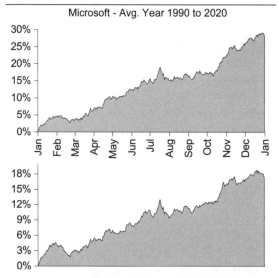

Microsoft - Avg. Year 1990 to 2020

Microsoft / S&P 500 Rel. Strength - Avg Yr. 1990 - 2020

Relative to the S&P 500, it has only suffered one double digit underperformance (a relative loss of greater than 10%) in October, but has had eight double digit out performances.

Covid-19 Performance Update. In 2021, Microsoft performed well, particularly heading into its earnings reports. As interest in the cyclical sectors waned starting in late May, investors became more focused on Microsoft. The result was a strong outperformance of Microsoft over the summer months of 2021.

As Microsoft has grown over the decades, its strong performance in October has been fairly consistent.

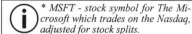

* MSFT - stock symbol for The Microsoft which trades on the Nasdaq, adjusted for stock splits.

Microsoft Performance

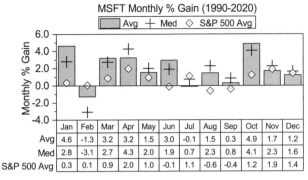

MSFT Monthly % Gain (1990-2020)

Legend: Avg | + Med | ◇ S&P 500 Avg

	Jan	Feb	Mar	Apr	May	Jun	Jul	Aug	Sep	Oct	Nov	Dec
Avg	4.6	-1.3	3.2	3.2	1.5	3.0	-0.1	1.5	0.3	4.9	1.7	1.2
Med	2.8	-3.1	2.7	4.3	2.0	1.9	0.7	2.3	0.8	4.1	2.3	1.6
S&P 500 Avg	0.3	0.1	0.9	2.0	1.0	-0.1	1.1	-0.6	-0.4	1.2	1.9	1.4

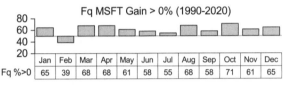

Fq MSFT Gain > 0% (1990-2020)

	Jan	Feb	Mar	Apr	May	Jun	Jul	Aug	Sep	Oct	Nov	Dec
Fq %>0	65	39	68	68	61	58	55	68	58	71	61	65

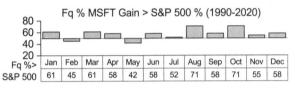

Fq % MSFT Gain > S&P 500 % (1990-2020)

	Jan	Feb	Mar	Apr	May	Jun	Jul	Aug	Sep	Oct	Nov	Dec
Fq %> S&P 500	61	45	61	58	42	58	52	71	58	71	55	58

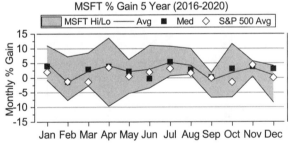

MSFT % Gain 5 Year (2016-2020)

Legend: MSFT Hi/Lo — Avg ■ Med ◇ S&P 500 Avg

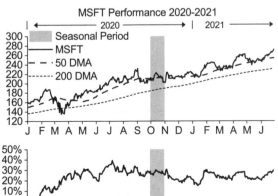

MSFT Performance 2020-2021

Seasonal Period | MSFT | 50 DMA | 200 DMA

Relative Strength, % Gain vs. S&P 500

WEEK 34

Market Indices & Rates
Weekly Values**

Stock Markets	2019	2020
Dow	25,629	27,930
S&P500	2,847	3,397
Nasdaq	7,752	11,312
TSX	16,038	16,518
FTSE	7,095	6,002
DAX	11,612	12,765
Nikkei	20,711	22,920
Hang Seng	26,179	25,114

Commodities	2019	2020
Oil	54.11	42.19
Gold	1503.8	1924.4

Bond Yields	2019	2020
USA 5 Yr Treasury	1.40	0.27
USA 10 Yr T	1.52	0.64
USA 20 Yr T	1.82	1.13
Moody's Aaa	2.88	2.30
Moody's Baa	3.79	3.28
CAN 5 Yr T	1.21	0.36
CAN 10 Yr T	1.17	0.54

Money Market	2019	2020
USA Fed Funds	2.25	0.25
USA 3 Mo T-B	1.93	0.10
CAN tgt overnight rate	1.75	0.25
CAN 3 Mo T-B	1.63	0.15

Foreign Exchange	2019	2020
EUR/USD	1.11	1.18
GBP/USD	1.23	1.31
USD/CAD	1.33	1.32
USD/JPY	105.39	105.80

AUGUST

M	T	W	T	F	S	S
1	2	3	4	5	6	7
8	9	10	11	12	13	14
15	16	17	18	19	20	21
22	23	24	25	26	27	28
29	30	31				

SEPTEMBER

M	T	W	T	F	S	S
			1	2	3	4
5	6	7	8	9	10	11
12	13	14	15	16	17	18
19	20	21	22	23	24	25
26	27	28	29	30		

OCTOBER

M	T	W	T	F	S	S
					1	2
3	4	5	6	7	8	9
10	11	12	13	14	15	16
17	18	19	20	21	22	23
24	25	26	27	28	29	30
31						

HEALTH CARE – PRESCRIPTION RENEWAL
①LONG (May1-Aug2) ②SELL SHORT (Aug3-Aug11) ③LONG (Aug12-Oct24)

Health care stocks have traditionally been classified as defensive stocks because of their stable earnings. Pharmaceutical and other health care companies typically still perform relatively well in an economic downturn.

7% gain & positive

The health care sector has on average been one of the top performing sectors in the month of May. Although the returns tend to be lower in June and July, there is value investing in the health care sector from the beginning of May to early August. The sector does take a pause in early August, when the stock market tends to perform poorly.

The period from August 12 to October 24 tends to be positive for the health care sector as investor interest increases ahead of the many health care conferences that take place in autumn.

Covid-19 Pandemic Update. In 2021, the health care sector underperformed the S&P 500 into April and then started to turn higher into the beginning of its strong seasonal period that started on May 1. In May and June, the sector was volatile relative to the S&P 500.

*Health Care SP GIC Sector# 35: An index designed to represent a cross section of health care companies. For more information see www.standardandpoors.com.

Health Care* vs. S&P 500 1990 to 2020
Negative Short [ ]   Positive Long [ ]

Year	May 1 to Aug 2		Aug 3 to Aug 11		Aug 12 to Oct 24		Compound Growth	
	S&P 500	Health Care	S&P 500	Health Care	S&P 500	Health Care	S&P 500	Health Care
1990	6.3 %	18.4 %	-4.5 %	-4.5 %	-6.8 %	2.8 %	-5.5 %	27.2 %
1991	3.2	7.9	0.0	-0.1	-0.5	1.8	2.6	9.9
1992	2.2	1.0	-1.3	-0.2	-1.2	-9.6	-0.2	-8.5
1993	2.3	-9.3	0.1	-4.2	2.8	12.2	5.2	6.0
1994	2.1	5.5	-0.4	3.6	0.4	7.4	2.2	9.2
1995	8.6	10.5	-0.7	-0.9	5.7	15.3	14.0	28.5
1996	1.3	4.7	-0.1	0.8	6.1	8.7	7.4	12.9
1997	18.2	16.3	-1.1	-3.9	0.5	6.1	17.5	28.0
1998	0.8	5.3	-4.6	-4.2	0.2	4.6	-3.7	14.8
1999	-0.5	-3.7	-2.0	-5.8	0.0	10.2	-2.5	12.2
2000	-1.0	13.0	2.3	-4.2	-5.0	7.1	-3.7	26.1
2001	-2.3	-0.1	-2.5	0.3	-8.8	0.9	-13.2	0.4
2002	-19.8	-16.1	5.1	4.8	-2.9	-1.1	-18.1	-20.9
2003	6.9	2.8	0.0	0.4	4.9	-2.3	12.2	0.0
2004	-0.1	-6.1	-2.8	-1.1	1.9	-5.5	-1.1	-10.3
2005	7.5	3.7	-0.5	-0.4	-3.1	-4.6	3.7	-0.7
2006	-2.5	3.8	-0.9	-1.8	8.7	7.3	5.1	13.2
2007	-0.7	-5.2	-1.3	-0.6	4.3	4.2	2.3	-0.6
2008	-9.0	0.7	3.6	5.2	-32.8	-23.4	-36.7	-26.9
2009	13.1	15.5	0.7	-0.5	8.6	3.4	23.7	20.0
2010	-5.1	-5.8	-3.2	-0.2	8.6	7.6	-0.3	1.6
2011	-8.0	-7.0	-6.5	-4.4	7.0	7.1	-8.0	4.0
2012	-2.4	1.4	3.0	1.8	0.2	3.7	0.8	3.3
2013	7.0	8.4	-1.1	-0.9	3.6	3.5	9.7	13.2
2014	2.2	4.6	0.6	-0.6	1.4	7.8	4.3	13.4
2015	0.9	6.7	-0.9	-1.7	-0.4	-8.0	-0.5	-0.1
2016	4.4	8.1	1.3	-0.6	-1.6	-7.1	4.2	1.0
2017	3.9	5.4	-1.5	-1.2	5.2	5.9	7.8	12.9
2018	6.8	8.5	0.2	0.4	-6.3	-2.5	0.3	5.3
2019	-0.4	1.9	-0.5	0.4	3.1	0.6	2.2	2.0
2020	12.3	5.7	1.9	-0.1	4.0	2.4	19.0	8.4
Avg.	1.9 %	3.4 %	-0.6 %	-0.8 %	2.5 %	2.1 %	1.6 %	6.6 %
Fq>0	61 %	74 %	35	29 %	61 %	71 %	61 %	74 %

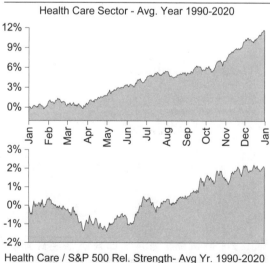

Health Care Sector - Avg. Year 1990-2020

Health Care / S&P 500 Rel. Strength- Avg Yr. 1990-2020

Health Care Performance

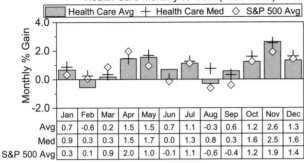

Health Care Monthly % Gain (1990-2020)

	Jan	Feb	Mar	Apr	May	Jun	Jul	Aug	Sep	Oct	Nov	Dec
Avg	0.7	-0.6	0.2	1.5	1.5	0.7	1.1	-0.3	0.6	1.2	2.6	1.3
Med	0.9	0.3	0.3	1.5	1.7	0.0	1.3	0.8	0.3	1.6	2.5	1.6
S&P 500 Avg	0.3	0.1	0.9	2.0	1.0	-0.1	1.1	-0.6	-0.4	1.2	1.9	1.4

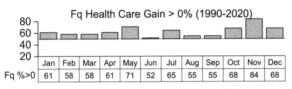

Fq Health Care Gain > 0% (1990-2020)

	Jan	Feb	Mar	Apr	May	Jun	Jul	Aug	Sep	Oct	Nov	Dec
Fq %>0	61	58	58	61	71	52	65	55	55	68	84	68

Fq % Health Care Gain > S&P 500 % (1990-2020)

	Jan	Feb	Mar	Apr	May	Jun	Jul	Aug	Sep	Oct	Nov	Dec
Fq %> S&P 500	58	39	32	48	52	65	45	65	61	45	58	52

Health Care % Gain 5 Year (2016-2020)

Health Care Performance 2020-2021

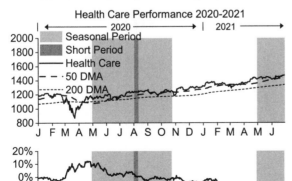

Relative Strength, % Gain vs. S&P 500

Market Indices & Rates
Weekly Values**

Stock Markets	2019	2020
Dow	26,403	28,654
S&P500	2,926	3,508
Nasdaq	7,963	11,696
TSX	16,442	16,706
FTSE	7,207	5,964
DAX	11,939	13,033
Nikkei	20,704	22,883
Hang Seng	25,725	25,422

Commodities	2019	2020
Oil	55.10	42.97
Gold	1528.4	1957.4

Bond Yields	2019	2020
USA 5 Yr Treasury	1.39	0.28
USA 10 Yr T	1.50	0.74
USA 20 Yr T	1.78	1.29
Moody's Aaa	2.85	2.40
Moody's Baa	3.76	3.45
CAN 5 Yr T	1.19	0.40
CAN 10 Yr T	1.16	0.63

Money Market	2019	2020
USA Fed Funds	2.25	0.25
USA 3 Mo T-B	1.95	0.10
CAN tgt overnight rate	1.75	0.25
CAN 3 Mo T-B	1.62	0.15

Foreign Exchange	2019	2020
EUR/USD	1.10	1.19
GBP/USD	1.22	1.34
USD/CAD	1.33	1.31
USD/JPY	106.28	105.37

AUGUST
M	T	W	T	F	S	S
1	2	3	4	5	6	7
8	9	10	11	12	13	14
15	16	17	18	19	20	21
22	23	24	25	26	27	28
29	30	31				

SEPTEMBER
M	T	W	T	F	S	S
			1	2	3	4
5	6	7	8	9	10	11
12	13	14	15	16	17	18
19	20	21	22	23	24	25
26	27	28	29	30		

OCTOBER
M	T	W	T	F	S	S
					1	2
3	4	5	6	7	8	9
10	11	12	13	14	15	16
17	18	19	20	21	22	23
24	25	26	27	28	29	30
31						

SEPTEMBER

	MONDAY	TUESDAY	WEDNESDAY
WEEK 35	29	30	31
WEEK 36	**5** 25 USA Market Closed- Labor Day CAN Market Closed- Labor Day	**6** 24	**7** 23
WEEK 37	**12** 18	**13** 17	**14** 16
WEEK 38	**19** 11	**20** 10	**21** 9
WEEK 39	**26** 4	**27** 3	**28** 2

THURSDAY	FRIDAY
1 29	**2** 28
8 22	**9** 21
15 15	**16** 14
22 8	**23** 7
29 1	**30**

OCTOBER

M	T	W	T	F	S	S
					1	2
3	4	5	6	7	8	9
10	11	12	13	14	15	16
17	18	19	20	21	22	23
24	25	26	27	28	29	30
31						

NOVEMBER

M	T	W	T	F	S	S
	1	2	3	4	5	6
7	8	9	10	11	12	13
14	15	16	17	18	19	20
21	22	23	24	25	26	27
28	29	30				

DECEMBER

M	T	W	T	F	S	S
			1	2	3	4
5	6	7	8	9	10	11
12	13	14	15	16	17	18
19	20	21	22	23	24	25
26	27	28	29	30	31	

JANUARY

M	T	W	T	F	S	S
						1
2	3	4	5	6	7	8
9	10	11	12	13	14	15
16	17	18	19	20	21	22
23	24	25	26	27	28	29
31						

SEPTEMBER
S U M M A R Y

S&P500 Cumulative Daily Gains for Avg Month 1950 to 2020

	Dow Jones	S&P 500	Nasdaq	TSX Comp
Month Rank	12	12	12	12
# Up	29	32	26	15
# Down	42	39	23	21
% Pos	41	45	53	42
% Avg. Gain	-0.7	-0.5	-0.6	-1.4

Dow & S&P 1950-2020, Nasdaq 1972-2020, TSX 1985-2020

♦ September has the reputation of being the worst month of the year for the S&P 500. From 1950 to 2020, September has produced an average loss of 0.5% and has only been positive 45% of the time. ♦ In particular, the last part of September tends to be negative. ♦ The defensive sectors are typically the favored sectors in September as investors seek more stable earnings in a month that is often volatile ♦ The materials sector on average performs poorly in September and has outperformed the S&P 500 only 29% of the time from 1990 to 2020.

BEST / WORST SEPTEMBER BROAD MKTS. 2011-2020

BEST SEPTEMBER MARKETS
- ♦ Nikkei 225 (2013) 8.0%
- ♦ Russell 2000 (2013) 6.2%
- ♦ Russell 2000 (2017) 6.1%

WORST SEPTEMBER MARKETS
- ♦ Russell 2000 (2011) -11.4%
- ♦ TSX Comp. (2011) -9.0%
- ♦ Nikkei 225 (2015) -8.0%

Index Values End of Month

	2011	2012	2013	2014	2015	2016	2017	2018	2019	2020
Dow	10,913	13,437	15,130	17,043	16,285	18,308	22,405	26,458	26,917	27,782
S&P 500	1,131	1,441	1,682	1,972	1,920	2,168	2,519	2,914	2,977	3,363
Nasdaq	2,415	3,116	3,771	4,493	4,620	5,312	6,496	8,046	7,999	11,168
TSX Comp.	11,624	12,317	12,787	14,961	13,307	14,726	15,635	16,073	16,659	16,121
Russell 1000	623	794	940	1,096	1,068	1,202	1,397	1,615	1,644	1,873
Russell 2000	644	837	1,074	1,102	1,101	1,252	1,491	1,697	1,523	1,508
FTSE 100	5,128	5,742	6,462	6,623	6,062	6,899	7,373	7,510	7,408	5,866
Nikkei 225	8,700	8,870	14,456	16,174	17,388	16,450	20,356	24,120	21,756	23,185

Percent Gain for September

	2011	2012	2013	2014	2015	2016	2017	2018	2019	2020
Dow	-6.0	2.6	2.2	-0.3	-1.5	-0.5	2.1	1.9	1.9	-2.3
S&P 500	-7.2	2.4	3.0	-1.6	-2.6	-0.1	1.9	0.4	1.7	-3.9
Nasdaq	-6.4	1.6	5.1	-1.9	-3.3	1.9	1.0	-0.8	0.5	-5.2
TSX Comp.	-9.0	3.1	1.1	-4.3	-4.0	0.9	2.8	-1.2	1.3	-2.4
Russell 1000	-7.6	2.4	3.3	-1.9	-2.9	-0.1	2.0	0.2	1.6	-3.8
Russell 2000	-11.4	3.1	6.2	-6.2	-5.1	0.9	6.1	-2.5	1.9	-3.5
FTSE 100	-4.9	0.5	0.8	-2.9	-3.0	1.7	-0.8	1.0	2.8	-1.6
Nikkei 225	-2.8	0.3	8.0	4.9	-8.0	-2.6	3.6	5.5	5.1	0.2

September Market Avg. Performance 2011 to 2020[1]

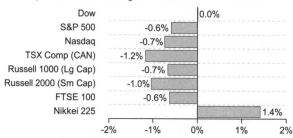

Dow	0.0%
S&P 500	-0.6%
Nasdaq	-0.7%
TSX Comp (CAN)	-1.2%
Russell 1000 (Lg Cap)	-0.7%
Russell 2000 (Sm Cap)	-1.0%
FTSE 100	-0.6%
Nikkei 225	1.4%

Interest Corner Sep[2]

	Fed Funds %[3]	3 Mo. T-Bill %[4]	10 Yr %[5]	20 Yr %[6]
2020	0.25	0.10	0.69	1.23
2019	2.00	1.88	1.68	1.94
2018	2.25	2.19	3.05	3.13
2017	1.25	1.06	2.33	2.63
2016	0.50	0.29	1.60	1.99

(1) Russell Data provided by Russell (2) Federal Reserve Bank of St. Louis- end of month values (3) Target rate set by FOMC (4)(5)(6) Constant yield maturities.

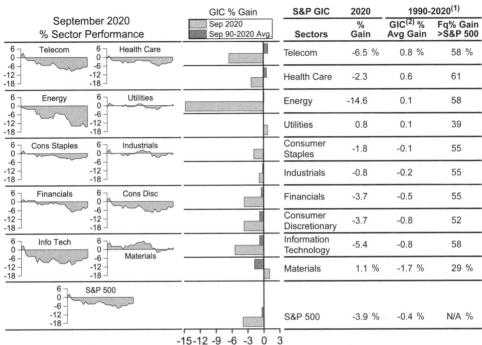

S&P GIC Sectors	2020 % Gain	1990-2020[1] GIC[2] % Avg Gain	Fq% Gain >S&P 500
Telecom	-6.5 %	0.8 %	58 %
Health Care	-2.3	0.6	61
Energy	-14.6	0.1	58
Utilities	0.8	0.1	39
Consumer Staples	-1.8	-0.1	55
Industrials	-0.8	-0.2	55
Financials	-3.7	-0.5	55
Consumer Discretionary	-3.7	-0.8	52
Information Technology	-5.4	-0.8	58
Materials	1.1 %	-1.7 %	29 %
S&P 500	-3.9 %	-0.4 %	N/A %

SELECTED SUB-SECTORS[3]

Gold	-3.6 %	1.8 %	61 %
Biotech (1993-2020)	-4.5	1.2	61
Silver	-13.3	0.7	61
Pharma	-2.3	0.7	58
Agriculture (1994-2020)	3.9	0.2	56
Railroads	1.6	0.0	48
Transportation	1.9	-0.2	58
Retail	-5.8	-0.5	48
Homebuilders	4.9	-0.6	58
Banks	-5.2	-0.8	52
Chemicals	0.3	-1.5	35
Metals & Mining	-3.6	-1.8	42
Automotive & Components	0.5	-1.9	42
SOX (1995-2020)	-0.7	-2.0	50
Steel	-1.3	-3.0	48

Sector Commentary

♦ In September, it is often the defensive sectors of the stock market that perform well relative to the S&P 500. In September 2020, the top performing sector was the materials sector with a gain of 1.1% ♦ The next best performing sector was the utilities sector with a gain of 0.8%. ♦ All other major sectors of the stock market were negative in September ♦ The energy sector was sharply lower for the third month in a row. ♦ Overall, the stock market corrected sharply in September, dragging most sectors of the stock market lower.

Sub-Sector Commentary

♦ September is typically the month when precious metals tend to perform well. ♦ In September 2020, both gold and silver performed poorly. ♦ The top performing sub-sector from the list of selected sub-sectors was the transportation sector with a gain of 1.9%. The agriculture sub-sector typically starts outperforming the S&P 500 late in September on a seasonal basis and performed well in September 2020. ♦ Homebuilders were uncharacteristically strong in September.

(1) Sector data provided by Standard and Poors (2) GIC is short form for Global Industry Classification (3) Sub Sector data provided by Standard and Poors, except where marked by symbol.

SHERWIN-WILLIAMS – TIME TO PAINT
①SELL SHORT (Aug13-Sep23) ②LONG(Sep24-Apr19)

Sherwin-Williams is known for its paints, stains and other coatings. Approximately 70% of its business is derived from residential orders.

In the summer months, homebuilders tend to languish with poor stock performance. Sherwin-Williams follows the same trend and tends to underperform the S&P 500 from August 13 until September 23.

15% gain

On the other hand, Sherwin-Williams tends to outperform the S&P 500 from September 24 to April 19. This performance tendency is very similar to the seasonal trend for the homebuilders sector which tends to outperform in approximately the same time period.

It is interesting to note the contrast of large gains and losses for Sherwin-Williams, comparing the seasonally strong period to the seasonally weak period. From August 13 to September 23, from 1990 to 2020, Sherwin-Williams has produced losses of 10% or greater, four times and gains of 10% or greater only once. In comparison, in the same yearly period, from September 24 to April 19, Sherwin-Williams has produced losses of 10% or greater once and gains of 10% or greater twenty-three times.

Covid-19 Performance Update. In 2021, Sherwin-Williams corrected at the beginning of the year and found its footing in late February and outperformed into June. Generally, Sherwin-Williams' performance tracked the homebuilders performance in the first half of 2021.

 * *The Sherwin-Williams Company is a consumer discretionary company. Data adjusted for stock splits.*

SHW vs. S&P 500 1990/91 to 2020/21

Negative Short ☐ Positive Long ☐

Year	Aug 13 to Sep 23		Sep 24 to Apr 19		Compound Growth	
	S&P 500	SHW	S&P 500	SHW	S&P 500	SHW
1990/91	-7.2 %	-5.6 %	23.4 %	43.3 %	14.5 %	51.3 %
1991/92	-0.5	-5.1	7.8	24.5	7.2	30.8
1992/93	-0.1	-4.7	7.2	20.1	7.1	25.7
1993/94	2.0	8.9	-3.3	-9.2	-1.4	-17.3
1994/95	-0.5	-4.2	9.8	10.4	9.3	15.0
1995/96	4.8	-0.4	10.9	27.2	16.2	27.6
1996/97	3.1	-1.9	11.6	19.2	15.1	21.5
1997/98	2.7	-2.4	17.9	20.0	21.2	22.9
1998/99	-1.7	-31.6	21.0	54.5	18.9	103.3
1999/00	-1.4	-24.8	11.5	25.8	10.0	57.0
2001/01	-1.6	-9.0	-13.5	3.2	-14.8	12.4
2001/02	-18.9	-8.4	16.5	49.2	-5.5	61.7
2002/03	-7.8	-17.7	7.2	17.4	-1.1	38.1
2003/04	3.9	0.3	10.4	30.3	14.7	29.9
2004/05	4.2	10.1	4.0	7.7	8.4	-3.2
2005/06	-1.2	-6.9	7.8	20.0	6.5	28.2
2006/07	3.8	8.1	11.9	22.5	16.1	12.6
2007/08	5.0	-4.7	-8.9	-14.7	-4.4	-10.7
2008/09	-7.9	2.0	-26.8	-5.5	-32.6	-7.4
2009/10	5.5	-0.8	12.9	19.9	19.1	20.8
2010/11	3.8	7.3	16.7	14.3	21.1	6.0
2011/12	-3.6	-5.8	21.2	63.5	16.8	73.0
2012/13	3.9	6.1	6.5	19.3	10.6	12.0
2013/14	0.7	2.1	9.6	8.9	10.4	6.6
2014/15	2.5	3.7	5.0	29.1	7.6	24.3
2015/16	-7.1	-14.8	8.4	28.2	0.7	47.3
2016/17	-0.9	-4.3	8.0	10.1	7.0	14.8
2017/18	2.5	5.4	7.6	13.3	10.3	7.2
2018/19	3.4	6.1	-0.8	-3.7	2.5	-9.6
2019/20	3.8	5.0	-3.9	-4.6	-0.3	-9.4
2020/21	-4.2	0.8	28.6	17.6	23.2	-6.5
Avg.	-2.9 %	-2.8 %	7.9 %	18.8 %	7.6 %	15.3 %
Fq>0	52 %	42 %	81 %	84 %	77 %	68 %

SHW - Avg. Year 1990 to 2020

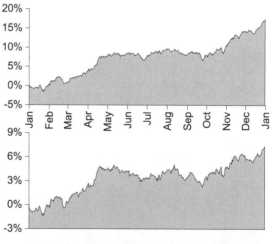

SHW / S&P 500 Rel. Strength- Avg Yr. 1990-2020

Sherwin-Williams Performance

SHW Monthly % Gain (1990-2020)

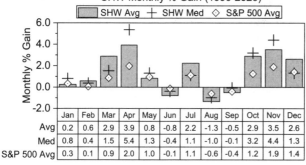

	Jan	Feb	Mar	Apr	May	Jun	Jul	Aug	Sep	Oct	Nov	Dec
Avg	0.2	0.6	2.9	3.9	0.8	-0.8	2.2	-1.3	-0.5	2.9	3.5	2.6
Med	0.8	0.4	1.5	5.4	1.3	-0.4	1.1	-1.0	-0.1	3.2	4.4	1.3
S&P 500 Avg	0.3	0.1	0.9	2.0	1.0	-0.1	1.1	-0.6	-0.4	1.2	1.9	1.4

Fq SHW Gain > 0% (1990-2020)

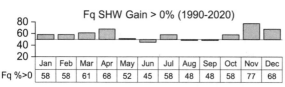

	Jan	Feb	Mar	Apr	May	Jun	Jul	Aug	Sep	Oct	Nov	Dec
Fq %>0	58	58	61	68	52	45	58	48	48	58	77	68

Fq % SHW Gain > S&P 500 % (1990-2020)

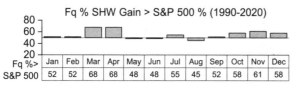

	Jan	Feb	Mar	Apr	May	Jun	Jul	Aug	Sep	Oct	Nov	Dec
Fq %> S&P 500	52	52	68	68	48	48	55	45	52	58	61	58

SHW % Gain 5 Year (2016-2020)

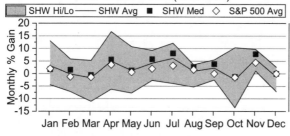

SHW Performance 2020-2021

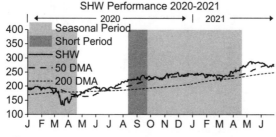

Relative Strength, % Gain vs. S&P 500

WEEK 36

Market Indices & Rates
Weekly Values**

Stock Markets	2019	2020
Dow	26,797	28,133
S&P500	2,979	3,427
Nasdaq	8,103	11,313
TSX	16,535	16,218
FTSE	7,282	5,799
DAX	12,192	12,843
Nikkei	21,200	23,205
Hang Seng	26,691	24,695

Commodities	2019	2020
Oil	56.52	39.77
Gold	1523.7	1926.3

Bond Yields	2019	2020
USA 5 Yr Treasury	1.42	0.30
USA 10 Yr T	1.55	0.72
USA 20 Yr T	1.83	1.25
Moody's Aaa	2.91	2.34
Moody's Baa	3.81	3.40
CAN 5 Yr T	1.32	0.39
CAN 10 Yr T	1.28	0.60

Money Market	2019	2020
USA Fed Funds	2.25	0.25
USA 3 Mo T-B	1.92	0.11
CAN tgt overnight rate	1.75	0.25
CAN 3 Mo T-B	1.61	0.15

Foreign Exchange	2019	2020
EUR/USD	1.10	1.18
GBP/USD	1.23	1.33
USD/CAD	1.32	1.31
USD/JPY	106.92	106.24

SEPTEMBER

M	T	W	T	F	S	S
			1	2	3	4
5	6	7	8	9	10	11
12	13	14	15	16	17	18
19	20	21	22	23	24	25
26	27	28	29	30		

OCTOBER

M	T	W	T	F	S	S
					1	2
3	4	5	6	7	8	9
10	11	12	13	14	15	16
17	18	19	20	21	22	23
24	25	26	27	28	29	30
31						

NOVEMBER

M	T	W	T	F	S	S
	1	2	3	4	5	6
7	8	9	10	11	12	13
14	15	16	17	18	19	20
21	22	23	24	25	26	27
28	28	30				

LOCKHEED MARTIN
September 1 to September 30

Lockheed Martin has a few months when it tends to outperform the S&P 500. If there were only one month to invest in Lockheed Martin versus the S&P 500 on a seasonal basis, it would be September.

April is also a good month for Lockheed. From 1990 to 2020, the average gain is higher than in September, but its frequency of outperformance compared to the S&P 500 is lower.

68% of the time better than the S&P 500

Lockheed is an aerospace company and by definition is part of the industrial sector. Most industrial companies start their strong seasonal period in late October. Although Lockheed is an industrial company, the nature of its business with government defense contracts tends to be less sensitive to economic conditions than the average industrial company.

LMT vs. S&P 500 1990 to 2020

Sep 1 to Sep 30	S&P 500	Positive LMT	Diff
1990	-5.1 %	2.0 %	7.1 %
1991	-1.9	-6.7	-4.8
1992	0.9	1.6	0.7
1993	-1.0	0.4	1.4
1994	-2.7	-11.6	-8.9
1995	4.0	10.3	6.3
1996	5.4	7.1	1.7
1997	5.3	2.8	-2.5
1998	6.2	15.1	8.9
1999	-2.9	-11.7	-8.8
2000	-5.3	16.1	21.4
2001	-8.2	9.8	17.9
2002	-11.0	2.1	13.1
2003	-1.2	-9.9	-8.7
2004	0.9	3.7	2.8
2005	0.7	-1.9	-2.6
2006	2.5	4.2	1.7
2007	3.6	9.4	5.9
2008	-9.1	-5.8	3.3
2009	3.6	4.1	0.6
2010	8.8	2.5	-6.2
2011	-7.2	-2.1	5.1
2012	2.4	2.5	0.0
2013	3.0	4.2	1.2
2014	-1.6	5.0	6.6
2015	-2.6	3.0	5.7
2016	-0.1	-1.3	-1.2
2017	1.9	1.6	-0.3
2018	0.4	8.0	7.5
2019	1.7	1.5	-0.2
2020	-3.9	-1.8	2.1
Avg.	-0.4 %	2.1 %	2.5 %
Fq > 0	52 %	71 %	68 %

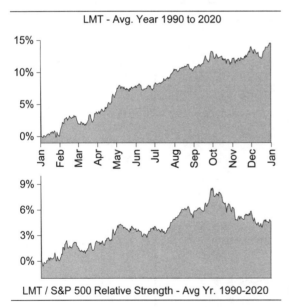

LMT - Avg. Year 1990 to 2020

LMT / S&P 500 Relative Strength - Avg Yr. 1990-2020

careful as Lockheed tends to perform poorly in October, leading up to its third quarter earnings report.

Covid-19 Performance Update. In 2021, Lockheed started the year outperforming the S&P 500, but started to underperform the S&P 500 in May, at the same time that many other cyclical stocks started their underperformance.

During the summer months, investors generally take on less risk in their equity portfolios. In autumn, investors generally increase their risk. The process is not typically a binary event. For investors looking to increase their industrial sector exposure, Lockheed can provide a good stepping stone in the month of September, before investors shift make a large shift into equity holdings in October. Investors should be

 LMT - stock symbol for Lockheed Martin, which trades on the NYSE, adjusted for stock splits.

Lockheed Martin Performance

Lockheed Martin Monthly % Gain (1990-2020)

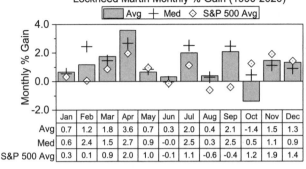

	Jan	Feb	Mar	Apr	May	Jun	Jul	Aug	Sep	Oct	Nov	Dec
Avg	0.7	1.2	1.8	3.6	0.7	0.3	2.0	0.4	2.1	-1.4	1.5	1.3
Med	0.6	2.4	1.5	2.7	0.9	-0.0	2.5	0.3	2.5	0.5	1.1	0.9
S&P 500 Avg	0.3	0.1	0.9	2.0	1.0	-0.1	1.1	-0.6	-0.4	1.2	1.9	1.4

Fq Lockheed Martin Gain > 0% (1990-2020)

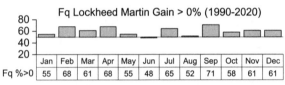

	Jan	Feb	Mar	Apr	May	Jun	Jul	Aug	Sep	Oct	Nov	Dec
Fq %>0	55	68	61	68	55	48	65	52	71	58	61	61

Fq % Lockheed Martin Gain > S&P 500 % (1990-2020)

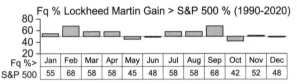

	Jan	Feb	Mar	Apr	May	Jun	Jul	Aug	Sep	Oct	Nov	Dec
Fq %> S&P 500	55	68	58	58	45	48	58	58	68	42	52	48

Lockheed Martin % Gain 5 Year (2016-2020)

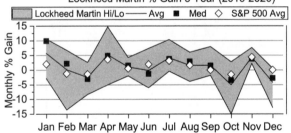

Lockheed Martin Performance 2020-2021

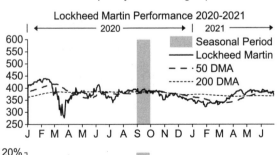

Relative Strength, % Gain vs. S&P 500

Market Indices & Rates
Weekly Values**

Stock Markets	2019	2020
Dow	27,220	27,666
S&P500	3,007	3,341
Nasdaq	8,177	10,854
TSX	16,682	16,222
FTSE	7,367	6,032
DAX	12,469	13,203
Nikkei	21,988	23,406
Hang Seng	27,353	24,503

Commodities	2019	2020
Oil	54.85	37.33
Gold	1503.1	1947.4

Bond Yields	2019	2020
USA 5 Yr Treasury	1.75	0.26
USA 10 Yr T	1.90	0.67
USA 20 Yr T	2.17	1.21
Moody's Aaa	3.25	2.32
Moody's Baa	4.11	3.36
CAN 5 Yr T	1.51	0.36
CAN 10 Yr T	1.51	0.55

Money Market	2019	2020
USA Fed Funds	2.25	0.25
USA 3 Mo T-B	1.92	0.11
CAN tgt overnight rate	1.75	0.25
CAN 3 Mo T-B	1.62	0.15

Foreign Exchange	2019	2020
EUR/USD	1.11	1.18
GBP/USD	1.25	1.28
USD/CAD	1.33	1.32
USD/JPY	108.09	106.16

SEPTEMBER

M	T	W	T	F	S	S
		1	2	3	4	
5	6	7	8	9	10	11
12	13	14	15	16	17	18
19	20	21	22	23	24	25
26	27	28	29	30		

OCTOBER

M	T	W	T	F	S	S
					1	2
3	4	5	6	7	8	9
10	11	12	13	14	15	16
17	18	19	20	21	22	23
24	25	26	27	28	29	30
31						

NOVEMBER

M	T	W	T	F	S	S
	1	2	3	4	5	6
7	8	9	10	11	12	13
14	15	16	17	18	19	20
21	22	23	24	25	26	27
28	29	30				

INFORMATION TECHNOLOGY
①Oct9-Dec5 ②Dec15-Jan17
③Apr16-Jun5 ④Jun28-Jul17

Over the long-term, since 1990, the technology sector has performed better at certain times of the year compared to other sectors.

The technology sector performs well from October 9 to December 5 and then from December 15 to January 17. The interim period in between these two periods tends to be negative.

20% gain

The technology sector also tends to perform well from April 16 to June 5 and then from June 28 to Jul 17. The interim period in between these two periods tends to be negative.

If the technology sector has strong momentum in the first leg of its seasonal period from either October 9 to December 5, or from April 16 to June 5, it is possible to continue holding a position in the sector at the end of the seasonal periods for a few weeks until the next leg of the strong seasonal periods.

Info Tech vs. S&P 500 1990 to 2020   Positive Long [ ]

	Oct 9 to Dec 5		Dec 15 to Jan 17		Apr 16 to Jun 5		Jun 28 to Jul 17		Compound Growth	
Year	S&P 500	Info Tech	S&P 500	Info Tech	S&P 500	Info Tech	S&P 500	Info Tech	S&P 500	Info Tech
1989/90	-2.6 %	-5.7 %	-3.9 %	3.8 %	6.5 %	10.8 %	3.5 %	2.8 %	3.2 %	11.5 %
1990/91	5.2	11.2	0.4	5.5	1.0	-1.8	1.8	1.0	8.6	16.2
1991/92	-0.9	-1.4	8.9	17.6	-0.7	-3.6	3.0	2.6	10.5	14.7
1992/93	6.0	6.8	1.0	7.4	0.4	9.5	-0.4	-7.0	7.0	16.8
1993/94	1.0	6.9	2.2	8.8	3.1	6.9	1.5	-0.3	8.1	23.9
1994/95	-0.4	8.5	3.3	9.6	5.2	11.9	3.7	14.1	12.3	51.8
1995/96	6.0	3.2	-1.7	-8.0	5.6	11.6	-5.2	-7.2	4.4	-1.6
1996/97	2.4	14.4	6.5	7.3	11.8	16.6	5.0	17.5	32.8	68.2
1997/98	1.0	-8.1	0.9	4.0	-0.5	-0.8	4.7	10.3	6.2	4.6
1998/99	22.6	46.8	8.9	18.7	0.4	1.6	7.9	15.8	44.7	105.0
1999/00	7.3	18.7	4.4	9.7	8.2	13.4	4.1	8.1	26.2	59.8
2000/01	-2.3	-12.8	-0.9	-3.3	8.5	9.7	0.3	-0.4	5.3	-7.9
2001/02	10.2	31.9	1.4	2.3	-4.8	-7.4	-8.5	-0.4	-2.7	24.4
2002/03	13.5	37.2	1.4	-0.6	11.2	16.7	0.6	4.0	28.7	65.6
2003/04	2.7	2.3	6.1	11.1	-0.6	-1.2	-2.9	-8.7	5.2	2.5
2004/05	6.2	11.7	-1.6	-4.1	4.7	10.4	3.1	6.5	12.8	26.0
2005/06	5.5	8.4	0.8	1.5	-1.8	-8.9	-0.4	-3.9	4.0	-3.7
2006/07	4.8	6.5	0.4	0.8	5.4	7.0	2.9	5.2	14.0	20.9
2007/08	-4.4	-2.6	-9.2	-12.7	5.2	13.5	-1.4	-0.9	-9.9	-4.3
2008/09	-11.1	-14.2	-3.4	-1.9	10.3	13.0	2.3	5.7	-3.0	0.6
2009/10	3.8	6.3	2.0	2.7	-12.1	-11.7	-1.1	-0.3	-8.0	-3.9
2010/11	5.1	7.0	4.2	4.9	-1.5	-0.9	2.8	5.0	10.9	16.8
2011/12	8.8	7.6	6.8	4.9	-6.2	-9.3	2.4	0.0	11.6	2.3
2012/13	-3.2	-6.4	4.8	4.0	3.6	6.6	4.2	4.8	9.5	8.8
2013/14	7.8	10.2	3.6	5.5	5.3	6.8	-0.1	1.6	17.4	26.1
2014/15	5.4	6.8	0.9	-0.7	-0.7	1.8	1.2	3.1	6.9	11.4
2015/16	3.9	8.2	-7.0	-9.4	0.9	-1.4	8.1	9.1	5.3	5.5
2016/17	2.4	-1.5	0.6	1.5	4.6	10.3	1.6	3.7	9.5	14.4
2017/18	3.1	4.6	5.7	6.3	3.5	9.1	4.1	6.3	17.4	29.0
2018/19	-6.4	-8.5	1.4	0.0	-2.7	-3.9	2.0	3.0	-5.8	-9.5
2019/20	7.8	10.0	5.1	8.9	14.8	16.4	7.2	5.2	39.2	46.6
2020/21	7.3	6.3	3.3	2.3	1.4	-2.5	1.1	4.5	13.7	10.8
Avg.	3.8 %	6.9 %	1.8 %	3.4 %	2.8 %	4.7 %	1.8 %	3.5 %	10.8 %	20.4 %
Fq>0	75 %	72 %	78 %	75 %	69 %	63 %	75 %	69 %	84 %	81 %

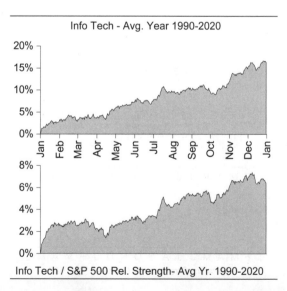

Info Tech - Avg. Year 1990-2020

Info Tech / S&P 500 Rel. Strength- Avg Yr. 1990-2020

Information Technology Performance

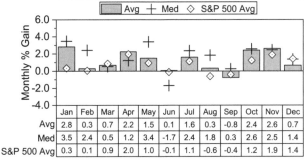

Information Technology Monthly % Gain (1990-2020)

	Jan	Feb	Mar	Apr	May	Jun	Jul	Aug	Sep	Oct	Nov	Dec
Avg	2.8	0.3	0.7	2.2	1.5	0.1	1.6	0.3	-0.8	2.4	2.6	0.7
Med	3.5	2.4	0.5	1.2	3.4	-1.7	2.4	1.8	0.3	2.6	2.5	1.4
S&P 500 Avg	0.3	0.1	0.9	2.0	1.0	-0.1	1.1	-0.6	-0.4	1.2	1.9	1.4

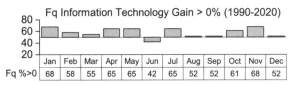

Fq Information Technology Gain > 0% (1990-2020)

	Jan	Feb	Mar	Apr	May	Jun	Jul	Aug	Sep	Oct	Nov	Dec
Fq %>0	68	58	55	65	65	42	65	52	52	61	68	52

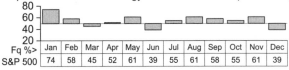

Fq % Information Technology Gain > S&P 500 % (1990-2020)

	Jan	Feb	Mar	Apr	May	Jun	Jul	Aug	Sep	Oct	Nov	Dec
Fq %> S&P 500	74	58	45	52	61	39	55	61	58	55	61	39

Information Technology % Gain 5 Year (2016-2020)

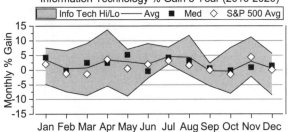

Information Technology Performance 2020-2021

Relative Strength, % Gain vs. S&P 500

Market Indices & Rates
Weekly Values**

Stock Markets	2019	2020
Dow	26,935	27,657
S&P500	2,992	3,319
Nasdaq	8,118	10,793
TSX	16,900	16,199
FTSE	7,345	6,007
DAX	12,468	13,116
Nikkei	22,079	23,360
Hang Seng	26,436	24,455

Commodities	2019	2020
Oil	58.09	41.11
Gold	1501.9	1950.9

Bond Yields	2019	2020
USA 5 Yr Treasury	1.61	0.29
USA 10 Yr T	1.74	0.70
USA 20 Yr T	1.99	1.24
Moody's Aaa	3.03	2.30
Moody's Baa	3.93	3.36
CAN 5 Yr T	1.42	0.37
CAN 10 Yr T	1.39	0.58

Money Market	2019	2020
USA Fed Funds	2.00	0.25
USA 3 Mo T-B	1.87	0.10
CAN tgt overnight rate	1.75	0.25
CAN 3 Mo T-B	1.63	0.15

Foreign Exchange	2019	2020
EUR/USD	1.10	1.18
GBP/USD	1.25	1.29
USD/CAD	1.33	1.32
USD/JPY	107.56	104.57

SEPTEMBER

M	T	W	T	F	S	S
			1	2	3	4
5	6	7	8	9	10	11
12	13	14	15	16	17	18
19	20	21	22	23	24	25
26	27	28	29	30		

OCTOBER

M	T	W	T	F	S	S
					1	2
3	4	5	6	7	8	9
10	11	12	13	14	15	16
17	18	19	20	21	22	23
24	25	26	27	28	29	30
31						

NOVEMBER

M	T	W	T	F	S	S
	1	2	3	4	5	6
7	8	9	10	11	12	13
14	15	16	17	18	19	20
21	22	23	24	25	26	27
28	29	30				

CANADIAN BANKS
① Oct10-Dec 31   ② Jan23-Apr13

The Canadian bank sector, has a strong seasonal period from October 10 to December 31 and then from January 23 to April 13.

Canadian banks have their year-end on October 31st. Why does this matter? In the past Canadian banks have announced most of their dividend increases and stock splits when they announce their typically optimistic full year fiscal reports at the end of November and beginning of December. Investors tend to push up bank stocks ahead of their earnings announcement. Canadian banks also tend to perform well in early in the year as economic reports tend to be favorable at this time.

Canadian bank returns in December have been separated out from their autumn seasonal period to show the impact of bank earnings on returns. In December, Canadian banks on average have provided gains 72% of the time, but they have underperformed the TSX Composite. If Canadian banks have performed well leading into their earnings, they often pause in December.

Covid-19 Performance Update. In 2021, the Canadian banking sector performed well in the first part of the year as economic growth was expanding at a rapid pace.

Canadian Banks* vs. S&P 500 1989/90 to 2020/21
Positive ▢

Year	Oct 10 to Dec 31 TSX-Comp	Oct 10 to Dec 31 Cdn. Banks	Jan 23 to Apr 13 TSX-Comp	Jan 23 to Apr 13 Cdn. Banks	Compound Growth TSX-Comp	Compound Growth Cdn. Banks	Dec 1 Dec 31 TSX-Comp	Dec 1 Dec 31 Cdn. Banks
89/90	-1.7 %	-1.8 %	-6.3 %	-9.1 %	-7.9 %	-10.8 %	0.7 %	-1.4 %
90/91	3.7	8.9	9.8	14.6	13.9	24.8	3.4	5.5
91/92	5.2	10.2	-6.8	-11.6	-2.0	-2.6	1.9	4.6
92/93	4.1	2.5	10.7	14.4	15.2	17.3	2.1	1.8
93/94	6.3	6.8	-5.6	-13.3	0.3	-7.4	3.4	5.1
94/95	-1.8	3.4	5.0	10.0	3.1	13.8	2.9	0.9
95/96	4.9	3.5	3.6	-3.2	8.6	0.1	1.1	1.5
96/97	9.0	15.1	-6.2	0.7	2.3	15.9	-1.5	-1.9
97/98	-6.1	7.6	19.9	38.8	12.6	49.4	2.9	4.2
98/99	18.3	28.0	4.8	13.0	24.0	44.6	2.2	3.0
99/00	18.2	5.1	3.8	22.1	22.8	28.3	11.8	0.7
00/01	-14.4	1.7	-14.1	-6.7	-26.4	-5.1	1.3	9.6
01/02	11.9	6.5	2.3	8.2	14.5	15.1	3.5	3.4
02/03	16.1	21.3	-4.3	2.6	11.1	24.4	0.7	2.6
03/04	8.1	5.1	2.0	2.1	10.3	7.4	4.6	2.0
04/05	4.9	6.2	4.5	6.9	9.6	13.5	2.4	4.7
05/06	6.2	8.4	5.5	2.7	12.1	11.3	4.1	2.1
06/07	10.4	8.4	6.9	3.2	18.0	11.8	1.2	3.7
07/08	-3.0	-10.4	8.2	-3.5	5.0	-13.5	1.1	-7.7
08/09	-6.4	-14.8	9.4	24.4	2.4	6.1	-3.1	-11.2
09/10	2.7	2.4	6.7	15.2	9.6	18.0	2.6	0.1
10/11	7.2	-0.2	4.3	9.1	11.9	8.9	3.8	-0.5
11/12	3.2	3.1	-2.9	1.1	0.2	4.2	-2.0	2.7
12/13	1.3	4.4	-3.8	-2.0	-2.5	2.3	1.6	1.5
13/14	7.0	9.0	1.9	1.6	9.1	10.7	1.7	0.9
14/15	1.2	-0.9	4.2	4.4	5.4	3.5	-0.8	-4.3
15/16	-6.8	-1.5	10.4	11.0	2.8	9.4	-3.4	-3.6
16/17	5.0	11.8	-0.1	-1.5	4.9	10.2	1.4	4.3
17/18	3.1	4.4	-6.6	-8.8	-3.7	-4.8	0.9	1.1
18/19	-9.7	-11.1	8.2	2.5	-2.3	-8.8	-5.8	-6.8
19/20	4.2	0.0	-20.0	-22.8	-16.7	-22.9	0.1	-4.0
20/21	5.3	13.3	7.6	12.1	13.3	27.1	1.4	2.3
Avg.	3.7 %	4.9 %	2.0 %	4.3 %	5.7 %	9.4 %	1.5 %	0.8 %
Fq>0	75 %	75 %	66 %	69 %	78 %	75 %	81 %	72 %

1989 to 2020

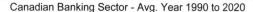

Canadian Banking Sector - Avg. Year 1990 to 2020

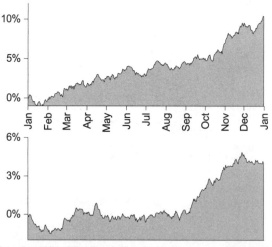

Cdn. Banking / TSX Comp Rel. Strength- Avg Yr. 1990-2020

Canadian Banks Performance

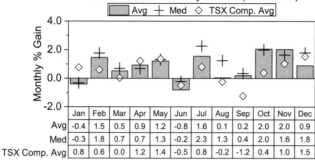

Canadian Banks Monthly % Gain (1990-2020)

Legend: Avg + Med ◇ TSX Comp. Avg

	Jan	Feb	Mar	Apr	May	Jun	Jul	Aug	Sep	Oct	Nov	Dec
Avg	-0.4	1.5	0.5	0.9	1.2	-0.8	1.6	0.1	0.2	2.0	2.0	0.9
Med	-0.3	1.8	0.7	0.7	1.3	-0.2	2.3	1.3	0.4	2.0	1.6	1.8
TSX Comp. Avg	0.8	0.6	0.0	1.2	1.4	-0.5	0.8	-0.2	-1.2	0.4	1.0	1.5

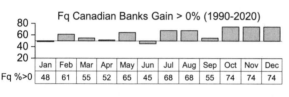

Fq Canadian Banks Gain > 0% (1990-2020)

	Jan	Feb	Mar	Apr	May	Jun	Jul	Aug	Sep	Oct	Nov	Dec
Fq %>0	48	61	55	52	65	45	68	68	55	74	74	74

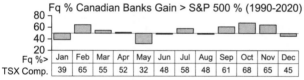

Fq % Canadian Banks Gain > S&P 500 % (1990-2020)

	Jan	Feb	Mar	Apr	May	Jun	Jul	Aug	Sep	Oct	Nov	Dec
Fq %> TSX Comp.	39	65	55	52	32	48	58	48	61	68	65	45

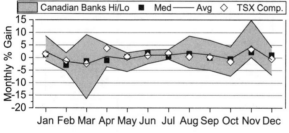

Canadian Banks % Gain 5 Year (2016-2020)

Legend: Canadian Banks Hi/Lo ■ Med — Avg ◇ TSX Comp.

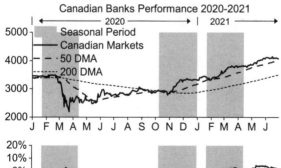

Canadian Banks Performance 2020-2021

Seasonal Period
Canadian Markets
- - 50 DMA
····· 200 DMA

Relative Strength, % Gain vs. TSX Comp.

Market Indices & Rates
Weekly Values**

Stock Markets	2019	2020
Dow	26,820	27,174
S&P500	2,962	3,298
Nasdaq	7,940	10,914
TSX	16,694	16,065
FTSE	7,426	5,843
DAX	12,381	12,469
Nikkei	21,879	23,205
Hang Seng	25,955	23,235

Commodities	2019	2020
Oil	55.91	40.10
Gold	1489.9	1859.7

Bond Yields	2019	2020
USA 5 Yr Treasury	1.56	0.26
USA 10 Yr T	1.69	0.66
USA 20 Yr T	1.95	1.19
Moody's Aaa	3.00	2.31
Moody's Baa	3.88	3.40
CAN 5 Yr T	1.40	0.35
CAN 10 Yr T	1.36	0.54

Money Market	2019	2020
USA Fed Funds	2.00	0.25
USA 3 Mo T-B	1.76	0.10
CAN tgt overnight rate	1.75	0.25
CAN 3 Mo T-B	1.65	0.14

Foreign Exchange	2019	2020
EUR/USD	1.09	1.16
GBP/USD	1.23	1.27
USD/CAD	1.32	1.34
USD/JPY	107.92	105.58

SEPTEMBER

M	T	W	T	F	S	S
			1	2	3	4
5	6	7	8	9	10	11
12	13	14	15	16	17	18
19	20	21	22	23	24	25
26	27	28	29	30		

OCTOBER

M	T	W	T	F	S	S
					1	2
3	4	5	6	7	8	9
10	11	12	13	14	15	16
17	18	19	20	21	22	23
24	25	26	27	28	29	30
31						

NOVEMBER

M	T	W	T	F	S	S
	1	2	3	4	5	6
7	8	9	10	11	12	13
14	15	16	17	18	19	20
21	22	23	24	25	26	27
28	29	30				

OCTOBER

	MONDAY	TUESDAY	WEDNESDAY
WEEK 40	**3** 28	**4** 27	**5** 26

WEEK 41	**10** 21
	
	 USA Bond Market Closed-
	        Columbus Day
	
	 CAN Market Closed-
	        Thanksgiving Day
		11 20	**12** 19

WEEK 42	**17** 14	**18** 13	**19** 12
WEEK 43	**24** 7	**25** 6	**26** 5
WEEK 44	**31**	1	2

THURSDAY	FRIDAY
6 25	**7** 24
13 18	**14** 17
20 11	**21** 10
27 4	**28** 3
3	4

NOVEMBER

M	T	W	T	F	S	S
	1	2	3	4	5	6
7	8	9	10	11	12	13
14	15	16	17	18	19	20
21	22	23	24	25	26	27
28	29	30				

DECEMBER

M	T	W	T	F	S	S
			1	2	3	4
5	6	7	8	9	10	11
12	13	14	15	16	17	18
19	20	21	22	23	24	25
26	27	28	29	30	31	

JANUARY

M	T	W	T	F	S	S
						1
2	3	4	5	6	7	8
9	10	11	12	13	14	15
16	17	18	19	20	21	22
23	24	25	26	27	28	29
31						

FEBRUARY

M	T	W	T	F	S	S
		1	2	3	4	5
6	7	8	9	10	11	12
13	14	15	16	17	18	19
20	21	22	23	24	25	26
27	28					

OCTOBER
S U M M A R Y

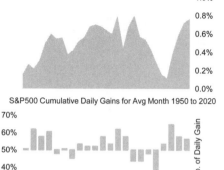

S&P500 Cumulative Daily Gains for Avg Month 1950 to 2020

	Dow Jones	S&P 500	Nasdaq	TSX Comp
Month Rank	7	7	7	9
# Up	42	42	27	22
# Down	29	29	22	14
% Pos	59	59	55	61
% Avg. Gain	0.5	0.8	0.7	-0.1

Dow & S&P 1950-2020, Nasdaq 1972-2020, TSX 1985-2020

♦ October, on average, is the most volatile month of the year for the stock market and often provides opportunities for short-term traders. The first half of October tends to be positive. ♦ The second half of the month, leading up to the last four days, tends to be negative, and prone to large drops. ♦ Seasonal opportunities in mid-October include Canadian banks, technology and transportation sectors. ♦ In late October, a lot of sectors start their seasonal period, including the materials, industrials, consumer discretionary and retail sectors.

BEST / WORST OCTOBER BROAD MKTS. 2011-2020

BEST OCTOBER MARKETS
- Russell 2000 (2011) 15.0%
- Nasdaq (2011) 11.1%
- Russell 1000 (2011) 11.1%

WORST OCTOBER MARKETS
- Russell 2000 (2018) -10.9%
- Nasdaq (2018) -9.2%
- Nikkei 225 (2018) -9.1%

Index Values End of Month

	2011	2012	2013	2014	2015	2016	2017	2018	2019	2020
Dow	11,955	13,096	15,546	17,391	17,664	18,142	23,377	25,116	27,046	26,502
S&P 500	1,253	1,412	1,757	2,018	2,079	2,126	2,575	2,712	3,038	3,270
Nasdaq	2,684	2,977	3,920	4,631	5,054	5,189	6,728	7,306	8,292	10,912
TSX Comp.	12,252	12,423	13,361	14,613	13,529	14,787	16,026	15,027	16,483	15,581
Russell 1000	692	779	980	1,122	1,154	1,177	1,427	1,499	1,677	1,826
Russell 2000	741	819	1,100	1,174	1,162	1,191	1,503	1,511	1,562	1,538
FTSE 100	5,544	5,783	6,731	6,546	6,361	6,954	7,493	7,128	7,248	5,577
Nikkei 225	8,988	8,928	14,328	16,414	19,083	17,425	22,012	21,920	22,927	22,977

Percent Gain for October

	2011	2012	2013	2014	2015	2016	2017	2018	2019	2020
Dow	9.5	-2.5	2.8	2.0	8.5	-0.9	4.3	-5.1	0.5	-4.6
S&P 500	10.8	-2.0	4.5	2.3	8.3	-1.9	2.2	-6.9	2.0	-2.8
Nasdaq	11.1	-4.5	3.9	3.1	9.4	-2.3	3.6	-9.2	3.7	-2.3
TSX Comp.	5.4	0.9	4.5	-2.3	1.7	0.4	2.5	-6.5	-1.1	-3.4
Russell 1000	11.1	-1.8	4.3	2.3	8.0	-2.1	2.2	-7.2	2.0	-2.5
Russell 2000	15.0	-2.2	2.5	6.5	5.6	-4.8	0.8	-10.9	2.6	2.0
FTSE 100	8.1	0.7	4.2	-1.2	4.9	0.8	1.6	-5.1	-2.2	-4.9
Nikkei 225	3.3	0.7	-0.9	1.5	9.7	5.9	8.1	-9.1	5.4	-0.9

October Market Avg. Performance 2011 to 2020[1]

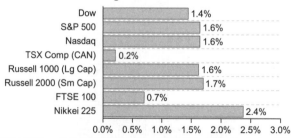

- Dow — 1.4%
- S&P 500 — 1.6%
- Nasdaq — 1.6%
- TSX Comp (CAN) — 0.2%
- Russell 1000 (Lg Cap) — 1.6%
- Russell 2000 (Sm Cap) — 1.7%
- FTSE 100 — 0.7%
- Nikkei 225 — 2.4%

Interest Corner Oct[2]

	Fed Funds % [3]	3 Mo. T-Bill % [4]	10 Yr % [5]	20 Yr % [6]
2020	0.25	0.09	0.88	1.43
2019	1.75	1.54	1.69	2.00
2018	2.25	2.34	3.15	3.30
2017	1.25	1.15	2.38	2.66
2016	0.50	0.34	1.84	2.25

(1) Russell Data provided by Russell (2) Federal Reserve Bank of St. Louis- end of month values (3) Target rate set by FOMC (4)(5)(6) Constant yield maturities.

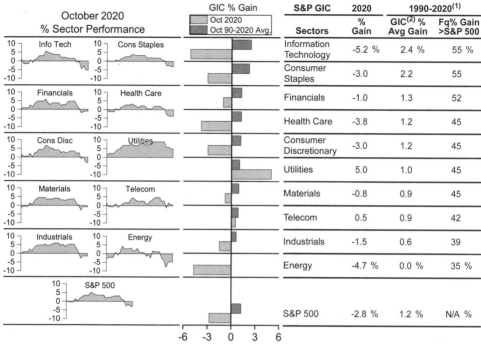

October 2020 % Sector Performance

S&P GIC Sectors	2020 % Gain	1990-2020[1] GIC[2] % Avg Gain	1990-2020[1] Fq% Gain >S&P 500
Information Technology	-5.2 %	2.4 %	55 %
Consumer Staples	-3.0	2.2	55
Financials	-1.0	1.3	52
Health Care	-3.8	1.2	45
Consumer Discretionary	-3.0	1.2	45
Utilities	5.0	1.0	45
Materials	-0.8	0.9	45
Telecom	0.5	0.9	42
Industrials	-1.5	0.6	39
Energy	-4.7 %	0.0 %	35 %
S&P 500	-2.8 %	1.2 %	N/A %

SELECTED SUB-SECTORS[3]

	2020 % Gain	GIC % Avg Gain	Fq% Gain >S&P 500
Agriculture (1994-2020)	-0.5 %	4.8 %	78 %
Transportation	-3.5	3.0	65
Railroads	-5.3	2.9	58
Steel	6.5	2.4	52
SOX (1995-2020)	0.1	1.8	50
Pharma	-6.8	1.7	55
Chemicals	-3.2	1.6	52
Retail	-3.7	1.3	55
Banks	1.7	1.2	45
Automotive & Components	11.1	1.0	45
Biotech (1993-2020)	-9.4	0.6	43
Homebuilders	-10.8	0.5	39
Metals & Mining	3.3	0.2	39
Gold	-0.3	-0.9	26
Silver	-0.4	-1.1	35

Sector Commentary

♦ In October 2020, the S&P 500 was volatile and produced a loss of 2.8%. ♦ A rapidly rising yield on the US 10-Year Treasury Note took its toll on the growth sectors of the stock market. ♦ The technology sector was the worst performing major sector of the market, producing a loss of 5.2%. ♦ The consumer discretionary sector lost 3.0%. ♦ The top performing sector was the utilities sector, which produced a gain of 5.0%, despite rising interest rates.

Sub-Sector Commentary

♦ In October 2020, the homebuilders sub-sector performed very poorly, producing a loss of 10.8%. ♦ Rising interest rates took its tool on the home-builders. ♦ The biotech sector produced a loss of 9.4%. ♦ On a positive note, the auto sub-sector managed to produce a gain of 11.1%. ♦ Generally speaking there was not a strong pattern of outperformance between different sub-sectors of the market compared to their seasonal trends.

VALERO

VLO ①SELL SHORT (May11-Jun26)
②LONG (Oct19-Nov2) ③LONG (Dec12-Apr1)

Valero acknowledges the seasonality of its business in its 10k report as of December 31, 2020.

"Demand for gasoline, diesel, and asphalt is higher during the spring and summer months than during the winter months in most of our markets, primarily due to seasonal increases in highway traffic and construction."

28% gain & positive 90% of the time

The time to be in a stock is typically well before the seasonal event. With Valero, this has been from December 12 until April 1. This provides an exit before the driving season starts in May. One of the better times to short sell the stock has been from May 11 to June 26 as the driving season gets underway. Valero also performs well from October 19 to November 2.

Covid-19 Performance Update. In 2021, Valero started the year outperforming the S&P 500 as demand for oil was increasing. It stalled in March and started its weak seasonal trend early. Valero managed to rally in May, but turned sharply lower at the beginning of June, underperforming the S&P 500 in its weak seasonal period.

Valero vs. S&P 500 1990 to 2020

Negative Short ☐   Positive Long ▨

	May 11 to Jun 26		Oct 19 to Nov 2		Dec 12 to Apr 1		Compound Growth	
Year	S&P 500	VLO	S&P 500	VLO	S&P 500	VLO	S&P 500	VLO
1990	2.4 %	8.5 %	2.0 %	9.4 %	13.7 %	37.2 %	18.8 %	37.3 %
1991	-1.1	-11.7	-0.3	3.3	7.0	18.1	5.5	36.4
1992	-3.0	-22.7	2.7	3.4	3.8	9.4	3.4	38.7
1993	1.1	-8.3	0.0	-6.8	-3.9	-0.6	-2.9	0.3
1994	-0.7	-19.8	-0.2	4.8	12.0	-0.7	10.9	24.7
1995	3.8	-5.9	0.4	2.7	5.5	-4.9	9.9	3.5
1996	1.9	-10.2	-1.0	3.8	2.6	24.9	3.5	42.9
1997	7.1	-1.4	-3.1	-4.7	16.0	12.9	20.4	9.0
1998	2.3	-5.3	5.2	35.0	10.9	29.4	19.3	84.0
1999	-1.9	-6.5	7.5	-0.3	5.8	58.9	11.5	68.6
2000	5.2	0.4	6.4	-1.5	-15.9	7.2	-5.9	5.2
2001	-3.1	-23.6	1.7	5.6	0.9	30.7	-0.5	70.5
2002	-7.7	-10.9	1.9	12.3	-5.1	23.5	-10.8	53.9
2003	5.6	2.7	1.1	7.3	5.7	31.6	12.8	37.4
2004	4.4	16.9	1.5	4.2	-1.3	80.8	4.6	56.6
2005	2.2	17.2	3.1	8.2	2.8	13.4	8.3	1.5
2006	-5.5	-4.2	0.1	-3.2	0.6	15.7	-4.8	16.7
2007	0.1	2.9	-2.0	-2.2	-7.3	-20.1	-9.0	-24.1
2008	-7.6	-7.4	3.0	13.6	-7.2	-5.5	-11.6	15.3
2009	-1.1	-29.3	-4.1	-10.1	6.5	20.5	1.0	40.1
2010	-7.2	-4.9	0.7	-2.4	7.4	38.9	0.5	42.1
2011	-6.5	-18.6	1.0	7.5	12.2	21.8	5.9	55.4
2012	-2.8	3.5	-3.0	-4.9	9.4	37.7	3.2	26.4
2013	-1.9	-8.8	1.0	4.9	5.8	20.6	4.8	37.5
2014	4.2	-6.5	7.0	10.9	1.2	35.5	12.8	60.2
2015	-0.7	3.1	3.5	6.7	3.0	-6.8	5.9	-3.6
2016	-2.3	-6.1	-1.9	5.4	4.6	-2.5	0.2	9.0
2017	1.6	-1.0	0.7	5.1	-0.7	6.4	1.6	12.9
2018	0.0	-3.7	-1.7	-11.2	8.7	18.0	6.9	8.7
2019	1.1	1.4	2.7	9.7	-21.4	-55.9	-18.3	-52.3
2020	2.7	-14.6	-5.0	-0.8	9.7	27.6	7.1	45.0
Avg.	-0.2 %	-5.6 %	1.0 %	3.7 %	3.0 %	16.9 %	3.7 %	27.7 %
Fq>0	48 %	29 %	65	65 %	74 %	74 %	74 %	90 %

Valero - Avg. Year 1990-2020

Valero / S&P 500 Rel. Strength- Avg Yr. 1990-2020

Valero Performance

Valero Monthly % Gain (1990-2020)

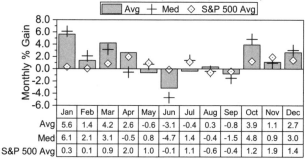

	Jan	Feb	Mar	Apr	May	Jun	Jul	Aug	Sep	Oct	Nov	Dec
Avg	5.6	1.4	4.2	2.6	-0.6	-3.1	-0.4	0.3	-0.8	3.9	1.1	2.7
Med	6.1	2.1	3.1	-0.5	0.8	-4.7	1.4	-0.4	-1.5	4.8	0.9	3.0
S&P 500 Avg	0.3	0.1	0.9	2.0	1.0	-0.1	1.1	-0.6	-0.4	1.2	1.9	1.4

Fq Valero Gain > 0% (1990-2020)

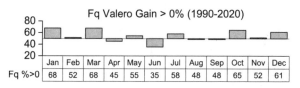

	Jan	Feb	Mar	Apr	May	Jun	Jul	Aug	Sep	Oct	Nov	Dec
Fq %>0	68	52	68	45	55	35	58	48	48	65	52	61

Fq % Valero Gain > S&P 500 % (1990-2020)

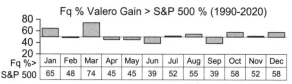

	Jan	Feb	Mar	Apr	May	Jun	Jul	Aug	Sep	Oct	Nov	Dec
Fq %> S&P 500	65	48	74	45	45	39	52	55	39	58	52	58

Valero % Gain 5 Year (2016-2020)

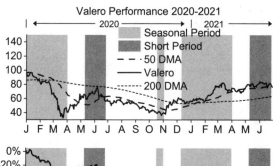

Valero Performance 2020-2021

Relative Strength, % Gain vs. S&P 500

Market Indices & Rates
Weekly Values**

Stock Markets	2019	2020
Dow	26,574	27,683
S&P500	2,952	3,348
Nasdaq	7,982	11,075
TSX	16,449	16,199
FTSE	7,155	5,902
DAX	12,013	12,689
Nikkei	21,410	23,030
Hang Seng	25,821	23,459

Commodities	2019	2020
Oil	52.81	37.05
Gold	1499.2	1903.1

Bond Yields	2019	2020
USA 5 Yr Treasury	1.34	0.28
USA 10 Yr T	1.52	0.70
USA 20 Yr T	1.81	1.25
Moody's Aaa	2.88	2.37
Moody's Baa	3.81	3.46
CAN 5 Yr T	1.25	0.36
CAN 10 Yr T	1.23	0.57

Money Market	2019	2020
USA Fed Funds	2.00	0.25
USA 3 Mo T-B	1.68	0.09
CAN tgt overnight rate	1.75	0.25
CAN 3 Mo T-B	1.63	0.12

Foreign Exchange	2019	2020
EUR/USD	1.10	1.17
GBP/USD	1.23	1.29
USD/CAD	1.33	1.33
USD/JPY	106.94	105.29

OCTOBER

M	T	W	T	F	S	S
					1	2
3	4	5	6	7	8	9
10	11	12	13	14	15	16
17	18	19	20	21	22	23
24	25	26	27	28	29	30
31						

NOVEMBER

M	T	W	T	F	S	S
	1	2	3	4	5	6
7	8	9	10	11	12	13
14	15	16	17	18	19	20
21	22	23	24	25	26	27
28	29	30				

DECEMBER

M	T	W	T	F	S	S
			1	2	3	4
5	6	7	8	9	10	11
12	13	14	15	16	17	18
19	20	21	22	23	24	25
26	27	28	29	30	31	

HOMEBUILDERS –
TIME TO BREAK & TIME TO BUILD
① SELL SHORT (Apr27-Jun13)   ② LONG (Oct28-Feb3)

Historically, the best time to be in the homebuilders sector has been from October 28 to February 3. This period is the lead up to the spring build season. Investors strive to be in the sector well before the spring season takes place, which helps to push up the price of homebuilding stocks.

**18% gain &
positive 74% of the time**

Generally, the time period outside of the strong seasonal period for homebuilders should be avoided by investors, as not only has the average performance relative to the S&P 500 been negative, but the sector has produced both large gains and losses. In other words, the risk is substantially higher that a large draw-down could occur. This is particularly true for the time period from April 27 to June 13.

The weak seasonal period takes place when the spring home building season and house sales season gets underway. At this point, the sector has generally priced in expected gains.

Covid-19 Performance Update. The homebuilding sector performed well and outperformed the S&P 500 from the start of 2021 to the beginning of May. The homebuilders sector turned lower just after its weak seasonal period started. In May and June, the homebuilders sector was negative and underperformed the S&P 500. The negative performance was largely the result of investors expecting slower economic growth.

(i) *Homebuilders: SP GIC Sector: An index designed to represent a cross section of homebuilding companies.*
For more information, see www.standardandpoors.com.

Homebuilders (HB)* vs. S&P 500 1990/91 to 2020/21
Negative Short ☐   Positive Long ☐

Year	SHORT Apr 27 to Jun 13 S&P 500	HB.	LONG Oct 28 to Feb 3 S&P 500	HB.	Compound Growth S&P 500	HB.
1990/91	9.6 %	7.9 %	12.6 %	58.0 %	23.4 %	45.5 %
1991/92	-0.4	-4.8	6.6	41.2	6.2	48.0
1992/93	0.2	-11.5	6.9	26.7	7.1	41.2
1993/94	3.2	12.6	3.5	8.6	6.7	-5.1
1994/95	1.6	-4.0	2.8	-4.0	4.4	-0.2
1995/96	4.6	11.1	9.7	16.7	14.7	3.7
1996/97	2.2	10.6	12.2	6.3	14.7	-4.9
1997/98	16.7	22.6	14.7	24.8	33.9	-3.4
1998/99	-0.8	-10.6	19.4	12.4	18.4	24.2
1999/00	-4.9	-7.1	9.9	-3.9	4.5	2.9
2000/01	0.6	-3.8	-2.2	18.6	-1.6	23.1
2001/02	0.6	-17.5	1.6	43.1	2.2	68.1
2002/03	-6.2	-5.3	-4.2	6.7	-10.1	12.3
2003/04	10.0	31.5	10.2	7.6	21.2	-26.3
2004/05	0.1	-2.6	5.7	23.7	5.8	26.9
2005/06	4.3	11.9	7.2	14.8	11.8	1.1
2006/07	-6.3	-27.1	5.2	16.8	-1.4	48.4
2007/08	1.4	-7.9	-9.1	8.8	-7.8	17.4
2008/09	-2.7	-25.3	-1.2	27.7	-3.9	60.0
2009/10	9.2	-25.1	3.2	15.5	12.7	44.4
2010/11	-9.9	-22.9	10.5	12.9	-0.4	38.7
2011/12	-5.6	-11.2	4.7	35.0	-1.2	50.1
2012/13	-6.1	-9.3	7.2	13.7	0.7	24.3
2013/14	3.4	-7.2	-1.0	10.1	2.4	18.1
2014/15	3.9	4.5	4.5	7.8	8.6	3.0
2015/16	-1.1	-0.8	-7.4	-15.3	-8.5	-14.6
2016/17	-0.6	-2.3	7.7	10.9	7.1	13.5
2017/18	2.2	4.6	7.0	4.2	9.4	-0.6
2018/19	4.1	-3.6	1.8	10.2	5.9	14.2
2019/20	-1.6	2.8	7.5	7.5	5.7	4.5
2020/21	7.2	29.0	13.0	13.4	21.1	-19.4
Avg.	1.3 %	-2.0 %	5.5 %	15.5 %	6.9 %	18.0 %
Fq>0	61 %	35 %	81 %	90 %	74 %	74 %

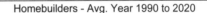

Homebuilders - Avg. Year 1990 to 2020

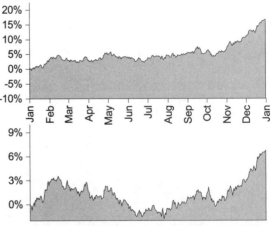

20%
15%
10%
5%
0%
-5%
-10%

Jan Feb Mar Apr May Jun Jul Aug Sep Oct Nov Dec Jan

9%
6%
3%
0%

Homebuilders / S&P 500 Rel. Strength- Avg Yr. 1990-2020

Homebuilders Performance

Homebuilders Monthly % Gain (1990-2020)

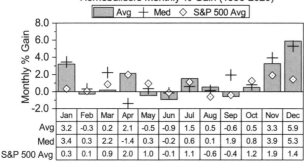

	Jan	Feb	Mar	Apr	May	Jun	Jul	Aug	Sep	Oct	Nov	Dec
Avg	3.2	-0.3	0.2	2.1	-0.5	-0.9	1.5	0.5	-0.6	0.5	3.3	5.9
Med	3.4	0.3	2.2	-1.4	0.3	-0.2	0.6	0.1	1.9	0.8	3.9	5.3
S&P 500 Avg	0.3	0.1	0.9	2.0	1.0	-0.1	1.1	-0.6	-0.4	1.2	1.9	1.4

Fq Homebuilders Gain > 0% (1990-2020)

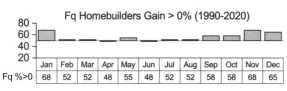

	Jan	Feb	Mar	Apr	May	Jun	Jul	Aug	Sep	Oct	Nov	Dec
Fq %>0	68	52	52	48	55	48	52	52	58	58	68	65

Fq % Homebuilders Gain > S&P 500 % (1990-2020)

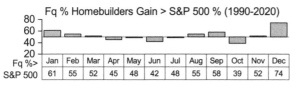

	Jan	Feb	Mar	Apr	May	Jun	Jul	Aug	Sep	Oct	Nov	Dec
Fq %> S&P 500	61	55	52	45	48	42	48	55	58	39	52	74

Homebuilders % Gain 5 Year (2016-2020)

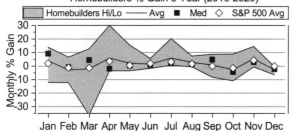

Homebuilders Performance 2020-2021

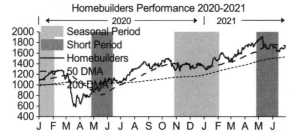

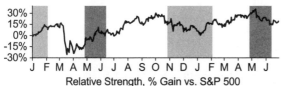

Relative Strength, % Gain vs. S&P 500

Market Indices & Rates
Weekly Values**

Stock Markets	2019	2020
Dow	26,817	28,587
S&P500	2,970	3,477
Nasdaq	8,057	11,580
TSX	16,415	16,563
FTSE	7,247	6,017
DAX	12,512	13,051
Nikkei	21,799	23,620
Hang Seng	26,308	24,119

Commodities	2019	2020
Oil	54.70	40.60
Gold	1479.2	1923.3

Bond Yields	2019	2020
USA 5 Yr Treasury	1.59	0.34
USA 10 Yr T	1.76	0.79
USA 20 Yr T	2.04	1.34
Moody's Aaa	3.06	2.34
Moody's Baa	3.98	3.46
CAN 5 Yr T	1.53	0.38
CAN 10 Yr T	1.52	0.63

Money Market	2019	2020
USA Fed Funds	2.00	0.25
USA 3 Mo T-B	1.65	0.10
CAN tgt overnight rate	1.75	0.25
CAN 3 Mo T-B	1.65	0.09

Foreign Exchange	2019	2020
EUR/USD	1.10	1.18
GBP/USD	1.27	1.30
USD/CAD	1.32	1.31
USD/JPY	108.29	105.62

OCTOBER

M	T	W	T	F	S	S
					1	2
3	4	5	6	7	8	9
10	11	12	13	14	15	16
17	18	19	20	21	22	23
24	25	26	27	28	29	30
31						

NOVEMBER

M	T	W	T	F	S	S
	1	2	3	4	5	6
7	8	9	10	11	12	13
14	15	16	17	18	19	20
21	22	23	24	25	26	27
28	29	30				

DECEMBER

M	T	W	T	F	S	S
			1	2	3	4
5	6	7	8	9	10	11
12	13	14	15	16	17	18
19	20	21	22	23	24	25
26	27	28	29	30	31	

TOLL BROTHERS
October 28 to March 7

Toll Brothers in its 10-K report dated October 31, 2020, discussed seasonality in its business.

"Our quarterly operating results fluctuate with the seasons; normally, a significant portion of our agreements of sale are entered into with customers in the winter and spring months. Construction of one of our traditional homes typically proceeds after signing the agreement of sale with our customer and can require seven months or more to complete."

The busiest build and sell time for the homebuilding industry is in the spring. Toll Brothers has a similar trend to the homebuilders industry, but its seasonal period of strength finishes slightly earlier.

15% gain &
71% of the time better than the S&P 500

From 1990 to 2021, in the period from October 28 to March 7, Toll brothers has produced an average gain of 20.5% and has been positive 68% of the time.

Toll Brothers vs. S&P 500 1990 to 2020

Oct 28 to Mar 7	S&P 500	Positive Agri	Diff
1990/91	23.4 %	152.4 %	129.0 %
1991/92	5.3	67.2	62.0
1992/93	6.6	60.8	54.2
1993/94	0.5	0.0	-0.5
1994/95	3.5	9.3	5.8
1995/96	12.8	16.4	3.7
1996/97	14.8	17.0	2.2
1997/98	20.4	33.0	12.6
1998/99	19.7	-16.7	-36.4
1999/00	4.5	5.8	1.3
2000/01	-8.5	34.8	43.3
2001/02	4.8	66.3	61.5
2002/03	-7.7	-14.2	-6.5
2003/04	12.2	37.1	25.0
2004/05	8.9	93.5	84.6
2005/06	8.2	-9.6	-17.8
2006/07	1.1	-1.4	-2.4
2007/08	-15.8	-15.5	0.2
2008/09	-19.5	-18.2	1.3
2009/10	7.1	8.9	1.8
2010/11	10.8	16.4	5.6
2011/12	5.3	23.8	18.5
2012/13	9.4	4.3	-5.1
2013/14	6.7	16.0	9.3
2014/15	5.6	14.9	9.3
2015/16	-3.1	-20.2	-17.1
2016/17	11.0	30.4	19.4
2017/18	5.6	-1.8	-7.4
2018/19	3.4	13.4	10.0
2019/20	-1.7	-9.7	-8.0
2020/21	13.3	21.4	8.1
Avg.	5.4 %	20.5 %	15.1 %
Fq > 0	81 %	68 %	71 %

Toll Brothers - Avg. Year 1990 to 2020

Toll Brothers / S&P 500 Relative Strength - Avg Yr.

Covid-19 Performance Update. Toll Brothers started 2021 on a strong note, strongly outperforming the S&P 500. Toll Brothers benefited from investors anticipating strong economic growth. The company continued to perform well into May and then started to turn lower and underperform the S&P 500.

It should be noted that Toll Brothers tends to perform poorly in September and the beginning part of October. This trend can make an entry into Toll Brothers a challenging affair as its strong seasonal period starts in late October.

*TOL - stock symbol for Toll Brothers, which trades on the NYSE, adjusted for stock splits.

Toll Brothers Performance

Toll Brothers Monthly % Gain (1990-2020)

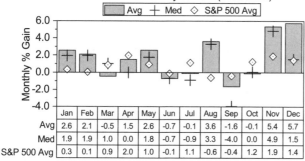

	Jan	Feb	Mar	Apr	May	Jun	Jul	Aug	Sep	Oct	Nov	Dec
Avg	2.6	2.1	-0.5	1.5	2.6	-0.7	-0.1	3.6	-1.6	-0.1	5.4	5.7
Med	1.9	1.9	1.0	0.0	1.8	-0.7	-0.9	3.3	-4.0	0.0	4.9	1.5
S&P 500 Avg	0.3	0.1	0.9	2.0	1.0	-0.1	1.1	-0.6	-0.4	1.2	1.9	1.4

Fq Toll Brothers Gain > 0% (1990-2020)

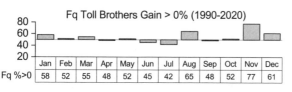

	Jan	Feb	Mar	Apr	May	Jun	Jul	Aug	Sep	Oct	Nov	Dec
Fq %>0	58	52	55	48	52	45	42	65	48	52	77	61

Fq % Toll Brothers Gain > S&P 500 % (1990-2020)

	Jan	Feb	Mar	Apr	May	Jun	Jul	Aug	Sep	Oct	Nov	Dec
Fq %> S&P 500	65	52	45	39	55	42	35	68	45	39	65	58

Toll Brothers % Gain 5 Year (2016-2020)

Toll Brothers Performance 2020-2021

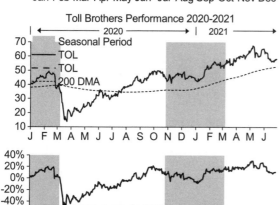

Relative Strength, % Gain vs. S&P 500

WEEK 42

Market Indices & Rates
Weekly Values**

Stock Markets	2019	2020
Dow	26,770	28,606
S&P500	2,986	3,484
Nasdaq	8,090	11,672
TSX	16,377	16,439
FTSE	7,151	5,920
DAX	12,634	12,909
Nikkei	22,493	23,411
Hang Seng	26,720	24,387

Commodities	2019	2020
Oil	53.78	40.88
Gold	1490.0	1905.1

Bond Yields	2019	2020
USA 5 Yr Treasury	1.56	0.32
USA 10 Yr T	1.76	0.76
USA 20 Yr T	2.06	1.30
Moody's Aaa	3.03	2.29
Moody's Baa	3.97	3.40
CAN 5 Yr T	1.55	0.35
CAN 10 Yr T	1.55	0.58

Money Market	2019	2020
USA Fed Funds	2.00	0.25
USA 3 Mo T-B	1.63	0.11
CAN tgt overnight rate	1.75	0.25
CAN 3 Mo T-B	1.67	0.09

Foreign Exchange	2019	2020
EUR/USD	1.12	1.17
GBP/USD	1.30	1.29
USD/CAD	1.31	1.32
USD/JPY	108.45	105.40

OCTOBER

M	T	W	T	F	S	S
					1	2
3	4	5	6	7	8	9
10	11	12	13	14	15	16
17	18	19	20	21	22	23
24	25	26	27	28	29	30
31						

NOVEMBER

M	T	W	T	F	S	S
	1	2	3	4	5	6
7	8	9	10	11	12	13
14	15	16	17	18	19	20
21	22	23	24	25	26	27
28	29	30				

DECEMBER

M	T	W	T	F	S	S
			1	2	3	4
5	6	7	8	9	10	11
12	13	14	15	16	17	18
19	20	21	22	23	24	25
26	27	28	29	30	31	

RETAIL
① Jan21 to Apr12 ② Oct28 to Nov29

The retail sector has two strong seasonal periods. The late January to mid-April seasonal period is the result of the retail sector's response to analysts putting forward positive economic expectations for the economy and consumer spending at the beginning of the year. The retail sector also performs well at this time of the year as it bounces of a weaker period from late December to mid-January.

The second seasonal period for the retail sector occurs in the run-up period to Black Friday, from late October to late November. The retail sector tends to perform well in this period as the result of investors increasing their interest in the sector anticipating retail companies to benefit from increased sales during the holiday shopping season.

13% gain

The frequency of success in the late October to late November seasonal period is stronger than the spring seasonal period. On the other hand, the average percentage gain of spring seasonal period is stronger. Overall, the spring seasonal period when considering both frequency and gain, is the best seasonal period.

Covid-19 Performance Update. In the first half of 2021, the broad based retail sector continued to underperform the S&P 500 as shoppers continued to favor on-line shopping versus shopping at physical locations.

Retail* vs. S&P 500 - 1990 to 2020   Positive

Year	Jan 21 to Apr 12 S&P 500	Retail	Oct 28 to Nov 29 S&P 500	Retail	Compound Growth S&P 500	Retail
1990	1.5 %	9.6 %	3.8 %	9.9 %	5.4 %	20.5 %
1991	14.5	29.9	-2.3	2.7	11.8	33.4
1992	-2.9	-2.7	2.8	5.5	-0.2	2.7
1993	3.5	-0.6	-0.6	6.3	2.9	5.7
1994	-5.8	2.0	-2.3	0.4	-7.9	2.4
1995	9.1	7.4	4.8	9.5	14.4	17.6
1996	4.1	19.7	8.0	0.4	12.4	20.2
1997	-5.0	6.0	8.9	16.9	3.5	23.9
1998	13.5	20.1	11.9	20.4	27.0	44.5
1999	8.1	23.4	8.6	14.1	17.4	40.7
2000	1.5	5.8	-2.7	9.9	-1.3	16.2
2001	-11.8	-0.5	3.2	7.9	-9.0	7.4
2002	-1.5	6.7	4.3	-1.7	2.8	4.9
2003	-3.7	6.5	2.6	2.5	-1.2	9.2
2004	0.6	6.7	4.7	7.0	5.3	14.1
2005	1.1	-1.6	6.7	9.9	7.8	8.1
2006	2.1	3.4	1.6	0.2	3.8	3.6
2007	1.2	-0.7	-4.3	-7.5	-3.1	-8.1
2008	0.6	3.5	5.6	7.5	6.2	11.3
2009	6.4	25.1	2.6	3.6	9.2	29.6
2010	5.1	15.5	0.4	5.2	5.6	21.5
2011	2.6	4.4	-7.0	-4.5	-4.5	-0.3
2012	5.5	12.1	0.3	5.1	5.8	17.8
2013	6.9	10.1	2.6	5.0	9.7	15.5
2014	-1.3	-7.1	5.4	8.9	4.1	1.2
2015	3.9	15.5	1.2	3.9	5.2	19.9
2016	10.9	9.7	3.4	2.8	14.6	12.8
2017	3.2	4.6	1.7	4.4	5.0	9.2
2018	-5.2	1.6	3.0	0.9	-2.4	2.5
2019	8.9	10.7	3.9	0.4	13.1	11.1
2020	-16.2	-6.0	7.3	0.5	-10.1	-5.5
Avg.	2.0 %	7.8 %	2.9 %	5.1 %	4.9 %	13.3 %
Fq>0	71 %	77 %	81 %	90 %	71 %	90 %

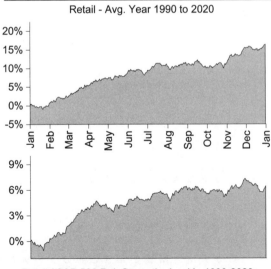

Retail - Avg. Year 1990 to 2020

Retail / S&P 500 Rel. Strength- Avg Yr. 1990-2020

ⓘ *Retail SP GIC Sector # 2550:
An index of retail companies.
For more information on the retail sector, see www.standardandpoors.com.*

OCTOBER

Retail Performance

Retail Monthly % Gain (1990-2020)

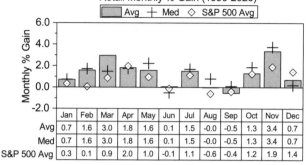

	Jan	Feb	Mar	Apr	May	Jun	Jul	Aug	Sep	Oct	Nov	Dec
Avg	0.7	1.6	3.0	1.8	1.6	0.1	1.5	-0.0	-0.5	1.3	3.4	0.7
Med	0.7	1.6	3.0	1.8	1.6	0.1	1.5	-0.0	-0.5	1.3	3.4	0.7
S&P 500 Avg	0.3	0.1	0.9	2.0	1.0	-0.1	1.1	-0.6	-0.4	1.2	1.9	1.4

Fq Retail Gain > 0% (1990-2020)

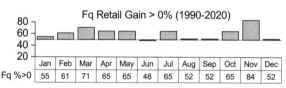

	Jan	Feb	Mar	Apr	May	Jun	Jul	Aug	Sep	Oct	Nov	Dec
Fq %>0	55	61	71	65	65	48	65	52	52	65	84	52

Fq % Retail Gain > S&P 500 % (1990-2020)

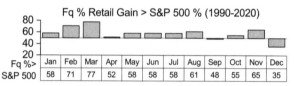

	Jan	Feb	Mar	Apr	May	Jun	Jul	Aug	Sep	Oct	Nov	Dec
Fq %> S&P 500	58	71	77	52	58	58	58	61	48	55	65	35

Retail % Gain 5 Year (2016-2020)

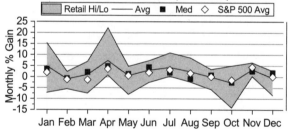

Retail Performance 2020-2021

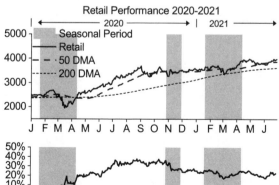

Relative Strength, % Gain vs. S&P 500

WEEK 43

Market Indices & Rates
Weekly Values**

Stock Markets	2019	2020
Dow	26,958	28,336
S&P500	3,023	3,465
Nasdaq	8,243	11,548
TSX	16,404	16,304
FTSE	7,324	5,860
DAX	12,895	12,646
Nikkei	22,800	23,517
Hang Seng	26,667	24,919

Commodities	2019	2020
Oil	56.46	39.67
Gold	1513.5	1903.7

Bond Yields	2019	2020
USA 5 Yr Treasury	1.62	0.37
USA 10 Yr T	1.80	0.85
USA 20 Yr T	2.10	1.41
Moody's Aaa	3.04	2.41
Moody's Baa	3.96	3.45
CAN 5 Yr T	1.57	0.39
CAN 10 Yr T	1.54	0.64

Money Market	2019	2020
USA Fed Funds	2.00	0.25
USA 3 Mo T-B	1.63	0.10
CAN tgt overnight rate	1.75	0.25
CAN 3 Mo T-B	1.65	0.09

Foreign Exchange	2019	2020
EUR/USD	1.11	1.19
GBP/USD	1.28	1.30
USD/CAD	1.31	1.31
USD/JPY	108.67	104.71

OCTOBER

M	T	W	T	F	S	S
					1	2
3	4	5	6	7	8	9
10	11	12	13	14	15	16
17	18	19	20	21	22	23
24	25	26	27	28	29	30
31						

NOVEMBER

M	T	W	T	F	S	S
	1	2	3	4	5	6
7	8	9	10	11	12	13
14	15	16	17	18	19	20
21	22	23	24	25	26	27
28	29	30				

DECEMBER

M	T	W	T	F	S	S
		1	2	3	4
5	6	7	8	9	10	11
12	13	14	15	16	17	18
19	20	21	22	23	24	25
26	27	28	29	30	31	

INDUSTRIAL STRENGTH
① Oct28-Dec31 ② Jan23-May5

The industrial sector's seasonal trends are largely the same as the broad market, such as the S&P 500. Although the trends are similar, there still exists an opportunity to take advantage of the time period when the industrial sector tends to outperform.

11% gain &
positive 88% of the time

Industrials tend to outperform in the favorable six month period for the stock market, but there is an opportunity to temporarily get out of the industrial sector in order to avoid a time period when the sector has on average, decreased before turning positive again.

The overall strategy is to be invested in the industrial sector from October 28 to December 31, sell at the end of the day on the 31, and re-enter the sector to be invested from January 23 to May 5.

It should be noted that longer term investors may decide to be invested during the whole time period from October 28 to May 5. Shorter term investors may decide to use technical analysis to determine, if and when, they should temporarily sell the industrials sector during its weak period from January 1 to January 22.

Covid-19 Pandemic Update. In 2021, the industrial sector relative to the S&P 500 bottomed in late January, just before its strong seasonal period started. The sector strongly outperformed the S&P 500 until early May, when its strong seasonal period ended. In May and June, the industrial sector underperformed the S&P 500.

Industrials* vs. S&P 500 1989/90 to 2020/21 Positive ☐

Year	Oct 28 to Dec 31 S&P 500	Ind.	Jan 23 to May 5 S&P 500	Ind.	Compound Growth S&P 500	Ind.
1989/90	5.5 %	6.9 %	2.4 %	5.5 %	8.0 %	12.7 %
1990/91	8.4	10.7	16.0	15.2	25.7	27.5
1991/92	8.6	7.2	-0.3	-1.0	8.2	6.1
1992/93	4.1	6.3	1.9	5.4	6.1	12.0
1993/94	0.4	5.1	-4.9	-6.7	-4.5	-2.0
1994/95	-1.4	-0.5	11.9	12.4	10.3	11.8
1995/96	6.3	10.7	4.6	7.6	11.1	19.1
1996/97	5.7	4.5	5.6	5.2	11.6	9.9
1997/98	10.7	10.5	15.8	11.5	28.2	23.2
1998/99	15.4	10.5	10.0	19.5	26.9	32.1
1999/00	13.3	10.8	-0.6	4.5	12.6	15.8
2000/01	-4.3	1.8	-5.7	4.7	-9.7	6.6
2001/02	3.9	8.1	-4.1	-5.3	-0.3	2.4
2002/03	-2.0	-1.3	5.5	8.6	3.4	7.1
2003/04	7.8	11.6	-2.0	-3.3	5.7	7.9
2004/05	7.7	8.7	0.4	0.2	8.1	8.9
2005/06	5.9	7.6	5.1	14.3	11.3	23.0
2006/07	3.0	3.1	5.8	6.8	9.0	10.1
2007/08	-4.4	-3.4	7.4	9.7	2.7	6.0
2008/09	6.4	7.1	9.2	6.1	16.2	13.7
2009/10	4.9	6.4	6.8	13.4	12.0	20.6
2010/11	6.4	8.1	4.0	4.9	10.6	13.5
2011/12	-2.1	-1.0	4.1	0.3	1.9	-0.7
2012/13	1.0	4.1	8.2	4.9	9.3	9.2
2013/14	5.0	7.3	2.2	1.6	7.3	9.0
2014/15	5.0	5.2	1.3	-1.0	6.3	4.1
2015/16	-1.1	-1.2	7.5	12.8	6.4	11.4
2016/17	5.0	9.7	5.6	5.0	10.9	15.2
2017/18	3.6	4.2	-6.0	-9.5	-2.6	-5.7
2018/19	-5.7	-6.7	11.9	14.2	5.5	6.6
2019/20	6.9	3.8	-13.6	-25.5	-7.7	-22.7
2020/21	10.8	14.6	8.5	16.9	20.2	34.0
Avg.	4.4 %	5.6 %	3.9 %	5.0 %	8.5 %	10.9 %
Fq > 0	78 %	81 %	75 %	78 %	84 %	88 %

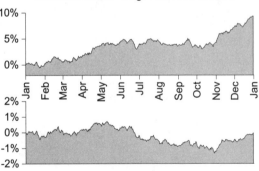

Industrials Sector - Avg. Year 1990 to 2020

Industrials / S&P 500 Rel. Strength - Avg Yr. 1990 - 2020

> Ⓨ *Alternate Strategy—*
> *Investors can bridge the gap between the two positive seasonal trends for the industrials sector by holding from October 28th to May 5th. Longer term investors may prefer this strategy, shorter term investors can use technical tools to determine the appropriate strategy.*

> ⓘ *The SP GICS Industrial Sector. For more information on the industrials sector, see www.standardandpoors.com*

Industrials Performance

Industrials Monthly % Gain (1990-2020)

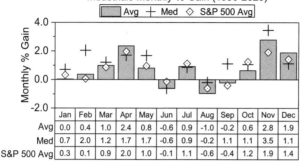

Legend: ☐ Avg + Med ◇ S&P 500 Avg

	Jan	Feb	Mar	Apr	May	Jun	Jul	Aug	Sep	Oct	Nov	Dec
Avg	0.0	0.4	1.0	2.4	0.8	-0.6	0.9	-1.0	-0.2	0.6	2.8	1.9
Med	0.7	2.0	1.2	1.7	1.7	-0.6	0.9	-0.2	1.1	1.1	3.5	1.1
S&P 500 Avg	0.3	0.1	0.9	2.0	1.0	-0.1	1.1	-0.6	-0.4	1.2	1.9	1.4

Fq Industrials Gain > 0% (1990-2020)

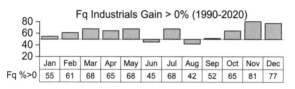

	Jan	Feb	Mar	Apr	May	Jun	Jul	Aug	Sep	Oct	Nov	Dec
Fq %>0	55	61	68	65	68	45	68	42	52	65	81	77

Fq % Industrials Gain > S&P 500 % (1990-2020)

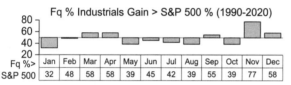

	Jan	Feb	Mar	Apr	May	Jun	Jul	Aug	Sep	Oct	Nov	Dec
Fq %> S&P 500	32	48	58	58	39	45	42	39	55	39	77	58

Industrials % Gain 5 Year (2016-2020)

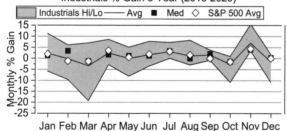

Legend: ☐ Industrials Hi/Lo — Avg ■ Med ◇ S&P 500 Avg

Industrials Performance 2020-2021

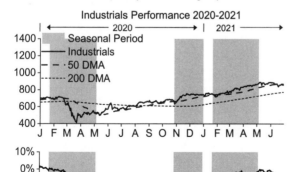

Relative Strength, % Gain vs. S&P 500

WEEK 44

**Market Indices & Rates
Weekly Values****

Stock Markets	2019	2020
Dow	27,347	26,502
S&P500	3,067	3,270
Nasdaq	8,386	10,912
TSX	16,594	15,581
FTSE	7,302	5,577
DAX	12,961	11,556
Nikkei	22,851	22,977
Hang Seng	27,101	24,107

Commodities	2019	2020
Oil	56.20	35.79
Gold	1508.8	1881.9

Bond Yields	2019	2020
USA 5 Yr Treasury	1.55	0.38
USA 10 Yr T	1.73	0.88
USA 20 Yr T	2.03	1.43
Moody's Aaa	3.02	2.39
Moody's Baa	3.89	3.49
CAN 5 Yr T	1.47	0.40
CAN 10 Yr T	1.45	0.66

Money Market	2019	2020
USA Fed Funds	1.75	0.25
USA 3 Mo T-B	1.49	0.09
CAN tgt overnight rate	1.75	0.25
CAN 3 Mo T-B	1.68	0.09

Foreign Exchange	2019	2020
EUR/USD	1.12	1.16
GBP/USD	1.29	1.29
USD/CAD	1.31	1.33
USD/JPY	108.19	104.66

OCTOBER

M	T	W	T	F	S	S
					1	2
3	4	5	6	7	8	9
10	11	12	13	14	15	16
17	18	19	20	21	22	23
24	25	26	27	28	29	30
31						

NOVEMBER

M	T	W	T	F	S	S
	1	2	3	4	5	6
7	8	9	10	11	12	13
14	15	16	17	18	19	20
21	22	23	24	25	26	27
28	29	30				

DECEMBER

M	T	W	T	F	S	S
			1	2	3	4
5	6	7	8	9	10	11
12	13	14	15	16	17	18
19	20	21	22	23	24	25
26	27	28	29	30	31	

NOVEMBER

	MONDAY	TUESDAY	WEDNESDAY
WEEK 44	31	1 29	2 28
WEEK 45	7 23	8 22	9 21
WEEK 46	14 16	15 15	16 14
WEEK 47	21 9	22 8	23 7
WEEK 48	28 2	29 1	30

THURSDAY		FRIDAY	
3	27	**4**	26
10	20	**11**	19
		USA Bond Market Closed-Veterans Day	
		CAD Bond Market Closed-Remembrance Day	
17	13	**18**	12
24	6	**25**	5
USA Market Closed-Thanksgiving Day		USA Early Market Close Thanksgiving	
1		2	

DECEMBER

M	T	W	T	F	S	S
			1	2	3	4
5	6	7	8	9	10	11
12	13	14	15	16	17	18
19	20	21	22	23	24	25
26	27	28	29	30	31	

JANUARY

M	T	W	T	F	S	S
						1
2	3	4	5	6	7	8
9	10	11	12	13	14	15
16	17	18	19	20	21	22
23	24	25	26	27	28	29
31						

FEBRUARY

M	T	W	T	F	S	S
		1	2	3	4	5
6	7	8	9	10	11	12
13	14	15	16	17	18	19
20	21	22	23	24	25	26
27	28					

MARCH

M	T	W	T	F	S	S
		1	2	3	4	5
6	7	8	9	10	11	12
13	14	15	16	17	18	19
20	21	22	23	24	25	26
27	28	29	30	31		

NOVEMBER
S U M M A R Y

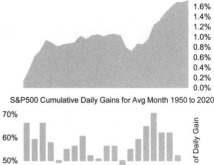

S&P500 Cumulative Daily Gains for Avg Month 1950 to 2020

	Dow Jones	S&P 500	Nasdaq	TSX Comp
Month Rank	2	1	2	5
# Up	50	49	35	23
# Down	21	22	14	13
% Pos	70	69	71	64
% Avg. Gain	1.8	1.7	1.9	1.0

Dow & S&P 1950-2020, Nasdaq 1972-2020, TSX 1985-2020

Prob. of Daily Gain

♦ November, on average, is one of the better months of the year for the S&P 500. From 1950 to 2020, it has produced an average gain of 1.7% and has been positive 69% of the time. ♦ In November, the cyclical sectors tend to start increasing their relative performance compared to the S&P 500. The metals and mining sector starts its period of seasonal strength on November 19th. ♦ For investors looking for a short-term investment, the day before and the day after Thanksgiving are on average the two strongest days of the year for the S&P 500.

BEST / WORST NOVEMBER BROAD MKTS. 2011-2020

BEST NOVEMBER MARKETS
♦ Russell 2000 (2020) 18.3%
♦ Nikkei 225 (2020) 15.0%
♦ FTSE 100 (2020) 12.4%

WORST NOVEMBER MARKETS
♦ Nikkei 225 (2011) -6.2%
♦ FTSE 100 (2016) -2.5%
♦ Nasdaq (2011) -2.4%

Index Values End of Month

	2011	2012	2013	2014	2015	2016	2017	2018	2019	2020
Dow	12,046	13,026	16,086	17,828	17,720	19,124	24,272	25,538	28,051	29,639
S&P 500	1,247	1,416	1,806	2,068	2,080	2,199	2,648	2,760	3,141	3,622
Nasdaq	2,620	3,010	4,060	4,792	5,109	5,324	6,874	7,331	8,665	12,199
TSX Comp.	12,204	12,239	13,395	14,745	13,470	15,083	16,067	15,198	17,040	17,190
Russell 1000	689	783	1,005	1,149	1,155	1,221	1,467	1,526	1,737	2,037
Russell 2000	737	822	1,143	1,173	1,198	1,322	1,544	1,533	1,625	1,820
FTSE 100	5,505	5,867	6,651	6,723	6,356	6,784	7,327	6,980	7,347	6,266
Nikkei 225	8,435	9,446	15,662	17,460	19,747	18,308	22,725	22,351	23,294	26,434

Percent Gain for November

	2011	2012	2013	2014	2015	2016	2017	2018	2019	2020
Dow	0.8	-0.5	3.5	2.5	0.3	5.4	3.8	1.7	3.7	11.8
S&P 500	-0.5	0.3	2.8	2.5	0.1	3.4	2.8	1.8	3.4	10.8
Nasdaq	-2.4	1.1	3.6	3.5	1.1	2.6	2.2	0.3	4.5	11.8
TSX Comp.	-0.4	-1.5	0.3	0.9	-0.4	2.0	0.3	1.1	3.4	10.3
Russell 1000	-0.5	0.5	2.6	2.4	0.1	3.7	2.8	1.8	3.6	11.6
Russell 2000	-0.5	0.4	3.9	0.0	3.1	11.0	2.8	1.4	4.0	18.3
FTSE 100	-0.7	1.5	-1.2	2.7	-0.1	-2.5	-2.2	-2.1	1.4	12.4
Nikkei 225	-6.2	5.8	9.3	6.4	3.5	5.1	3.2	2.0	1.6	15.0

November Market Avg. Performance 2011 to 2020[1]

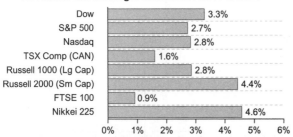

Dow 3.3%
S&P 500 2.7%
Nasdaq 2.8%
TSX Comp (CAN) 1.6%
Russell 1000 (Lg Cap) 2.8%
Russell 2000 (Sm Cap) 4.4%
FTSE 100 0.9%
Nikkei 225 4.6%

Interest Corner Nov[2]

	Fed Funds % [3]	3 Mo. T-Bill % [4]	10 Yr % [5]	20 Yr % [6]
2020	0.25	0.08	0.84	1.37
2019	1.75	1.59	1.78	2.07
2018	2.25	2.37	3.01	3.19
2017	1.25	1.27	2.42	2.65
2016	0.50	0.48	2.37	2.73

(1) Russell Data provided by Russell (2) Federal Reserve Bank of St. Louis- end of month values (3) Target rate set by FOMC (4)(5)(6) Constant yield maturities.

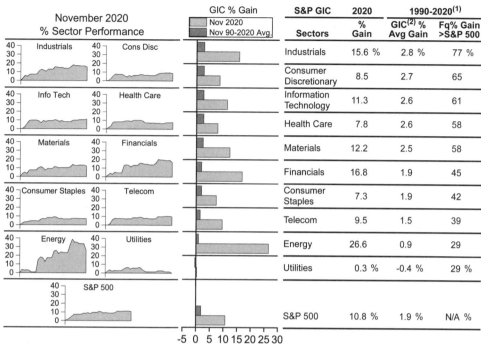

S&P GIC Sectors	2020 % Gain	1990-2020[1] GIC[2] % Avg Gain	1990-2020[1] Fq% Gain >S&P 500
Industrials	15.6 %	2.8 %	77 %
Consumer Discretionary	8.5	2.7	65
Information Technology	11.3	2.6	61
Health Care	7.8	2.6	58
Materials	12.2	2.5	58
Financials	16.8	1.9	45
Consumer Staples	7.3	1.9	42
Telecom	9.5	1.5	39
Energy	26.6	0.9	29
Utilities	0.3 %	-0.4 %	29 %
S&P 500	10.8 %	1.9 %	N/A %

Sector Commentary

♦ In November 2020, the S&P 500 managed to produce a gain of 10.8%. ♦ Information technology, which is typically one of the better performing sectors in November lived up to its reputation with a gain of 11.3%. ♦ The cyclical sectors performed well, with the energy sector gaining 26.6%. ♦ The financial sector gained 16.8%. Rising interest rates helped to bolster the financials sector. ♦ The utilities sector has on average been the weakest sector in November since 1990. In 2020, the utilities sector was the worst performing sector with a gain of 0.3%.

Sub-Sector Commentary

♦ In November 2020, the cyclical sub-sectors performed well. ♦ Typically, the semi-conductor sub-sector is one of the better performing sub-sectors. In November it produced a gain of 18.6%. ♦ The banking sub-sector produced a gain of 19.9%. ♦ Gold and silver typically perform poorly in November. In 2020, they lived up to their reputation with losses of 6.3% and 6.2% respectively.

SELECTED SUB-SECTORS[3]			
SOX (1995-2020)	18.6 %	3.9 %	62 %
Steel	12.4	3.8	55
Retail	6.5	3.4	65
Home-builders	7.6	3.3	52
Transportation	13.1	3.1	55
Agriculture (1994-2020)	7.6	2.7	37
Biotech (1993-2020)	7.7	2.5	46
Chemicals	14.4	2.4	52
Railroads	13.9	2.3	61
Automotive & Components	22.1	2.3	52
Pharma	7.9	2.3	52
Banks	19.9	2.2	52
Metals & Mining	8.2	1.8	48
Gold	-6.3	0.6	45
Silver	-6.2	0.1	42

(1) Sector data provided by Standard and Poors (2) GIC is short form for Global Industry Classification (3) Sub Sector data provided by Standard and Poors, except where marked by symbol.

MATERIAL STOCKS – MATERIAL GAINS
① Oct28-Jan6   ② Jan23-May5

The materials sector (U.S.) generally performs well during the favorable six months of the year, from the end of October to the beginning of May. The sector is economically sensitive and is leveraged to economic forecasts.

Positive 91% of the time

The materials sector has two seasonal periods. The first period is from October 28 to January 6 and the second period is from January 23 to May 5.

The time period in between the two seasonal periods, from January 7 to January 22, has had an average loss of 2.1% and only been positive 44% of the time (1990 to 2021).

Investors may decide to bridge the gap between the two seasonal periods if the materials sector has strong momentum at the beginning of January. The complete materials strategy is to be invested from October 28 to January 6, out of the sector from January 7 to the 22, and back in from January 23 to May 5.

Covid-19 Performance Update. In 2021, the materials sector relative to the S&P 500 bottomed in late January, just before its strong seasonal period started. The sector strongly outperformed the S&P 500 until early May, when its strong seasonal period ended. In May and June, the materials sector underperformed the S&P 500.

Materials* vs S&P 500 1989/90 to 2020/21 Positive ☐

Year	Oct 28 to Jan 6 S&P 500	Oct 28 to Jan 6 Mat.	Jan 23 to May 5 S&P 500	Jan 23 to May 5 Mat.	Compound Growth S&P 500	Compound Growth Mat.
1989/90	5.1 %	9.1 %	2.4 %	-3.1 %	7.7 %	5.7 %
1990/91	5.4	9.2	16.0	15.3	22.2	26.0
1991/92	8.8	1.5	-0.3	5.5	8.5	7.1
1992/93	3.8	5.6	1.9	4.3	5.8	10.2
1993/94	0.5	9.4	-4.9	-5.3	-4.4	3.6
1994/95	-1.1	-3.5	11.9	6.1	10.7	2.4
1995/96	6.4	7.6	4.6	11.1	11.3	19.5
1996/97	6.7	2.3	5.6	2.3	12.6	4.6
1997/98	10.2	1.4	15.8	20.9	27.7	22.6
1998/99	19.4	6.1	10.0	31.5	31.3	39.6
1999/00	8.2	15.7	-0.6	-7.1	7.6	7.5
2000/01	-5.9	19.2	-5.7	15.1	-11.2	37.2
2001/02	6.2	8.5	-4.1	14.9	1.8	24.7
2002/03	3.5	9.2	5.5	2.7	9.2	12.1
2003/04	9.0	16.6	-2.0	-3.0	6.8	13.1
2004/05	5.6	5.4	0.4	0.3	6.0	5.8
2005/06	9.0	16.3	5.1	14.7	14.6	33.5
2006/07	2.4	3.2	5.8	10.7	8.3	14.2
2007/08	-8.1	-5.1	7.4	16.7	-1.2	10.8
2008/09	10.1	12.0	9.2	23.3	20.3	38.1
2009/10	6.9	13.8	6.8	3.0	14.2	17.2
2010/11	7.7	11.7	4.0	4.2	12.1	16.4
2011/12	-0.5	-2.3	4.1	-2.7	3.5	-4.9
2012/13	3.9	7.2	8.2	0.0	12.3	7.2
2013/14	3.8	3.1	2.2	4.3	6.1	7.5
2014/15	2.1	-0.7	1.3	2.9	3.4	2.2
2015/16	-3.7	-6.2	7.5	18.3	3.6	11.0
2016/17	6.8	8.6	5.6	4.5	12.8	13.5
2017/18	6.3	6.4	-6.0	-8.6	-0.1	-2,8
2018/19	-4.8	1.0	11.9	7.4	6.5	8.5
2019/20	7.4	2.2	-13.6	-15.0	-7.3	-13.2
2020/21	10.5	19.9	8.4	15.6	19.9	38.6
Avg.	4.7 %	6.7 %	3.9 %	6.6 %	8.8 %	13.7 %
Fq > 0	81 %	84 %	75 %	75 %	84 %	91 %

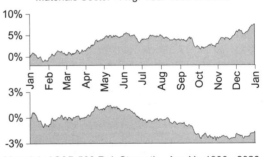

Materials Sector - Avg. Year 1990 to 2020

Materials / S&P 500 Rel. Strength - Avg Yr. 1990 - 2020

> Ⓨ *Alternate Strategy—*
> *Investors can bridge the gap between the two positive seasonal trends for the materials sector by holding from October 28 to May 5. Longer term investors may prefer this strategy. Shorter term investors can use technical tools to determine the appropriate strategy.*

> ⓘ *The SP GICS Materials Sector encompasses a wide range of materials based companies.*
> *For more information on the materials sector, see www.standardandpoors.com*

Materials Performance

Materials Monthly % Gain (1990-2020)

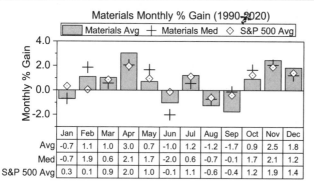

	Jan	Feb	Mar	Apr	May	Jun	Jul	Aug	Sep	Oct	Nov	Dec
Avg	-0.7	1.1	1.0	3.0	0.7	-1.0	1.2	-1.2	-1.7	0.9	2.5	1.8
Med	-0.7	1.9	0.6	2.1	1.7	-2.0	0.6	-0.7	-0.1	1.7	2.1	1.2
S&P 500 Avg	0.3	0.1	0.9	2.0	1.0	-0.1	1.1	-0.6	-0.4	1.2	1.9	1.4

Fq Materials Gain > 0% (1990-2020)

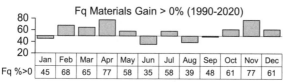

	Jan	Feb	Mar	Apr	May	Jun	Jul	Aug	Sep	Oct	Nov	Dec
Fq %>0	45	68	65	77	58	35	58	39	48	61	77	61

Fq % Materials Gain > S&P 500 % (1990-2020)

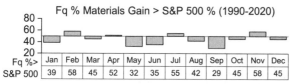

	Jan	Feb	Mar	Apr	May	Jun	Jul	Aug	Sep	Oct	Nov	Dec
Fq %> S&P 500	39	58	45	52	32	35	55	42	29	45	58	45

Materials % Gain 5 Year (2016-2020)

Materials Performance 2020-2021

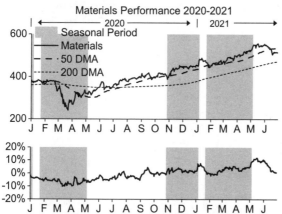

Relative Strength, % Gain vs. S&P 500

Market Indices & Rates
Weekly Values**

Stock Markets	2019	2020
Dow	27,681	28,323
S&P500	3,093	3,509
Nasdaq	8,475	11,895
TSX	16,877	16,283
FTSE	7,359	5,910
DAX	13,229	12,480
Nikkei	23,392	24,325
Hang Seng	27,651	25,713

Commodities	2019	2020
Oil	57.24	37.14
Gold	1464.2	1940.8

Bond Yields	2019	2020
USA 5 Yr Treasury	1.74	0.36
USA 10 Yr T	1.94	0.83
USA 20 Yr T	2.27	1.37
Moody's Aaa	3.17	2.31
Moody's Baa	4.05	3.34
CAN 5 Yr T	1.56	0.40
CAN 10 Yr T	1.58	0.65

Money Market	2019	2020
USA Fed Funds	1.75	0.25
USA 3 Mo T-B	1.52	0.10
CAN tgt overnight rate	1.75	0.25
CAN 3 Mo T-B	1.68	0.09

Foreign Exchange	2019	2020
EUR/USD	1.10	1.19
GBP/USD	1.28	1.32
USD/CAD	1.32	1.31
USD/JPY	109.26	103.35

NOVEMBER

M	T	W	T	F	S	S
	1	2	3	4	5	6
7	8	9	10	11	12	13
14	15	16	17	18	19	20
21	22	23	24	25	26	27
28	29	30				

DECEMBER

M	T	W	T	F	S	S
			1	2	3	4
5	6	7	8	9	10	11
12	13	14	15	16	17	18
19	20	21	22	23	24	25
26	27	28	29	30	31	

JANUARY

M	T	W	T	F	S	S
						1
2	3	4	5	6	7	8
9	10	11	12	13	14	15
16	17	18	19	20	21	22
23	24	25	26	27	28	29
30	31					

HOME DEPOT – BUILDING GAINS
① Oct28-Dec31　② Jan9-Apr15

Home Depot is part of the consumer discretionary sector, and as such, has a similar seasonal period. Both Home Depot and the consumer discretionary sector start their seasonal periods on October 28. In the seasonal period from October 28 to December 31 (1989 to 2020), Home Depot has produced an average gain of 10.6% and has been positive 78% of the time

> ### *19% gain &*
> ### *positive 84% of the time*

Home Depot has a second seasonal period from January 9 to April 15. In this period, Home Depot's strong seasonal period occurs at a similar time to the consumer discretionary and retail sectors' strong seasonal period.

Comparing the two seasonal periods, Home Depot has better performance in its October 28 to December 31 period compared to the January 9 to April 15 period.

Home Depot has a short period (January 1 to January 8) at the beginning of January where it tends to underperform the S&P 500. In this time period, during the years 1990 to 2021, on average Home Depot has lost 1.4% and has only outperformed the S&P 500, 38% of the time.

Covid-19 Performance Update. In 2021, Home Depot initially underperformed the S&P 500 as its strong seasonal period started in early January. It bottomed relative to the market in early February and then strongly outperformed in March and April. In early May, Home Depot turned lower on an absolute basis and relative to the market.

In the first half of 2021, Home Depot benefited from the do-it-yourself home renovation trend, despite rising inflation.

HD* vs. S&P 500 1989/90 to 2020/21 Positive

Year	Oct 28 to Dec 31 S&P 500	HD	Jan 9 to Apr 15 S&P 500	HD	Compound Growth S&P 500	HD
1989/90	5.5 %	9.3 %	-2.7 %	26.2 %	2.7 %	37.9 %
1990/91	8.4	28.8	21.1	64.2	31.2	111.4
1991/92	8.6	23.3	-0.4	-0.2	8.1	23.1
1992/93	4.1	18.4	4.5	-9.6	8.8	7.0
1993/94	0.4	1.6	-5.1	8.1	-4.7	9.8
1994/95	-1.4	3.1	10.5	-3.4	9.0	-0.4
1995/96	6.3	29.5	3.9	4.3	10.4	35.0
1996/97	5.7	-9.3	0.8	10.7	6.6	0.5
1997/98	10.7	15.4	17.1	23.6	29.5	42.7
1998/99	15.4	49.7	3.8	8.4	19.7	62.2
1999/00	13.3	48.0	-5.9	-5.1	6.6	40.4
2000/01	-4.3	16.0	-8.7	-12.7	-12.6	1.3
2001/02	3.9	26.6	-5.0	-3.7	-1.3	21.9
2002/03	-2.0	-21.5	-2.1	28.4	-4.0	0.8
2003/04	7.8	-1.4	-0.3	0.7	7.5	-0.7
2004/05	7.7	4.8	-3.7	-12.8	3.7	-8.7
2005/06	5.9	2.8	0.3	1.8	6.2	4.7
2006/07	3.0	8.3	2.8	-4.1	5.9	4.0
2007/08	-4.4	-14.1	-4.0	12.9	-8.2	-3.0
2008/09	6.4	21.7	-6.3	5.3	-0.3	28.1
2009/10	4.9	11.3	5.8	21.3	11.0	34.9
2010/11	6.4	13.5	3.8	11.0	10.4	26.0
2011/12	-2.1	13.0	7.2	18.0	5.0	33.2
2012/13	1.0	3.0	6.5	14.3	7.6	17.7
2013/14	5.0	8.0	0.3	-7.4	5.3	0.0
2014/15	5.0	10.0	2.2	6.3	7.2	16.9
2015/16	-1.1	6.3	8.3	9.0	7.1	15.8
2016/17	5.0	9.7	2.3	9.3	7.4	19.8
2017/18	3.6	13.3	-3.3	-10.0	0.1	1.9
2018/19	-5.7	-0.2	12.9	15.2	6.4	14.9
2019/20	6.9	-6.8	-14.4	-10.5	-8.5	-16.6
2020/21	10.8	-4.1	9.0	19.9	20.8	15.1
Avg.	4.4 %	10.6 %	1.9 %	7.5 %	6.4 %	18.7 %
Fq > 0	78 %	78 %	59 %	66 %	78 %	84 %

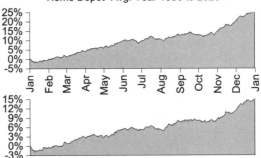

Home Depot- Avg. Year 1990 to 2020

Home Depot / S&P 500 Rel. Str. - Avg Yr. 1990 - 2020

> ⓨ *Alternate Strategy—*
> *Investors can bridge the gap between the two positive seasonal trends for Home Depot by holding from October 28th to April 15th. Longer term investors may prefer this strategy, shorter term investors can use technical tools to determine the appropriate strategy.*

> * *Home Depot trades on the NYSE, adjusted for splits.*

Home Depot Performance

HD Monthly % Gain (1990-2020)

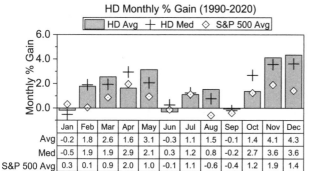

	Jan	Feb	Mar	Apr	May	Jun	Jul	Aug	Sep	Oct	Nov	Dec
Avg	-0.2	1.8	2.6	1.6	3.1	-0.3	1.1	1.5	-0.1	1.4	4.1	4.3
Med	-0.5	1.9	1.9	2.9	2.1	0.3	1.2	0.8	-0.2	2.7	3.6	3.6
S&P 500 Avg	0.3	0.1	0.9	2.0	1.0	-0.1	1.1	-0.6	-0.4	1.2	1.9	1.4

Fq HD Gain > 0% (1990-2020)

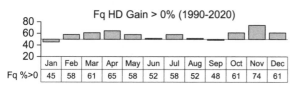

	Jan	Feb	Mar	Apr	May	Jun	Jul	Aug	Sep	Oct	Nov	Dec
Fq %>0	45	58	61	65	58	52	58	52	48	61	74	61

Fq % HD Gain > S&P 500 % (1990-2020)

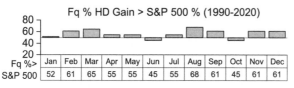

	Jan	Feb	Mar	Apr	May	Jun	Jul	Aug	Sep	Oct	Nov	Dec
Fq %> S&P 500	52	61	65	55	55	45	55	68	61	45	61	61

HD % Gain 5 Year (2016-2020)

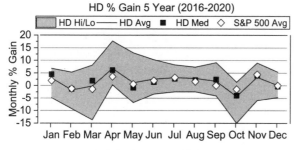

HD Performance 2020-2021

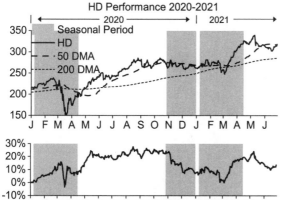

Relative Strength, % Gain vs. S&P 500

Market Indices & Rates
Weekly Values**

Stock Markets	2019	2020
Dow	28,005	29,480
S&P500	3,120	3,585
Nasdaq	8,541	11,829
TSX	17,028	16,676
FTSE	7,303	6,316
DAX	13,242	13,077
Nikkei	23,303	25,386
Hang Seng	26,327	26,157

Commodities	2019	2020
Oil	57.72	40.13
Gold	1466.9	1890.9

Bond Yields	2019	2020
USA 5 Yr Treasury	1.65	0.41
USA 10 Yr T	1.84	0.89
USA 20 Yr T	2.16	1.43
Moody's Aaa	3.10	2.35
Moody's Baa	3.97	3.33
CAN 5 Yr T	1.48	0.46
CAN 10 Yr T	1.48	0.73

Money Market	2019	2020
USA Fed Funds	1.75	0.25
USA 3 Mo T-B	1.54	0.09
CAN tgt overnight rate	1.75	0.25
CAN 3 Mo T-B	1.71	0.11

Foreign Exchange	2019	2020
EUR/USD	1.11	1.18
GBP/USD	1.29	1.32
USD/CAD	1.32	1.31
USD/JPY	108.80	104.63

NOVEMBER

M	T	W	T	F	S	S
	1	2	3	4	5	6
7	8	9	10	11	12	13
14	15	16	17	18	19	20
21	22	23	24	25	26	27
28	29	30				

DECEMBER

M	T	W	T	F	S	S
			1	2	3	4
5	6	7	8	9	10	11
12	13	14	15	16	17	18
19	20	21	22	23	24	25
26	27	28	29	30	31	

JANUARY

M	T	W	T	F	S	S
						1
2	3	4	5	6	7	8
9	10	11	12	13	14	15
16	17	18	19	20	21	22
23	24	25	26	27	28	29
30	31					

METALS AND MINING – STRONG TWO TIMES
①Nov19-Jan 5   ②Jan23-May5

At the macro level, the metals and mining (M&M) sector is driven by future economic growth expectations. When worldwide growth expectations are increasing, there is a greater need for raw materials, and vice versa.

Within the macro trend, the M&M sector has traditionally followed the overall market cycle of performing well from autumn until spring. This is the time of year that investors have a positive outlook on the economy and as a result, the cyclical sectors tend to outperform, including the metals and mining sector.

14% gain

The metals and mining sector has two seasonal "sweet spots" – the first from November 19 to January 5 and the second from January 23 to May 5.

Investors have the option to hold and "bridge the gap" across the two sweet spots, but over the long-term, nimble traders have been able to capture extra value by being out of the sector from January 6 to the 22.

From a portfolio perspective, it is important to consider reducing exposure at the beginning of May. The danger of holding on too long is that the sector tends not to perform well in the late summer, particularly in September.

Covid-19 Pandemic Update. In the first part of 2021, the metals and mining sector performed well in its strong seasonal period. The sector turned lower in May, shortly after its strong seasonal period ended.

For more information on the metals and mining sector, see www.standardandpoors.com

Metals & Mining* vs. S&P 500
1989/90 to 2020/21   Positive ▢

Year	Nov 19 to Jan 5 S&P 500	M&M	Jan 23 to May 5 S&P 500	M&M	Compound Growth S&P 500	M&M
1989/90	3.1 %	6.3 %	2.4 %	-4.6 %	5.6 %	1.4 %
1990/91	1.2	6.4	16.0	7.1	17.4	13.9
1991/92	8.9	1.0	-0.3	-1.7	8.5	-0.7
1992/93	2.7	12.5	1.9	3.2	4.7	16.1
1993/94	0.9	9.0	-4.9	-11.1	-4.1	-3.1
1994/95	-0.2	-1.2	11.9	-3.0	11.6	-4.1
1995/96	2.8	8.3	4.6	5.8	7.5	14.6
1996/97	1.5	-1.9	5.6	-1.2	7.2	-3.0
1997/98	4.1	-4.5	15.8	19.3	20.6	13.9
1998/99	8.8	-7.9	10.0	31.0	19.6	20.6
1999/00	-1.6	21.7	-0.6	-10.4	-2.2	9.1
2000/01	-5.1	17.0	-5.7	19.6	-10.5	40.0
2001/02	3.0	5.5	-4.1	12.8	-1.3	19.0
2002/03	0.9	9.3	5.5	3.2	6.4	12.8
2003/04	8.5	18.2	-2.0	-12.1	6.4	3.9
2004/05	0.0	-8.4	0.4	-4.0	0.4	-12.0
2005/06	2.0	17.3	5.1	27.3	7.2	49.4
2006/07	0.6	3.0	5.8	17.2	6.5	20.8
2007/08	-3.2	0.9	7.4	27.4	3.9	28.5
2008/09	8.0	43.8	9.2	30.6	17.9	87.8
2009/10	2.4	6.3	6.8	4.8	9.4	11.3
2010/11	6.7	15.0	4.0	-1.6	11.0	13.1
2011/12	5.4	1.2	4.1	-16.0	9.7	-15.0
2012/13	7.8	3.9	8.2	-16.8	16.6	-13.6
2013/14	2.2	1.2	2.2	2.6	4.4	3.8
2014/15	-1.5	-14.2	1.3	5.3	-0.3	-9.7
2015/16	-3.2	-3.4	7.5	76.3	4.1	70.2
2016/17	4.0	7.2	5.6	-10.8	9.8	-4.4
2017/18	6.4	24.3	-6.0	-11.5	0.0	9.9
2018/19	-7.5	-7.4	11.9	-2.6	3.5	-9.8
2019/20	3.6	9.7	-13.6	12.7	-10.5	23.6
2020/21	4.5	13.6	8.5	27.2	13.3	44.4
Avg.	2.4 %	6.7 %	3.9 %	7.1 %	6.4 %	14.4 %
Fq > 0	78 %	75 %	75 %	56 %	81 %	69 %

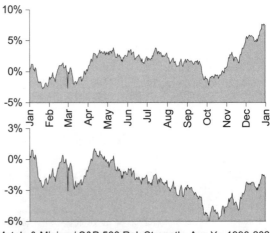

Metals & Mining - Avg. Year 1990 to 2020

Metals & Mining / S&P 500 Rel. Strength- Avg Yr. 1990-2020

Metals & Mining Performance

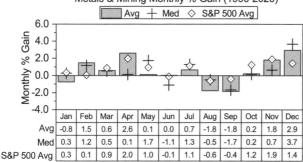

Metals & Mining Monthly % Gain (1990-2020)

Avg + Med ◇ S&P 500 Avg

	Jan	Feb	Mar	Apr	May	Jun	Jul	Aug	Sep	Oct	Nov	Dec
Avg	-0.8	1.5	0.6	2.6	0.1	0.0	0.7	-1.8	-1.8	0.2	1.8	2.9
Med	0.3	1.2	0.5	0.1	1.7	-1.1	1.3	-0.5	-1.7	0.2	0.7	3.7
S&P 500 Avg	0.3	0.1	0.9	2.0	1.0	-0.1	1.1	-0.6	-0.4	1.2	1.9	1.4

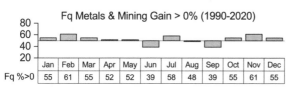

Fq Metals & Mining Gain > 0% (1990-2020)

	Jan	Feb	Mar	Apr	May	Jun	Jul	Aug	Sep	Oct	Nov	Dec
Fq %>0	55	61	55	52	52	39	58	48	39	55	61	55

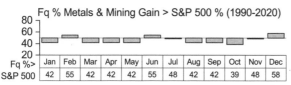

Fq % Metals & Mining Gain > S&P 500 % (1990-2020)

	Jan	Feb	Mar	Apr	May	Jun	Jul	Aug	Sep	Oct	Nov	Dec
Fq %> S&P 500	42	55	42	42	42	55	48	42	42	39	48	58

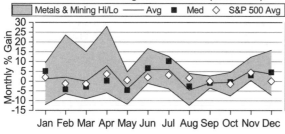

Metals & Mining % Gain 5 Year (2016-2020)

Metals & Mining Hi/Lo —— Avg ■ Med ◇ S&P 500 Avg

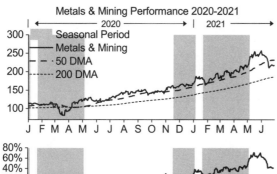

Metals & Mining Performance 2020-2021

2020 | 2021
Seasonal Period
Metals & Mining
50 DMA
200 DMA

Relative Strength, % Gain vs. S&P 500

Market Indices & Rates
Weekly Values**

Stock Markets	2019	2020
Dow	27,876	29,263
S&P500	3,110	3,558
Nasdaq	8,520	11,855
TSX	16,955	17,019
FTSE	7,327	6,351
DAX	13,164	13,137
Nikkei	23,113	25,527
Hang Seng	26,595	26,452

Commodities	2019	2020
Oil	57.70	42.15
Gold	1464.5	1875.7

Bond Yields	2019	2020
USA 5 Yr Treasury	1.62	0.38
USA 10 Yr T	1.77	0.83
USA 20 Yr T	2.08	1.33
Moody's Aaa	3.03	2.24
Moody's Baa	3.91	3.18
CAN 5 Yr T	1.50	0.42
CAN 10 Yr T	1.47	0.65

Money Market	2019	2020
USA Fed Funds	1.75	0.25
USA 3 Mo T-B	1.55	0.07
CAN tgt overnight rate	1.75	0.25
CAN 3 Mo T-B	1.66	0.11

Foreign Exchange	2019	2020
EUR/USD	1.10	1.19
GBP/USD	1.28	1.33
USD/CAD	1.33	1.31
USD/JPY	108.66	103.86

NOVEMBER

M	T	W	T	F	S	S
	1	2	3	4	5	6
7	8	9	10	11	12	13
14	15	16	17	18	19	20
21	22	23	24	25	26	27
28	29	30				

DECEMBER

M	T	W	T	F	S	S
		1	2	3	4	
5	6	7	8	9	10	11
12	13	14	15	16	17	18
19	20	21	22	23	24	25
26	27	28	29	30	31	

JANUARY

M	T	W	T	F	S	S
						1
2	3	4	5	6	7	8
9	10	11	12	13	14	15
16	17	18	19	20	21	22
23	24	25	26	27	28	29
30	31					

UPS – DELIVERING RETURNS

UPS
① LONG (Oct10-Dec8)
② SELL SHORT (Dec9-Mar1)

In recent years, Amazon has shown an increasing interest in delivering its own packages, rather than using package delivery companies. Although this trend is expected to continue, consideration should still be given to investing in UPS in its seasonal period before Christmas, as this is when UPS would still be expected to outperform the S&P 500.

Investors look for an activity that could drive a stock price higher. In UPS' case investors typically become more interested in the stock just before the holiday season. The logic is that a busy time of year will help increase earnings, which should raise the stock price.

12% growth & positive 86% of the time

The best time to get into UPS is before most investors become excited about the stock. When maximum investor interest for the stock occurs, it has been best to exit.

"Get in before everyone else and exit once everyone is in." In other words, the seasonal trend takes advantage of human behavioral tendencies.

Investors typically do not want to invest in UPS at the times of the year when its stock price lacks a near-term catalyst. January and February are low activity months for UPS. As a result, investors tend to reduce their buying of package delivery companies at the end of the year and into the beginning of March.

Covid-19 Pandemic Update. In its weak seasonal period from mid-December of 2020 to early March 2021,

UPS* vs. S&P 500 2000/01 to 2020/21

Positive Long | Negative Short

Year	Oct 10 to Dec 8 S&P 500	UPS	Dec 9 to Mar 1 S&P 500	UPS	Compound Growth S&P 500	UPS
2000/01	-2.3 %	12.0 %	-9.4 %	-12.1 %	-11.5 %	25.5 %
2001/02	9.6	12.1	-2.3	3.3	7.1	8.5
2002/03	17.4	6.5	-7.8	-10.2	8.3	17.4
2003/04	2.9	11.1	8.1	-4.9	11.3	16.5
2004/05	5.4	14.5	2.3	-11.0	7.9	27.1
2005/06	5.0	9.6	2.8	0.4	8.0	9.2
2006/07	4.4	5.6	-0.5	-10.2	3.9	16.3
2007/08	-3.9	-3.5	-11.6	-5.3	-15.0	1.6
2008/09	0.0	10.6	-19.2	-29.8	-19.2	43.5
2009/10	1.9	3.2	2.2	1.9	4.1	1.2
2010/11	5.4	6.6	6.4	0.5	12.1	6.1
2011/12	6.8	8.7	11.3	6.8	18.9	1.3
2012/13	-1.6	0.2	7.1	13.3	5.3	-13.1
2013/14	9.0	15.5	3.0	-6.5	12.3	23.0
2014/15	6.9	14.2	2.1	-7.7	9.1	22.9
2015/16	2.4	-2.4	-4.1	-2.8	-1.8	0.3
2016/17	4.3	9.4	6.7	-10.2	11.2	20.5
2017/18	4.2	2.1	1.0	-11.0	5.2	13.3
2018/19	-8.6	-10.7	6.5	6.5	-2.7	-16.5
2019/20	7.8	3.2	-6.1	-23.0	1.2	27.0
2020/21	6.5	-4.8	5.4	-3.0	12.2	-1.9
Avg.	4.0 %	5.9 %	0.2 %	-5.5 %	4.2 %	11.9 %
Fq>0	76 %	81 %	62 %	33 %	76 %	86 %

UPS was negative and underperformed the S&P 500. In April 2021, UPS started to outperform the S&P 500 and strong earnings gave it a boost into early May. Shortly afterwards, UPS started to perform poorly.

UPS - Avg. Year 2000 to 2020

UPS / S&P 500 Rel. Strength- Avg Yr. 2000-2020

ⓘ *UPS trades on the NYSE, adjusted for splits.*

UPS Performance

UPS Monthly % Gain (2000-2020)

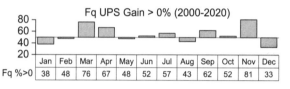

Legend: UPS Avg + UPS Med ◇ S&P 500 Avg

	Jan	Feb	Mar	Apr	May	Jun	Jul	Aug	Sep	Oct	Nov	Dec
Avg	-3.0	-1.8	3.4	1.7	-1.0	0.1	3.1	-0.0	0.4	1.0	4.5	-1.8
Med	-3.1	-0.3	1.7	0.9	-0.6	0.7	0.4	-0.5	1.0	1.0	4.2	-1.6
S&P 500 Avg	-0.3	-0.6	0.9	2.3	0.3	-0.5	1.1	0.1	-1.0	1.0	1.7	0.7

Fq UPS Gain > 0% (2000-2020)

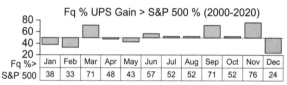

	Jan	Feb	Mar	Apr	May	Jun	Jul	Aug	Sep	Oct	Nov	Dec
Fq %>0	38	48	76	67	48	52	57	43	62	52	81	33

Fq % UPS Gain > S&P 500 % (2000-2020)

	Jan	Feb	Mar	Apr	May	Jun	Jul	Aug	Sep	Oct	Nov	Dec
Fq %> S&P 500	38	33	71	48	43	57	52	52	71	52	76	24

UPS % Gain 5 Year (2016-2020)

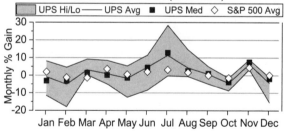

Legend: UPS Hi/Lo — UPS Avg ■ UPS Med ◇ S&P 500 Avg

UPS Performance 2020-2021

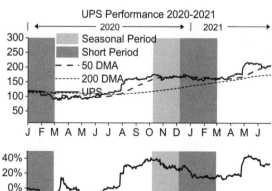

Relative Strength, % Gain vs. S&P 500

Market Indices & Rates
Weekly Values**

Stock Markets	2019	2020
Dow	28,051	29,910
S&P500	3,141	3,638
Nasdaq	8,665	12,206
TSX	17,040	17,397
FTSE	7,347	6,368
DAX	13,236	13,336
Nikkei	23,294	26,645
Hang Seng	26,346	26,895

Commodities	2019	2020
Oil	55.17	45.51
Gold	1460.2	1779.3

Bond Yields	2019	2020
USA 5 Yr Treasury	1.62	0.37
USA 10 Yr T	1.78	0.84
USA 20 Yr T	2.07	1.36
Moody's Aaa	2.95	2.20
Moody's Baa	3.86	3.16
CAN 5 Yr T	1.49	0.43
CAN 10 Yr T	1.46	0.68

Money Market	2019	2020
USA Fed Funds	1.75	0.25
USA 3 Mo T-B	1.56	0.09
CAN tgt overnight rate	1.75	0.25
CAN 3 Mo T-B	1.65	0.12

Foreign Exchange	2019	2020
EUR/USD	1.10	1.20
GBP/USD	1.29	1.33
USD/CAD	1.33	1.30
USD/JPY	109.49	104.09

NOVEMBER

M	T	W	T	F	S	S
	1	2	3	4	5	6
7	8	9	10	11	12	13
14	15	16	17	18	19	20
21	22	23	24	25	26	27
28	29	30				

DECEMBER

M	T	W	T	F	S	S
			1	2	3	4
5	6	7	8	9	10	11
12	13	14	15	16	17	18
19	20	21	22	23	24	25
26	27	28	29	30	31	

JANUARY

M	T	W	T	F	S	S
						1
2	3	4	5	6	7	8
9	10	11	12	13	14	15
16	17	18	19	20	21	22
23	24	25	26	27	28	29
30	31					

DECEMBER

	MONDAY	TUESDAY	WEDNESDAY
WEEK 48	28	29	30
WEEK 49	**5** 26	**6** 25	**7** 24
WEEK 50	**12** 19	**13** 18	**14** 17
WEEK 51	**19** 12	**20** 11	**21** 10
WEEK 52	**26** 5 CAN Market Closed- Christmas Day USA Market Closed- Christmas Day	**27** 4 CAN Market Closed- Boxing Day	**28** 3

THURSDAY		FRIDAY	
1	30	**2**	29
8	23	**9**	22
15	16	**16**	15
22	9	**23**	8
29	2	**30**	1

JANUARY

M	T	W	T	F	S	S
						1
2	3	4	5	6	7	8
9	10	11	12	13	14	15
16	17	18	19	20	21	22
23	24	25	26	27	28	29
31						

FEBRUARY

M	T	W	T	F	S	S
		1	2	3	4	5
6	7	8	9	10	11	12
13	14	15	16	17	18	19
20	21	22	23	24	25	26
27	28					

MARCH

M	T	W	T	F	S	S
		1	2	3	4	5
6	7	8	9	10	11	12
13	14	15	16	17	18	19
20	21	22	23	24	25	26
27	28	29	30	31		

APRIL

M	T	W	T	F	S	S
					1	2
3	4	5	6	7	8	9
10	11	12	13	14	15	16
17	18	19	20	21	22	23
24	25	26	27	28	29	30

DECEMBER
S U M M A R Y

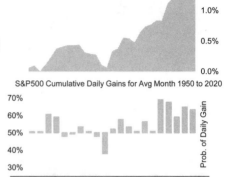

S&P500 Cumulative Daily Gains for Avg Month 1950 to 2020

	Dow Jones	S&P 500	Nasdaq	TSX Comp
Month Rank	3	3	4	1
# Up	50	53	29	30
# Down	21	18	20	6
% Pos	70	75	59	83
% Avg. Gain	1.5	1.5	1.5	1.6

Dow & S&P 1950-2020, Nasdaq 1972-2020 TSX 1985-2020

◆ December is typically one of the strongest months of the year for the S&P 500. From 1950 to 2020, the S&P 500 produced an average gain of 1.5% and was positive 75% of the time. ◆ Most of the gains for the S&P 500 tend to occur in the second half of the month. ◆ The Nasdaq tends to outperform the S&P 500 starting mid-December. ◆ The small cap sector typically starts to outperform the S&P 500 mid-month. ◆ In 2020, the S&P 500 rallied strongly for most of December.

BEST / WORST DECEMBER BROAD MKTS. 2011-2020

BEST DECEMBER MARKETS
- Nikkei 225 (2012) 10.0%
- Russell 2000 (2020) 8.5%
- Nasdaq (2020) 5.7%

WORST DECEMBER MARKETS
- Russell 2000 (2018) -12.0%
- Nikkei 225 (2018) -10.5%
- Nasdaq (2018) -9.5%

Index Values End of Month

	2011	2012	2013	2014	2015	2016	2017	2018	2019	2020
Dow	12,218	13,104	16,577	17,823	17,425	19,763	24,719	23,327	28,538	30,606
S&P 500	1,258	1,426	1,848	2,059	2,044	2,239	2,674	2,507	3,231	3,756
Nasdaq	2,605	3,020	4,177	4,736	5,007	5,383	6,903	6,635	8,973	12,888
TSX Comp.	11,955	12,434	13,622	14,632	13,010	15,288	16,209	14,323	17,063	17,433
Russell 1000	693	790	1,030	1,144	1,132	1,242	1,482	1,384	1,784	2,121
Russell 2000	741	849	1,164	1,205	1,136	1,357	1,536	1,349	1,668	1,975
FTSE 100	5,572	5,898	6,749	6,566	6,242	7,143	7,688	6,728	7,542	6,461
Nikkei 225	8,455	10,395	16,291	17,451	19,034	19,114	22,765	20,015	23,657	27,444

Percent Gain for December

	2011	2012	2013	2014	2015	2016	2017	2018	2019	2020
Dow	1.4	0.6	3.0	0.0	-1.7	3.3	1.8	-8.7	1.7	3.3
S&P 500	0.9	0.7	2.4	-0.4	-1.8	1.8	1.0	-9.2	2.9	3.7
Nasdaq	-0.6	0.3	2.9	-1.2	-2.0	1.1	0.4	-9.5	3.5	5.7
TSX Comp.	-2.0	1.6	1.7	-0.8	-3.4	1.4	0.9	-5.8	0.1	1.4
Russell 1000	0.7	0.8	2.5	-0.4	-2.0	1.7	1.0	-9.3	2.7	4.1
Russell 2000	0.5	3.3	1.8	2.7	-5.2	2.6	-0.6	-12.0	2.7	8.5
FTSE 100	1.2	0.5	1.5	-2.3	-1.8	5.3	4.9	-3.6	2.7	3.1
Nikkei 225	0.2	10.0	4.0	-0.1	-3.6	4.4	0.2	-10.5	1.6	3.8

December Market Avg. Performance 2011 to 2020[1]

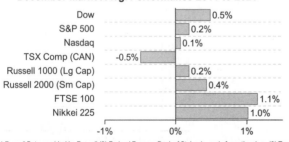

Dow	0.5%
S&P 500	0.2%
Nasdaq	0.1%
TSX Comp (CAN)	-0.5%
Russell 1000 (Lg Cap)	0.2%
Russell 2000 (Sm Cap)	0.4%
FTSE 100	1.1%
Nikkei 225	1.0%

Interest Corner Dec[2]

	Fed Funds % [3]	3 Mo. T-Bill % [4]	10 Yr % [5]	20 Yr % [6]
2021	0.25	0.09	0.93	1.45
2020	1.75	1.55	1.92	2.25
2019	2.50	2.45	2.69	2.87
2018	1.50	1.39	2.40	2.58
2017	0.75	0.51	2.45	2.79

(1) Russell Data provided by Russell (2) Federal Reserve Bank of St. Louis- end of month values (3) Target rate set by FOMC (4)(5)(6) Constant yield maturities.

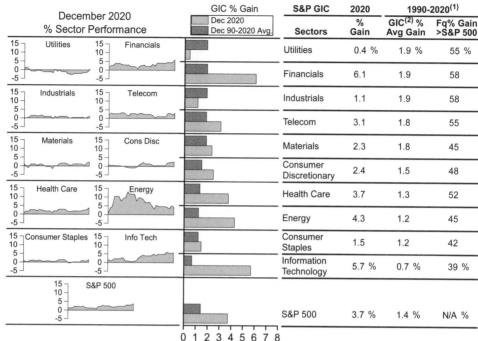

S&P GIC Sectors	2020 % Gain	1990-2020[1] GIC[2] % Avg Gain	1990-2020[1] Fq% Gain >S&P 500
Utilities	0.4 %	1.9 %	55 %
Financials	6.1	1.9	58
Industrials	1.1	1.9	58
Telecom	3.1	1.8	55
Materials	2.3	1.8	45
Consumer Discretionary	2.4	1.5	48
Health Care	3.7	1.3	52
Energy	4.3	1.2	45
Consumer Staples	1.5	1.2	42
Information Technology	5.7 %	0.7 %	39 %
S&P 500	3.7 %	1.4 %	N/A %

Sector Commentary

♦ In December 2020, all of the major sectors were positive ♦ The strongest performing sector was the information technology sector with a gain of 5.7%. Typically, the energy sector is one of the weaker sectors in December. ♦ The energy sector also performed well with a gain of 4.3%. It is also typically weak in December. ♦ The utilities sector has been the strongest performing sector since 1990. In December, the utilities sector produced a nominal gain of 0.4%.

Sub-Sector Commentary

♦ In December 2020, silver produced a gain of 19.6%. Silver benefited from investors trying to short squeeze the precious metal (buying silver in order to force investors that are short silver, to buy silver). ♦ Generally, the cyclical sub-sectors performed well. ♦ The metals and mining sub-sector gained 4.6%. Banks gained 8.4%. ♦ The home-builders sub-sector is typically a strong sub-sector in December. ♦ Rising interest rates took its toll on the homebuilders sub-sector and it produced a loss of 2.2% in December.

SELECTED SUB-SECTORS[3]			
Homebuilders	-2.2 %	5.9 %	74 %
Steel	-0.9	3.8	58
Biotech (1993-2020)	2.3	3.2	46
Metals & Mining	4.6	3.0	58
Silver	19.6	2.0	52
Agriculture (1994-2020)	1.3	1.9	52
Banks	8.4	1.8	61
Chemicals	1.8	1.5	52
Pharma	4.4	1.2	48
SOX (1995-2020)	5.0	1.1	50
Railroads	1.8	1.1	45
Retail	2.0	0.7	35
Automotive & Components	-0.5	0.6	32
Transportation	-0.4	0.5	35
Gold	7.1	0.4	39

EMERGING MARKETS (USD) – TRUNCATED SIX MONTH SEASONAL
November 24 to April 18

Emerging markets become popular periodically, mainly after they have had a strong run, or if they have suffered a major correction and investors perceive them as having a lot of value.

Markets around the world tend to have the same broad seasonal trends, including emerging markets.

Emerging markets outperform the S&P 500 more often, when the S&P 500 is increasing, and underperform when the S&P 500 is decreasing. Given that the S&P 500 has a higher probability of increasing in the favorable six-month period for stocks, from October 27 to May 5, emerging markets will have a higher probability of outperforming the S&P 500 sometime within the six-month favorable for stocks.

9% gain & positive 84% of the time positive

Seasonal investors have benefited from concentrating their emerging market exposure in a truncated, or shorter time period within the favorable six month seasonal period. The seasonally strong period for the emerging markets sector is from November 24 to April 18.

Emerging Markets (USD)* vs. S&P 500 1989/90 to 2020/21			
Nov 24 to Apr 18	S&P 500	Positive Em. Mkts.	Diff
1989/90	-0.3%	4.5%	4.9%
1990/91	23.3	33.8	10.5
1991/92	10.6	37.5	26.8
1992/93	5.6	11.8	6.2
1993/94	-4.0	3.7	7.8
1994/95	12.3	-16.4	-28.7
1995/96	7.6	14.7	7.1
1996/97	2.4	7.1	4.7
1997/98	16.6	6.7	-9.9
1998/99	11.0	18.1	7.1
1999/00	2.6	3.5	0.8
2000/01	-6.4	-4.6	1.8
2001/02	-2.3	22.3	24.5
2002/03	-4.0	0.0	4.0
2003/04	9.6	19.5	9.9
2004/05	-2.6	4.3	7.0
2005/06	3.3	24.7	21.4
2006/07	4.7	13.2	8.5
2007/08	-3.5	-0.9	2.6
2008/09	8.7	37.6	28.9
2009/10	7.8	5.6	-2.2
2010/11	10.5	6.6	-3.9
2011/12	19.2	15.6	-3.6
2012/13	9.4	0.1	-9.3
2013/14	3.3	0.3	-3.1
2014/15	0.9	3.8	3.0
2015/16	0.4	0.3	-0.1
2016/17	6.2	11.9	5.7
2017/18	4.3	2.1	-2.2
2018/19	10.4	12.7	2.4
2019/20	-7.6	-14.0	-6.5
2020/21	17.0	10.5	-6.5
Avg	5.5%	9.3%	3.7%
Fq > 0	75%	84%	66%

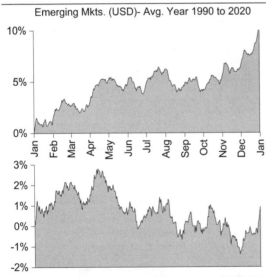

Emerging Mkts. (USD)- Avg. Year 1990 to 2020

Emerg. Mkts. (USD)/S&P 500 Rel. Str. - Avg Yr. 1990-2020

Covid-19 Performance Update. The emerging markets initially performed well in 2020 as the economic recovery took place from the Covid-19 pandemic. In 2021, after an initial rally into February, the emerging markets turned lower and underperformed the S&P 500, as the US dollar strengthened relative to world currencies. The emerging markets continued to underperform the S&P 500 in the remainder of the first half of 2021.

* Emerging Markets (USD)- For more information on the emerging markets, see www.standardandpoors.com

Emerging Markets Performance

Emerging Mkts. Monthly % Gain (1990-2020)

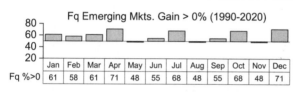

Legend: Avg, + Med, ◇ S&P 500 Avg

	Jan	Feb	Mar	Apr	May	Jun	Jul	Aug	Sep	Oct	Nov	Dec
Avg	1.2	1.3	0.3	2.4	-0.4	-0.2	1.5	-1.8	-0.9	1.0	0.7	3.2
Med	0.6	0.9	0.7	1.8	-0.6	0.2	1.6	-0.5	0.6	2.2	-0.2	3.5
S&P 500 Avg	0.3	0.1	0.9	2.0	1.0	-0.1	1.1	-0.6	-0.4	1.2	1.9	1.4

Fq Emerging Mkts. Gain > 0% (1990-2020)

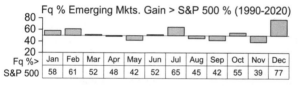

	Jan	Feb	Mar	Apr	May	Jun	Jul	Aug	Sep	Oct	Nov	Dec
Fq %>0	61	58	61	71	48	55	68	48	55	68	48	71

Fq % Emerging Mkts. Gain > S&P 500 % (1990-2020)

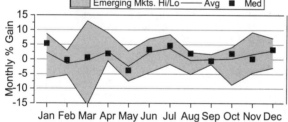

	Jan	Feb	Mar	Apr	May	Jun	Jul	Aug	Sep	Oct	Nov	Dec
Fq %> S&P 500	58	61	52	48	42	52	65	45	42	55	39	77

Emerging Mkts. % Gain 5 Year (2016-2020)

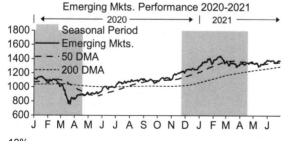

Legend: Emerging Mkts. Hi/Lo — Avg ■ Med

Emerging Mkts. Performance 2020-2021

- Seasonal Period
- Emerging Mkts.
- 50 DMA
- 200 DMA

Relative Strength, % Gain vs. S&P 500

WEEK 49

Market Indices & Rates
Weekly Values**

Stock Markets	2019	2020
Dow	28,015	30,218
S&P500	3,146	3,699
Nasdaq	8,657	12,464
TSX	16,997	17,521
FTSE	7,240	6,550
DAX	13,167	13,299
Nikkei	23,354	26,751
Hang Seng	26,498	26,836

Commodities	2019	2020
Oil	59.20	46.26
Gold	1459.7	1843.0

Bond Yields	2019	2020
USA 5 Yr Treasury	1.67	0.42
USA 10 Yr T	1.84	0.97
USA 20 Yr T	2.14	1.53
Moody's Aaa	3.03	2.26
Moody's Baa	3.91	3.20
CAN 5 Yr T	1.59	0.50
CAN 10 Yr T	1.58	0.80

Money Market	2019	2020
USA Fed Funds	1.75	0.25
USA 3 Mo T-B	1.50	0.09
CAN tgt overnight rate	1.75	0.25
CAN 3 Mo T-B	1.65	0.12

Foreign Exchange	2019	2020
EUR/USD	1.11	1.21
GBP/USD	1.31	1.34
USD/CAD	1.33	1.28
USD/JPY	108.58	104.17

DECEMBER

M	T	W	T	F	S	S
			1	2	3	4
5	6	7	8	9	10	11
12	13	14	15	16	17	18
19	20	21	22	23	24	25
26	27	28	29	30	31	

JANUARY

M	T	W	T	F	S	S
						1
2	3	4	5	6	7	8
9	10	11	12	13	14	15
16	17	18	19	20	21	22
23	24	25	26	27	28	29
30	31					

FEBRUARY

M	T	W	T	F	S
	1	2	3	4	5
6	7	8	9	10	11	12
13	14	15	16	17	18	19
20	21	22	23	24	25	26
27	28					

10-YR INFLATION BREAK-EVEN (B/E) RATE
December 20th to Mar 7th

10-YR Inflation Break-Even (B/E) rate

The 10YR inflation break-even rate is representative of investors' expectations for inflation over the next ten years. It is approximately calculated by subtracting the yield on the 10 Year Treasury Inflation Protected bonds (TIPS) from the yield on 10 Year US Treasury 10 year bonds.

The mantra that is inflation is dead has been prevalent in the bull market that started after the Great Financial Crash (GFC). There are undoubtedly reasons why there is downward pressure on inflation, including aging demographics and increasing productivity from computerization, but inflation is not dead.

5% increase & positive 82% of the time

There will be a time when inflation once again makes a comeback. It could be stoked by too much money printing trying to stimulate the economy or rising supply costs. The point is that at some point it will be a problem again.

Since the GFC, as inflation expectations have remained subdued, investors have on average adjusted their expectations upwards for inflation towards the end of the year and into early March of the following year. The most probably cause of this phenomenon is investors adjusting their expectations based upon overly optimistic full year analyst forecasts that generally get published at the end of the year and the beginning of the next year.

10 YR Inflation Break-Even* 2003/04 to 2020/21	
Positive	
Dec 20 to Mar 7	B/E
2003/04	8.6 %
2004/05	4.3
2005/06	10.3
2006/07	2.2
2007/08	9.4
2008/09	440.0*
2009/10	-1.3
2010/11	10.1
2011/12	13.4
2012/13	3.2
2013/14	3.7
2014/15	8.9
2015/16	1.4
2016/17	9.1
2017/18	11.5
2018/19	5.6
2019/20	-26.0
2020/21	13.8
Avg	5.2* %
Fq > 0	83* %

*2008/09 data has been excluded from average and frequency % positive data.

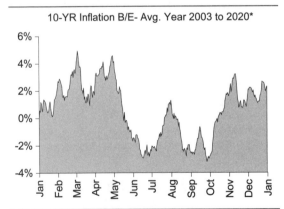

10-YR Inflation B/E- Avg. Year 2003 to 2020*

* Excludes 2008-2009 due to extreme volatility

At the retail level, one of the better methods of taking advantage of the 10YR-B/E strategy is to invest in an ETF that invests in Treasury Inflation Protected TIPS bonds and to short sell an ETF that represents the US 10YR Government bonds of the same maturity. It is important to consider the full risk of the trade, including all of the costs that go along with short selling.

Although most investors will probably not invest directly in a B/E spread trade, investors can still benefit from understanding the impact of investing in other sectors of the stock and bond markets that are affected by changing inflation expectations.

Covid-19 Performance Update. The inflation break-even rose rapidly at the beginning of the 2021 in its strong seasonal period. In May, the inflation break-even turned lower. May is one of the weakest months of the year for the inflation break-even rate.

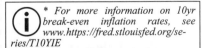 *For more information on 10yr break-even inflation rates, see www.https://fred.stlouisfed.org/series/T10YIE*

10YR Inflation Break-Even Performance

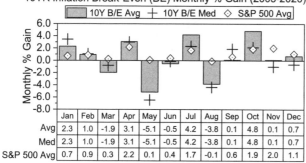

10YR Inflation Break-Even (BE) Monthly % Gain (2003-2020)*

Legend: 10Y B/E Avg | 10Y B/E Med | S&P 500 Avg

	Jan	Feb	Mar	Apr	May	Jun	Jul	Aug	Sep	Oct	Nov	Dec
Avg	2.3	1.0	-1.9	3.1	-5.1	-0.5	4.2	-3.8	0.1	4.8	0.1	0.7
Med	2.3	1.0	-1.9	3.1	-5.1	-0.5	4.2	-3.8	0.1	4.8	0.1	0.7
S&P 500 Avg	0.7	0.9	0.3	2.2	0.1	0.4	1.7	-0.1	0.6	1.9	2.0	1.1

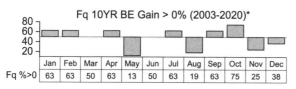

Fq 10YR BE Gain > 0% (2003-2020)*

	Jan	Feb	Mar	Apr	May	Jun	Jul	Aug	Sep	Oct	Nov	Dec
Fq %>0	63	63	50	63	13	50	63	19	63	75	25	38

Fq % 10YR BE Gain > S&P 500 % (2003-2020)*

	Jan	Feb	Mar	Apr	May	Jun	Jul	Aug	Sep	Oct	Nov	Dec
Fq %> S&P 500	69	50	31	56	19	38	75	25	50	63	31	38

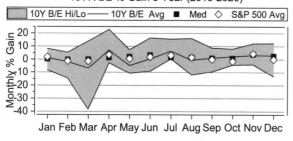

10YR BE % Gain 5 Year (2016-2020)

Legend: 10Y B/E Hi/Lo | 10Y B/E Avg | Med | S&P 500 Avg

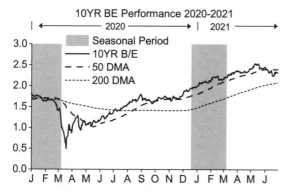

10YR BE Performance 2020-2021

2020 → | 2021 →

Legend: Seasonal Period | 10YR B/E | 50 DMA | 200 DMA

*2008 & 2009 excluded due to extreme volatility

Market Indices & Rates
Weekly Values**

Stock Markets	2019	2020
Dow	28,135	30,046
S&P500	3,169	3,663
Nasdaq	8,735	12,378
TSX	17,003	17,549
FTSE	7,353	6,547
DAX	13,283	13,114
Nikkei	24,023	26,653
Hang Seng	27,688	26,506

Commodities	2019	2020
Oil	60.07	46.57
Gold	1466.6	1842.0

Bond Yields	2019	2020
USA 5 Yr Treasury	1.66	0.37
USA 10 Yr T	1.82	0.90
USA 20 Yr T	2.11	1.42
Moody's Aaa	2.97	2.27
Moody's Baa	3.84	3.13
CAN 5 Yr T	1.59	0.44
CAN 10 Yr T	1.58	0.71

Money Market	2019	2020
USA Fed Funds	1.75	0.25
USA 3 Mo T-B	1.54	0.08
CAN tgt overnight rate	1.75	0.25
CAN 3 Mo T-B	1.66	0.13

Foreign Exchange	2019	2020
EUR/USD	1.11	1.21
GBP/USD	1.33	1.32
USD/CAD	1.32	1.28
USD/JPY	109.38	104.04

DECEMBER

M	T	W	T	F	S	S
			1	2	3	4
5	6	7	8	9	10	11
12	13	14	15	16	17	18
19	20	21	22	23	24	25
26	27	28	29	30	31	

JANUARY

M	T	W	T	F	S	S
						1
2	3	4	5	6	7	8
9	10	11	12	13	14	15
16	17	18	19	20	21	22
23	24	25	26	27	28	29
30	31					

FEBRUARY

M	T	W	T	F	S	
	1	2	3	4	5	
6	7	8	9	10	11	12
13	14	15	16	17	18	19
20	21	22	23	24	25	26
27	28					

DO THE "NAZ" WITH SANTA
Nasdaq Gives More at Christmas – Dec 15th to Jan 23rd

One of the best times to invest in the major stock markets is the period around Christmas. The markets are generally positive at this time of the year as investors reposition their portfolios for the start of the new year. A lot of investors are familiar with the *Small Cap Effect* opportunity that starts approximately at this time of the year, where small caps tend to outperform from mid-December until the beginning of March (*see Small Cap Effect*), but few investors know that the last half of December and the first half of January is also a seasonally strong period for the Nasdaq.

82% of time better than S&P 500

The Nasdaq tends to perform well in the last two weeks of December, as investors typically increase their investment allocation to higher beta investments, including the Nasdaq, to finish the year.

In addition, the major sector drivers of the Nasdaq (biotech and technology), tend to perform well in the second half of December and the first half of January. Biotech tends to perform well in the last half of December, and technology tends to perform well in the first half of January. The end result is a Nasdaq Christmas trade that lasts from December 15 to January 23. In this time period, for the years 1971/72 to 2020/21, the Nasdaq has outperformed the S&P 500 by an average 2.1% per year. This rate of return is considered to be very high given that the length of the favorable period is just over one month. Even more impressive is the 82% frequency that the Nasdaq has outperformed the S&P 500.

Nasdaq vs. S&P 500 Dec 15th to Jan 23rd 1971/72 To 2020/21

Dec 15 to Jan 23	S&P 500	Positive Nasdaq	Diff
1971/72	6.1 %	7.5 %	1.3 %
1972/73	0.0	-0.7	-0.7
1973/74	4.1	6.8	2.8
1974/75	7.5	8.9	1.4
1975/76	13.0	13.8	0.9
1976/77	-1.7	2.8	4.5
1977/78	-5.1	-3.5	1.6
1978/79	4.7	6.2	1.4
1979/80	4.1	5.6	1.5
1980/81	0.8	3.3	2.5
1981/82	-6.0	-5.0	1.0
1982/83	4.7	5.5	0.8
1983/84	0.9	1.4	0.4
1984/85	9.0	13.3	4.3
1985/86	-2.7	0.8	3.5
1986/87	9.2	10.2	1.0
1987/88	1.8	9.1	7.3
1988/89	3.3	4.6	1.3
1989/90	-5.5	-3.8	1.7
1990/91	1.0	4.1	3.1
1991/92	7.9	15.2	7.2
1992/93	0.8	7.2	6.4
1993/94	2.5	5.7	3.2
1994/95	2.4	4.7	2.3
1995/96	-0.7	-1.0	-0.3
1996/97	6.7	7.3	0.6
1997/98	0.4	2.6	2.1
1998/99	7.4	18.9	11.6
1999/00	2.7	18.6	15.9
2000/01	1.5	4.1	2.6
2001/02	0.5	-1.6	-2.0
2002/03	-0.2	1.9	2.1
2003/04	6.3	9.0	2.7
2004/05	-3.0	-5.8	-2.9
2005/06	-0.7	-0.6	0.1
2006/07	0.2	-0.9	-1.1
2007/08	-8.8	-12.1	-3.3
2008/09	-5.4	-4.1	1.3
2009/10	-2.0	-0.3	1.7
2010/11	3.4	2.4	-1.0
2011/12	8.6	9.6	1.1
2012/13	5.8	6.1	0.4
2013/14	3.0	5.5	2.5
2014/15	2.5	2.2	-0.2
2015/16	-5.7	-7.3	-1.6
2016/17	0.5	2.1	1.6
2017/18	7.1	8.8	1.8
2018/19	1.5	1.7	0.2
2019/20	4.9	7.6	2.7
2020/21	5.3	8.9	3.5
Avg	2.1 %	4.1 %	2.1 %
Fq > 0	72 %	74 %	82 %

Nasdaq - Avg. Year 1972 to 2020

Nasdaq / SP 500 Relative Strength - Avg Yr. 1972 - 2020

Alternate Strategy — For those investors who favor the Nasdaq, an alternative strategy is to invest in the Nasdaq at an earlier date: October 28th. Historically, on average the Nasdaq has started its outperformance at this time. The "Do the Naz with Santa" strategy focuses on the sweet spot of the Nasdaq's outperformance.

Nasdaq Performance

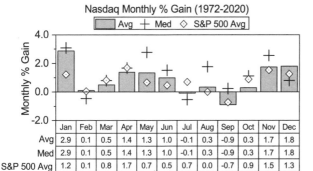

Nasdaq Monthly % Gain (1972-2020)

	Jan	Feb	Mar	Apr	May	Jun	Jul	Aug	Sep	Oct	Nov	Dec
Avg	2.9	0.1	0.5	1.4	1.3	1.0	-0.1	0.3	-0.9	0.3	1.7	1.8
Med	2.9	0.1	0.5	1.4	1.3	1.0	-0.1	0.3	-0.9	0.3	1.7	1.8
S&P 500 Avg	1.2	0.1	0.8	1.7	0.7	0.5	0.7	0.0	-0.7	0.9	1.5	1.3

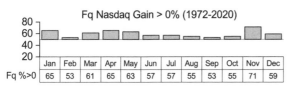

Fq Nasdaq Gain > 0% (1972-2020)

	Jan	Feb	Mar	Apr	May	Jun	Jul	Aug	Sep	Oct	Nov	Dec
Fq %>0	65	53	61	65	63	57	57	55	53	55	71	59

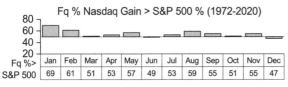

Fq % Nasdaq Gain > S&P 500 % (1972-2020)

	Jan	Feb	Mar	Apr	May	Jun	Jul	Aug	Sep	Oct	Nov	Dec
Fq %> S&P 500	69	61	51	53	57	49	53	59	55	51	55	47

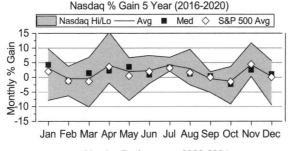

Nasdaq % Gain 5 Year (2016-2020)

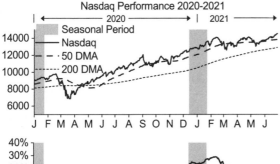

Nasdaq Performance 2020-2021

Relative Strength, % Gain vs. S&P 500

Market Indices & Rates
Weekly Values**

Stock Markets	2019	2020
Dow	28,455	30,179
S&P500	3,221	3,709
Nasdaq	8,925	12,756
TSX	17,118	17,535
FTSE	7,582	6,529
DAX	13,319	13,631
Nikkei	23,817	26,763
Hang Seng	27,871	26,499

Commodities	2019	2020
Oil	60.41	49.10
Gold	1479.0	1879.8

Bond Yields	2019	2020
USA 5 Yr Treasury	1.73	0.39
USA 10 Yr T	1.92	0.95
USA 20 Yr T	2.21	1.49
Moody's Aaa	3.01	2.32
Moody's Baa	3.88	3.19
CAN 5 Yr T	1.63	0.45
CAN 10 Yr T	1.62	0.75

Money Market	2019	2020
USA Fed Funds	1.75	0.25
USA 3 Mo T-B	1.55	0.08
CAN tgt overnight rate	1.75	0.25
CAN 3 Mo T-B	1.66	0.10

Foreign Exchange	2019	2020
EUR/USD	1.11	1.23
GBP/USD	1.30	1.35
USD/CAD	1.32	1.28
USD/JPY	109.44	103.30

DECEMBER

M	T	W	T	F	S	S
			1	2	3	4
5	6	7	8	9	10	11
12	13	14	15	16	17	18
19	20	21	22	23	24	25
26	27	28	29	30	31	

JANUARY

M	T	W	T	F	S	S
						1
2	3	4	5	6	7	8
9	10	11	12	13	14	15
16	17	18	19	20	21	22
23	24	25	26	27	28	29
30	31					

FEBRUARY

M	T	W	T	F	S	
	1	2	3	4	5	
6	7	8	9	10	11	12
13	14	15	16	17	18	19
20	21	22	23	24	25	26
27	28					

SMALL CAP (SMALL COMPANY) EFFECT
Small Companies Outperform - Dec 19 to Mar 7

At different stages of the business cycle, small capitalization companies (small caps represented by Russell 2000), perform better than large capitalization companies (large caps represented by Russell 1000).

Evidence shows that the small caps relative outperformance also has a seasonal component as they typically outperform large caps from December 19 to March 7.

3% extra and positive 67% of the time

Russell 2000 - Avg. Year 1979 to 2020

Russell 2000 / Russell 1000 - Avg Yr. 1979 - 2020

Russell 2000 vs. Russell 1000* % Gains
Dec 19th to Mar 7th 1979/80 to 2020/21
Positive [ ]

Dec 19 - Mar7	Russell 1000	Russell 2000	Diff
1979/80	-1.3 %	-0.4 %	0.9 %
1980/81	-2.8	4.0	6.8
1981/82	-12.4	-12.1	0.3
1982/83	11.8	19.8	8.0
1983/84	-6.4	-7.5	-1.1
1984/85	7.7	17.1	9.4
1985/86	8.2	11.7	3.5
1986/87	17.2	21.3	4.1
1987/88	8.3	16.4	8.0
1988/89	6.9	9.1	2.5
1989/90	-2.0	-1.9	0.2
1990/91	14.6	29.0	14.4
1991/92	6.0	16.8	10.8
1992/93	1.4	5.0	3.5
1993/94	0.5	5.7	5.3
1994/95	5.3	5.5	0.2
1995/96	8.3	7.8	-0.5
1996/97	9.5	3.5	-6.0
1997/98	10.2	10.3	0.1
1998/99	7.3	0.2	-7.2
1999/00	-1.7	27.7	29.4
2000/01	-5.2	4.7	9.8
2001/02	1.6	1.9	0.4
2002/03	-6.7	-7.8	-1.0
2003/04	6.4	9.6	3.3
2004/05	2.8	0.3	-2.5
2005/06	0.8	5.6	4.7
2006/07	-1.6	-0.8	0.9
2007/08	-10.9	-12.5	-1.5
2008/09	-22.2	-26.7	-4.5
2009/10	3.6	9.1	5.5
2010/11	5.5	4.2	-1.3
2011/12	11.3	10.2	-1.1
2012/13	7.1	10.3	3.1
2013/14	4.2	6.1	2.0
2014/15	1.0	2.1	1.1
2015/16	-0.3	-2.4	-2.1
2016/17	4.8	0.8	-4.1
2017/18	1.5	1.7	0.2
2018/19	8.4	10.6	2.2
2019/20	-6.8	-12.8	-5.9
2020/21	3.2	11.3	7.7
Avg.	2.5 %	5.1 %	2.8 %
Fq > 0	69 %	76 %	67 %

In recent times, the January Effect start date has shifted to mid-December and is more pronounced for small caps as their prices are more volatile than large caps. At the beginning of the year, small cap stocks benefit from a phenomenon that I have coined, "beta out of the gate, and coast." If small cap stocks are outperforming at the beginning of the year, money managers will gravitate to the sector in order to produce returns that are above their index benchmark. Once above average returns have been "locked in," the managers then rotate from their small cap overweight positions back to index large cap positions and coast for the rest of the year with above average returns. The overall process boosts small cap stocks at the beginning of the year.

Covid-19 Pandemic Update. In 2021, the small cap sector in its strong seasonal period, initially outperformed the Russell 1000. Just after the small cap sector seasonal period finished in March, the sector started to underperform the Russell 1000.

(i) *Russell 2000 (small cap index): The 2000 smallest companies in the Russell 3000 stock index (a broad market index). Russell 1000 (large cap index): The 1000 largest companies in the Russell 3000 stock index.*

Small Caps Performance

Russell 2000 Monthly % Gain (1979-2020)

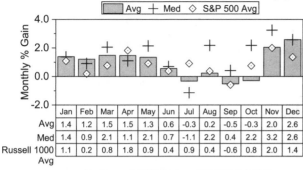

	Jan	Feb	Mar	Apr	May	Jun	Jul	Aug	Sep	Oct	Nov	Dec
Avg	1.4	1.2	1.5	1.5	1.3	0.6	-0.3	0.2	-0.5	-0.3	2.0	2.6
Med	1.4	0.9	2.1	1.1	2.1	0.7	-1.1	2.2	0.4	2.2	3.2	2.6
Russell 1000 Avg	1.1	0.2	0.8	1.8	0.9	0.4	0.9	0.4	-0.6	0.8	2.0	1.4

Fq Russell 2000 Gain > 0% (1979-2020)

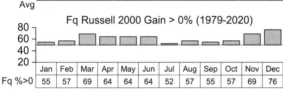

	Jan	Feb	Mar	Apr	May	Jun	Jul	Aug	Sep	Oct	Nov	Dec
Fq %>0	55	57	69	64	64	64	52	57	55	57	69	76

Fq % Russell 2000 Gain > S&P 500 % (1979-2020)

	Jan	Feb	Mar	Apr	May	Jun	Jul	Aug	Sep	Oct	Nov	Dec
Fq %> Russell 1000	48	55	57	40	60	64	33	50	60	38	50	57

Russell 2000 % Gain 5 Year (2016-2020)

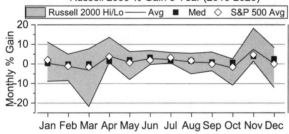

Russell 2000 Performance 2020-2021

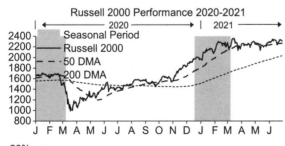

Relative Strength, % Gain vs. Russell 1000

Stock Markets	2019	2020
Dow	28,645	30,200
S&P500	3,240	3,703
Nasdaq	9,007	12,805
TSX	17,168	17,624
FTSE	7,645	6,502
DAX	13,337	13,587
Nikkei	23,838	26,657
Hang Seng	28,225	26,387

Commodities	2019	2020
Oil	61.72	48.08
Gold	1511.5	1875.0

Bond Yields	2019	2020
USA 5 Yr Treasury	1.68	0.37
USA 10 Yr T	1.88	0.94
USA 20 Yr T	2.18	1.46
Moody's Aaa	2.98	2.26
Moody's Baa	3.84	3.17
CAN 5 Yr T	1.63	0.43
CAN 10 Yr T	1.60	0.72

Money Market	2019	2020
USA Fed Funds	1.75	0.25
USA 3 Mo T-B	1.54	0.09
CAN tgt overnight rate	1.75	0.25
CAN 3 Mo T-B	1.66	0.09

Foreign Exchange	2019	2020
EUR/USD	1.12	1.22
GBP/USD	1.31	1.36
USD/CAD	1.31	1.29
USD/JPY	109.44	103.43

DECEMBER

M	T	W	T	F	S	S
			1	2	3	4
5	6	7	8	9	10	11
12	13	14	15	16	17	18
19	20	21	22	23	24	25
26	27	28	29	30	31	

JANUARY

M	T	W	T	F	S	S
						1
2	3	4	5	6	7	8
9	10	11	12	13	14	15
16	17	18	19	20	21	22
23	24	25	26	27	28	29
30	31					

FEBRUARY

M	T	W	T	F	S	
	1	2	3	4	5	
6	7	8	9	10	11	12
13	14	15	16	17	18	19
20	21	22	23	24	25	26
27	28					

FINANCIALS (U.S.) YEAR END CLEAN UP
December 15th to April 13th

The main driver for the strong seasonal performance of the financial sector has been the year-end earnings of the banks that start to report in mid-January. A strong performance from mid-December has been the result of investors getting into the market early to take advantage of positive year-end earnings.

Extra 1% & 59% of the time better than the S&P 500

It is possible for the bank sector to start its strong seasonal period early. November can be a good month for the banking sector. On an average and median basis, the banking sector performs better than the S&P 500 in November. However, on a frequency basis of outperforming the S&P 500, the success rate is less than 50%.

Financials Sector - Avg. Year 1990 to 2020

Financials / S&P 500 Relative Strength - Avg Yr. 1990-2020

The return profile of the banking sector in November translates to the sector performing very well sometimes and other times not as well as the S&P 500. The average and the median are skewed higher by a few good years. Nevertheless, it makes sense to consider an early entry if the sector has positive momentum and a favorable macro backdrop. This is particularly true if interest rates are rising, helping to boost the net interest margin of the banks and therefore their profits.

Financials* vs. S&P 500 1989/90 to 2020/21			
Dec 15 to Apr 13	S&P 500	Positive Finan- cials	Diff
1989/90	-1.9 %	-9.9 %	-8.0 %
1990/91	16.4	29.2	12.8
1991/92	5.6	9.2	3.5
1992/93	3.8	17.9	14.1
1993/94	-3.6	-0.4	3.2
1994/95	11.9	14.0	2.1
1995/96	3.2	5.5	2.3
1996/97	1.2	4.7	3.4
19/9798	16.4	19.7	3.3
1998/99	18.3	24.9	6.6
1999/00	2.7	4.0	1.3
2000/01	-11.7	-4.8	6.9
2001/02	-1.1	6.5	7.6
2002/03	-2.4	-1.8	0.6
2003/04	5.2	6.7	1.5
2004/05	-2.5	-6.2	-3.7
2005/06	1.3	1.1	-0.2
2006/07	1.9	-2.2	-4.1
2007/08	-9.2	-14.1	-4.9
2008/09	-2.4	-7.0	-4.6
2009/10	7.5	15.2	7.8
2010/11	5.9	4.6	-1.3
2011/12	13.1	20.7	7.7
2012/13	12.4	16.0	3.6
2013/14	2.3	1.0	-1.3
2014/15	4.5	1.1	-3.4
2015/16	3.0	-2.0	-5.0
2016/17	3.4	-2.0	-5.4
2017/18	0.2	-0.6	-0.7
2018/19	11.8	12.5	0.6
2019/20	-12.8	-26.2	-13.4
2020/21	13.5	24.7	11.2
Avg.	3.7 %	5.1 %	1.4 %
Fq > 0	72 %	63 %	59 %

Covid-19 Performance Update. In December 2020, the financial sector was already on a roll as it started its strong seasonal period mid-month. The sector continued to perform well into mid-April 2021, when it finished its seasonal period. It continued to perform well into the beginning of June, at which time it started to head lower as interest rates headed lower.

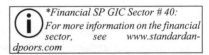

Financial SP GIC Sector # 40:
For more information on the financial sector, see www.standardandpoors.com

Financials Performance

Financials Monthly % Gain (1990-2020)

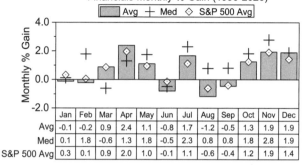

	Jan	Feb	Mar	Apr	May	Jun	Jul	Aug	Sep	Oct	Nov	Dec
Avg	-0.1	-0.2	0.9	2.4	1.1	-0.8	1.7	-1.2	-0.5	1.3	1.9	1.9
Med	0.1	1.8	-0.6	1.3	1.8	-0.5	2.3	0.8	0.8	1.8	2.8	1.9
S&P 500 Avg	0.3	0.1	0.9	2.0	1.0	-0.1	1.1	-0.6	-0.4	1.2	1.9	1.4

Fq Financials Gain > 0% (1990-2020)

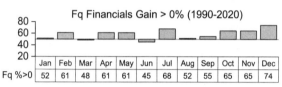

	Jan	Feb	Mar	Apr	May	Jun	Jul	Aug	Sep	Oct	Nov	Dec
Fq %>0	52	61	48	61	61	45	68	52	55	65	65	74

Fq % Financials Gain > S&P 500 % (1990-2020)

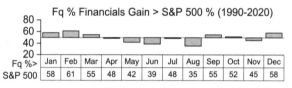

	Jan	Feb	Mar	Apr	May	Jun	Jul	Aug	Sep	Oct	Nov	Dec
Fq %> S&P 500	58	61	55	48	42	39	48	35	55	52	45	58

Financials % Gain 5 Year (2016-2020)

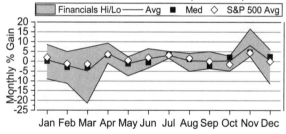

Financials Performance 2020-2021

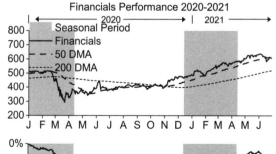

Relative Strength, % Gain vs. S&P 500

JANUARY

M	T	W	T	F	S	S
						1
2	3	4	5	6	7	8
9	10	11	12	13	14	15
16	17	18	19	20	21	22
23	24	25	26	27	28	29
30	31					

FEBRUARY

M	T	W	T	F	S	S
		1	2	3	4	5
6	7	8	9	10	11	12
13	14	15	16	17	18	19
20	21	22	23	24	25	26
27	28					

MARCH

M	T	W	T	F	S	S
1		1	2	3	4	5
6	7	8	9	10	11	12
13	14	15	16	17	18	19
20	21	22	23	24	25	26
27	28	29	30	31		

APRIL

M	T	W	T	F	S	S
					1	2
3	4	5	6	7	8	9
10	11	12	13	14	15	16
17	18	19	20	21	22	23
24	25	26	27	28	29	30

MAY

M	T	W	T	F	S	S
1	2	3	4	5	6	7
8	9	10	11	12	13	14
15	16	17	18	19	20	21
22	23	24	25	26	27	28
29	30	31				

JUNE

M	T	W	T	F	S	S
		1	2	3	4	
5	6	7	8	9	10	11
12	13	14	15	16	17	18
19	20	21	22	23	24	25
29	30					

APPENDIX

STOCK MARKET RETURNS

STOCK MKT S&P 500 PERCENT CHANGES

	JAN	FEB	MAR	APR	MAY	JUN
1950	1.5 %	1.0 %	0.4 %	4.5 %	3.9 %	— 5.8 %
1951	6.1	0.6	— 1.8	4.8	— 4.1	— 2.6
1952	1.6	— 3.6	4.8	— 4.3	2.3	4.6
1953	— 0.7	— 1.8	— 2.4	— 2.6	— 0.3	— 1.6
1954	5.1	0.3	3.0	4.9	3.3	0.1
1955	1.8	0.4	— 0.5	3.8	— 0.1	8.2
1956	— 3.6	3.5	6.9	— 0.2	— 6.6	3.9
1957	— 4.2	— 3.3	2.0	3.7	3.7	— 0.1
1958	4.3	2.1	3.1	3.2	1.5	2.6
1959	0.4	— 0.1	0.1	3.9	1.9	— 0.4
1960	— 7.1	0.9	— 1.4	— 1.8	2.7	2.0
1961	6.3	2.7	2.6	0.4	1.9	— 2.9
1962	— 3.8	1.6	— 0.6	— 6.2	— 8.6	— 8.2
1963	4.9	— 2.9	3.5	4.9	1.4	— 2.0
1964	2.7	1.0	1.5	0.6	1.1	1.6
1965	3.3	— 0.1	— 1.5	3.4	— 0.8	— 4.9
1966	0.5	— 1.8	— 2.2	2.1	— 5.4	— 1.6
1967	7.8	0.2	3.9	4.2	— 5.2	1.8
1968	— 4.4	— 3.1	0.9	8.0	1.3	0.9
1969	— 0.8	— 4.7	3.4	2.1	— 0.2	— 5.6
1970	— 7.6	5.3	0.1	— 9.0	— 6.1	— 5.0
1971	4.0	0.9	3.7	3.6	— 4.2	— 0.9
1972	1.8	2.5	0.6	0.4	1.7	— 2.2
1973	— 1.7	— 3.7	— 0.1	— 4.1	— 1.9	— 0.7
1974	— 1.0	— 0.4	— 2.3	— 3.9	— 3.4	— 1.5
1975	12.3	6.0	2.2	4.7	4.4	4.4
1976	11.8	— 1.1	3.1	— 1.1	— 1.4	4.1
1977	— 5.1	— 2.2	— 1.4	0.0	— 2.4	4.5
1978	— 6.2	— 2.5	2.5	8.5	0.4	— 1.8
1979	4.0	— 3.7	5.5	0.2	— 2.6	3.9
1980	5.8	— 0.4	— 10.2	4.1	4.7	2.7
1981	— 4.6	1.3	3.6	— 2.3	0.2	— 1.0
1982	— 1.8	— 6.1	— 1.0	4.0	— 3.9	— 2.0
1983	3.3	1.9	3.3	7.5	— 1.2	3.2
1984	— 0.9	— 3.9	1.3	0.5	— 5.9	1.7
1985	7.4	0.9	— 0.3	— 0.5	5.4	1.2
1986	0.2	7.1	5.3	— 1.4	5.0	1.4
1987	13.2	3.7	2.6	— 1.1	0.6	4.8
1988	4.0	4.2	— 3.3	0.9	0.3	4.3
1989	7.1	— 2.9	2.1	5.0	3.5	— 0.8
1990	— 6.9	0.9	2.4	— 2.7	9.2	— 0.9
1991	4.2	6.7	2.2	0.0	3.9	— 4.8
1992	— 2.0	1.0	— 2.2	2.8	0.1	— 1.7
1993	0.7	1.0	1.9	— 2.5	2.3	0.1
1994	3.3	— 3.0	— 4.6	1.2	1.2	— 2.7
1995	2.4	3.6	2.7	2.8	3.6	2.1
1996	3.3	0.7	0.8	1.3	2.3	0.2
1997	6.1	0.6	— 4.3	5.8	5.9	4.3
1998	1.0	7.0	5.0	0.9	— 1.9	3.9
1999	4.1	— 3.2	3.9	3.8	— 2.5	5.4
2000	— 5.1	— 2.0	9.7	— 3.1	— 2.2	2.4
2001	3.5	— 9.2	— 6.4	7.7	0.5	— 2.5
2002	— 1.6	— 2.1	3.7	— 6.1	— 0.9	— 7.2
2003	— 2.7	— 1.7	0.8	8.1	5.1	1.1
2004	1.7	1.2	— 1.6	— 1.7	1.2	1.8
2005	— 2.5	1.9	— 1.9	— 2.0	3.0	0.0
2006	2.5	0.0	1.1	1.2	— 3.1	0.0
2007	1.4	— 2.2	1.0	4.3	3.3	— 1.8
2008	— 6.1	— 3.5	— 0.6	4.8	1.1	— 8.6
2009	— 8.6	— 11.0	8.5	9.4	5.3	0.0
2010	— 3.7	2.9	5.9	1.5	— 8.2	— 5.4
2011	2.3	3.2	— 0.1	2.8	— 1.4	— 1.8
2012	4.4	4.1	3.1	— 0.7	— 6.3	4.0
2013	5.0	1.1	3.6	1.8	2.1	— 1.5
2014	— 3.6	4.3	0.7	0.6	2.1	1.9
2015	— 3.1	5.5	— 1.7	0.9	1.0	— 2.1
2016	— 5.1	— 0.4	6.6	0.3	1.5	0.1
2017	1.8	3.7	0.0	0.9	1.2	0.5
2018	5.6	— 3.9	— 2.7	0.3	2.2	0.5
2019	7.9	3.0	1.8	3.9	— 6.6	6.9
2020	— 0.2	— 8.4	— 12.5	12.7	4.5	1.8
FQ POS*	43/71	39/71	45/71	50/71	42/71	39/71
% FQ POS*	61 %	55 %	63 %	70 %	59 %	55 %
AVG GAIN*	1.1 %	0.0 %	1.0 %	1.6 %	0.2 %	0.1 %
RANK GAIN*	5	11	6	2	8	9

JUL	AUG	SEP	OCT	NOV	DEC		YEAR
0.8 %	3.3 %	5.6 %	0.4 %	— 0.1 %	4.6 %	1950	21.7 %
6.9	3.9	— 0.1	— 1.4	— 0.3	3.9	1951	16.5
1.8	— 1.5	— 2.0	— 0.1	4.6	3.5	1952	11.8
2.5	— 5.8	0.1	5.1	0.9	0.2	1953	— 6.6
5.7	— 3.4	8.3	— 1.9	8.1	5.1	1954	45.0
6.1	— 0.8	1.1	— 3.0	7.5	— 0.1	1955	26.4
5.2	— 3.8	— 4.5	0.5	— 1.1	3.5	1956	2.6
1.1	— 5.6	— 6.2	— 3.2	1.6	— 4.1	1957	— 14.3
4.3	1.2	4.8	2.5	2.2	5.2	1958	38.1
3.5	— 1.5	— 4.6	1.1	1.3	2.8	1959	8.5
— 2.5	2.6	— 6.0	— 0.2	4.0	4.6	1960	— 3.0
3.3	2.0	— 2.0	2.8	3.9	0.3	1961	23.1
6.4	1.5	— 4.8	0.4	10.2	1.3	1962	— 11.8
— 0.3	4.9	— 1.1	3.2	— 1.1	2.4	1963	18.9
1.8	— 1.6	2.9	0.8	— 0.5	0.4	1964	13.0
1.3	2.3	3.2	2.7	— 0.9	0.9	1965	9.1
1.3	— 7.8	— 0.7	4.8	0.3	— 0.1	1966	— 13.1
4.5	— 1.2	3.3	— 3.5	0.8	2.6	1967	20.1
— 1.8	1.1	3.9	0.7	4.8	— 4.2	1968	7.7
— 6.0	4.0	— 2.5	4.3	— 3.4	— 1.9	1969	— 11.4
7.3	4.4	3.4	— 1.2	4.7	5.7	1970	0.1
— 3.2	3.6	— 0.7	— 4.2	— 0.3	8.6	1971	10.8
0.2	3.4	— 0.5	0.9	4.6	1.2	1972	15.6
3.8	— 3.7	4.0	— 0.1	— 11.4	1.7	1973	— 17.4
— 7.8	— 9.0	— 11.9	16.3	— 5.3	— 2.0	1974	— 29.7
— 6.8	— 2.1	— 3.5	6.2	2.5	— 1.2	1975	31.5
— 0.8	— 0.5	2.3	— 2.2	— 0.8	5.2	1976	19.1
— 1.6	— 2.1	— 0.2	— 4.3	2.7	0.3	1977	— 11.5
5.4	2.6	— 0.7	— 9.2	1.7	1.5	1978	1.1
0.9	5.3	0.0	— 6.9	4.3	1.7	1979	12.3
6.5	0.6	2.5	1.6	10.2	— 3.4	1980	25.8
— 0.2	— 6.2	— 5.4	4.9	3.7	— 3.0	1981	— 9.7
— 2.3	11.6	0.8	11.0	3.6	1.5	1982	14.8
— 3.0	1.1	1.0	— 1.5	1.7	— 0.9	1983	17.3
— 1.6	10.6	— 0.3	0.0	— 1.5	2.2	1984	1.4
— 0.5	— 1.2	— 3.5	4.3	6.5	4.5	1985	26.3
— 5.9	7.1	— 8.5	5.5	2.1	— 2.8	1986	14.6
4.8	3.5	— 2.4	— 21.8	— 8.5	7.3	1987	2.0
— 0.5	— 3.9	4.0	2.6	— 1.9	1.5	1988	12.4
8.8	1.6	— 0.7	— 2.5	1.7	2.1	1989	27.3
— 0.5	— 9.4	— 5.1	— 0.7	6.0	2.5	1990	— 6.6
4.5	2.0	— 1.9	1.2	— 4.4	11.2	1991	26.3
3.9	— 2.4	0.9	0.2	3.0	1.0	1992	4.5
0.5	3.4	— 1.0	1.9	— 1.3	1.0	1993	7.1
3.1	3.8	— 2.7	2.1	— 4.0	1.2	1994	— 1.5
3.2	0.0	4.0	— 0.5	4.1	1.7	1995	34.1
— 4.6	1.9	5.4	2.6	7.3	— 2.2	1996	20.3
7.8	— 5.7	5.3	— 3.4	4.5	1.6	1997	31.0
1.2	— 14.6	6.2	8.0	5.9	5.6	1998	26.7
— 3.2	— 0.6	— 2.9	6.3	1.9	5.8	1999	19.5
— 1.6	6.1	— 5.3	— 0.5	— 8.0	0.4	2000	— 10.1
— 1.1	— 6.4	— 8.2	1.8	7.5	0.8	2001	— 13.0
— 7.9	0.5	— 11.0	8.6	5.7	— 6.0	2002	— 23.4
1.6	1.8	— 1.2	5.5	0.7	5.1	2003	26.4
-3.4	0.2	0.9	1.4	3.9	3.2	2004	9.0
3.6	— 1.1	0.7	— 1.8	3.5	— 0.1	2005	3.0
0.5	2.1	2.5	3.2	1.6	1.3	2006	13.6
— 3.2	1.3	3.6	1.5	— 4.4	— 0.9	2007	3.5
— 1.0	1.2	— 9.1	— 16.9	— 7.5	0.8	2008	-38.5
7.4	3.4	3.6	— 2.0	5.7	1.8	2009	23.5
6.9	— 4.7	8.8	3.7	— 0.2	6.5	2010	12.8
— 2.1	— 5.7	— 7.2	10.8	— 0.5	0.9	2011	0.0
1.3	2.0	2.4	— 2.0	0.3	0.7	2012	13.4
4.9	— 3.1	3.0	4.5	2.8	2.4	2013	29.6
— 1.5	3.8	— 1.6	2.3	2.5	— 0.4	2014	11.4
2.0	— 6.3	— 2.6	8.3	0.1	— 1.8	2015	— 0.7
3.6	— 0.1	— 0.1	— 1.9	3.4	1.8	2016	9.5
1.9	0.1	1.9	2.2	2.8	1.0	2017	19.4
3.6	3.0	0.4	— 6.9	1.8	— 9.2	2018	6.2
1.3	— 1.8	1.7	2.0	3.4	2.9	2019	28.9
5.5	7.0	— 3.9	— 2.8	10.8	3.7	2020	16.3
41/71	39/71	32/71	42/71	49/71	53/71		52/71
58 %	55 %	45 %	59 %	69 %	75 %		73 %
1.1 %	0.0 %	— 0.5 %	0.8 %	1.7 %	1.5 %		9.2 %
4	10	12	7	1	3		

S&P 500 MONTH CLOSING VALUES

	JAN	FEB	MAR	APR	MAY	JUN
1950	17	17	17	18	19	18
1951	22	22	21	22	22	21
1952	24	23	24	23	24	25
1953	26	26	25	25	25	24
1954	26	26	27	28	29	29
1955	37	37	37	38	38	41
1956	44	45	48	48	45	47
1957	45	43	44	46	47	47
1958	42	41	42	43	44	45
1959	55	55	55	58	59	58
1960	56	56	55	54	56	57
1961	62	63	65	65	67	65
1962	69	70	70	65	60	55
1963	66	64	67	70	71	69
1964	77	78	79	79	80	82
1965	88	87	86	89	88	84
1966	93	91	89	91	86	85
1967	87	87	90	94	89	91
1968	92	89	90	97	99	100
1969	103	98	102	104	103	98
1970	85	90	90	82	77	73
1971	96	97	100	104	100	99
1972	104	107	107	108	110	107
1973	116	112	112	107	105	104
1974	97	96	94	90	87	86
1975	77	82	83	87	91	95
1976	101	100	103	102	100	104
1977	102	100	98	98	96	100
1978	89	87	89	97	97	96
1979	100	96	102	102	99	103
1980	114	114	102	106	111	114
1981	130	131	136	133	133	131
1982	120	113	112	116	112	110
1983	145	148	153	164	162	168
1984	163	157	159	160	151	153
1985	180	181	181	180	190	192
1986	212	227	239	236	247	251
1987	274	284	292	288	290	304
1988	257	268	259	261	262	274
1989	297	289	295	310	321	318
1990	329	332	340	331	361	358
1991	344	367	375	375	390	371
1992	409	413	404	415	415	408
1993	439	443	452	440	450	451
1994	482	467	446	451	457	444
1995	470	487	501	515	533	545
1996	636	640	646	654	669	671
1997	786	791	757	801	848	885
1998	980	1049	1102	1112	1091	1134
1999	1280	1238	1286	1335	1302	1373
2000	1394	1366	1499	1452	1421	1455
2001	1366	1240	1160	1249	1256	1224
2002	1130	1107	1147	1077	1067	990
2003	856	841	848	917	964	975
2004	1131	1145	1126	1107	1121	1141
2005	1181	1204	1181	1157	1192	1191
2006	1280	1281	1295	1311	1270	1270
2007	1438	1407	1421	1482	1531	1503
2008	1379	1331	1323	1386	1400	1280
2009	826	735	798	873	919	919
2010	1074	1104	1169	1187	1089	1031
2011	1286	1327	1326	1364	1345	1321
2012	1312	1366	1408	1398	1310	1362
2013	1498	1515	1569	1598	1631	1606
2014	1783	1869	1872	1884	1924	1960
2015	1995	2105	2068	2086	2107	2063
2016	1940	1932	2060	2065	2097	2099
2017	2279	2364	2363	2384	2412	2423
2018	2824	2714	2641	2648	2705	2718
2019	2704	2784	2834	2946	2752	2942
2020	3226	2954	2585	2912	3044	3100

JUL	AUG	SEP	OCT	NOV	DEC	
18	18	19	20	20	20	**1950**
22	23	23	23	23	24	**1951**
25	25	25	25	26	27	**1952**
25	23	23	25	25	25	**1953**
31	30	32	32	34	36	**1954**
44	43	44	42	46	45	**1955**
49	48	45	46	45	47	**1956**
48	45	42	41	42	40	**1957**
47	48	50	51	52	55	**1958**
61	60	57	58	58	60	**1959**
56	57	54	53	56	58	**1960**
67	68	67	69	71	72	**1961**
58	59	56	57	62	63	**1962**
69	73	72	74	73	75	**1963**
83	82	84	85	84	85	**1964**
85	87	90	92	92	92	**1965**
84	77	77	80	80	80	**1966**
95	94	97	93	94	96	**1967**
98	99	103	103	108	104	**1968**
92	96	93	97	94	92	**1969**
78	82	84	83	87	92	**1970**
96	99	98	94	94	102	**1971**
107	111	111	112	117	118	**1972**
108	104	108	108	96	98	**1973**
79	72	64	74	70	69	**1974**
89	87	84	89	91	90	**1975**
103	103	105	103	102	107	**1976**
99	97	97	92	95	95	**1977**
101	103	103	93	95	96	**1978**
104	109	109	102	106	108	**1979**
122	122	125	127	141	136	**1980**
131	123	116	122	126	123	**1981**
107	120	120	134	139	141	**1982**
163	164	166	164	166	165	**1983**
151	167	166	166	164	167	**1984**
191	189	182	190	202	211	**1985**
236	253	231	244	249	242	**1986**
319	330	322	252	230	247	**1987**
272	262	272	279	274	278	**1988**
346	351	349	340	346	353	**1989**
356	323	306	304	322	330	**1990**
388	395	388	392	375	417	**1991**
424	414	418	419	431	436	**1992**
448	464	459	468	462	466	**1993**
458	475	463	472	454	459	**1994**
562	562	584	582	605	616	**1995**
640	652	687	705	757	741	**1996**
954	899	947	915	955	970	**1997**
1121	957	1017	1099	1164	1229	**1998**
1329	1320	1283	1363	1389	1469	**1999**
1431	1518	1437	1429	1315	1320	**2000**
1211	1134	1041	1060	1139	1148	**2001**
912	916	815	886	936	880	**2002**
990	1008	996	1051	1058	1112	**2003**
1102	1104	1115	1130	1174	1212	**2004**
1234	1220	1229	1207	1249	1248	**2005**
1277	1304	1336	1378	1401	1418	**2006**
1455	1474	1527	1549	1481	1468	**2007**
1267	1283	1165	969	896	903	**2008**
987	1021	1057	1036	1096	1115	**2009**
1102	1049	1141	1183	1181	1258	**2010**
1292	1219	1131	1253	1247	1258	**2011**
1379	1407	1441	1412	1416	1426	**2012**
1686	1633	1682	1757	1806	1848	**2013**
1931	2003	1972	2018	2068	2059	**2014**
2104	1972	1920	2079	2080	2044	**2015**
2174	2171	2168	2126	2199	2239	**2016**
2470	2472	2519	2575	2648	2674	**2017**
2816	2902	2914	2712	2760	2507	**2018**
2980	2926	2977	3038	3141	3231	**2019**
3271	3500	3363	3270	3622	3756	**2020**

DOW JONES PERCENT MONTH CHANGES

	JAN	FEB	MAR	APR	MAY	JUN
1950	0.8 %	0.8 %	1.3 %	4.0 %	4.2 %	− 6.4 %
1951	5.7	1.3	− 1.7	4.5	− 3.6	− 2.8
1952	0.6	− 3.9	3.6	− 4.4	2.1	4.3
1953	− 0.7	− 2.0	− 1.5	− 1.8	− 0.9	− 1.5
1954	4.1	0.7	3.1	5.2	2.6	1.8
1955	1.1	0.8	− 0.5	3.9	− 0.2	6.2
1956	− 3.6	2.8	5.8	0.8	− 7.4	3.1
1957	− 4.1	− 3.0	2.2	4.1	2.1	− 0.3
1958	3.3	− 2.2	1.6	2.0	1.5	3.3
1959	1.8	1.6	− 0.3	3.7	3.2	0.0
1960	− 8.4	1.2	− 2.1	− 2.4	4.0	2.4
1961	5.2	2.1	2.2	0.3	2.7	− 1.8
1962	− 4.3	1.2	− 0.2	− 5.9	− 7.8	− 8.5
1963	4.7	− 2.9	3.0	5.2	1.3	− 2.8
1964	2.9	1.9	1.6	− 0.3	1.2	1.3
1965	3.3	0.1	− 1.6	3.7	− 0.5	− 5.4
1966	1.5	− 3.2	− 2.8	1.0	− 5.3	− 1.6
1967	8.2	− 1.2	3.2	3.6	− 5.0	0.9
1968	− 5.5	− 1.8	0.0	8.5	− 1.4	− 0.1
1969	0.2	− 4.3	3.3	1.6	− 1.3	− 6.9
1970	− 7.0	4.5	1.0	− 6.3	− 4.8	− 2.4
1971	3.5	1.2	2.9	4.1	− 3.6	− 1.8
1972	1.3	2.9	1.4	1.4	0.7	− 3.3
1973	− 2.1	− 4.4	− 0.4	− 3.1	− 2.2	− 1.1
1974	0.6	0.6	− 1.6	− 1.2	− 4.1	0.0
1975	14.2	5.0	3.9	6.9	1.3	5.6
1976	14.4	− 0.3	2.8	− 0.3	− 2.2	2.8
1977	− 5.0	− 1.9	− 1.8	0.8	− 3.0	2.0
1978	− 7.4	− 3.6	2.1	10.5	0.4	− 2.6
1979	4.2	− 3.6	6.6	− 0.8	− 3.8	2.4
1980	4.4	− 1.5	− 9.0	4.0	4.1	2.0
1981	− 1.7	2.9	3.0	− 0.6	− 0.6	− 1.5
1982	− 0.4	− 5.4	− 0.2	3.1	− 3.4	− 0.9
1983	2.8	3.4	1.6	8.5	− 2.1	1.8
1984	− 3.0	− 5.4	0.9	0.5	− 5.6	2.5
1985	6.2	− 0.2	− 1.3	− 0.7	4.6	1.5
1986	1.6	8.8	6.4	− 1.9	5.2	0.9
1987	13.8	3.1	3.6	− 0.8	0.2	5.5
1988	1.0	5.8	− 4.0	2.2	− 0.1	5.4
1989	8.0	− 3.6	1.6	5.5	2.5	− 1.6
1990	− 5.9	1.4	3.0	− 1.9	8.3	0.1
1991	3.9	5.3	1.1	− 0.9	4.8	− 4.0
1992	1.7	1.4	− 1.0	3.8	1.1	− 2.3
1993	0.3	1.8	1.9	− 0.2	2.9	− 0.3
1994	6.0	− 3.7	− 5.1	1.3	2.1	− 3.5
1995	0.2	4.3	3.7	3.9	3.3	2.0
1996	5.4	1.7	1.9	− 0.3	1.3	0.2
1997	5.7	0.9	− 4.3	6.5	4.6	4.7
1998	0.0	8.1	3.0	3.0	− 1.8	0.6
1999	1.9	− 0.6	5.2	10.2	− 2.1	3.9
2000	− 4.5	− 7.4	7.8	− 1.7	− 2.0	− 0.7
2001	0.9	− 3.6	− 5.9	8.7	1.6	− 3.8
2002	− 1.0	1.9	2.9	− 4.4	− 0.2	− 6.9
2003	− 3.5	− 2.0	1.3	6.1	4.4	1.5
2004	0.3	0.9	− 2.1	− 1.3	− 0.4	2.4
2005	− 2.7	2.6	− 2.4	− 3.0	2.7	− 1.8
2006	1.4	1.2	1.1	2.3	− 1.7	− 0.2
2007	1.3	− 2.8	0.7	5.7	4.3	− 1.6
2008	− 4.6	− 3.0	0.0	4.5	− 1.4	− 10.2
2009	− 8.8	− 11.7	7.7	7.3	4.1	− 0.6
2010	− 3.5	2.6	5.1	1.4	− 7.9	− 3.6
2011	2.7	2.8	0.8	4.0	− 1.9	− 1.2
2012	3.4	3.8	2.0	0.0	− 6.2	3.9
2013	5.8	4.8	3.7	1.8	1.9	− 1.4
2014	− 5.3	5.8	0.8	0.7	0.8	0.7
2015	− 3.7	6.8	− 2.0	0.4	1.0	− 2.2
2016	− 5.5	0.3	7.1	0.5	0.1	0.8
2017	0.5	4.8	− 0.7	1.3	0.3	1.6
2018	5.8	− 4.3	− 3.7	0.2	1.0	− 0.6
2019	7.2	3.7	0.0	2.6	− 6.7	7.2
2020	− 0.2	− 8.4	− 12.5	12.7	4.5	1.8
FQ POS	45/71	41/71	45/71	49/71	38/71	34/71
% FQ POS	63 %	58 %	63 %	69 %	54 %	48 %
AVG GAIN	1.0 %	0.2 %	0.9 %	2.0 %	0.0 %	− 0.1 %
RANK GAIN	5	8	6	1	9	11

DOW JONES PERCENT MONTH CHANGES 🇺🇸

JUL	AUG	SEP	OCT	NOV	DEC		YEAR
0.1 %	3.6 %	4.4 %	− 0.6 %	1.2 %	3.4 %	**1950**	17.6 %
6.3	4.8	0.3	− 3.2	− 0.4	3.0	**1951**	14.4
1.9	− 1.6	− 0.5		5.4	2.9	**1952**	8.4
2.6	− 5.2	1.1	4.5	2.0	− 0.2	**1953**	− 3.8
4.3	− 3.5	7.4	− 2.3	9.9	4.6	**1954**	44.0
3.2	0.5	− 0.3	− 2.5	6.2	1.1	**1955**	20.8
5.1	− 3.1	− 5.3	1.0	− 1.5	5.6	**1956**	2.3
1.0	− 4.7	− 5.8	− 3.4	2.0	− 3.2	**1957**	− 12.8
5.2	1.1	4.6	2.1	2.6	4.7	**1958**	34.0
4.9	− 1.6	− 4.9	2.4	1.9	3.1	**1959**	16.4
− 3.7	1.5	− 7.3	0.1	2.9	3.1	**1960**	− 9.3
3.1	2.1	− 2.6	0.4	2.5	1.3	**1961**	18.7
6.5	1.9	− 5.0	1.9	10.1	0.4	**1962**	− 10.8
− 1.6	4.9	0.5	3.1	− 0.6	1.7	**1963**	17.0
1.2	− 0.3	4.4	− 0.3	0.3	− 0.1	**1964**	14.6
1.6	1.3	4.2	3.2	− 1.5	2.4	**1965**	10.9
2.6	− 7.0	− 1.8	4.2	− 1.9	− 0.7	**1966**	− 18.9
5.1	− 0.3	2.8	− 5.1	− 0.4	3.3	**1967**	15.2
− 1.6	1.5	4.4	1.8	3.4	− 4.2	**1968**	4.3
− 6.6	2.6	− 2.8	5.3	− 5.1	− 1.5	**1969**	− 15.2
7.4	4.2	− 0.5	− 0.7	5.1	5.6	**1970**	4.8
− 3.7	4.6	− 1.2	− 5.4	− 0.9	7.1	**1971**	6.1
− 0.5	4.2	− 1.1	0.2	6.6	0.2	**1972**	14.6
3.9	− 4.2	6.7	1.0	− 14.0	3.5	**1973**	16.6
− 5.6	− 10.4	− 10.4	9.5	− 7.0	− 0.4	**1974**	− 27.6
− 5.4	0.5	− 5.0	5.3	3.0	− 1.0	**1975**	38.3
− 1.8	− 1.1	1.7	− 2.6	− 1.8	6.1	**1976**	17.9
− 2.9	− 3.2	− 1.7	− 3.4	1.4	0.2	**1977**	− 17.3
5.3	1.7	− 1.3	− 8.5	0.8	0.8	**1978**	3.2
0.5	4.9	− 1.0	− 7.2	0.8	2.0	**1979**	4.2
7.8	− 0.3	0.0	− 0.8	7.4	− 2.9	**1980**	14.9
− 2.5	− 7.4	− 3.6	0.3	4.3	− 1.6	**1981**	9.2
− 0.4	11.5	− 0.6	10.6	4.8	0.7	**1982**	19.6
− 1.9	1.4	1.4	− 0.6	4.1	− 1.4	**1983**	20.3
− 1.5	9.8	− 1.4	0.1	− 1.5	1.9	**1984**	− 3.7
0.9	− 1.0	− 0.4	3.4	7.1	5.1	**1985**	27.7
− 6.2	6.9	− 6.9	6.2	1.9	− 1.0	**1986**	22.6
6.4	3.5	− 2.5	− 23.2	− 8.0	5.7	**1987**	2.3
0.6	− 4.6	4.0	1.7	− 1.6	2.6	**1988**	11.9
9.0	2.9	− 1.6	− 1.8	2.3	1.7	**1989**	27.0
0.9	− 10.0	− 6.2	− 0.4	4.8	2.9	**1990**	− 4.3
4.1	0.6	− 0.9	1.7	− 5.7	9.5	**1991**	20.3
2.3	− 4.0	0.4	− 1.4	2.4	− 0.1	**1992**	4.2
0.7	3.2	− 2.6	3.5	0.1	1.9	**1993**	13.7
3.8	4.0	− 1.8	1.7	− 4.3	2.5	**1994**	2.1
3.3	− 2.1	3.9	− 0.7	6.7	0.8	**1995**	33.5
− 2.2	1.6	4.7	2.5	8.2	− 1.1	**1996**	26.0
7.2	− 7.3	4.2	− 6.3	5.1	1.1	**1997**	22.6
− 0.8	− 15.1	4.0	9.6	6.1	0.7	**1998**	16.1
− 2.9	1.6	− 4.5	3.8	1.4	5.3	**1999**	24.7
0.7	6.6	− 5.0	3.0	− 5.1	3.6	**2000**	− 5.8
0.2	− 5.4	− 11.1	2.6	8.6	1.7	**2001**	− 7.1
− 5.5	− 0.8	− 12.4	10.6	5.9	− 6.2	**2002**	− 16.8
2.8	2.0	− 1.5	5.7	− 0.2	6.9	**2003**	25.3
− 2.8	0.3	− 0.9	− 0.5	4.0	3.4	**2004**	3.1
3.6	− 1.5	0.8	− 1.2	3.5	− 0.8	**2005**	0.6
0.3	1.7	2.6	3.4	1.2	2.0	**2006**	16.3
− 1.5	1.1	4.0	0.2	− 4.0	− 0.8	**2007**	6.4
0.2	1.5	− 6.0	− 14.1	− 5.3	− 0.6	**2008**	− 33.8
8.6	3.5	2.3	0.0	6.5	0.8	**2009**	18.8
7.1	− 4.3	7.7	3.1	− 1.0	5.2	**2010**	11.0
− 2.2	− 4.4	− 6.0	9.5	0.8	1.4	**2011**	5.5
1.0	0.6	2.6	− 2.5	− 0.5	0.6	**2012**	7.3
4.0	− 4.4	2.2	2.8	3.5	3.0	**2013**	26.5
− 1.6	3.2	− 0.3	2.0	2.5	0.0	**2014**	7.5
0.4	− 6.6	− 1.5	8.5	0.3	− 2.2	**2015**	− 2.2
2.8	− 0.2	− 0.5	− 0.9	5.4	3.3	**2016**	13.4
2.5	0.3	2.1	4.3	3.8	1.8	**2017**	25.1
4.7	2.2	1.9	− 5.1	1.7	− 8.7	**2018**	− 5.6
1.0	− 1.7	1.9	0.5	3.7	1.7	**2019**	22.3
5.5	7.0	− 3.9	− 2.8	10.8	3.7	**2020**	16.3
46/71	40/71	29/71	42/71	50/71	50/71		51/71
65 %	56 %	41 %	59 %	70 %	70 %		71 %
1.3 %	− 0.1 %	− 0.7 %	0.5 %	1.8 %	1.5 %		8.3 %
4	10	12	7	2	3		

DOW JONES
MONTH CLOSING VALUES

	JAN	FEB	MAR	APR	MAY	JUN
1950	202	203	206	214	223	209
1951	249	252	248	259	250	243
1952	271	260	270	258	263	274
1953	290	284	280	275	272	268
1954	292	295	304	319	328	334
1955	409	412	410	426	425	451
1956	471	484	512	516	478	493
1957	479	465	475	494	505	503
1958	450	440	447	456	463	478
1959	594	604	602	624	644	644
1960	623	630	617	602	626	641
1961	648	662	677	679	697	684
1962	700	708	707	665	613	561
1963	683	663	683	718	727	707
1964	785	800	813	811	821	832
1965	903	904	889	922	918	868
1966	984	952	925	934	884	870
1967	850	839	866	897	853	860
1968	856	841	841	912	899	898
1969	946	905	936	950	938	873
1970	744	778	786	736	700	684
1971	869	879	904	942	908	891
1972	902	928	941	954	961	929
1973	999	955	951	921	901	892
1974	856	861	847	837	802	802
1975	704	739	768	821	832	879
1976	975	973	1000	997	975	1003
1977	954	936	919	927	899	916
1978	770	742	757	837	841	819
1979	839	809	862	855	822	842
1980	876	863	786	817	851	868
1981	947	975	1004	998	992	977
1982	871	824	823	848	820	812
1983	1076	1113	1130	1226	1200	1222
1984	1221	1155	1165	1171	1105	1132
1985	1287	1284	1267	1258	1315	1336
1986	1571	1709	1819	1784	1877	1893
1987	2158	2224	2305	2286	2292	2419
1988	1958	2072	1988	2032	2031	2142
1989	2342	2258	2294	2419	2480	2440
1990	2591	2627	2707	2657	2877	2881
1991	2736	2882	2914	2888	3028	2907
1992	3223	3268	3236	3359	3397	3319
1993	3310	3371	3435	3428	3527	3516
1994	3978	3832	3636	3682	3758	3625
1995	3844	4011	4158	4321	4465	4556
1996	5395	5486	5587	5569	5643	5655
1997	6813	6878	6584	7009	7331	7673
1998	7907	8546	8800	9063	8900	8952
1999	9359	9307	9786	10789	10560	10971
2000	10941	10128	10922	10734	10522	10448
2001	10887	10495	9879	10735	10912	10502
2002	9920	10106	10404	9946	9925	9243
2003	8054	7891	7992	8480	8850	8985
2004	10488	10584	10358	10226	10188	10435
2005	10490	10766	10504	10193	10467	10275
2006	10865	10993	11109	11367	11168	11150
2007	12622	12269	12354	13063	13628	13409
2008	12650	12266	12263	12820	12638	11350
2009	8001	7063	7609	8168	8500	8447
2010	10067	10325	10857	11009	10137	9774
2011	11892	12226	12320	12811	12570	12414
2012	12633	12952	13212	13214	12393	12880
2013	13861	14054	14579	14840	15116	14910
2014	15699	16322	16458	16581	16717	16827
2015	17165	18133	17776	17841	18011	17620
2016	16466	16517	17685	17774	17787	17930
2017	19864	20812	20663	20941	21009	21350
2018	26149	25029	24103	24163	24416	24271
2019	25000	25916	25929	26593	24815	26600
2020	28256	25409	21917	24346	25383	25813

DOW JONES
MONTH CLOSING VALUES — STOCK MKT

JUL	AUG	SEP	OCT	NOV	DEC	
209	217	226	225	228	235	**1950**
258	270	271	262	261	269	**1951**
280	275	271	269	284	292	**1952**
275	261	264	276	281	281	**1953**
348	336	361	352	387	404	**1954**
466	468	467	455	483	488	**1955**
518	502	475	480	473	500	**1956**
509	484	456	441	450	436	**1957**
503	509	532	543	558	584	**1958**
675	664	632	647	659	679	**1959**
617	626	580	580	597	616	**1960**
705	720	701	704	722	731	**1961**
598	609	579	590	649	652	**1962**
695	729	733	755	751	763	**1963**
841	839	875	873	875	874	**1964**
882	893	931	961	947	969	**1965**
847	788	774	807	792	786	**1966**
904	901	927	880	876	905	**1967**
883	896	936	952	985	944	**1968**
816	837	813	856	812	800	**1969**
734	765	761	756	794	839	**1970**
858	898	887	839	831	890	**1971**
925	964	953	956	1018	1020	**1972**
926	888	947	957	822	851	**1973**
757	679	608	666	619	616	**1974**
832	835	794	836	861	852	**1975**
985	974	990	965	947	1005	**1976**
890	862	847	818	830	831	**1977**
862	877	866	793	799	805	**1978**
846	888	879	816	822	839	**1979**
935	933	932	925	993	964	**1980**
952	882	850	853	889	875	**1981**
809	901	896	992	1039	1047	**1982**
1199	1216	1233	1225	1276	1259	**1983**
1115	1224	1207	1207	1189	1212	**1984**
1348	1334	1329	1374	1472	1547	**1985**
1775	1898	1768	1878	1914	1896	**1986**
2572	2663	2596	1994	1834	1939	**1987**
2129	2032	2113	2149	2115	2169	**1988**
2661	2737	2693	2645	2706	2753	**1989**
2905	2614	2453	2442	2560	2634	**1990**
3025	3044	3017	3069	2895	3169	**1991**
3394	3257	3272	3226	3305	3301	**1992**
3540	3651	3555	3681	3684	3754	**1993**
3765	3913	3843	3908	3739	3834	**1994**
4709	4611	4789	4756	5075	5117	**1995**
5529	5616	5882	6029	6522	6448	**1996**
8223	7622	7945	7442	7823	7908	**1997**
8883	7539	7843	8592	9117	9181	**1998**
10655	10829	10337	10730	10878	11453	**1999**
10522	11215	10651	10971	10415	10788	**2000**
10523	9950	8848	9075	9852	10022	**2001**
8737	8664	7592	8397	8896	8342	**2002**
9234	9416	9275	9801	9782	10454	**2003**
10140	10174	10080	10027	10428	10783	**2004**
10641	10482	10569	10440	10806	10718	**2005**
11186	11381	11679	12801	12222	12463	**2006**
13212	13358	13896	13930	13372	13265	**2007**
11378	11544	10851	9325	8829	8776	**2008**
9172	9496	9712	9713	10345	10428	**2009**
10466	10015	10788	11118	11006	11578	**2010**
12143	11614	10913	11955	12046	12218	**2011**
13009	13091	13437	13096	13026	13104	**2012**
15500	14810	15130	15546	16086	16577	**2013**
16563	17098	17043	17391	17828	17823	**2014**
17690	16528	16285	17664	17720	17425	**2015**
18432	18401	18308	18142	19124	19763	**2016**
21891	21948	22405	23377	24272	24719	**2017**
25415	25965	26458	25166	25538	23327	**2018**
26864	26403	26917	27046	28051	28538	**2019**
26428	28430	27782	26502	29639	30606	**2020**

NASDAQ PERCENT MONTH CHANGES

	JAN	FEB	MAR	APR	MAY	JUN
1972	4.2	5.5	2.2	2.5	0.9	− 1.8
1973	− 4.0	− 6.2	− 2.4	− 8.2	− 4.8	− 1.6
1974	3.0	− 0.6	− 2.2	− 5.9	− 7.7	− 5.3
1975	16.6	4.6	3.6	3.8	5.8	4.7
1976	12.1	3.7	0.4	− 0.6	− 2.3	2.6
1977	− 2.4	− 1.0	− 0.5	1.4	0.1	4.3
1978	− 4.0	0.6	4.7	8.5	4.4	0.0
1979	6.6	− 2.6	7.5	1.6	− 1.8	5.1
1980	7.0	− 2.3	− 17.1	6.9	7.5	4.9
1981	− 2.2	0.1	6.1	3.1	3.1	− 3.5
1982	− 3.8	− 4.8	− 2.1	5.2	− 3.3	− 4.1
1983	6.9	5.0	3.9	8.2	5.3	3.2
1984	− 3.7	− 5.9	− 0.7	− 1.3	− 5.9	2.9
1985	12.8	2.0	− 1.8	0.5	3.6	1.9
1986	3.4	7.1	4.2	2.3	4.4	1.3
1987	12.4	8.4	1.2	− 2.9	− 0.3	2.0
1988	4.3	6.5	2.1	1.2	− 2.3	6.6
1989	5.2	− 0.4	1.8	5.1	4.3	− 2.4
1990	− 8.6	2.4	2.3	− 3.5	9.3	0.7
1991	10.8	9.4	6.4	0.5	4.4	− 6.0
1992	5.8	2.1	− 4.7	− 4.2	1.1	− 3.7
1993	2.9	− 3.7	2.9	− 4.2	5.9	0.5
1994	3.0	− 1.0	− 6.2	− 1.3	0.2	− 4.0
1995	0.4	5.1	3.0	3.3	2.4	8.0
1996	0.7	3.8	0.1	8.1	4.4	− 4.7
1997	6.9	− 5.1	− 6.7	3.2	11.1	3.0
1998	3.1	9.3	3.7	1.8	− 4.8	6.5
1999	14.3	− 8.7	7.6	3.3	− 2.8	8.7
2000	− 3.2	19.2	− 2.6	− 15.6	− 11.9	16.6
2001	12.2	− 22.4	− 14.5	15.0	− 0.3	2.4
2002	− 0.8	− 10.5	6.6	− 8.5	− 4.3	− 9.4
2003	− 1.1	1.3	0.3	9.2	9.0	1.7
2004	3.1	− 1.8	− 1.8	− 3.7	3.5	3.1
2005	− 5.2	− 0.5	− 2.6	− 3.9	7.6	− 0.5
2006	4.6	− 1.1	2.6	− 0.7	− 6.2	− 0.3
2007	2.0	− 1.9	0.2	4.3	3.1	0.0
2008	− 9.9	− 5.0	0.3	5.9	4.6	− 9.1
2009	− 6.4	− 6.7	10.9	12.3	3.3	3.4
2010	− 5.4	4.2	7.1	2.6	− 8.3	− 6.5
2011	1.8	3.0	0.0	3.3	− 1.3	− 2.2
2012	8.0	5.4	4.2	− 1.5	− 7.2	3.8
2013	4.1	0.6	3.4	1.9	3.8	− 1.5
2014	− 1.7	5.0	− 2.5	− 2.0	3.1	3.9
2015	− 2.1	7.1	− 1.3	0.8	2.6	− 1.6
2016	− 7.9	− 1.2	6.8	− 1.9	3.6	− 2.1
2017	4.3	3.8	1.5	2.3	2.5	− 0.9
2018	7.4	− 1.9	− 2.9	0.0	5.3	0.9
2019	9.7	3.4	2.6	4.7	− 7.9	7.4
2020	2.0	− 6.4	− 10.1	15.4	6.8	6.0
FQ POS	32/49	26/49	30/49	32/49	31/49	28/49
% FQ POS	65 %	53 %	61 %	65 %	63 %	57 %
AVG GAIN	2.6 %	0.6 %	0.6 %	1.6 %	1.1 %	0.9 %
RANK GAIN	1	10	9	3	5	6

NASDAQ PERCENT MONTH CHANGES 🇺🇸 STOCK MKT

JUL	AUG	SEP	OCT	NOV	DEC		YEAR
− 1.8	1.7	− 0.3	0.5	2.1	0.6	**1972**	17.2
7.6	− 3.5	6.0	− 0.9	− 15.1	− 1.4	**1973**	− 31.1
− 7.9	− 10.9	− 10.7	17.2	− 3.5	− 5.0	**1974**	− 35.1
− 4.4	− 5.0	− 5.9	3.6	2.4	− 1.5	**1975**	29.8
1.1	− 1.7	1.7	− 1.0	0.9	7.4	**1976**	26.1
0.9	− 0.5	0.7	− 3.3	5.8	1.8	**1977**	7.3
5.0	6.9	− 1.6	− 16.4	3.2	2.9	**1978**	12.3
2.3	6.4	− 0.3	− 9.6	6.4	4.8	**1979**	28.1
8.9	5.7	3.4	2.7	8.0	− 2.8	**1980**	33.9
− 1.9	− 7.5	− 8.0	8.4	3.1	− 2.7	**1981**	− 3.2
− 2.3	6.2	5.6	13.3	9.3	0.0	**1982**	18.7
− 4.6	− 3.8	1.4	− 7.4	4.1	− 2.5	**1983**	19.9
− 4.2	10.9	− 1.8	− 1.2	− 1.9	1.9	**1984**	− 11.3
1.7	− 1.2	− 5.8	4.4	7.4	3.5	**1985**	31.5
− 8.4	3.1	− 8.4	2.9	− 0.3	− 3.0	**1986**	7.4
2.4	4.6	− 2.4	− 27.2	− 5.6	8.3	**1987**	− 5.2
− 1.9	− 2.8	2.9	− 1.3	− 2.9	2.7	**1988**	15.4
4.2	3.4	0.8	− 3.7	0.1	− 0.3	**1989**	19.2
− 5.2	− 13.0	− 9.6	− 4.3	8.9	4.1	**1990**	− 17.8
5.5	4.7	0.2	3.1	− 3.5	11.9	**1991**	56.9
3.1	− 3.0	3.6	3.8	7.9	3.7	**1992**	15.5
0.1	5.4	2.7	2.2	− 3.2	3.0	**1993**	14.7
2.3	6.0	− 0.2	1.7	− 3.5	0.2	**1994**	− 3.2
7.3	1.9	2.3	− 0.7	2.2	− 0.7	**1995**	39.9
− 8.8	5.6	7.5	− 0.4	5.8	− 0.1	**1996**	22.7
10.5	− 0.4	6.2	− -5.5	0.4	− 1.9	**1997**	21.6
− 1.2	− 19.9	13.0	4.6	10.1	12.5	**1998**	39.6
− 1.8	3.8	0.2	8.0	12.5	22.0	**1999**	85.6
− 5.0	11.7	− 12.7	− 8.3	− 22.9	− 4.9	**2000**	− 39.3
− 6.2	− 10.9	− 17.0	12.8	14.2	1.0	**2001**	− 21.1
− 9.2	− 1.0	− 10.9	13.5	11.2	− 9.7	**2002**	− 31.5
6.9	4.3	− 1.3	8.1	1.5	2.2	**2003**	50.0
− 7.8	− 2.6	3.2	4.1	6.2	3.7	**2004**	8.6
6.2	− 1.5	0.0	− 1.5	5.3	− 1.2	**2005**	1.4
− 3.7	4.4	3.4	4.8	2.7	− 0.7	**2006**	9.5
− 2.2	2.0	4.0	5.8	− 6.9	− 0.3	**2007**	9.8
1.4	1.8	− 11.6	− 17.7	− 10.8	2.7	**2008**	− 40.5
7.8	1.5	5.6	− 3.6	4.9	5.8	**2009**	43.9
6.9	− 6.2	12.0	5.9	− 0.4	6.2	**2010**	16.9
− 0.6	− 6.4	− 6.4	11.1	− 2.4	− 0.6	**2011**	− 1.8
0.2	4.3	1.6	− 4.5	1.1	0.3	**2012**	15.9
6.6	− 1.0	5.1	3.9	3.6	2.9	**2013**	38.3
− 0.9	4.8	− 1.9	3.1	3.5	− 1.2	**2014**	13.4
2.8	− 6.9	− 3.3	9.4	1.1	− 2.0	**2015**	5.7
6.6	1.0	1.9	− 2.3	2.6	1.1	**2016**	7.5
3.4	1.3	1.0	3.6	2.2	0.4	**2017**	28.2
2.2	5.7	− 0.8	− 9.2	0.3	− 9.5	**2018**	− 3.9
2.1	− 2.6	0.5	3.7	4.5	3.5	**2019**	35.2
6.8	9.6	− 5.2	− 2.3	11.8	5.7	**2020**	43.6
28/49	27/49	26/49	27/49	35/49	29/49		36/49
57 %	55 %	53 %	55 %	71 %	59 %		73 %
0.7 %	0.3 %	− 0.6 %	0.7 %	1.9 %	1.5 %		13.2 %
8	11	12	7	2	4		

NASDAQ MONTH
CLOSING VALUES

	JAN	FEB	MAR	APR	MAY	JUN
1972	119	125	128	131	133	130
1973	128	120	117	108	103	101
1974	95	94	92	87	80	76
1975	70	73	76	79	83	87
1976	87	90	91	90	88	90
1977	96	95	94	95	96	100
1978	101	101	106	115	120	120
1979	126	123	132	134	131	138
1980	162	158	131	140	150	158
1981	198	198	210	217	223	216
1982	188	179	176	185	179	171
1983	248	261	271	293	309	319
1984	268	253	251	247	233	240
1985	279	284	279	281	291	296
1986	336	360	375	383	400	406
1987	392	425	430	418	417	425
1988	345	367	375	379	370	395
1989	401	400	407	428	446	435
1990	416	426	436	420	459	462
1991	414	453	482	485	506	476
1992	620	633	604	579	585	564
1993	696	671	690	661	701	704
1994	800	793	743	734	735	706
1995	755	794	817	844	865	933
1996	1060	1100	1101	1191	1243	1185
1997	1380	1309	1222	1261	1400	1442
1998	1619	1771	1836	1868	1779	1895
1999	2506	2288	2461	2543	2471	2686
2000	3940	4697	4573	3861	3401	3966
2001	2773	2152	1840	2116	2110	2161
2002	1934	1731	1845	1688	1616	1463
2003	1321	1338	1341	1464	1596	1623
2004	2066	2030	1994	1920	1987	2048
2005	2062	2052	1999	1922	2068	2057
2006	2306	2281	2340	2323	2179	2172
2007	2464	2416	2422	2525	2605	2603
2008	2390	2271	2279	2413	2523	2293
2009	1476	1378	1529	1717	1774	1835
2010	2147	2238	2398	2461	2257	2109
2011	2700	2782	2781	2874	2835	2774
2012	2814	2967	3092	3046	2827	2935
2013	3142	3160	3268	3329	3456	3403
2014	4104	4308	4199	4115	4243	4408
2015	4635	4964	4901	4941	5070	4987
2016	4614	4558	4870	4775	4948	4843
2017	5615	5825	5912	6048	6199	6140
2018	7411	7273	7063	7066	7442	7510
2019	7282	7533	7729	8095	7453	8006
2020	9151	8567	7700	8890	9490	10059

NASDAQ MONTH CLOSING VALUES 🇺🇸 STOCK MKT

JUL	AUG	SEP	OCT	NOV	DEC	
128	130	130	130	133	134	**1972**
109	105	111	110	94	92	**1973**
70	62	56	65	63	60	**1974**
83	79	74	77	79	78	**1975**
91	90	91	90	91	98	**1976**
101	100	101	98	103	105	**1977**
126	135	133	111	115	118	**1978**
141	150	150	136	144	151	**1979**
172	182	188	193	208	202	**1980**
212	196	180	195	201	196	**1981**
167	178	188	213	232	232	**1982**
304	292	297	275	286	279	**1983**
230	255	250	247	242	247	**1984**
301	298	280	293	314	325	**1985**
371	383	351	361	360	349	**1986**
435	455	444	323	305	331	**1987**
387	377	388	383	372	381	**1988**
454	469	473	456	456	455	**1989**
438	381	345	330	359	374	**1990**
502	526	527	543	524	586	**1991**
581	563	583	605	653	677	**1992**
705	743	763	779	754	777	**1993**
722	766	764	777	750	752	**1994**
1001	1020	1044	1036	1059	1052	**1995**
1081	1142	1227	1222	1293	1291	**1996**
1594	1587	1686	1594	1601	1570	**1997**
1872	1499	1694	1771	1950	2193	**1998**
2638	2739	2746	2966	3336	4069	**1999**
3767	4206	3673	3370	2598	2471	**2000**
2027	1805	1499	1690	1931	1950	**2001**
1328	1315	1172	1330	1479	1336	**2002**
1735	1810	1787	1932	1960	2003	**2003**
1887	1838	1897	1975	2097	2175	**2004**
2185	2152	2152	2120	2233	2205	**2005**
2091	2184	2258	2367	2432	2415	**2006**
2546	2596	2702	2859	2661	2652	**2007**
2326	2368	2092	1721	1536	1577	**2008**
1979	2009	2122	2045	2145	2269	**2009**
2255	2114	2369	2507	2498	2653	**2010**
2756	2579	2415	2684	2620	2605	**2011**
2940	3067	3116	2977	3010	3020	**2012**
3626	3590	3771	3920	4060	4177	**2013**
4370	4580	4493	4631	4792	4736	**2014**
5128	4777	4620	5054	5109	5007	**2015**
5162	5213	5312	5189	5324	5383	**2016**
6348	6429	6496	6728	6874	6903	**2017**
7672	8110	8046	7306	7331	6635	**2018**
8175	7963	7999	8292	8665	8973	**2019**
10745	11775	11168	10912	12199	12888	**2020**

S&P/TSX MONTH PERCENT CHANGES

	JAN	FEB	MAR	APR	MAY	JUN
1985	8.1	0.0	0.7	0.8	3.8	— 0.8
1986	— 1.7	0.5	6.7	1.1	1.4	— 1.2
1987	9.2	4.5	6.9	— 0.6	— 0.9	1.5
1988	— 3.3	4.8	3.4	0.8	— 2.7	5.9
1989	6.7	— 1.2	0.2	1.4	2.2	1.5
1990	— 6.7	— 0.5	— 1.3	— 8.2	6.7	— 0.6
1991	0.5	5.8	1.0	-0.8	2.2	— 2.3
1992	2.4	— 0.4	— 4.7	— 1.7	1.0	0.0
1993	— 1.3	4.4	4.4	5.2	2.5	2.2
1994	5.4	— 2.9	— 2.1	— 1.4	1.4	— 7.0
1995	— 4.7	2.7	4.6	— -0.8	4.0	1.8
1996	5.4	— 0.7	0.8	3.5	1.9	— 3.9
1997	3.1	0.8	— 5.0	2.2	6.8	0.9
1998	0.0	5.9	6.6	1.4	— 1.0	— 2.9
1999	3.8	— 6.2	4.5	6.3	— 2.5	2.5
2000	0.8	7.6	3.7	— 1.2	— 1.0	10.2
2001	4.3	— 13.3	— 5.8	4.5	2.7	— 5.2
2002	— 0.5	— 0.1	2.8	— 2.4	— 0.1	— 6.7
2003	— 0.7	— 0.2	— 3.2	3.8	4.2	1.8
2004	3.7	3.1	— 2.3	— 4.0	2.1	1.5
2005	— 0.5	5.0	— 0.6	— 3.5	3.6	3.1
2006	6.0	— 2.2	3.6	0.8	— 3.8	— 1.1
2007	1.0	0.1	0.9	1.9	4.8	— 1.1
2008	— 4.9	3.3	— 1.7	4.4	5.6	— 1.7
2009	— 3.3	— 6.6	7.4	6.9	11.2	0.0
2010	— 5.5	4.8	3.5	1.4	— 3.7	— 4.0
2011	0.8	4.3	— 0.1	— 1.2	— 1.0	— 3.6
2012	4.2	1.5	— 2.0	— 0.8	— 6.3	0.7
2013	2.0	1.1	— 0.6	— 2.3	1.6	— 4.1
2014	0.5	3.8	0.9	2.2	— 0.3	3.7
2015	0.3	3.8	— 2.2	2.2	— 1.4	— 3.1
2016	— 1.4	0.3	4.9	3.4	0.8	0.0
2017	0.6	0.1	1.0	0.2	— 1.5	— 1.1
2018	— 1.6	— 3.2	— 0.5	1.6	2.9	1.3
2019	8.5	2.9	0.6	3.0	— 3.3	2.1
2020	1.5	— 6.1	— 17.7	10.5	2.8	2.1
FQ POS	23/36	22/36	21/36	23/36	22/36	17/36
% FQ POS	64 %	61 %	58 %	64 %	61 %	47 %
AVG GAIN	1.2 %	0.8 %	0.5 %	1.2 %	1.3 %	-0.2 %
RANK GAIN	3	7	8	4	2	11

S&P/TSX MONTH PERCENT CHANGES 🍁 STOCK MKT

JUL	AUG	SEP	OCT	NOV	DEC		YEAR
2.4	1.5	— 6.7	1.6	6.8	1.3	**1985**	20.5
— 4.9	3.2	— 1.6	1.6	0.7	0.6	**1986**	6.0
7.8	— 0.9	— 2.3	— 22.6	— 1.4	6.1	**1987**	3.1
— 1.9	— 2.7	— 0.1	3.4	— 3.0	2.9	**1988**	7.3
5.6	1.0	— 1.7	— 0.6	0.6	0.7	**1989**	17.1
0.5	— 6.0	— 5.6	— 2.5	2.3	3.4	**1990**	— 18.0
2.1	— 0.6	— 3.7	3.8	— 1.9	1.9	**1991**	7.8
1.6	— 1.2	— 3.1	1.2	— 1.6	2.1	**1992**	— 4.6
0.0	4.3	— 3.6	6.6	— 1.8	3.4	**1993**	29.0
3.8	4.1	0.1	— 1.4	— 4.6	2.9	**1994**	— 2.5
1.9	— 2.1	0.3	— 1.6	4.5	1.1	**1995**	11.9
— 2.3	4.3	2.9	5.8	7.5	— 1.5	**1996**	25.7
6.8	— 3.9	6.5	— 2.8	— 4.8	2.9	**1997**	13.0
— 5.9	— 20.2	1.5	10.6	2.2	2.2	**1998**	— 3.2
1.0	— 1.6	— 0.2	4.3	3.6	11.9	**1999**	29.7
2.1	8.1	— 7.7	— 7.1	— 8.5	1.3	**2000**	6.2
— 0.6	— 3.8	— 7.6	0.7	7.8	3.5	**2001**	— 13.9
— 7.6	0.1	— 6.5	1.1	5.1	0.7	**2002**	— 14.0
3.9	3.6	— 1.3	4.7	1.1	4.6	**2003**	24.3
— 1.0	— 1.0	3.5	2.3	1.8	2.4	**2004**	12.5
5.3	2.4	3.2	— 5.7	4.2	4.1	**2005**	21.9
1.9	2.1	— 2.6	5.0	3.3	1.2	**2006**	14.5
— 0.3	— 1.5	3.2	3.7	— 6.4	1.1	**2007**	7.2
— 6.0	1.3	— 14.7	— 16.9	— 5.0	— 3.1	**2008**	— 35.0
4.0	0.8	4.8	— 4.2	4.9	2.6	**2009**	30.7
3.7	1.7	3.8	2.5	2.2	3.8	**2010**	14.4
— 2.7	— 1.4	— 9.0	5.4	— 0.4	— 2.0	**2011**	— 11.1
0.6	2.4	3.1	0.9	— 1.5	1.6	**2012**	4.0
2.9	1.3	1.1	4.5	0.3	1.7	**2013**	9.6
1.2	1.9	— 4.3	— 2.3	0.9	— 0.8	**2014**	7.4
— 0.6	— 4.2	— 4.0	1.7	— 0.4	— 3.4	**2015**	— 11.1
3.7	0.1	0.9	0.4	2.0	1.4	**2016**	17.5
— 0.3	0.4	2.8	2.5	0.3	0.9	**2017**	6.0
1.0	— 1.0	— 1.2	— 6.5	1.1	— 5.8	**2018**	— 11.8
0.1	0.2	1.3	— 1.1	3.4	0.1	**2019**	19.1
4.2	2.1	— 2.4	— 3.4	10.3	1.4	**2020**	2.2
24/36	21/36	15/36	22/36	23/36	30/36		26/36
67 %	58 %	42 %	61 %	64 %	83 %		72 %
1.0 %	— 0.1 %	— 1.4 %	— 0.1 %	1.0 %	1.6 %		6.8 %
6	10	12	9	5	1		

S&P/TSX MONTH CLOSING VALUES

	JAN	FEB	MAR	APR	MAY	JUN
1985	2595	2595	2613	2635	2736	2713
1986	2843	2856	3047	3079	3122	3086
1987	3349	3499	3739	3717	3685	3740
1988	3057	3205	3314	3340	3249	3441
1989	3617	3572	3578	3628	3707	3761
1990	3704	3687	3640	3341	3565	3544
1991	3273	3462	3496	3469	3546	3466
1992	3596	3582	3412	3356	3388	3388
1993	3305	3452	3602	3789	3883	3966
1994	4555	4424	4330	4267	4327	4025
1995	4018	4125	4314	4280	4449	4527
1996	4968	4934	4971	5147	5246	5044
1997	6110	6158	5850	5977	6382	6438
1998	6700	7093	7559	7665	7590	7367
1999	6730	6313	6598	7015	6842	7010
2000	8481	9129	9462	9348	9252	10196
2001	9322	8079	7608	7947	8162	7736
2002	7649	7638	7852	7663	7656	7146
2003	6570	6555	6343	6586	6860	6983
2004	8521	8789	8586	8244	8417	8546
2005	9204	9668	9612	9275	9607	9903
2006	11946	11688	12111	12204	11745	11613
2007	13034	13045	13166	13417	14057	13907
2008	13155	13583	13350	13937	14715	14467
2009	8695	8123	8720	9325	10370	10375
2010	11094	11630	12038	12211	11763	11294
2011	13552	14137	14116	13945	13803	13301
2012	12452	12644	12392	12293	11513	11597
2013	12685	12822	12750	12457	12650	12129
2014	13695	14210	14335	14652	14604	15146
2015	14674	15234	14902	15225	15014	14553
2016	12822	12860	13494	13951	14066	14065
2017	15386	15399	15548	15586	15350	15182
2018	15952	15443	15367	15608	16062	16278
2019	15541	15999	16102	16581	16037	16382
2020	17318	16263	13379	14781	15193	15515

S&P/TSX PERCENT CLOSING VALUES

JUL	AUG	SEP	OCT	NOV	DEC	
2779	2820	2632	2675	2857	2893	1985
2935	3028	2979	3027	3047	3066	1986
4030	3994	3902	3019	2978	3160	1987
3377	3286	3284	3396	3295	3390	1988
3971	4010	3943	3919	3943	3970	1989
3561	3346	3159	3081	3151	3257	1990
3540	3518	3388	3516	3449	3512	1991
3443	3403	3298	3336	3283	3350	1992
3967	4138	3991	4256	4180	4321	1993
4179	4350	4354	4292	4093	4214	1994
4615	4517	4530	4459	4661	4714	1995
4929	5143	5291	5599	6017	5927	1996
6878	6612	7040	6842	6513	6699	1997
6931	5531	5614	6208	6344	6486	1998
7081	6971	6958	7256	7520	8414	1999
10406	11248	10378	9640	8820	8934	2000
7690	7399	6839	6886	7426	7688	2001
6605	6612	6180	6249	6570	6615	2002
7258	7517	7421	7773	7859	8221	2003
8458	8377	8668	8871	9030	9247	2004
10423	10669	11012	10383	10824	11272	2005
11831	12074	11761	12345	12752	12908	2006
13869	13660	14099	14625	13689	13833	2007
13593	13771	11753	9763	9271	8988	2008
10787	10868	11935	10911	11447	11746	2009
11713	11914	12369	12676	12953	13443	2010
12946	12769	11624	12252	12204	11955	2011
11665	11949	12317	12423	12239	12434	2012
12487	12654	12787	13361	13395	13622	2013
15331	15626	14961	14613	14745	14632	2014
14468	13859	13307	13529	13470	13010	2015
14583	14598	14726	14787	15083	15288	2016
15144	15212	15635	16026	16067	16209	2017
16434	16263	16073	15027	15198	14323	2018
16407	16442	16659	16483	17040	17063	2019
16169	16514	16121	15581	17190	17433	2020

S&P 500 1950 - 2020
BEST - WORST

10 BEST

YEARS

	Close	Change	Change
1954	36	11 pt	45.0 %
1958	55	15	38.1
1995	616	157	34.1
1975	90	22	31.5
1997	970	230	31.0
2013	1848	422	29.6
2019	3231	724	28.9
1989	353	76	27.3
1998	1229	259	26.7
1955	45	10	26.4

MONTHS

	Close	Change	Change
Oct 1974	74	10 pt	16.3 %
Apr 2020	2912	328	12.7
Aug 1982	120	12	11.6
Dec 1991	417	42	11.2
Oct 1982	134	13	11.0
Oct 2011	1253	122	10.8
Nov 2020	3622	352	10.8
Aug 1984	167	16	10.6
Nov 1980	141	13	10.2
Nov 1962	62	6	10.2

DAYS

		Close	Change	Change
Mon	2008 Oct 13	1003	104 pt	11.6 %
Tue	2008 Oct 28	941	92	10.8
Tue	2020 Mar 24	2447	210	9.4
Fri	2020 Mar 13	2711	230	9.3
Wed	1987 Oct 21	258	22	9.1
Mon	2009 Mar 23	883	54	7.1
Mon	2020 Apr 6	2667	175	7.0
Thu	2008 Nov 13	911	59	6.9
Mon	2008 Nov 24	852	52	6.5
Tues	2009 Mar 10	720	43	6.4

10 WORST

YEARS

	Close	Change	Change
2008	903	– 566 pt	– 38.5 %
1974	69	– 29	– 29.7
2002	880	– 268	– 23.4
1973	98	– 21	– 17.4
1957	40	– 7	– 14.3
1966	80	– 12	– 13.1
2001	1148	– 172	– 13.0
1962	63	– 8	– 11.8
1977	95	– 12	– 11.5
1969	92	– 12	– 11.4

MONTHS

	Close	Change	Change
Oct 1987	252	– 70 pt	– 21.8 %
Oct 2008	969	– 196	– 16.8
Aug 1998	957	– 163	– 14.6
Mar 2020	2584	– 370	– 12.5
Sep 1974	64	– 9	– 11.9
Nov 1973	96	– 12	– 11.4
Sep 2002	815	– 101	– 11.0
Feb 2009	735	– 91	– 11.0
Mar 1980	102	– 12	– 10.2
Aug 1990	323	– 34	– 9.4

DAYS

		Close	Change	Change
Mon	1987 Oct 19	225	– 58 pt	– 20.5 %
Mon	2020 Mar 16	2386	– 325	– 12.0
Thu	2020 Mar 12	2481	– 261	– 9.5
Wed	2008 Oct 15	908	– 90	– 9.0
Mon	2008 Dec 01	816	– 80	– 8.9
Mon	2008 Sep 29	1106	– 107	– 8.8
Mon	1987 Oct 26	228	– 21	– 8.3
Thu	2008 Oct 09	910	– 75	– 7.6
Mon	2020 Mar 9	2747	– 226	– 7.6
Mon	1997 Oct 27	877	– 65	– 6.9

10 BEST

YEARS

	Close	Change	Change
1954	404	124 pt	44.0 %
1975	852	236	38.3
1958	584	148	34.0
1995	5117	1283	33.5
1985	1547	335	27.7
1989	2753	585	27.0
2013	16577	3473	26.5
1996	6448	1331	26.0
2003	10454	2112	25.3
1999	11453	2272	25.2

MONTHS

	Close	Change	Change
Nov 2020	29639	3137 pt	11.8 %
Aug 1982	901	93	11.5
Oct 1982	992	95	10.6
Apr 2020	24246	2429	11.1
Oct 2002	8397	805	10.6
Apr 1978	837	80	10.5
Apr 1999	10789	1003	10.2
Nov 1962	649	60	10.1
Nov 1954	387	35	9.9
Aug 1984	1224	109	9.8

DAYS

		Close	Change	Change
Tue	2020 Mar 24	20705	2113 pt	11.4 %
Mon	2008 Oct 13	9388	936	11.1
Tue	2008 Oct 28	9065	889	10.9
Wed	1987 Oct 21	2028	187	10.2
Fri	2020 Mar 13	23186	1985	9.4
Mon	2020 Apr 6	22680	1627	7.7
Mon	2009 Mar 23	7776	497	6.8
Thu	2008 Nov 13	8835	553	6.7
Fri	2008 Nov 21	8046	494	6.5
Thu	2020 Mar 26	22552	1352	6.4

10 WORST

YEARS

	Close	Change	Change
2008	8776	− 4488 pt	− 33.8 %
1974	616	− 235	− 27.6
1966	786	− 184	− 18.9
1977	831	− 174	− 17.3
2002	8342	− 1680	− 16.8
1973	851	− 169	− 16.6
1969	800	− 143	− 15.2
1957	436	− 64	− 12.8
1962	652	− 79	− 10.8
1960	616	− 64	− 9.3

MONTHS

	Close	Change	Change
Oct 1987	1994	− 603 pt	− 23.2 %
Aug 1998	7539	− 1344	− 15.1
Oct 2008	9325	− 1526	− 14.1
Nov 1973	822	− 134	− 14.0
Mar 2020	21917	3492	13.7
Sep 2002	7592	− 1072	− 12.4
Feb 2009	7063	− 938	− 11.7
Sep 2001	8848	− 1102	− 11.1
Sep 1974	608	− 71	− 10.4
Aug 1974	679	− 79	− 10.4

DAYS

		Close	Change	Change
Mon	1987 Oct 19	1739	− 508 pt	− 22.6 %
Mon	2020 Mar 16	20189	− 2997	− 12.9
Thu	2020 Mar 12	20201	− 2353	− 10.0
Mon	1987 Oct 26	1794	− 157	− 8.0
Wed	2008 Oct 15	8578	− 733	− 7.9
Mon	2020 Mar 9	23851	2014	− 7.8
Mon	2008 Dec 01	8149	− 680	− 7.7
Thu	2008 Oct 09	8579	− 679	− 7.3
Mon	1997 Oct 27	8366	− 554	− 7.2
Mon	2001 Sep 17	8921	− 685	− 7.1

10 BEST   # 10 WORST

YEARS

	Close	Change	Change		Close	Change	Change
1999	4069	1877 pt	85.6 %	2008	1577	– 1075 pt	– 40.5 %
1991	586	213	56.9	2000	2471	– 1599	– 39.3
2003	2003	668	50.0	1974	60	– 32	– 35.1
2009	2269	692	43.9	2002	1336	– 615	– 31.5
1995	1052	300	39.9	1973	92	– 42	– 31.1
1998	2193	622	39.6	2001	1950	– 520	– 21.1
2013	4161	1157	38.3	1990	374	– 81	– 17.8
2019	8973	2337	35.2	1984	247	– 32	– 11.3
1980	202	51	33.9	1987	331	– 18	– 5.2
1985	325	78	31.5	2018	6635	– 268	– 3.9

MONTHS

	Close	Change	Change		Close	Change	Change
Dec 1999	4069	733 pt	22.0 %	Oct 1987	323	– 121 pt	– 27.2 %
Feb 2000	4697	756	19.2	Nov 2000	2598	– 772	– 22.9
Oct 1974	65	10	17.2	Feb 2001	2152	– 621	– 22.4
Jun 2000	3966	565	16.6	Aug 1998	1499	– 373	– 19.9
Apr 2020	8890	1189	15.4	Oct 2008	1721	– 371	– 17.7
Apr 2001	2116	276	15.0	Mar 1980	131	– 27	– 17.1
Nov 2001	1931	240	14.2	Sep 2001	1499	– 307	– 17.0
Oct 2002	1330	158	13.5	Oct 1978	111	– 22	– 16.4
Oct 1982	1771	25	13.3	Apr 2000	3861	– 712	– 15.6
Sep 1998	1694	195	13.0	Nov 1973	94	– 17	– 15.1

DAYS

		Close	Change	Change			Close	Change	Change
Wed	2001 Jan 3	2617	325 pt	14.2 %	Mon	2020 Mar 16	6905	– 970 pt	– 12.3 %
Mon	2008 Oct 13	1844	195	11.8	Mon	1987 Oct 19	360	– 46	– 11.3
Tue	2000 Dec 5	2890	274	10.5	Fri	2000 Apr 14	3321	– 355	– 9.7
Tue	2008 Oct 28	1649	144	9.5	Thu	2020 Mar 12	7202	– 750	– 9.4
Fri	2020 Mar 13	7875	673	9.3	Mon	2008 Sep 29	1984	– 200	– 9.1
Thu	2001 Apr 5	1785	146	8.9	Mon	1987 Oct 26	299	– 30	– 9.0
Wed	2001 Apr 18	2079	156	8.1	Tue	1987 Oct 20	328	– 32	– 9.0
	2020 Mar 24		557	8.1	Mon	2008 Dec 01	1398	– 138	– 9.0
Tue	2000 May 30	3459	254	7.9	Mon	1998 Aug 31	1499	– 140	– 8.6
Fri	2000 Oct 13	3317	242	7.9	Wed	2008 Oct 15	1628	– 151	– 8.5

10 BEST

10 WORST

YEARS

	Close	Change	Change
2009	8414	2758 pt	30.7 %
1999	4321	1928	29.7
1993	5927	971	29.0
1996	8221	1213	25.7
2003	11272	1606	24.3
2005	2893	2026	21.9
1985	3970	500	20.8
2019	17063	1842	27.4
1989	12908	580	17.1
2006	6699	1636	14.5

YEARS

	Close	Change	Change
2008	8988	– 4845 pt	– 35.0 %
1990	3257	– 713	– 18.0
2002	6615	– 1074	– 14.0
2001	7688	– 1245	– 13.9
2018	14323	– 1886	– 11.6
2015	13010	– 1622	– 11.1
2011	11955	– 1488	– 11.1
1992	3350	– 162	– 4.6
1998	6486	– 214	– 3.2
1994	4214	– 108	– 2.5

MONTHS

	Close	Change	Change
Dec 1999	8414	891 pt	11.8 %
May 2009	8500	1045	11.2
Oct 1998	6208	594	10.6
Apr 2020	14781	1402	10.5
Nov 2020	17190	1610	10.3
Jun 2000	10196	943	10.2
Jan 1985	2595	195	8.1
Aug 2000	11248	842	8.1
Nov 2001	7426	540	7.8
Jul 1987	4030	290	7.8

MONTHS

	Close	Change	Change
Oct 1987	3019	– 883 pt	– 22.6 %
Aug 1998	5531	– 1401	– 20.2
Mar 2020	13379	– 2884	– 17.7
Oct 2008	9763	– 1990	– 16.9
Sep 2008	11753	– 2018	– 14.7
Feb 2001	8079	– 1243	– 13.3
Sep 2011	11624	– 1145	– 9.0
Nov 2000	8820	– 820	– 8.5
Apr 1990	3341	– 299	– 8.2
Sep 2000	10378	– 870	– 7.7

DAYS

		Close	Change	Change
Tue	2020 Mar 24	12571	1342 pt	12.0 %
Tue	2008 Oct 14	9956	891	9.8
Mon	2020 Mar 13	13716	1208	9.7
Wed	1987 Oct 21	3246	269	9.0
Mon	2008 Oct 20	10251	689	7.2
Tue	2008 Oct 28	9152	614	7.2
Fri	2008 Sep 19	12913	848	7.0
Fri	2008 Nov 28	9271	517	5.9
Fri	2008 Nov 21	8155	431	5.6
Mon	2008 Dec 08	8567	450	5.5

DAYS

		Close	Change	Change
Wed	2020 Mar 12	12508	– 1762 pt	– 12.3 %
Mon	1987 Oct 19	3192	– 407	– 11.3
Mon	2020 Mar 9	14514	– 1661	– 10.3
Mon	2020 Mar 16	12360	– 1356	– 9.9
Mon	2008 Dec 01	8406	– 864	– 9.3
Thu	2008 Nov 20	7725	– 766	– 9.0
Mon	2008 Oct 27	8537	– 757	– 8.1
Wed	2000 Oct 25	9512	– 840	– 8.1
Wed	2020 Mar 18	11721	– 964	– 7.6
Mon	1987 Oct 26	2846	– 233	– 7.6

BOND YIELDS

	JAN	FEB	MAR	APR	MAY	JUN
1954	2.48	2.47	2.37	2.29	2.37	2.38
1955	2.61	2.65	2.68	2.75	2.76	2.78
1956	2.9	2.84	2.96	3.18	3.07	3
1957	3.46	3.34	3.41	3.48	3.6	3.8
1958	3.09	3.05	2.98	2.88	2.92	2.97
1959	4.02	3.96	3.99	4.12	4.31	4.34
1960	4.72	4.49	4.25	4.28	4.35	4.15
1961	3.84	3.78	3.74	3.78	3.71	3.88
1962	4.08	4.04	3.93	3.84	3.87	3.91
1963	3.83	3.92	3.93	3.97	3.93	3.99
1964	4.17	4.15	4.22	4.23	4.2	4.17
1965	4.19	4.21	4.21	4.2	4.21	4.21
1966	4.61	4.83	4.87	4.75	4.78	4.81
1967	4.58	4.63	4.54	4.59	4.85	5.02
1968	5.53	5.56	5.74	5.64	5.87	5.72
1969	6.04	6.19	6.3	6.17	6.32	6.57
1970	7.79	7.24	7.07	7.39	7.91	7.84
1971	6.24	6.11	5.7	5.83	6.39	6.52
1972	5.95	6.08	6.07	6.19	6.13	6.11
1973	6.46	6.64	6.71	6.67	6.85	6.9
1974	6.99	6.96	7.21	7.51	7.58	7.54
1975	7.5	7.39	7.73	8.23	8.06	7.86
1976	7.74	7.79	7.73	7.56	7.9	7.86
1977	7.21	7.39	7.46	7.37	7.46	7.28
1978	7.96	8.03	8.04	8.15	8.35	8.46
1979	9.1	9.1	9.12	9.18	9.25	8.91
1980	10.8	12.41	12.75	11.47	10.18	9.78
1981	12.57	13.19	13.12	13.68	14.1	13.47
1982	14.59	14.43	13.86	13.87	13.62	14.3
1983	10.46	10.72	10.51	10.4	10.38	10.85
1984	11.67	11.84	12.32	12.63	13.41	13.56
1985	11.38	11.51	11.86	11.43	10.85	10.16
1986	9.19	8.7	7.78	7.3	7.71	7.8
1987	7.08	7.25	7.25	8.02	8.61	8.4
1988	8.67	8.21	8.37	8.72	9.09	8.92
1989	9.09	9.17	9.36	9.18	8.86	8.28
1990	8.21	8.47	8.59	8.79	8.76	8.48
1991	8.09	7.85	8.11	8.04	8.07	8.28
1992	7.03	7.34	7.54	7.48	7.39	7.26
1993	6.6	6.26	5.98	5.97	6.04	5.96
1994	5.75	5.97	6.48	6.97	7.18	7.1
1995	7.78	7.47	7.2	7.06	6.63	6.17
1996	5.65	5.81	6.27	6.51	6.74	6.91
1997	6.58	6.42	6.69	6.89	6.71	6.49
1998	5.54	5.57	5.65	5.64	5.65	5.5
1999	4.72	5	5.23	5.18	5.54	5.9
2000	6.66	6.52	6.26	5.99	6.44	6.1
2001	5.16	5.1	4.89	5.14	5.39	5.28
2002	5.04	4.91	5.28	5.21	5.16	4.93
2003	4.05	3.9	3.81	3.96	3.57	3.33
2004	4.15	4.08	3.83	4.35	4.72	4.73
2005	4.22	4.17	4.5	4.34	4.14	4.00
2006	4.42	4.57	4.72	4.99	5.11	5.11
2007	4.76	4.72	4.56	4.69	4.75	5.10
2008	3.74	3.74	3.51	3.68	3.88	4.10
2009	2.52	2.87	2.82	2.93	3.29	3.72
2010	3.73	3.69	3.73	3.85	3.42	3.20
2011	3.39	3.58	3.41	3.46	3.17	3.00
2012	1.97	1.97	2.17	2.05	1.80	1.62
2013	1.91	1.98	1.96	1.76	1.93	2.30
2014	2.86	2.71	2.72	2.71	2.56	2.60
2015	1.88	1.98	2.04	1.94	2.20	2.36
2016	2.09	1.78	1.89	1.81	1.81	1.64
2017	2.43	2.42	2.48	2.30	2.30	2.19
2018	2.58	2.86	2.84	2.87	2.98	2.91
2019	2.71	2.68	2.57	2.53	2.40	2.07
2020	1.76	1.50	0.87	0.66	0.67	0.73

* Source: Federal Reserve Bank of St. Louis, monthly data calculated as average of business days

10 YEAR TREASURY BOND YIELDS

JUL	AUG	SEP	OCT	NOV	DEC	
2.3	2.36	2.38	2.43	2.48	2.51	**1954**
2.9	2.97	2.97	2.88	2.89	2.96	**1955**
3.11	3.33	3.38	3.34	3.49	3.59	**1956**
3.93	3.93	3.92	3.97	3.72	3.21	**1957**
3.2	3.54	3.76	3.8	3.74	3.86	**1958**
4.4	4.43	4.68	4.53	4.53	4.69	**1959**
3.9	3.8	3.8	3.89	3.93	3.84	**1960**
3.92	4.04	3.98	3.92	3.94	4.06	**1961**
4.01	3.98	3.98	3.93	3.92	3.86	**1962**
4.02	4	4.08	4.11	4.12	4.13	**1963**
4.19	4.19	4.2	4.19	4.15	4.18	**1964**
4.2	4.25	4.29	4.35	4.45	4.62	**1965**
5.02	5.22	5.18	5.01	5.16	4.84	**1966**
5.16	5.28	5.3	5.48	5.75	5.7	**1967**
5.5	5.42	5.46	5.58	5.7	6.03	**1968**
6.72	6.69	7.16	7.1	7.14	7.65	**1969**
7.46	7.53	7.39	7.33	6.84	6.39	**1970**
6.73	6.58	6.14	5.93	5.81	5.93	**1971**
6.11	6.21	6.55	6.48	6.28	6.36	**1972**
7.13	7.4	7.09	6.79	6.73	6.74	**1973**
7.81	8.04	8.04	7.9	7.68	7.43	**1974**
8.06	8.4	8.43	8.14	8.05	8	**1975**
7.83	7.77	7.59	7.41	7.29	6.87	**1976**
7.33	7.4	7.34	7.52	7.58	7.69	**1977**
8.64	8.41	8.42	8.64	8.81	9.01	**1978**
8.95	9.03	9.33	10.3	10.65	10.39	**1979**
10.25	11.1	11.51	11.75	12.68	12.84	**1980**
14.28	14.94	15.32	15.15	13.39	13.72	**1981**
13.95	13.06	12.34	10.91	10.55	10.54	**1982**
11.38	11.85	11.65	11.54	11.69	11.83	**1983**
13.36	12.72	12.52	12.16	11.57	11.5	**1984**
10.31	10.33	10.37	10.24	9.78	9.26	**1985**
7.3	7.17	7.45	7.43	7.25	7.11	**1986**
8.45	8.76	9.42	9.52	8.86	8.99	**1987**
9.06	9.26	8.98	8.8	8.96	9.11	**1988**
8.02	8.11	8.19	8.01	7.87	7.84	**1989**
8.47	8.75	8.89	8.72	8.39	8.08	**1990**
8.27	7.9	7.65	7.53	7.42	7.09	**1991**
6.84	6.59	6.42	6.59	6.87	6.77	**1992**
5.81	5.68	5.36	5.33	5.72	5.77	**1993**
7.3	7.24	7.46	7.74	7.96	7.81	**1994**
6.28	6.49	6.2	6.04	5.93	5.71	**1995**
6.87	6.64	6.83	6.53	6.2	6.3	**1996**
6.22	6.3	6.21	6.03	5.88	5.81	**1997**
5.46	5.34	4.81	4.53	4.83	4.65	**1998**
5.79	5.94	5.92	6.11	6.03	6.28	**1999**
6.05	5.83	5.8	5.74	5.72	5.24	**2000**
5.24	4.97	4.73	4.57	4.65	5.09	**2001**
4.65	4.26	3.87	3.94	4.05	4.03	**2002**
3.98	4.45	4.27	4.29	4.3	4.27	**2003**
4.5	4.28	4.13	4.1	4.19	4.23	**2004**
4.18	4.26	4.20	4.46	4.54	4.47	**2005**
5.09	4.88	4.72	4.73	4.60	4.56	**2006**
5.00	4.67	4.52	4.53	4.15	4.10	**2007**
4.01	3.89	3.69	3.81	3.53	2.42	**2008**
3.56	3.59	3.40	3.39	3.40	3.59	**2009**
3.01	2.70	2.65	2.54	2.76	3.29	**2010**
3.00	2.30	1.98	2.15	2.01	1.98	**2011**
1.53	1.68	1.72	1.75	1.65	1.72	**2012**
2.58	2.74	2.81	2.62	2.72	2.90	**2013**
2.54	2.42	2.53	2.30	2.33	2.21	**2014**
2.32	2.17	2.17	2.07	2.26	2.24	**2015**
1.50	1.56	1.63	1.76	2.14	2.49	**2016**
2.32	2.21	2.20	2.36	2.35	2.40	**2017**
2.89	2.89	3.00	3.15	3.12	2.83	**2018**
2.06	1.63	1.70	1.71	1.81	1.86	**2019**
0.62	0.65	0.68	0.79	0.87	0.93	**2020**

	JAN	FEB	MAR	APR	MAY	JUN
1954	2.17	2.04	1.93	1.87	1.92	1.92
1955	2.32	2.38	2.48	2.55	2.56	2.59
1956	2.84	2.74	2.93	3.20	3.08	2.97
1957	3.47	3.39	3.46	3.53	3.64	3.83
1958	2.88	2.78	2.64	2.46	2.41	2.46
1959	4.01	3.96	3.99	4.12	4.35	4.50
1960	4.92	4.69	4.31	4.29	4.49	4.12
1961	3.67	3.66	3.60	3.57	3.47	3.81
1962	3.94	3.89	3.68	3.60	3.66	3.64
1963	3.58	3.66	3.68	3.74	3.72	3.81
1964	4.07	4.03	4.14	4.15	4.05	4.02
1965	4.10	4.15	4.15	4.15	4.15	4.15
1966	4.86	4.98	4.92	4.83	4.89	4.97
1967	4.70	4.74	4.54	4.51	4.75	5.01
1968	5.54	5.59	5.76	5.69	6.04	5.85
1969	6.25	6.34	6.41	6.30	6.54	6.75
1970	8.17	7.82	7.21	7.50	7.97	7.85
1971	5.89	5.56	5.00	5.65	6.28	6.53
1972	5.59	5.69	5.87	6.17	5.85	5.91
1973	6.34	6.60	6.80	6.67	6.80	6.69
1974	6.95	6.82	7.31	7.92	8.18	8.10
1975	7.41	7.11	7.30	7.99	7.72	7.51
1976	7.46	7.45	7.49	7.25	7.59	7.61
1977	6.58	6.83	6.93	6.79	6.94	6.76
1978	7.77	7.83	7.86	7.98	8.18	8.36
1979	9.20	9.13	9.20	9.25	9.24	8.85
1980	10.74	12.60	13.47	11.84	9.95	9.21
1981	12.77	13.41	13.41	13.99	14.63	13.95
1982	14.65	14.54	13.98	14.00	13.75	14.43
1983	10.03	10.26	10.08	10.02	10.03	10.63
1984	11.37	11.54	12.02	12.37	13.17	13.48
1985	10.93	11.13	11.52	11.01	10.34	9.60
1986	8.68	8.34	7.46	7.05	7.52	7.64
1987	6.64	6.79	6.79	7.57	8.26	8.02
1988	8.18	7.71	7.83	8.19	8.58	8.49
1989	9.15	9.27	9.51	9.30	8.91	8.29
1990	8.12	8.42	8.60	8.77	8.74	8.43
1991	7.70	7.47	7.77	7.70	7.70	7.94
1992	6.24	6.58	6.95	6.78	6.69	6.48
1993	5.83	5.43	5.19	5.13	5.20	5.22
1994	5.09	5.40	5.94	6.52	6.78	6.70
1995	7.76	7.37	7.05	6.86	6.41	5.93
1996	5.36	5.38	5.97	6.30	6.48	6.69
1997	6.33	6.20	6.54	6.76	6.57	6.38
1998	5.42	5.49	5.61	5.61	5.63	5.52
1999	4.60	4.91	5.14	5.08	5.44	5.81
2000	6.58	6.68	6.50	6.26	6.69	6.30
2001	4.86	4.89	4.64	4.76	4.93	4.81
2002	4.34	4.30	4.74	4.65	4.49	4.19
2003	3.05	2.90	2.78	2.93	2.52	2.27
2004	3.12	3.07	2.79	3.39	3.85	3.93
2005	3.71	3.77	4.17	4.00	3.85	3.77
2006	4.35	4.57	4.72	4.90	5.00	5.07
2007	4.75	4.71	4.48	4.59	4.67	5.03
2008	2.98	2.78	2.48	2.84	3.15	3.49
2009	1.60	1.87	1.82	1.86	2.13	2.71
2010	2.48	2.36	2.43	2.58	2.18	2.00
2011	1.99	2.26	2.11	2.17	1.84	1.58
2012	0.84	0.83	1.02	0.89	0.76	0.71
2013	0.81	0.85	0.82	0.71	0.84	1.20
2014	1.65	1.52	1.64	1.70	1.59	1.68
2015	1.37	1.47	1.52	1.35	1.54	1.68
2016	1.52	1.22	1.38	1.26	1.30	1.17
2017	1.92	1.90	2.01	1.82	1.84	1.77
2018	2.38	2.60	2.63	2.70	2.82	2.78
2019	2.54	2.49	2.37	2.33	2.19	1.83
2020	1.56	1.32	0.59	0.39	0.34	0.34

* Source: Federal Reserve Bank of St. Louis, monthly data calculated as average of business days

5 YEAR TREASURY BOND YIELDS

JUL	AUG	SEP	OCT	NOV	DEC	
1.85	1.90	1.96	2.02	2.09	2.16	1954
2.72	2.86	2.85	2.76	2.81	2.93	1955
3.12	3.41	3.47	3.40	3.56	3.70	1956
4.00	4.00	4.03	4.08	3.72	3.08	1957
2.77	3.29	3.69	3.78	3.70	3.82	1958
4.58	4.57	4.90	4.72	4.75	5.01	1959
3.79	3.62	3.61	3.76	3.81	3.67	1960
3.84	3.96	3.90	3.80	3.82	3.91	1961
3.80	3.71	3.70	3.64	3.60	3.56	1962
3.89	3.89	3.96	3.97	4.01	4.04	1963
4.03	4.05	4.08	4.07	4.04	4.09	1964
4.15	4.20	4.25	4.34	4.46	4.72	1965
5.17	5.50	5.50	5.27	5.36	5.00	1966
5.23	5.31	5.40	5.57	5.78	5.75	1967
5.60	5.50	5.48	5.55	5.66	6.12	1968
7.01	7.03	7.57	7.51	7.53	7.96	1969
7.59	7.57	7.29	7.12	6.47	5.95	1970
6.85	6.55	6.14	5.93	5.78	5.69	1971
5.97	6.02	6.25	6.18	6.12	6.16	1972
7.33	7.63	7.05	6.77	6.92	6.80	1973
8.38	8.63	8.37	7.97	7.68	7.31	1974
7.92	8.33	8.37	7.97	7.80	7.76	1975
7.49	7.31	7.13	6.75	6.52	6.10	1976
6.84	7.03	7.04	7.32	7.34	7.48	1977
8.54	8.33	8.43	8.61	8.84	9.08	1978
8.90	9.06	9.41	10.63	10.93	10.42	1979
9.53	10.84	11.62	11.86	12.83	13.25	1980
14.79	15.56	15.93	15.41	13.38	13.60	1981
14.07	13.00	12.25	10.80	10.38	10.22	1982
11.21	11.63	11.43	11.28	11.41	11.54	1983
13.27	12.68	12.53	12.06	11.33	11.07	1984
9.70	9.81	9.81	9.69	9.28	8.73	1985
7.06	6.80	6.92	6.83	6.76	6.67	1986
8.01	8.32	8.94	9.08	8.35	8.45	1987
8.66	8.94	8.69	8.51	8.79	9.09	1988
7.83	8.09	8.17	7.97	7.81	7.75	1989
8.33	8.44	8.51	8.33	8.02	7.73	1990
7.91	7.43	7.14	6.87	6.62	6.19	1991
5.84	5.60	5.38	5.60	6.04	6.08	1992
5.09	5.03	4.73	4.71	5.06	5.15	1993
6.91	6.88	7.08	7.40	7.72	7.78	1994
6.01	6.24	6.00	5.86	5.69	5.51	1995
6.64	6.39	6.60	6.27	5.97	6.07	1996
6.12	6.16	6.11	5.93	5.80	5.77	1997
5.46	5.27	4.62	4.18	4.54	4.45	1998
5.68	5.84	5.80	6.03	5.97	6.19	1999
6.18	6.06	5.93	5.78	5.70	5.17	2000
4.76	4.57	4.12	3.91	3.97	4.39	2001
3.81	3.29	2.94	2.95	3.05	3.03	2002
2.87	3.37	3.18	3.19	3.29	3.27	2003
3.69	3.47	3.36	3.35	3.53	3.60	2004
3.98	4.12	4.01	4.33	4.45	4.39	2005
5.04	4.82	4.67	4.69	4.58	4.53	2006
4.88	4.43	4.20	4.20	3.67	3.49	2007
3.30	3.14	2.88	2.73	2.29	1.52	2008
2.46	2.57	2.37	2.33	2.23	2.34	2009
1.76	1.47	1.41	1.18	1.35	1.93	2010
1.54	1.02	0.90	1.06	0.91	0.89	2011
0.62	0.71	0.67	0.71	0.67	0.70	2012
1.40	1.52	1.60	1.37	1.37	1.58	2013
1.70	1.63	1.77	1.55	1.62	1.64	2014
1.63	1.54	1.49	1.39	1.67	1.70	2015
1.07	1.13	1.18	1.27	1.60	1.96	2016
1.87	1.78	1.80	1.98	2.05	2.18	2017
2.78	2.77	2.89	3.00	2.95	2.68	2018
1.83	1.49	1.57	1.53	1.64	1.68	2019
0.28	0.27	0.27	0.34	0.39	0.39	2020

	JAN	FEB	MAR	APR	MAY	JUN
1982	12.92	14.28	13.31	13.34	12.71	13.08
1983	8.12	8.39	8.66	8.51	8.50	9.14
1984	9.26	9.46	9.89	10.07	10.22	10.26
1985	8.02	8.56	8.83	8.22	7.73	7.18
1986	7.30	7.29	6.76	6.24	6.33	6.40
1987	5.58	5.75	5.77	5.82	5.85	5.85
1988	6.00	5.84	5.87	6.08	6.45	6.66
1999	8.56	8.84	9.14	8.96	8.74	8.43
1990	7.90	8.00	8.17	8.04	8.01	7.99
1991	6.41	6.12	6.09	5.83	5.63	5.75
1992	3.91	3.95	4.14	3.84	3.72	3.75
1993	3.07	2.99	3.01	2.93	3.03	3.14
1994	3.04	3.33	3.59	3.78	4.27	4.25
1995	5.90	5.94	5.91	5.84	5.85	5.64
1996	5.15	4.96	5.10	5.09	5.15	5.23
1997	5.17	5.14	5.28	5.30	5.20	5.07
1998	5.18	5.23	5.16	5.08	5.14	5.12
1999	4.45	4.56	4.57	4.41	4.63	4.72
2000	5.50	5.73	5.86	5.82	5.99	5.86
2001	5.29	5.01	4.54	3.97	3.70	3.57
2002	1.68	1.76	1.83	1.75	1.76	1.73
2003	1.19	1.19	1.15	1.15	1.09	0.94
2004	0.90	0.94	0.95	0.96	1.04	1.29
2005	2.37	2.58	2.80	2.84	2.90	3.04
2006	4.34	4.54	4.63	4.72	4.84	4.92
2007	5.11	5.16	5.08	5.01	4.87	4.74
2008	2.82	2.17	1.28	1.31	1.76	1.89
2009	0.13	0.30	0.22	0.16	0.18	0.18
2010	0.06	0.11	0.15	0.16	0.16	0.12
2011	0.15	0.13	0.10	0.06	0.04	0.04
2012	0.03	0.09	0.08	0.08	0.09	0.09
2013	0.07	0.10	0.09	0.06	0.04	0.05
2014	0.04	0.05	0.05	0.03	0.03	0.04
2015	0.03	0.02	0.03	0.02	0.02	0.02
2016	0.26	0.31	0.30	0.23	0.28	0.27
2017	0.52	0.53	0.75	0.81	0.90	1.00
2018	1.43	1.59	1.73	1.79	1.90	1.94
2019	2.42	2.44	2.45	2.43	2.40	2.22
2020	1.55	1.54	0.30	0.14	0.13	0.16

* Source: Federal Reserve Bank of St. Louis, monthly data calculated as average of business days

3 MONTH TREASURY BOND YIELDS

JUL	AUG	SEP	OCT	NOV	DEC	
11.86	9.00	8.19	7.97	8.35	8.20	**1982**
9.45	9.74	9.36	8.99	9.11	9.36	**1983**
10.53	10.90	10.80	10.12	8.92	8.34	**1984**
7.32	7.37	7.33	7.40	7.48	7.33	**1985**
6.00	5.69	5.35	5.32	5.50	5.68	**1986**
5.88	6.23	6.62	6.35	5.89	5.96	**1987**
6.95	7.30	7.48	7.60	8.03	8.35	**1988**
8.15	8.17	8.01	7.90	7.94	7.88	**1999**
7.87	7.69	7.60	7.40	7.29	6.95	**1990**
5.75	5.50	5.37	5.14	4.69	4.18	**1991**
3.28	3.20	2.97	2.93	3.21	3.29	**1992**
3.11	3.09	3.01	3.09	3.18	3.13	**1993**
4.46	4.61	4.75	5.10	5.45	5.76	**1994**
5.59	5.57	5.43	5.44	5.52	5.29	**1995**
5.30	5.19	5.24	5.12	5.17	5.04	**1996**
5.19	5.28	5.08	5.11	5.28	5.30	**1997**
5.09	5.04	4.74	4.07	4.53	4.50	**1998**
4.69	4.87	4.82	5.02	5.23	5.36	**1999**
6.14	6.28	6.18	6.29	6.36	5.94	**2000**
3.59	3.44	2.69	2.20	1.91	1.72	**2001**
1.71	1.65	1.66	1.61	1.25	1.21	**2002**
0.92	0.97	0.96	0.94	0.95	0.91	**2003**
1.36	1.50	1.68	1.79	2.11	2.22	**2004**
3.29	3.52	3.49	3.79	3.97	3.97	**2005**
5.08	5.09	4.93	5.05	5.07	4.97	**2006**
4.96	4.32	3.99	4.00	3.35	3.07	**2007**
1.66	1.75	1.15	0.69	0.19	0.03	**2008**
0.18	0.17	0.12	0.07	0.05	0.05	**2009**
0.16	0.16	0.15	0.13	0.14	0.14	**2010**
0.04	0.02	0.01	0.02	0.01	0.01	**2011**
0.10	0.10	0.11	0.10	0.09	0.07	**2012**
0.04	0.04	0.02	0.05	0.07	0.07	**2013**
0.03	0.03	0.02	0.02	0.02	0.03	**2014**
0.03	0.07	0.02	0.02	0.13	0.23	**2015**
0.30	0.30	0.29	0.33	0.45	0.51	**2016**
1.09	1.03	1.05	1.09	1.25	1.34	**2017**
1.99	2.07	2.17	2.29	2.37	2.41	**2018**
2.15	1.99	1.93	1.68	1.57	1.57	**2019**
0.13	0.10	0.11	0.10	0.09	0.09	**2020**

BOND YIELDS 🇺🇸 MOODY'S SEASONED CORPORATE Aaa*

	JAN	FEB	MAR	APR	MAY	JUN
1950	2.57	2.58	2.58	2.60	2.61	2.62
1951	2.66	2.66	2.78	2.87	2.89	2.94
1952	2.98	2.93	2.96	2.93	2.93	2.94
1953	3.02	3.07	3.12	3.23	3.34	3.40
1954	3.06	2.95	2.86	2.85	2.88	2.90
1955	2.93	2.93	3.02	3.01	3.04	3.05
1956	3.11	3.08	3.10	3.24	3.28	3.26
1957	3.77	3.67	3.66	3.67	3.74	3.91
1958	3.60	3.59	3.63	3.60	3.57	3.57
1959	4.12	4.14	4.13	4.23	4.37	4.46
1960	4.61	4.56	4.49	4.45	4.46	4.45
1961	4.32	4.27	4.22	4.25	4.27	4.33
1962	4.42	4.42	4.39	4.33	4.28	4.28
1963	4.21	4.19	4.19	4.21	4.22	4.23
1964	4.39	4.36	4.38	4.40	4.41	4.41
1965	4.43	4.41	4.42	4.43	4.44	4.46
1966	4.74	4.78	4.92	4.96	4.98	5.07
1967	5.20	5.03	5.13	5.11	5.24	5.44
1968	6.17	6.10	6.11	6.21	6.27	6.28
1969	6.59	6.66	6.85	6.89	6.79	6.98
1970	7.91	7.93	7.84	7.83	8.11	8.48
1971	7.36	7.08	7.21	7.25	7.53	7.64
1972	7.19	7.27	7.24	7.30	7.30	7.23
1973	7.15	7.22	7.29	7.26	7.29	7.37
1974	7.83	7.85	8.01	8.25	8.37	8.47
1975	8.83	8.62	8.67	8.95	8.90	8.77
1976	8.60	8.55	8.52	8.40	8.58	8.62
1977	7.96	8.04	8.10	8.04	8.05	7.95
1978	8.41	8.47	8.47	8.56	8.69	8.76
1979	9.25	9.26	9.37	9.38	9.50	9.29
1980	11.09	12.38	12.96	12.04	10.99	10.58
1981	12.81	13.35	13.33	13.88	14.32	13.75
1982	15.18	15.27	14.58	14.46	14.26	14.81
1983	11.79	12.01	11.73	11.51	11.46	11.74
1984	12.20	12.08	12.57	12.81	13.28	13.55
1985	12.08	12.13	12.56	12.23	11.72	10.94
1986	10.05	9.67	9.00	8.79	9.09	9.13
1987	8.36	8.38	8.36	8.85	9.33	9.32
1988	9.88	9.40	9.39	9.67	9.90	9.86
1989	9.62	9.64	9.80	9.79	9.57	9.10
1990	8.99	9.22	9.37	9.46	9.47	9.26
1991	9.04	8.83	8.93	8.86	8.86	9.01
1992	8.20	8.29	8.35	8.33	8.28	8.22
1993	7.91	7.71	7.58	7.46	7.43	7.33
1994	6.92	7.08	7.48	7.88	7.99	7.97
1995	8.46	8.26	8.12	8.03	7.65	7.30
1996	6.81	6.99	7.35	7.50	7.62	7.71
1997	7.42	7.31	7.55	7.73	7.58	7.41
1998	6.61	6.67	6.72	6.69	6.69	6.53
1999	6.24	6.40	6.62	6.64	6.93	7.23
2000	7.78	7.68	7.68	7.64	7.99	7.67
2001	7.15	7.10	6.98	7.20	7.29	7.18
2002	6.55	6.51	6.81	6.76	6.75	6.63
2003	6.17	5.95	5.89	5.74	5.22	4.97
2004	5.54	5.50	5.33	5.73	6.04	6.01
2005	5.36	5.20	5.40	5.33	5.15	4.96
2006	5.29	5.35	5.53	5.84	5.95	5.89
2007	5.40	5.39	5.30	5.47	5.47	5.79
2008	5.33	5.53	5.51	5.55	5.57	5.68
2009	5.05	5.27	5.50	5.39	5.54	5.61
2010	5.26	5.35	5.27	5.29	4.96	4.88
2011	5.04	5.22	5.13	5.16	4.96	4.99
2012	3.85	3.85	3.99	3.96	3.80	3.64
2013	3.80	3.90	3.93	3.73	3.89	4.27
2014	4.49	4.45	4.38	4.24	4.16	4.25
2015	3.46	3.61	3.64	3.52	3.98	4.19
2016	4.00	3.96	3.82	3.62	3.65	3.50
2017	3.92	3.95	4.01	3.87	3.85	3.68
2018	3.55	3.82	3.87	3.85	4.00	3.96
2019	3.93	3.79	3.77	3.69	3.67	3.42
2020	2.94	2.78	3.02	2.43	2.50	2.44

* Source: Federal Reserve Bank of St. Louis, monthly data calculated as average of business days

MOODY'S SEASONED CORPORATE Aaa ▦ BOND YIELDS

JUL	AUG	SEP	OCT	NOV	DEC	
2.65	2.61	2.64	2.67	2.67	2.67	**1950**
2.94	2.88	2.84	2.89	2.96	3.01	**1951**
2.95	2.94	2.95	3.01	2.98	2.97	**1952**
3.28	3.24	3.29	3.16	3.11	3.13	**1953**
2.89	2.87	2.89	2.87	2.89	2.90	**1954**
3.06	3.11	3.13	3.10	3.10	3.15	**1955**
3.28	3.43	3.56	3.59	3.69	3.75	**1956**
3.99	4.10	4.12	4.10	4.08	3.81	**1957**
3.67	3.85	4.09	4.11	4.09	4.08	**1958**
4.47	4.43	4.52	4.57	4.56	4.58	**1959**
4.41	4.28	4.25	4.30	4.31	4.35	**1960**
4.41	4.45	4.45	4.42	4.39	4.42	**1961**
4.34	4.35	4.32	4.28	4.25	4.24	**1962**
4.26	4.29	4.31	4.32	4.33	4.35	**1963**
4.40	4.41	4.42	4.42	4.43	4.44	**1964**
4.48	4.49	4.52	4.56	4.60	4.68	**1965**
5.16	5.31	5.49	5.41	5.35	5.39	**1966**
5.58	5.62	5.65	5.82	6.07	6.19	**1967**
6.24	6.02	5.97	6.09	6.19	6.45	**1968**
7.08	6.97	7.14	7.33	7.35	7.72	**1969**
8.44	8.13	8.09	8.03	8.05	7.64	**1970**
7.64	7.59	7.44	7.39	7.26	7.25	**1971**
7.21	7.19	7.22	7.21	7.12	7.08	**1972**
7.45	7.68	7.63	7.60	7.67	7.68	**1973**
8.72	9.00	9.24	9.27	8.89	8.89	**1974**
8.84	8.95	8.95	8.86	8.78	8.79	**1975**
8.56	8.45	8.38	8.32	8.25	7.98	**1976**
7.94	7.98	7.92	8.04	8.08	8.19	**1977**
8.88	8.69	8.69	8.89	9.03	9.16	**1978**
9.20	9.23	9.44	10.13	10.76	10.74	**1979**
11.07	11.64	12.02	12.31	12.97	13.21	**1980**
14.38	14.89	15.49	15.40	14.22	14.23	**1981**
14.61	13.71	12.94	12.12	11.68	11.83	**1982**
12.15	12.51	12.37	12.25	12.41	12.57	**1983**
13.44	12.87	12.66	12.63	12.29	12.13	**1984**
10.97	11.05	11.07	11.02	10.55	10.16	**1985**
8.88	8.72	8.89	8.86	8.68	8.49	**1986**
9.42	9.67	10.18	10.52	10.01	10.11	**1987**
9.96	10.11	9.82	9.51	9.45	9.57	**1988**
8.93	8.96	9.01	8.92	8.89	8.86	**1989**
9.24	9.41	9.56	9.53	9.30	9.05	**1990**
9.00	8.75	8.61	8.55	8.48	8.31	**1991**
8.07	7.95	7.92	7.99	8.10	7.98	**1992**
7.17	6.85	6.66	6.67	6.93	6.93	**1993**
8.11	8.07	8.34	8.57	8.68	8.46	**1994**
7.41	7.57	7.32	7.12	7.02	6.82	**1995**
7.65	7.46	7.66	7.39	7.10	7.20	**1996**
7.14	7.22	7.15	7.00	6.87	6.76	**1997**
6.55	6.52	6.40	6.37	6.41	6.22	**1998**
7.19	7.40	7.39	7.55	7.36	7.55	**1999**
7.65	7.55	7.62	7.55	7.45	7.21	**2000**
7.13	7.02	7.17	7.03	6.97	6.77	**2001**
6.53	6.37	6.15	6.32	6.31	6.21	**2002**
5.49	5.88	5.72	5.70	5.65	5.62	**2003**
5.82	5.65	5.46	5.47	5.52	5.47	**2004**
5.06	5.09	5.13	5.35	5.42	5.37	**2005**
5.85	5.68	5.51	5.51	5.33	5.32	**2006**
5.73	5.79	5.74	5.66	5.44	5.49	**2007**
5.67	5.64	5.65	6.28	6.12	5.05	**2008**
5.41	5.26	5.13	5.15	5.19	5.26	**2009**
4.72	4.49	4.53	4.68	4.87	5.02	**2010**
4.93	4.37	4.09	3.98	3.87	3.93	**2011**
3.40	3.48	3.49	3.47	3.50	3.65	**2012**
4.34	4.54	4.64	4.53	4.63	4.62	**2013**
4.16	4.08	4.11	3.92	3.92	3.79	**2014**
4.15	4.04	4.07	3.95	4.06	3.97	**2015**
3.28	3.32	3.41	3.51	3.86	4.06	**2016**
3.70	3.63	3.63	3.60	3.57	3.51	**2017**
3.87	3.88	3.98	4.14	4.22	4.02	**2018**
3.29	2.98	3.03	3.01	3.06	3.01	**2019**
2.14	2.25	2.31	2.35	2.30	2.26	**2020**

MOODY'S SEASONED
CORPORATE Baa*

	JAN	FEB	MAR	APR	MAY	JUN
1950	3.24	3.24	3.24	3.23	3.25	3.28
1951	3.17	3.16	3.23	3.35	3.40	3.49
1952	3.59	3.53	3.51	3.50	3.49	3.50
1953	3.51	3.53	3.57	3.65	3.78	3.86
1954	3.71	3.61	3.51	3.47	3.47	3.49
1955	3.45	3.47	3.48	3.49	3.50	3.51
1956	3.60	3.58	3.60	3.68	3.73	3.76
1957	4.49	4.47	4.43	4.44	4.52	4.63
1958	4.83	4.66	4.68	4.67	4.62	4.55
1959	4.87	4.89	4.85	4.86	4.96	5.04
1960	5.34	5.34	5.25	5.20	5.28	5.26
1961	5.10	5.07	5.02	5.01	5.01	5.03
1962	5.08	5.07	5.04	5.02	5.00	5.02
1963	4.91	4.89	4.88	4.87	4.85	4.84
1964	4.83	4.83	4.83	4.85	4.85	4.85
1965	4.80	4.78	4.78	4.80	4.81	4.85
1966	5.06	5.12	5.32	5.41	5.48	5.58
1967	5.97	5.82	5.85	5.83	5.96	6.15
1968	6.84	6.80	6.85	6.97	7.03	7.07
1969	7.32	7.30	7.51	7.54	7.52	7.70
1970	8.86	8.78	8.63	8.70	8.98	9.25
1971	8.74	8.39	8.46	8.45	8.62	8.75
1972	8.23	8.23	8.24	8.24	8.23	8.20
1973	7.90	7.97	8.03	8.09	8.06	8.13
1974	8.48	8.53	8.62	8.87	9.05	9.27
1975	10.81	10.65	10.48	10.58	10.69	10.62
1976	10.41	10.24	10.12	9.94	9.86	9.89
1977	9.08	9.12	9.12	9.07	9.01	8.91
1978	9.17	9.20	9.22	9.32	9.49	9.60
1979	10.13	10.08	10.26	10.33	10.47	10.38
1980	12.42	13.57	14.45	14.19	13.17	12.71
1981	15.03	15.37	15.34	15.56	15.95	15.80
1982	17.10	17.18	16.82	16.78	16.64	16.92
1983	13.94	13.95	13.61	13.29	13.09	13.37
1984	13.65	13.59	13.99	14.31	14.74	15.05
1985	13.26	13.23	13.69	13.51	13.15	12.40
1986	11.44	11.11	10.50	10.19	10.29	10.34
1987	9.72	9.65	9.61	10.04	10.51	10.52
1988	11.07	10.62	10.57	10.90	11.04	11.00
1989	10.65	10.61	10.67	10.61	10.46	10.03
1990	9.94	10.14	10.21	10.30	10.41	10.22
1991	10.45	10.07	10.09	9.94	9.86	9.96
1992	9.13	9.23	9.25	9.21	9.13	9.05
1993	8.67	8.39	8.15	8.14	8.21	8.07
1994	7.65	7.76	8.13	8.52	8.62	8.65
1995	9.08	8.85	8.70	8.60	8.20	7.90
1996	7.47	7.63	8.03	8.19	8.30	8.40
1997	8.09	7.94	8.18	8.34	8.20	8.02
1998	7.19	7.25	7.32	7.33	7.30	7.13
1999	7.29	7.39	7.53	7.48	7.72	8.02
2000	8.33	8.29	8.37	8.40	8.90	8.48
2001	7.93	7.87	7.84	8.07	8.07	7.97
2002	7.87	7.89	8.11	8.03	8.09	7.95
2003	7.35	7.06	6.95	6.85	6.38	6.19
2004	6.44	6.27	6.11	6.46	6.75	6.78
2005	6.02	5.82	6.06	6.05	6.01	5.86
2006	6.24	6.27	6.41	6.68	6.75	6.78
2007	6.34	6.28	6.27	6.39	6.39	6.70
2008	6.54	6.82	6.89	6.97	6.93	7.07
2009	8.14	8.08	8.42	8.39	8.06	7.50
2010	6.25	6.34	6.27	6.25	6.05	6.23
2011	6.09	6.15	6.03	6.02	5.78	5.75
2012	5.23	5.14	5.23	5.19	5.07	5.02
2013	4.73	4.85	4.85	4.59	4.73	5.19
2014	5.19	5.10	5.06	4.90	4.76	4.80
2015	4.45	4.51	4.54	4.48	4.89	5.13
2016	5.45	5.34	5.13	4.79	4.68	4.53
2017	4.66	4.64	4.68	4.57	4.55	4.37
2018	4.26	4.51	4.64	4.67	4.83	4.83
2019	5.12	4.95	4.84	4.70	4.63	4.46
2020	3.77	3.61	4.29	4.13	3.95	3.64

* Source: Federal Reserve Bank of St. Louis, monthly data calculated as average of business days

MOODY'S SEASONED CORPORATE Baa* ▦▦ BOND YIELDS

JUL	AUG	SEP	OCT	NOV	DEC	
3.32	3.23	3.21	3.22	3.22	3.20	**1950**
3.53	3.50	3.46	3.50	3.56	3.61	**1951**
3.50	3.51	3.52	3.54	3.53	3.51	**1952**
3.86	3.85	3.88	3.82	3.75	3.74	**1953**
3.50	3.49	3.47	3.46	3.45	3.45	**1954**
3.52	3.56	3.59	3.59	3.58	3.62	**1955**
3.80	3.93	4.07	4.17	4.24	4.37	**1956**
4.73	4.82	4.93	4.99	5.09	5.03	**1957**
4.53	4.67	4.87	4.92	4.87	4.85	**1958**
5.08	5.09	5.18	5.28	5.26	5.28	**1959**
5.22	5.08	5.01	5.11	5.08	5.10	**1960**
5.09	5.11	5.12	5.13	5.11	5.10	**1961**
5.05	5.06	5.03	4.99	4.96	4.92	**1962**
4.84	4.83	4.84	4.83	4.84	4.85	**1963**
4.83	4.82	4.82	4.81	4.81	4.81	**1964**
4.88	4.88	4.91	4.93	4.95	5.02	**1965**
5.68	5.83	6.09	6.10	6.13	6.18	**1966**
6.26	6.33	6.40	6.52	6.72	6.93	**1967**
6.98	6.82	6.79	6.84	7.01	7.23	**1968**
7.84	7.86	8.05	8.22	8.25	8.65	**1969**
9.40	9.44	9.39	9.33	9.38	9.12	**1970**
8.76	8.76	8.59	8.48	8.38	8.38	**1971**
8.23	8.19	8.09	8.06	7.99	7.93	**1972**
8.24	8.53	8.63	8.41	8.42	8.48	**1973**
9.48	9.77	10.18	10.48	10.60	10.63	**1974**
10.55	10.59	10.61	10.62	10.56	10.56	**1975**
9.82	9.64	9.40	9.29	9.23	9.12	**1976**
8.87	8.82	8.80	8.89	8.95	8.99	**1977**
9.60	9.48	9.42	9.59	9.83	9.94	**1978**
10.29	10.35	10.54	11.40	11.99	12.06	**1979**
12.65	13.15	13.70	14.23	14.64	15.14	**1980**
16.17	16.34	16.92	17.11	16.39	16.55	**1981**
16.80	16.32	15.63	14.73	14.30	14.14	**1982**
13.39	13.64	13.55	13.46	13.61	13.75	**1983**
15.15	14.63	14.35	13.94	13.48	13.40	**1984**
12.43	12.50	12.48	12.36	11.99	11.58	**1985**
10.16	10.18	10.20	10.24	10.07	9.97	**1986**
10.61	10.80	11.31	11.62	11.23	11.29	**1987**
11.11	11.21	10.90	10.41	10.48	10.65	**1988**
9.87	9.88	9.91	9.81	9.81	9.82	**1989**
10.20	10.41	10.64	10.74	10.62	10.43	**1990**
9.89	9.65	9.51	9.49	9.45	9.26	**1991**
8.84	8.65	8.62	8.84	8.96	8.81	**1992**
7.93	7.60	7.34	7.31	7.66	7.69	**1993**
8.80	8.74	8.98	9.20	9.32	9.10	**1994**
8.04	8.19	7.93	7.75	7.68	7.49	**1995**
8.35	8.18	8.35	8.07	7.79	7.89	**1996**
7.75	7.82	7.70	7.57	7.42	7.32	**1997**
7.15	7.14	7.09	7.18	7.34	7.23	**1998**
7.95	8.15	8.20	8.38	8.15	8.19	**1999**
8.35	8.26	8.35	8.34	8.28	8.02	**2000**
7.97	7.85	8.03	7.91	7.81	8.05	**2001**
7.90	7.58	7.40	7.73	7.62	7.45	**2002**
6.62	7.01	6.79	6.73	6.66	6.60	**2003**
6.62	6.46	6.27	6.21	6.20	6.15	**2004**
5.95	5.96	6.03	6.30	6.39	6.32	**2005**
6.76	6.59	6.43	6.42	6.20	6.22	**2006**
6.65	6.65	6.59	6.48	6.40	6.65	**2007**
7.16	7.15	7.31	8.88	9.21	8.43	**2008**
7.09	6.58	6.31	6.29	6.32	6.37	**2009**
6.01	5.66	5.66	5.72	5.92	6.10	**2010**
5.76	5.36	5.27	5.37	5.14	5.25	**2011**
4.87	4.91	4.84	4.58	4.51	4.63	**2012**
5.32	5.42	5.47	5.31	5.38	5.38	**2013**
4.73	4.69	4.80	4.69	4.79	4.74	**2014**
5.20	5.19	5.34	5.34	5.46	5.46	**2015**
4.22	4.24	4.31	4.38	4.71	4.83	**2016**
4.39	4.31	4.30	4.32	4.27	4.22	**2017**
4.79	4.77	4.88	5.07	5.22	5.13	**2018**
4.28	3.87	3.91	3.92	3.94	3.88	**2019**
3.31	3.27	3.36	3.44	3.30	3.16	**2020**

COMMODITIES

OIL - WEST TEXAS INTERMEDIATE
CLOSING VALUES $ / bbl

	JAN	FEB	MAR	APR	MAY	JUN
1950	2.6	2.6	2.6	2.6	2.6	2.6
1951	2.6	2.6	2.6	2.6	2.6	2.6
1952	2.6	2.6	2.6	2.6	2.6	2.6
1953	2.6	2.6	2.6	2.6	2.6	2.8
1954	2.8	2.8	2.8	2.8	2.8	2.8
1955	2.8	2.8	2.8	2.8	2.8	2.8
1956	2.8	2.8	2.8	2.8	2.8	2.8
1957	2.8	3.1	3.1	3.1	3.1	3.1
1958	3.1	3.1	3.1	3.1	3.1	3.1
1959	3.0	3.0	3.0	3.0	3.0	3.0
1960	3.0	3.0	3.0	3.0	3.0	3.0
1961	3.0	3.0	3.0	3.0	3.0	3.0
1962	3.0	3.0	3.0	3.0	3.0	3.0
1963	3.0	3.0	3.0	3.0	3.0	3.0
1964	3.0	3.0	3.0	3.0	3.0	3.0
1965	2.9	2.9	2.9	2.9	2.9	2.9
1966	2.9	2.9	2.9	2.9	2.9	2.9
1967	3.0	3.0	3.0	3.0	3.0	3.0
1968	3.1	3.1	3.1	3.1	3.1	3.1
1969	3.1	3.1	3.3	3.4	3.4	3.4
1970	3.4	3.4	3.4	3.4	3.4	3.4
1971	3.6	3.6	3.6	3.6	3.6	3.6
1972	3.6	3.6	3.6	3.6	3.6	3.6
1973	3.6	3.6	3.6	3.6	3.6	3.6
1974	10.1	10.1	10.1	10.1	10.1	10.1
1975	11.2	11.2	11.2	11.2	11.2	11.2
1976	11.2	12.0	12.1	12.2	12.2	12.2
1977	13.9	13.9	13.9	13.9	13.9	13.9
1978	14.9	14.9	14.9	14.9	14.9	14.9
1979	14.9	15.9	15.9	15.9	18.1	19.1
1980	32.5	37.0	38.0	39.5	39.5	39.5
1981	38.0	38.0	38.0	38.0	38.0	36.0
1982	33.9	31.6	28.5	33.5	35.9	35.1
1983	31.2	29.0	28.8	30.6	30.0	31.0
1984	29.7	30.1	30.8	30.6	30.5	30.0
1985	25.6	27.3	28.2	28.8	27.6	27.1
1986	22.9	15.4	12.6	12.8	15.4	13.5
1987	18.7	17.7	18.3	18.6	19.4	20.0
1988	17.2	16.8	16.2	17.9	17.4	16.5
1989	18.0	17.8	19.4	21.0	20.0	20.0
1990	22.6	22.1	20.4	18.6	18.2	16.9
1991	25.0	20.5	19.9	20.8	21.2	20.2
1992	18.8	19.0	18.9	20.2	20.9	22.4
1993	19.1	20.1	20.3	20.3	19.9	19.1
1994	15.0	14.8	14.7	16.4	17.9	19.1
1995	18.0	18.5	18.6	19.9	19.7	18.4
1996	18.9	19.1	21.4	23.6	21.3	20.5
1997	25.2	22.2	21.0	19.7	20.8	19.2
1998	16.7	16.1	15.0	15.4	14.9	13.7
1999	12.5	12.0	14.7	17.3	17.8	17.9
2000	27.2	29.4	29.9	25.7	28.8	31.8
2001	29.6	29.6	27.2	27.4	28.6	27.6
2002	19.7	20.7	24.4	26.3	27.0	25.5
2003	32.9	35.9	33.6	28.3	28.1	30.7
2004	34.3	34.7	36.8	36.7	40.3	38.0
2005	46.8	48.0	54.3	53.0	49.8	56.3
2006	65.5	61.6	62.9	69.7	70.9	71.0
2007	54.6	59.3	60.6	64.0	63.5	67.5
2008	93.0	95.4	105.6	112.6	125.4	133.9
2009	41.7	39.2	48.0	49.8	59.2	69.7
2010	78.2	76.4	81.2	84.5	73.8	75.4
2011	89.4	89.6	102.9	110.0	101.3	96.3
2012	100.3	102.3	106.2	103.3	94.7	82.3
2013	94.8	95.3	92.9	92.0	94.5	95.8
2014	94.6	100.8	100.8	102.1	102.2	105.8
2015	47.2	50.6	47.8	54.5	59.3	59.8
2016	31.7	30.3	37.6	40.8	46.7	48.8
2017	52.5	53.5	49.3	51.1	48.5	45.2
2018	63.7	62.2	62.7	66.3	70.0	67.9
2019	51.4	55.0	58.2	63.9	60.8	54.7
2020	57.5	50.5	29.2	16.6	28.6	38.3

* Source: Federal Reserve

OIL - WEST TEXAS INTERMEDIATE
CLOSING VALUES $ / bbl

JUL	AUG	SEP	OCT	NOV	DEC	
2.6	2.6	2.6	2.6	2.6	2.6	1950
2.6	2.6	2.6	2.6	2.6	2.6	1951
2.6	2.6	2.6	2.6	2.6	2.6	1952
2.8	2.8	2.8	2.8	2.8	2.8	1953
2.8	2.8	2.8	2.8	2.8	2.8	1954
2.8	2.8	2.8	2.8	2.8	2.8	1955
2.8	2.8	2.8	2.8	2.8	2.8	1956
3.1	3.1	3.1	3.1	3.1	3.0	1957
3.1	3.1	3.1	3.1	3.0	3.0	1958
3.0	3.0	3.0	3.0	3.0	3.0	1959
3.0	3.0	3.0	3.0	3.0	3.0	1960
3.0	3.0	3.0	3.0	3.0	3.0	1961
3.0	3.0	3.0	3.0	3.0	3.0	1962
3.0	3.0	3.0	3.0	3.0	3.0	1963
2.9	2.9	2.9	2.9	2.9	2.9	1964
2.9	2.9	2.9	2.9	2.9	2.9	1965
2.9	2.9	3.0	3.0	3.0	3.0	1966
3.0	3.1	3.1	3.1	3.1	3.1	1967
3.1	3.1	3.1	3.1	3.1	3.1	1968
3.4	3.4	3.4	3.4	3.4	3.4	1969
3.3	3.3	3.3	3.3	3.3	3.6	1970
3.6	3.6	3.6	3.6	3.6	3.6	1971
3.6	3.6	3.6	3.6	3.6	3.6	1972
3.6	4.3	4.3	4.3	4.3	4.3	1973
10.1	10.1	10.1	11.2	11.2	11.2	1974
11.2	11.2	11.2	11.2	11.2	11.2	1975
12.2	12.2	13.9	13.9	13.9	13.9	1976
13.9	14.9	14.9	14.9	14.9	14.9	1977
14.9	14.9	14.9	14.9	14.9	14.9	1978
21.8	26.5	28.5	29.0	31.0	32.5	1979
39.5	38.0	36.0	36.0	36.0	37.0	1980
36.0	36.0	36.0	35.0	36.0	35.0	1981
34.2	34.0	35.6	35.7	34.2	31.7	1982
31.7	31.9	31.1	30.4	29.8	29.2	1983
28.8	29.3	29.3	28.8	28.1	25.4	1984
27.3	27.8	28.3	29.5	30.8	27.2	1985
11.6	15.1	14.9	14.9	15.2	16.1	1986
21.4	20.3	19.5	19.8	18.9	17.2	1987
15.5	15.5	14.5	13.8	14.0	16.3	1988
19.6	18.5	19.6	20.1	19.8	21.1	1989
18.6	27.2	33.7	35.9	32.3	27.3	1990
21.4	21.7	21.9	23.2	22.5	19.5	1991
21.8	21.4	21.9	21.7	20.3	19.4	1992
17.9	18.0	17.5	18.1	16.7	14.5	1993
19.7	18.4	17.5	17.7	18.1	17.2	1994
17.3	18.0	18.2	17.4	18.0	19.0	1995
21.3	22.0	24.0	24.9	23.7	25.4	1996
19.6	19.9	19.8	21.3	20.2	18.3	1997
14.1	13.4	15.0	14.4	12.9	11.3	1998
20.1	21.3	23.9	22.6	25.0	26.1	1999
29.8	31.2	33.9	33.1	34.4	28.5	2000
26.5	27.5	25.9	22.2	19.7	19.3	2001
26.9	28.4	29.7	28.9	26.3	29.4	2002
30.8	31.6	28.3	30.3	31.1	32.2	2003
40.7	44.9	46.0	53.1	48.5	43.3	2004
58.7	65.0	65.6	62.4	58.3	59.4	2005
74.4	73.1	63.9	58.9	59.4	62.0	2006
74.2	72.4	79.9	86.2	94.6	91.7	2007
133.4	116.6	103.9	76.7	57.4	41.0	2008
64.1	71.1	69.5	75.6	78.1	74.3	2009
76.4	76.8	75.3	81.9	84.1	89.0	2010
97.2	86.3	85.6	86.4	97.2	98.6	2011
87.9	94.2	94.7	89.6	86.7	88.3	2012
104.7	106.6	106.3	100.5	93.9	97.6	2013
103.6	96.5	93.2	84.4	75.8	59.3	2014
50.9	42.9	45.5	46.2	42.4	37.2	2015
44.7	44.7	45.2	49.8	45.7	52.0	2016
46.6	48.0	49.8	51.6	56.6	57.9	2017
71.0	68.1	70.2	70.8	57.1	49.5	2018
57.4	54.8	57.0	54.0	57.0	59.9	2019
40.7	42.3	39.6	39.4	40.9	47.0	2020

	JAN	FEB	MAR	APR	MAY	JUN
1970	34.9	35.0	35.1	35.6	36.0	35.4
1971	37.9	38.7	38.9	39.0	40.5	40.1
1972	45.8	48.3	48.3	49.0	54.6	62.1
1973	65.1	74.2	84.4	90.5	102.0	120.1
1974	129.2	150.2	168.4	172.2	163.3	154.1
1975	175.8	181.8	178.2	167.0	167.0	166.3
1976	128.2	132.3	129.6	128.4	125.5	123.8
1977	132.3	142.8	148.9	147.3	143.0	143.0
1978	175.8	182.3	181.6	170.9	184.2	183.1
1979	233.7	251.3	240.1	245.3	274.6	277.5
1980	653.0	637.0	494.5	518.0	535.5	653.5
1981	506.5	489.0	513.8	482.8	479.3	426.0
1982	387.0	362.6	320.0	361.3	325.3	317.5
1983	499.5	408.5	414.8	429.3	437.5	416.0
1984	373.8	394.3	388.5	375.8	384.3	373.1
1985	306.7	287.8	329.3	321.4	314.0	317.8
1986	350.5	338.2	344.0	345.8	343.2	345.5
1987	400.5	405.9	405.9	453.3	451.0	447.3
1988	458.0	426.2	457.0	449.0	455.5	436.6
1989	394.0	387.0	383.2	377.6	361.8	373.0
1990	415.1	407.7	368.5	367.8	363.1	352.2
1991	366.0	362.7	355.7	357.8	360.4	368.4
1992	354.1	353.1	341.7	336.4	337.5	343.4
1993	330.5	327.6	337.8	354.3	374.8	378.5
1994	377.9	381.6	389.2	376.5	387.6	388.3
1995	374.9	376.4	392.0	389.8	384.3	387.1
1996	405.6	400.7	396.4	391.3	390.6	382.0
1997	345.5	358.6	348.2	340.2	345.6	334.6
1998	304.9	297.4	301.0	310.7	293.6	296.3
1999	285.4	287.1	279.5	286.6	268.6	261.0
2000	283.3	293.7	276.8	275.1	272.3	288.2
2001	264.5	266.7	257.7	263.2	267.5	270.6
2002	282.3	296.9	301.4	308.2	326.6	318.5
2003	367.5	347.5	334.9	336.8	361.4	346.0
2004	399.8	395.9	423.7	388.5	393.3	395.8
2005	422.2	435.5	427.5	435.7	414.5	437.1
2006	568.8	556.0	582.0	644.0	653.0	613.5
2007	650.5	664.2	661.8	677.0	659.1	650.5
2008	923.3	971.5	933.5	871.0	885.8	930.3
2009	919.5	952.0	916.5	883.3	975.5	934.5
2010	1078.5	1108.3	1115.5	1179.3	1207.5	1244.0
2011	1327.0	1411.0	1439.0	1535.5	1536.5	1505.5
2012	1744.0	1770.0	1662.5	1651.3	1558.0	1598.5
2013	1664.8	1588.5	1598.3	1469.0	1394.5	1192.0
2014	1251.0	1326.5	1291.75	1288.5	1250.5	1315.0
2015	1260.3	1214.0	1187.0	1180.3	1191.4	1171.0
2016	1111.8	1234.9	1237.0	1285.7	1212.1	1320.8
2017	1212.8	1255.0	1244.9	1266.4	1266.2	1242.3
2018	1345.1	1317.9	1323.9	1313.2	1305.4	1250.5
2019	1323.3	1319.2	1295.4	1282.3	1295.6	1409.0
2020	1584.2	1609.9	1609.0	1702.8	1728.7	1768.1

* Source: Bank of England

GOLD $US/OZ LONDON PM MONTH CLOSE

JUL	AUG	SEP	OCT	NOV	DEC	
35.3	35.4	36.2	37.5	37.4	37.4	1970
41.0	42.7	42.0	42.5	42.9	43.5	1971
65.7	67.0	65.5	64.9	62.9	63.9	1972
120.2	106.8	103.0	100.1	94.8	106.7	1973
143.0	154.6	151.8	158.8	181.7	183.9	1974
166.7	159.8	141.3	142.9	138.2	140.3	1975
112.5	104.0	116.0	123.2	130.3	134.5	1976
144.1	146.0	154.1	161.5	160.1	165.0	1977
200.3	208.7	217.1	242.6	193.4	226.0	1978
296.5	315.1	397.3	382.0	415.7	512.0	1979
614.3	631.3	666.8	629.0	619.8	589.8	1980
406.0	425.5	428.8	427.0	414.5	397.5	1981
342.9	411.5	397.0	423.3	436.0	456.9	1982
422.0	414.3	405.0	382.0	405.0	382.4	1983
342.4	348.3	343.8	333.5	329.0	309.0	1984
327.5	333.3	326.5	325.1	325.3	326.8	1985
357.5	384.7	423.2	401.0	383.5	388.8	1986
462.5	453.4	459.5	468.8	492.5	484.1	1987
436.8	427.8	397.7	412.4	422.6	410.3	1988
368.3	359.8	366.5	375.3	408.2	398.6	1989
372.3	387.8	408.4	379.5	384.9	386.2	1990
362.9	347.4	354.9	357.5	366.3	353.2	1991
357.9	340.0	349.0	339.3	334.2	332.9	1992
401.8	371.6	355.5	369.6	370.9	391.8	1993
384.0	385.8	394.9	383.9	383.1	383.3	1994
383.4	382.4	384.0	382.7	387.8	387.0	1995
385.3	386.5	379.0	379.5	371.3	369.3	1996
326.4	325.4	332.1	311.4	296.8	290.2	1997
288.9	273.4	293.9	292.3	294.7	287.8	1998
255.6	254.8	299.0	299.1	291.4	290.3	1999
276.8	277.0	273.7	264.5	269.1	274.5	2000
265.9	273.0	293.1	278.8	275.5	276.5	2001
304.7	312.8	323.7	316.9	319.1	347.2	2002
354.8	375.6	388.0	386.3	398.4	416.3	2003
391.4	407.3	415.7	425.6	453.4	435.6	2004
429.0	433.3	473.3	470.8	495.7	513.0	2005
632.5	623.5	599.3	603.8	646.7	632.0	2006
665.5	672.0	743.0	789.5	783.5	833.8	2007
918.0	833.0	884.5	730.8	814.5	869.8	2008
939.0	955.5	995.8	1040.0	1175.8	1087.5	2009
1169.0	1246.0	1307.0	1346.8	1383.5	1405.5	2010
1628.5	1813.5	1620.0	1722.0	1746.0	1531.0	2011
1622.0	1648.5	1776.0	1719.0	1726.0	1657.5	2012
1314.5	1394.8	1326.5	1324.0	1253.0	1204.5	2013
1285.3	1285.8	1216.5	1164.8	1282.8	1206.0	2014
1098.4	1135.0	1114.0	1142.4	1061.9	1060.0	2015
1342.0	1309.3	1322.5	1272.0	1178.1	1145.9	2016
1267.6	1311.8	1283.1	1270.2	1280.2	1291.0	2017
1221.0	1202.5	1187.3	1215.0	1217.6	1279.0	2018
1427.6	1528.4	1485.3	1511.0	1460.2	1514.8	2019
1964.9	1957.4	1886.9	1881.9	1752.6	1887.6	2020

FOREIGN EXCHANGE

US DOLLAR vs CDN DOLLAR
MONTHLY AVG. VALUES*

	JAN		FEB		MAR		APR		MAY		JUN	
	US / CDN	CDN / US	US / CDN	CDN / US	US / CDN	CDN /US	US / CDN	CDN / US	US / CDN	CDN / US	US / CDN	CDN / US
1971	1.01	0.99	1.01	0.99	1.01	0.99	1.01	0.99	1.01	0.99	1.02	0.98
1972	1.01	0.99	1.00	1.00	1.00	1.00	1.00	1.00	0.99	1.01	0.98	1.02
1973	1.00	1.00	1.00	1.00	1.00	1.00	1.00	1.00	1.00	1.00	1.00	1.00
1974	0.99	1.01	0.98	1.02	0.97	1.03	0.97	1.03	0.96	1.04	0.97	1.03
1975	0.99	1.01	1.00	1.00	1.00	1.00	1.01	0.99	1.03	0.97	1.03	0.97
1976	1.01	0.99	0.99	1.01	0.99	1.01	0.98	1.02	0.98	1.02	0.97	1.03
1977	1.01	0.99	1.03	0.97	1.05	0.95	1.05	0.95	1.05	0.95	1.06	0.95
1978	1.10	0.91	1.11	0.90	1.13	0.89	1.14	0.88	1.12	0.89	1.12	0.89
1979	1.19	0.84	1.20	0.84	1.17	0.85	1.15	0.87	1.16	0.87	1.17	0.85
1980	1.16	0.86	1.16	0.87	1.17	0.85	1.19	0.84	1.17	0.85	1.15	0.87
1981	1.19	0.84	1.20	0.83	1.19	0.84	1.19	0.84	1.20	0.83	1.20	0.83
1982	1.19	0.84	1.21	0.82	1.22	0.82	1.23	0.82	1.23	0.81	1.28	0.78
1983	1.23	0.81	1.23	0.81	1.23	0.82	1.23	0.81	1.23	0.81	1.23	0.81
1984	1.25	0.80	1.25	0.80	1.27	0.79	1.28	0.78	1.29	0.77	1.30	0.77
1985	1.32	0.76	1.35	0.74	1.38	0.72	1.37	0.73	1.38	0.73	1.37	0.73
1986	1.41	0.71	1.40	0.71	1.40	0.71	1.39	0.72	1.38	0.73	1.39	0.72
1987	1.36	0.73	1.33	0.75	1.32	0.76	1.32	0.76	1.34	0.75	1.34	0.75
1988	1.29	0.78	1.27	0.79	1.25	0.80	1.24	0.81	1.24	0.81	1.22	0.82
1989	1.19	0.84	1.19	0.84	1.20	0.84	1.19	0.84	1.19	0.84	1.20	0.83
1990	1.17	0.85	1.20	0.84	1.18	0.85	1.16	0.86	1.17	0.85	1.17	0.85
1991	1.16	0.87	1.15	0.87	1.16	0.86	1.15	0.87	1.15	0.87	1.14	0.87
1992	1.16	0.86	1.18	0.85	1.19	0.84	1.19	0.84	1.20	0.83	1.20	0.84
1993	1.28	0.78	1.26	0.79	1.25	0.80	1.26	0.79	1.27	0.79	1.28	0.78
1994	1.32	0.76	1.34	0.74	1.36	0.73	1.38	0.72	1.38	0.72	1.38	0.72
1995	1.41	0.71	1.40	0.71	1.41	0.71	1.38	0.73	1.36	0.73	1.38	0.73
1996	1.37	0.73	1.38	0.73	1.37	0.73	1.36	0.74	1.37	0.73	1.37	0.73
1997	1.35	0.74	1.36	0.74	1.37	0.73	1.39	0.72	1.38	0.72	1.38	0.72
1998	1.44	0.69	1.43	0.70	1.42	0.71	1.43	0.70	1.45	0.69	1.47	0.68
1999	1.52	0.66	1.50	0.67	1.52	0.66	1.49	0.67	1.46	0.68	1.47	0.68
2000	1.45	0.69	1.45	0.69	1.46	0.68	1.47	0.68	1.50	0.67	1.48	0.68
2001	1.50	0.67	1.52	0.66	1.56	0.64	1.56	0.64	1.54	0.65	1.52	0.66
2002	1.60	0.63	1.60	0.63	1.59	0.63	1.58	0.63	1.55	0.65	1.53	0.65
2003	1.54	0.65	1.51	0.66	1.48	0.68	1.46	0.69	1.38	0.72	1.35	0.74
2004	1.30	0.77	1.33	0.75	1.33	0.75	1.34	0.75	1.38	0.73	1.36	0.74
2005	1.22	0.82	1.24	0.81	1.22	0.82	1.24	0.81	1.26	0.80	1.24	0.81
2006	1.16	0.86	1.15	0.87	1.16	0.86	1.14	0.87	1.11	0.90	1.11	0.90
2007	1.18	0.85	1.17	0.85	1.17	0.86	1.14	0.88	1.10	0.91	1.07	0.94
2008	1.01	0.99	1.00	1.00	1.00	1.00	1.01	0.99	1.00	1.00	1.02	0.98
2009	1.22	0.82	1.25	0.80	1.26	0.79	1.22	0.82	1.15	0.87	1.13	0.89
2010	1.04	0.96	1.06	0.95	1.02	0.98	1.01	0.99	1.04	0.96	1.04	0.96
2011	0.99	1.01	0.99	1.01	0.98	1.02	0.96	1.04	0.97	1.03	0.98	1.02
2012	1.01	0.99	1.00	1.00	0.99	1.01	0.99	1.01	1.01	0.99	1.03	0.97
2013	0.99	1.01	1.01	0.99	1.02	.098	1.02	0.98	1.02	0.98	1.03	0.97
2014	1.09	0.91	1.11	0.90	1.11	0.90	1.10	0.91	1.09	0.92	1.08	0.92
2015	1.21	0.82	1.25	0.80	1.26	0.79	1.23	0.81	1.22	0.82	1.24	0.81
2016	1.42	0.70	1.38	0.72	1.32	0.76	1,28	0.78	1.29	0.77	1.29	0.78
2017	1.30	0.77	1.32	0.75	1.33	0.75	1.37	0.73	1.35	0.74	1.30	0.77
2018	1.24	0.80	1.26	0.79	1.29	0.77	1.27	0.79	1.29	0.78	1.31	0.76
2019	1.33	0.75	1.32	0.76	1.34	0.75	1.34	0.75	1.35	0.74	1.33	0.75
2020	1.32	0.76	1.34	0.75	1.41	0.71	1.39	0.72	1.38	0.72	1.36	0.73

Source: Federal Reserve: Avg of daily rates, noon buying rates in New York City for transfers payable in foreign currencies